ITALIAN FOR YOU

A Practical Grammar

By Delia Lennie
Selected Prose Passages for Translation into Italian
35 Novelle Contemporanee
Posso presentarle . . . ?

ITALIAN FOR YOU

A Practical Grammar

DELIA LENNIE
AND MOIRA GREGO

LONGMAN

LONGMAN GROUP LIMITED
London

Associated companies, branches and representatives throughout the world

First published 1960
Second edition 1962
Third edition 1966
Tenth impression 1977

ISBN 582 0 36407 8

Printed in Hong Kong by
Commonwealth Printing Press Ltd

CONTENTS

ACKNOWLEDGEMENTS

We are indebted to the following for permission to quote copyright material:

Casa Editrice Valentino Bompiani & C. for an extract from *I sogni del pigro* by Alberto Moravia; Messrs. Chatto & Windus Ltd. for an extract from *Vision and Design* by Roger Fry; Giulio Einaudi Editore for extracts from *Cristo si è fermato a Eboli* by Carlo Levi, and *Prima che il gallo canti* by Cesare Pavese; Arnoldo Mondadori Editore for extracts from *Paura alla Scala* by Dino Buzzati, and *Tempo migliore* by Marino Moretti; Messrs. Routledge & Kegan Paul Ltd. for an extract from *The History of Music* by Cecil Gray; the Executors of Luigi Pirandello for an extract from *Marsina Stretta*; University Tutorial Press Ltd. for extracts from *French Prose Composition* by E. Weekley; Vallecchi Editore, Firenze for extracts from *Un uomo finito* by Giovanni Papini, and *Maledetti toscani* by Curzio Malaparte; the Literary Executors of Sir Hugh Walpole, Messrs. Macmillan & Co. Ltd. and St. Martin's Press Inc. New York for an extract from *Rogue Herries.*

FOREWORD

The study of a foreign language cannot be separated from the study of the grammar which forms its very backbone, and which, whether it precedes, accompanies or follows practice in speaking, is indispensable. This is particularly true of the Italian language, especially for students whose native tongue is English, since the two languages are so different in construction: the first still very near to Latin from which it is derived, characterized by complex sentences, based on subordinate clauses; the second looser and more flexible, its sentences mostly based on co-ordinate clauses.

This grammar is the result of collaboration between two teachers, one Italian the other English. In it we have tried to resolve the problems and overcome the difficulties that appeared to us, each from her own angle. Since the constantly recurring differences between the two languages demand a knowledge of grammar which we have found by experience to be rare even among people who are well educated, we have thought it advisable to clarify points of English grammar before treating them in Italian.

An ideal grammar should group together all the instruction referring to each part of speech and all the rules of syntax; this being impossible in the case of a foreign language, since no enthusiasm would survive a surfeit of irregular verbs or of pronouns presented without discrimination, the next best thing is to provide as accurate an index as possible, where the student can find any reference he requires, and this we have given. We have, however, throughout the grammar tried to observe the principle of continuity and unity wherever possible, especially in the more important sections, such as those dealing with the present participle, the subjunctive mood, prepositions governing verbs, etc.

In compiling this grammar we have borne in mind the two main categories of people using it: students at a university and students attending continuation classes. To suit the needs of the former, who must complete the course in a term and a half, we have made the lessons fairly substantial, while for the latter there is ample material in each lesson to be studied weekly or, if necessary, to be divided.

Section C of each lesson has been inspired by the desire to combine instruction in formal grammar with some facility in speaking the language, and again in the case of continuation classes, to suggest matter for conversation as well as acquainting the student with Italian customs and ways of life. Though the exercises included in the A and B sections are grammatically complete in themselves, an enterprising student would profit much from studying and memorizing the C sections. Obviously they could not be graded, but their intelligent use will give the student a knowledge of the living language in the same way as children learn their native tongue long before they are aware of the grammar and syntax involved.

We hope that this grammar will be studied with the same interest with which it has been written and that the same determination to finish it, which has compelled us, will help the student to overcome the inevitable periods of discouragement.

Our gratitude goes to all those who have helped us in our work, first of all to the late Prof. Manfredi Porena of the University of Rome, whose advice we frequently sought and to whom we should so much have liked to give a copy of this book inspired by that love for the Italian language which he so well knew how to convey to his pupil.

Our grateful thanks go also in anticipation to all those who will help us by pointing out the mistakes inevitable in a first edition.

Publisher's Note

This third edition contains, in addition to revisions covering changes in prices, social conditions and political developments, a completely new section on the most common idioms, with special reference to spoken Italian; a paragraph dealing with compound nouns has been added together with suitable examples in the exercises. Certain passages, notably those on the treatment of the past descriptive, past absolute and past perfect tenses, have been re-arranged.

INTRODUCTION

The Alphabet

The Italian alphabet consists of 5 vowels and 16 consonants.

The vowels are: **a, e, i, o, u.**

The consonants are: **b, c, d, f, g, h, l, m, n, p, q, r, s, t, v, z. K, w, x,** and **y** are used in the writing of foreign words, **x** and **y** in algebraic expressions and **x** in such expressions as: ex-presidente.

PRONUNCIATION

LETTER	NAME	SOUND
A	a	**ask**
B	bi	**been**
C	ci	**cheek**
D	di	**deacon**
E	e	**age**
F	effe	**effeh**
G	gi	**genial**
H	acca	**akkah**
I	i	**east**
L	elle	**elleh**
M	emme	**emmeh**
N	enne	**enneh**
O	o	**tot**
P	p	**Peter**
Q	cu	**cool**
R	erre	**erreh**
S	esse	**esseh**
T	ti	**tee**
U	u	**coot**
V	vi	**veto**
Z	zeta	**dzayta**
K	cappa	**kappa**
W	doppio vi	
X	ics	**icks**
Y	ipsilon	**ipsilon**

To ensure correct pronunciation in Italian it is necessary to bear in mind these points:

1. Italian vowels represent pure sounds and therefore each must be accurately pronounced. This rule applies to *all* vowels, irrespective of position or stress. The sound is quite different from that of long vowels in English which tend to become diphthongs. This is never the case in Italian.

2. Words should be pronounced well forward in the mouth.

3. No type of nasal intonation exists in Italian, except where **n** is followed by another consonant: canto, banca, lungo.

4. Double consonants call for special care as each must be sounded.

5. The treatment of words beginning with "s impure", that is **s** followed by another consonant, is dealt with in Lesson I but demands constant vigilance on the part of an English-speaking person whose ear is no guide in this matter.

Vowels

a, **e**, and **o** are called "hard vowels", **i** and **u** are called "soft vowels". For the 5 vowels there are 7 sounds as follows:

A	like **a** in **ask**	mamma, pane, capo
E	(closed) like **a** in **age**	stella, fede, nembo
E	(open) like **e** in **sell**	sɛlla, dɛnte, pɛrdita
I	like **ea** in **east**	vino, divo, mito
O	(closed) like **o** in **dote**	ponte, conto, sordo
O	(open) like **o** in **hot**	cɔsta, fɔlla, rɔsa
U	like **oo** in **coot**	**u**nico, **u**tile, **u**rgente

There are two ways of pronouncing the vowels **o** and **e**: "closed" as in *ponte* and *fede*, and "open" as in *cɔsta* and *sɛlla*. The pronunciation of these vowels varies considerably from one province to another throughout Italy, but that of Tuscany is regarded as the most correct.

The **o** and **e** have always the closed sound in any unaccented syllable. For their pronunciation in accented syllables it is not possible to formulate rules that are simple and at the same time completely comprehensive to establish when an accented **o** and an accented **e** are closed and when open.[1] Any such attempt leads inevitably to obvious inaccuracy, or to discouragingly long and involved lists of instructions.

For the benefit of students, however, we shall indicate in the vocabularies by means of the usual signs (ɔ=**o** open; ɛ=**e** open) the accepted Tuscan pronunciation of these two vowels, although in Italy it is not at all considered a lack of education to pronounce them differently.[2]

[1] See *Prontuario di pronunzia e di ortografia* a cura di G. Bertoni e F. A. Ugolini, edito dalla Radio Italiana.

[2] Since open ɔ and open ɛ are *always* stressed these vowels will not be printed in bold type (see p. xvii).

Semivowels

The **i** and **u** preceded or followed by another vowel and not accented are called semivowels and have a sound similar to **y**: reietto; and **w**: uovo, auto.

Diphthongs and Hiatus

A group of two vowels that are pronounced as one compound sound, is called a diphthong: squadra, piɛtra, fiore, aurɔra. Similarly three vowels pronounced as one compound sound are known as a triphthong: tuɔi, miɛi, puɔi. The modern use prefers to shorten the triphthong **iuo** to the diphthong **io**: giuɔco—giɔco, figliuɔlo—figliɔlo. Diphthongs usually occur when a hard vowel (**a, e, o**) combines with a soft vowel (**i, u**), in which case the stress always falls on the hard vowel; or where the two soft vowels combine—here the stress falls on the second one; less frequently, two hard vowels form a diphthong: aere, oceano.

The diphthongs are:

ia, ie, io **ai, ei, oi**
ua, ue, uo **au, eu, ou**
iu, ui

Uo and **ie** are called movable diphthongs because in many cases they lose their first vowel, when in words of a common source, the accent does not fall on them:

buɔno—bontà scuɔla—scolaro
ciɛlo—celeste liɛto—letizia

When in poetry it is necessary, for metrical reasons, to separate the sounds of two vowels that form a diphthong, two dots (or diaeresis) are placed above one of the vowels.

O animal grazïoso e benigno (Dante)

The juxtaposition of two vowels that are pronounced separately is called hiatus: re-ale, pa-ura. The exceptions (aere, oceano) have been mentioned above.

Consonants

The following have nearly the same sound as in English: **b, d, f, l, m, n, p, t,** and **v.**

C and **G** can be pronounced in two ways:

1. *Guttural* (or hard) in front of **a, o, u**: ca, co, cu—cane, cɔsta, cuneo (**c**=English **k**): ga, go, gu—gala, gola, gufo (**g** as in 'got').

2. *Palatal* (or soft) in front of **e, i**: ce, ci—cena, cinque (**ch** in 'chin'): ge, gi—gɛlo, giro (**g** in 'gin').

H. The letter **h** interposed between **c** and **e**, **c** and **i**, **g** and **e**, **g** and **i**, changes the palatal sound into a guttural: che, chi—che, chino (**k** in 'keen'): ghe, ghi—ghetto, ghiro (**g** in 'get', 'gear'). Apart from this change effected in the pronunciation of the **c** and **g**, the letter **h** is always silent and only appears in a few words for the most part solely to distinguish them from other words similarly pronounced but with entirely different meanings: ho—I have; o—or: hai—you have; ai—to the: ah!—oh!; a—to, at.

I. The letter **i** placed between **c** and **a**, **o**, **u**, or between **g** and **a**, **o**, **u** is hardly pronounced at all, but changes the guttural sound into a palatal: cia, cio, ciu—ciarpame, ciɔcca, ciurma (**ch** in 'char', 'chocolate', etc.): gia, gio, giu—giacca, giɔstra, giusto (**j** in 'jar', 'John', 'Jew').

GL. The combination **gl** has two ways of being pronounced. When it precedes **a**, **e**, **o**, **u**, it is always pronounced as a guttural **g**, followed by an **l** as in English: gladiatore, glɛba, glɔria, glucɔsio (**gl** as in glass, glen, glow, glue).

When it is followed by **i** it has that same sound only in a *few* words: Anglia, Anglicano, ganglio, geroglifico, glicerina, negligɛnza, glicine, glicosio, glitico and some other derivatives. It has instead a sound very similar to **lli** followed by a vowel as in millions, billiards, in *all* other words: miglio, vaglia, sɔglia.[1]

GN. The combination **gn** has a sound very similar to the English 'newt': regno, cagna, gnɔmo, ogni.

QU. Is pronounced as if it were followed by **w**: quadro, quindi, quesito (**qu** in 'qualm', 'quinsy', 'quest').

R. Is always rolled or trilled: Roma, rete.

S. Has two sounds:

Unvoiced as in soap—sera, sano, passo.

Voiced as in rose—svago, snɛllo, esame.

The **s** is always unvoiced when it is at the beginning of a word and followed by a vowel, when it is double **ss** and in front of the consonants **c**, **f**, **p**, **q**, **t**. In front of any other consonants at the beginning and generally in the middle of a word, it is voiced.[2]

SC. Is sounded like the **sh** of 'shame' before **e** and **i**: scena, scirɔcco. It is sounded like **sk** in 'sky' before **a**, **o**, **u**: scala, scopa, scure. The letter **h** interposed between **sc** and **e** and **i** changes the sound from **sh** to **sk**: schiavo, scherzo.

[1] This sound, with slight variations, is found represented with different groupings of letters in all Romance languages: Spanish double **l**—caudillo; French double **l**—mouillé, famille, or **il**—ail; Portuguese **lh**—batalha.

[2] For the pronunciation of **s** between vowels and of **z** whether at the beginning or in the middle of a word, which varies in different parts of Italy, see: *Il Prontuario di pronunzia e di ortografia* a cura di G. Bertoni e di F. A. Ugolini edito dalla Radio Italiana.

The letter **i** interposed between **sc** and **a, o, u**, changes the sound conversely from **sk** to **sh**: **sciɔcco, sciame.**

Z. Has a double sound:

Unvoiced like **ts**: **quarzo, fɔrza, zucchero.**

Voiced like **dz**: **zɛro, zɛnit.**

Double consonants must be pronounced distinctly and strongly since many words vary in meaning according to whether they have a single or a double consonant: **nɔno—ninth; nɔnno—grandfather.**

Accents

In Italian there are two accents: the acute and the grave; the circumflex, employed to indicate the fusion of two identical vowels: studii—studî, or a contraction; tɔgliere—tôrre, being rarely used. The acute and grave accents have a double function:

(a) to indicate where the stress falls (in the cases in which the stress must be signified by a written accent) and

(b) to indicate the pronunciation open (` grave accent) or closed (´ acute accent) of the two vowels **e** and **o.**

In the first function which applies:

(1) to all nouns where the stress falls on the last syllable:

beltà, falò, virtù, mezzodì

(2) to some monosyllabic words:

ciò, giù, già, può, più

(3) to certain monosyllabic words which could otherwise be mistaken with others spelt in the same way:

dà (he gives)	**da (by, from)**
lì, là (there)	**li, la (them, the)**
sì (yes)	**si (refl. pron.)**

the grave accent is used in hand writing, whatever the vowel; in printing the grave accent is generally used too except when e appears as the final vowel in:

(a) **affé, testé, mercé, né, sé**

(b) **ché, perché, poiché, giacché, and derivatives**

(c) the third person singular of the past absolute of regular verbs of II conjugation:

temé, godé

In the second function (to indicate the open and closed sound of **o** and **e**), the written accent is only used in vocabularies or treatises on pronunciation, except in the case of words in which a different pronunciation of the vowel could cause confusion with another word spelt in the same way:

accétta	axe	accètta (v.)	do accept
affétto (v.)	I slice	affètto	affection

In this case the accent might even be indicated in an ordinary book, but never in hand writing.

Division of Words according to Position of Stress

According to where the stress falls words are divided into:

Tronche when the stress falls on the last syllable[1]:
città, virtù, carità

Piane when the stress falls on the second last syllable:
libro, amore, arazzo

Sdrucciole when the stress falls on the third last syllable:
anima, scatola, pɔpolo

Bisdrucciole when the stress falls on the fourth from the end:
illuminano, stritolano

The majority of Italian words have the stress on the second last syllable, some on the last, a few on the third last and very few on the fourth last syllable. In the case of words which fall into the third and fourth categories the vowel of the stressed syllable will be printed in bold type, as above, and in bold italic in the vocabularies.

Elision

When a word ending in an unaccented vowel is followed by a word beginning with a vowel, the final vowel of the first word is normally suppressed, in order to avoid the two vowels jarring.

This suppression is called elision and is indicated by an apostrophe: un'amica (una), l'attrazione (la), mezz'ora (mɛzza).

Elision usually occurs in the case of articles: (l'alunna), and in the corresponding combination of preposition + article (dell'alunna), in the simple preposition *di*: (d'amore) and with demonstrative adjectives (quest'onore, quell'articolo).

Ci: the vowel elides before **e** and **i**: c'era, c'entra, c'invita.

Che: the vowel sometimes elides before **i** and **e**: mi chiese *ch'io* gli scrivessi but it is preferable to avoid the elision. In the case of the plural definite article, elision is permitted only if the initial vowel of the word is identical to the final vowel of the preceding article, but it is preferable to avoid it, especially when it could cause confusion with the singular: *l'età* and *le età*; *l'ɛpoca* and *le ɛpoche* or *l'ɛpoche*.

Pɔvero elides at times before *uɔmo* and becomes *pɔver'uɔmo*.

Elision is *not* permitted:

(a) when the pronoun *ci* is followed by a word beginning with **a, o, *u***: ci ama, ci odia, ci urta.

[1] This is the only case in which the stress is signified by a written accent.

(b) when the definite article *gli* and prepositions combined with it, are followed by vowels other than **i**: gli orolɔgi, negli armadi, because in both cases the pronunciation of the consonants **c** and **gl** would alter.

(c) when using the pronoun *le* (a lɛi—to her): le auguro buɔna fortuna.

(d) when using the preposition *da*: legna da ardere, casa da affittare.

Apocopation

Apocopation consists in suppressing the final vowel, or entire syllable (when unaccented) even before a word beginning with a consonant—and this without using the apostrophe. It can only occur when the final unaccented vowel is preceded by one of the consonants **l, m, n, r**, amor(e), ciel(o), siam(o), etc., and between words logically connected: andar(e) piano, così fan(no) tutte. If any of these consonants are double, the second is omitted along with the final vowel: quel paese, bɛl bambino.

Contrary to the rule, an apostrophe is used in the following cases of apocopation: un po'—a little, di'—tell!

An accent is used in the case of: fè (fede), piè (piɛde), diè (diɛde), dà—he gives.

Syllabication

Words are divided into syllables in accordance with certain rules which must be known before a word can be correctly hyphenated at the end of a line, and also for the purpose of scansion.

(a) If two or more vowels form a diphthong or a triphthong they are considered as a single syllable: au-rɔ-ra, cuɔ-co, ciɛ-lo, a-iuɔ-la.

(b) A single consonant forms a syllable with the vowel following it: ca-sa, co-lo-re.

(c) **s** impure forms a syllable with the consonant that follows: a-sta, a-stro, fɛ-sta.

(d) Double consonants, and two consonants the first of which is **l, m, n, r**, are separated: mam-ma, ɔs-so, mɔl-le, can-to, ɔr-to, bal-do.

cq is treated as a double consonant, therefore: ac-qua, piac-que.

(e) Two consonants, other than those mentioned in (d), form a syllable with the vowel following: mi-glio, a-gnɛl-lo, a-cre.

(f) In groups of three consonants, the first forms part of the preceding syllable, except in the case of **s**: con-tro, in-tri-so, ar-tri-te, *but* a-stru-so, ra-strɛl-lo, pia-stra.

Punctuation Marks

Punctuation marks are similiar to those in English:

.	punto fermo	full stop
,	virgola	comma

;	punto e virgola	semi-colon
:	due punti	colon
!	punto esclamativo	exclamation mark
?	punto interrogativo	question mark
...	punti sospensivi	indicates omission
—	lineetta	dash
( )	parentesi tonda	round brackets
[ ]	parentesi quadra	square brackets
*	asterisco	asterisk
‘ ’	virgolette	inverted commas
-	stanghetta	hyphen
{	grappa	brace

Capital Letters

Contrary to the English usage, capital letters are not used in Italian in the following cases:

(a) In the pronoun: I—io.

(b) In titles followed by a proper name: Il principe Rospigliosi; il dottor Gigli.

(c) In the names of months and days of the week: il primo sabato di maggio.

(d) With adjectives indicating nationality unless they are used as nouns: la lingua italiana *but* gli Italiani.

Abbreviations

adj.	adjective	m.	masculine
adv.	adverb	n.	noun
aux.	auxiliary	pers.	person
comp.	comparative	pl.	plural
conj.	conjunction	prep.	preposition
contd.	continued	pron.	pronoun
f.	feminine	rel.	relative
inv.	invariable	s.	singular
inter.	interrogative	sup.	superlative
intrans.	intransitive	trans.	transitive

LESSON I

Nouns

All Italian nouns, with a few exceptions, end in a vowel.

Gender

With very few exceptions, notably *mano* (f.)—hand, all nouns ending in *o* are masculine. Those ending in *a* are mostly feminine. There is no neuter gender in Italian. Unlike English, names of inanimate objects are either masculine or feminine:

giardino (m.)	garden
finɛstra (f.)	window

Number

Nouns ending in *o* form their plural by changing the *o* to *i*:

giardino giardini

Nouns ending in *a* form their plural by changing the *a* to *e* if they are feminine, and the *a* to *i* if they are masculine:

pɔrta—pɔrte (f.)	door
problɛma—problɛmi (m.)	problem

Indefinite Article

Masculine	*Feminine*	
un	una	a, an
uno	un'	

The indefinite article varies according to the gender of the noun it precedes. *Un* is used before all masculine nouns, except those beginning with *s* impure (*s* followed by another consonant), *z, gn, ps, x* and the semi-vowel *i* (that is *i* followed by another vowel), which require *uno.*

un amico	a friend
un quadro	a painting
uno sbaglio	a mistake
uno zɛro	a nought
uno gnɔmo	a gnome
uno psichiatra	a psychiatrist
uno Iugoslavo	a Yugoslav

On page xiii of the introductory chapter, great stress was laid on this rule since it would be a serious mistake in Italian to use *un* in front of a word beginning with one of these letters. As the ear gives no warning of discordancy to English-speaking people, this rule should be carefully memorized and applied.

Una is the feminine form, which becomes *un'* before nouns beginning with a vowel.

una tavola	a table
un'amica	a friend

The article must be repeated before each noun to which it refers.

Uno (m.) and *una* (f.) are also the forms for the cardinal numeral ***one***.[1] The rest are indeclinable. Learn from 1 to 10.

uno, una	1	sɛi	6
due	2	sɛtte	7
tre	3	ɔtto	8
quattro	4	nɔve	9
cinque	5	diɛci	10

Present Indicative of Auxiliary Verbs

Ɛssere	To be	Avere	To have
sono	I am	ho	I have
sɛi	you are	hai	you have
è	he, she, it is	ha	he, she, it has
siamo	we are	abbiamo	we have
siɛte	you are	avete	you have
sono	they are	hanno	they have

N.B. So distinctive are the endings in any given tense—a different one for each person singular and plural—that normally no subject pronouns are required. Fuller instruction will be given later.

Vocabulary I

In all vocabularies, nouns ending in *a* are to be regarded as feminine unless otherwise stated.

casa	house, home	**cucina**	kitchen, cuisine, cooking
ingrɛsso	hall, admission, entrance	**giardino**	garden
scala	staircase, steps (pair of)	**pavimɛnto**	floor
camera da lɛtto	bedroom	**soffitto**	ceiling
salɔtto	drawing-room	**muro**	wall
sala da pranzo	dining-room	**credɛnza**	sideboard
stanza da bagno	bathroom	**sɛdia**	chair

[1] When used adjectively, the numeral *one* in Italian is treated in exactly the same way as the indefinite article.

divano divan
finɛstra window
lampada lamp
poltrona armchair, seat
spɛcchio mirror
rɔsa rose
garɔfano carnation
pɔrta door
tavola table
anche (adv.) also, too (always precedes the noun or pronoun it modifies)
dove (adv.) where; **dov'è** where is?
ɛcco (adv.) here is, here are
ci (adv.) there
c'è there is; **ci sono** there are
in (prep.) in, into, on, at
di (prep.) of
che (adj., inter. pron. & conj.) what? that
che cɔsa what? (thing)
ogni (adj. inv.) every, each
Maria Mary
Giulia Julia
Roberto Robert
o (conj.) or; **o . . . o** either . . . or
e, ed (conj.) and

Exercise 1

Translate into Italian inserting the indefinite article: chair, hall, ceiling, mirror, sideboard, mistake, floor, gnome, staircase, psychiatrist, garden, table, friend (f.), door, friend (m.).

Exercise 2

Make the following nouns plural, and put a numeral in front of each: finestra, sala da pranzo, tavola, salotto, cucina, giardino, scala, credenza, garofano, gnomo, porta, sedia, soffitto, camera da letto, Iugoslavo.

Exercise 3

Translate into Italian: we are, you have (pl.), they are, she is, you have (s.), you are (pl.), they have, I am, you are (s.), we have, I have, he is, she has.

A. *Translate into English:* 1. Maria, Giulia e Roberto hanno una casa. 2. In ogni casa ci sono un ingresso e una scala. 3. Ci sono anche tre o quattro camere da letto ed una stanza da bagno. 4. Una casa ha una sala da pranzo, un salotto ed una cucina. 5. In una sala da pranzo ci sono otto sedie, una tavola e una credenza. 6. Dov'è uno specchio? C'è uno specchio in ogni camera da letto e in ogni stanza da bagno. 7. Dove sei, Roberto? Roberto è in un giardino dove ci sono rose e garofani. 8. In ogni stanza ci sono un pavimento, un soffitto e quattro muri. 9. Ci sono anche una porta e una o due finestre. 10. Che cosa ha Maria? Maria ha tre rose. 11. Giulia ha cinque o sei garofani. 12. Dove siete? 13. Siamo in un salotto. 14. Che cosa c'è in un salotto? 15. In un salotto ci sono due poltrone, un divano, una tavola, uno specchio e tre o quattro sedie. 16. Che cosa c'è in un giardino? 17. In un giardino ci sono rose e garofani.[1] 18. Che cosa c'è in una cucina? 19. In una cucina ci sono una

[1] Nouns may be used without an article when they form a list.

tavola e due sedie. 20. Dov'è una scala? Ecco una scala ed ecco una porta.

B. *Translate into Italian*: 1. In every house there are two or three bedrooms, a dining-room, a drawing-room, a kitchen and a bathroom. 2. What is there in a dining-room? 3. In a dining-room there are four or six chairs, a table and a sideboard. 4. What is there in a drawing-room? 5. In a drawing-room there are two or three armchairs, a divan, a table and a lamp. 6. There is a mirror in every drawing-room, bedroom, and bathroom.[1] 7. Every room has four walls, a ceiling, a floor, one or two windows and one or two doors. 8. What is there in a kitchen? 9. In a kitchen there are two or three chairs and a table. 10. In a bedroom also there are one or two chairs. 11. Where is a table? 12. There is a table in every dining-room and in every kitchen. 13. Mary and Julia have a house and a garden. 14. What is there in a garden? 15. In a garden there are roses and carnations. 16. Where are Mary and Julia? 17. Mary and Julia are in a garden. 18. Mary has ten roses. 19. Robert has four carnations and Julia has three roses. 20. Where is a wall? Here is a wall.

C. Buon giorno.—Good morning, good day. Buona sera.—Good evening. Buona notte.—Good night.

Come stai?—How are you? (intimate form of address). Come sta?—How are you? (formal address). Sto bene, benissimo, grazie.—I am well, very well, thank you. Non troppo bene—not too well; così e così—so so; non c'è male—pretty well, pretty good.

Come ti chiami?—Mi chiamo Maria.—What is your name? My name is Mary. E tu come ti chiami?—And what are you called? (intimate form of address)

E lei come si chiama?—And what are you called? (formal address)

Dove siete? Siamo in Italia.—Where are you? We are in Italy; in Iscozia—in Scotland; in Inghilterra—in England; in Irlanda—in Ireland; in America—in America.

Che cosa desidera?—What do you want?

Per favore—please.

Come si chiama questo?—What is this called?

Come si dice 'attic' in italiano?—What is the Italian for 'attic'? In italiano 'attic' si dice 'soffitta'.

Repeat the above question for cellar (cantina); corridor (corridoio); lock (serratura); key (chiave).

Quante sedie ci sono in questa stanza?—How many chairs are there in this room?

Arrivederci, arrivederla.—Goodbye.

Dobbiamo imparare ogni giorno qualche nuova parola.—We must learn some new words every day.

[1] Repeat 'every' in front of each noun.

D. *Piacere*

Per piacere (or per favore)—Please.

Mi fa tanto piacere—I am so glad.

Piacere (di conoscerla)—How do you do? literally: pleased to know you).

Ma fammi il piacere (di non dire sciocchezze)—Please (don't talk nonsense).

LESSON II

Verbs

That part of the verb in English preceded by 'to' is called in Italian *modo infinito* (infinitive mood). According to the endings of the infinitive: *-are, -ere, -ire,* Italian verbs are divided into three conjugations.[1] The stem of the verb, which in regular verbs (those conforming to one of these three patterns) is the same for all tenses, is obtained by taking off the characteristic infinitive ending of each conjugation.

1. Am-are   2. Tem-ere   3. Dorm-ire

The various moods, tenses and persons are obtained by adding the appropriate endings to this stem.

Indicative Mood

In Italian a verb is in the *modo indicativo* (indicative mood) when, as in English, it is concerned with a statement of fact, e.g. I am reading a book —Leggo un libro: He is good—Egli è buɔno.

Present Indicative of Model Verbs

am-o	I love	tɛm-o	I fear	dɔrm-o	I sleep
am-i	you love	tɛm-i	you fear	dɔrm-i	you sleep
am-a	he / she / it loves	tɛm-e	he / she / it fears	dɔrm-e	he / she / it sleeps
am-iamo	we love	tem-iamo	we fear	dorm-iamo	we sleep
am-ate	you love	tem-ete	you fear	dorm-ite	you sleep
am-ano	they love	tɛm-ono	they fear	dɔrm-ono	they sleep

Note that the endings of the 1st and 2nd person singular and of the 1st plural are the same for all conjugations. The other endings differ from one conjugation to another although, in some cases, only in the vowels characteristic of each conjugation—*a, e, i.* Many verbs of the 3rd conjugation take between the stem and the ending, *isc* in the 1st, 2nd and 3rd persons singular and in the 3rd person plural of the present indicative, the present subjunctive and of the imperative, e.g. capire—to understand. From now on, these verbs will be indicated by means of an asterisk.

[1] To the second conjugation belong both verbs like *scrivere* where the stress falls on the third last syllable, and those like *vedere*, where the stress falls on the second last syllable: originally, in Latin, these verbs belonged to two different conjugations.

Present Indicative

cap-isc-o	I understand
cap-isc-i	you understand
cap-isc-e	he, she understands
cap-iamo	we understand
cap-ite	you understand
cap-isc-ono	they understand

Use of the Present

The present tense in Italian translates[1] not only the English simple present 'I love' but also the emphatic 'I do love' and the progressive 'I am loving', though a progressive form exists in Italian and will be studied later. The present tense also renders the English habitual action in the present.

I catch the tram every morning.
Prɛndo il tram ogni mattina.

Interrogative Form

1. In order to ask a question, Italians depend almost entirely on the intonation of the voice in speaking, and the question mark in written Italian: Has Mary (got) a book?—Maria ha un libro?

2. Questions in Italian are never rendered by introducing an auxiliary verb as we do in English: Do you speak Italian?—Parli italiano?

3. There is no fixed order for the words in an Italian interrogative sentence, but it is not usual to put the subject immediately after the verb as in English. Has Mary (got) a book?—Ha un libro Maria?

4. In a colloquial form of interrogation in Italian, when one expects or invites an affirmative reply, the expressions "no?" or "vero?" are added to the question, both being abbreviations of "non è vero?" and equivalent to the English "isn't it?", "don't you?" etc. Capisci l'italiano, vero?—You understand Italian, don't you? Voi avete un appartamento, no?—You have a flat, haven't you?

Vocabulary II

appartamento flat, apartments
stanza room (in general)
lɛtto bed
cassɛtto drawer
comodino bedside table
tolɛtta dressing table
tappɛto carpet, rug, mat
materasso mattress
lenzuɔlo sheet
cuscino pillow, cushion
copɛrta blanket, counterpane, rug
piumino quilt, eiderdown

[1] The Italian present tense is also used to render the English present perfect tense when the action is still continuing.
La conosco da molto tempo—I have known her for a long time

quadro picture, painting
libreria book-case, book-shop
st*u*dio study
scrivania writing desk
libro book
arm*a*dio wardrobe, cupboard
fɛdera pillowslip
penna pen
penna stilografica fountain pen
matita pencil
carta paper
con (prep.) with
quando (adv. & conj.) when
sɛmpre (adv.) always
su (prep.) on
ma (conj.) but
abitare to live in
conservare to keep *or* put away
vedere to see
aprire to open
appɛndere to hang
chiamare to call
m*e*ttere to put
preferire* to prefer
pulire* to clean

Exercise 1

1. *Repeat orally the present indicative of:* abitare, chiamare, mettere, aprire, vedere, dormire, pulire, preferire.
2. *Translate into Italian:* we live, they see, I open, they are calling, he puts, you (s.) prefer, we sleep, you (p.) clean, we call, they love, she cleans, you (p.) see, they put, you (p.) call, we open, they clean, you (s.) see, I sleep, she lives, I hang, he prefers, you (p.) open, you (s.) hang, we clean.

Exercise 2

Translate into Italian, inserting the indefinite article: wardrobe, lamp, desk, carpet, bed, mattress, pen, dressing table, study, book-shop, garden, window, door, mistake, painting, table, friend (f.), ceiling, bedroom, hall.

Exercise 3

Give the plural of the following nouns in Italian, inserting a numeral: drawer, book, pen, sheet, blanket, pillow, quilt, bookcase, desk, house, armchair, friend (m.), table, window, carnation, chair, rug, sideboard, rose.

A. *Translate into English:* 1. Dove abiti Roberto? 2. Abitiamo in un appartamento di sei stanze. 3. Preferite una casa o un appartamento? 4. Roberto e Maria preferiscono un appartamento. 5. Maria apre una finestra. Che cosa vedi, Maria? 6. Vedo un giardino. 7. Maria e Giulia sono in una camera da letto. 8. Che cosa c'è su un letto? 9. Ci sono un materasso, due lenzuoli, due o tre coperte, un cuscino e un piumino. 10. Maria ha due cuscini ma Roberto preferisce dormire con un cuscino. 11. Che cosa c'è su un comodino? 12. Su un comodino mettiamo una lampada. 13. Che cosa conservi in un armadio, Giulia?

Conservo coperte, lenzuoli e federe. 14. Maria apre una porta e chiama Roberto. 15. Dov'è Roberto? Roberto è in uno studio. 16. Che cosa metti in un cassetto di una scrivania, Roberto? 17. Metto penne e matite. 18. Giulia apre sempre ogni finestra quando pulisce una camera. 19. C'è un tappeto in ogni camera, Maria? 20. Mettiamo sempre un tappeto in un salotto e in una camera da letto.

B. *Translate into Italian* (until full instructions have been given (Lesson IV), use the 2nd person singular when addressing one person and 2nd person plural when addressing more than one): 1. Robert lives in a house with a garden. 2. Mary and Julia live in a flat. 3. Do you prefer a house or a flat? 4. In a flat of seven rooms, there are two or three bedrooms. 5. In every bedroom there is a bed, a dressing-table, a wardrobe, a bedside table, a carpet and a lamp. 6. Mary and Julia hang two or three pictures in a bedroom. 7. What do we keep in a desk? 8. In a desk we keep paper, pens and pencils.[1] 9. What do we see in a study? 10. We see a desk and three or four book-cases. 11. What is Mary cleaning? She is cleaning a mirror. 12. On a bed there are always two sheets, three blankets, and a quilt. 13. There are also a mattress and a pillow. 14. Mary has three blankets. 15. Julia prefers a quilt and two blankets. 16. Where do we keep sheets and blankets? 17. We keep sheets and blankets in a cupboard. 18. In a drawing-room there are always arm-chairs and a divan. 19. Robert keeps books, pens and pencils in a drawer. 20. Mary opens every window and cleans every room.

C. Mi capisce quando parlo in italiano?—Do you understand me when I speak in Italian? Sì, no, un poco, capisco qualche parola.—Yes, no, a little, I understand a few words. Mi rincresce non capisco.—I am sorry I do not understand. Che significa questa parola?—What does this word mean? Vuol ripetere per piacere?—Would you please repeat it? Come si dice 'sit down' in italiano?—How do you say 'sit down' in Italian? Si dice 'si accomodi' ad una persona e 'si accomodino' a due o tre persone.—You say 'si accomodi' to one person and 'si accomodino' to two or three people.

Repeat question for 'excuse me' supplying 'mi scusi' and 'mi scusino' in appropriate answer.

Che cosa c'è in una stanza da bagno?—What is there in a bathroom? In una stanza da bagno ci sono un bagno, un lavandino, uno specchio, uno sgabello o una sedia e un porta-asciugamano.—In a bathroom there is a bath, a washhand basin, a mirror, a stool or a chair and a towel-rail.

[1] When enumerating a list of things, the article is omitted. Similarly it can be omitted in Italian whenever English usage permits this, with certain exceptions, which will be taught later.

E che altro?—And what else? Sapone—soap; dentifricio—tooth paste; spazzolino da denti—tooth brush; spazzolino da unghie—nail brush; una lima per unghie—a nail file; un pettine—a comb; un rasoio di sicurezza o elettrico—a safety razor or an electric razor; crema da barba—shaving cream; borotalco—talcum powder; acqua di Colonia—eau de Cologne; una crema per pulire il viso—a cleansing cream; smalto per le unghie—nail varnish.

Repeat question and appropriate answers for dining-room, drawing-room, bedroom and study.

D. *Prɛgo*

Grazie. Prɛgo.—Thank you. Don't mention it.

Prɛgo, attenda un momento.—Please wait for a moment.

Si accɔmodi, Si accɔmodino

Prɛgo, si accɔmodi—Please take a seat
come in
come this way.

LESSON III

Definite Article

	Masculine		
Singular		*Plural*	
il		i	the
lo		gli	the
	Feminine		
la		le	the

The definite article, like the indefinite article, varies according to the gender and also the initial letter of the noun or adjective which it precedes. *Il* and *i* are used before all masculine nouns[1] beginning with a consonant, except *s* impure, *z*, *gn*, *ps*, *x* and the semi-vowel *i* which require *lo* and *gli*. All masculine nouns beginning with a vowel are preceded by *lo* and *gli*. *Lo* elides before any vowel; *gli* drops the *i* only before nouns beginning with an *i*:

il giardino	i giardini	garden(s)
lo zio	gli zii	uncle(s)
l'accɛnto	gli accɛnti	accent(s)
lo Ionio	gli Iugoslavi	Ionian Sea: Yugoslavs
l'ingrɛsso	gl'ingrɛssi	entrance(s)

La and *le* are used before all feminine nouns. *La* becomes *l'* before any vowel. *Le* can drop the *e* only in front of another *e*:

la camera	le camere	bedroom(s)
l'automɔbile	le automɔbili	car(s)
l'ɛrba	l'ɛrbe	grass

Nouns (*continued*)

Many nouns in Italian, both masculine and feminine, end in *e* in the singular; the *e* changes to *i* in the plural:

il lume (m.)	i lumi	lamp(s)
la luce (f.)	le luci	light(s)

Vocabulary III

campanɛllo bell
mɔbile (m.) piece of furniture
mob*i*lia furniture
cassettone (m.) chest of drawers
scaffale (m.) bookcase (open)
biro (f.) biro

[1] The sole exception to this rule is: gli Dei—the Gods. *Dei* was originally *Iddei.*

vestito dress; pl. clothes
biancheria underwear, linen
tov*a*glia tablecloth
settimana week
giorno day
anno year
lɛttera letter
balcone (m.) balcony
sera evening, night
giornale (m.) newspaper
Luisa Louise
spesso (adv.) often
sì (adv.) yes
cambiare to change
lavare to wash
spolverare to dust
entrare . . . in to go into, enter
suonare to ring, to play
scopare to sweep
scr*i*vere to write
lɛggere to read

Exercise 1

Translate into Italian inserting the definite article: bookcase, day, pillowcase, newspaper, ink, night, bell, tablecloth, study, paper, sideboard, armchair, wardrobe, year, week, kitchen, mirror, letter, balcony, underwear, chest of drawers.

Exercise 2

Give the plural of the following nouns supplying the definite article: lenzuolo, vestito, penna, settimana, giornale, tappeto, libro, materasso, sedia, divano, casa, salotto, rosa, lettera, federa, mobile, cuscino, matita, coperta, scaffale.

Exercise 3

Translate into Italian: we change, she sweeps, you play (p.), they dust, you wash (s.), they write, you are reading (p.), she prefers, we open, I am writing, we enter, you are changing (p.).

A. *Translate into English:* 1. Il campanello suona. 2. Roberto apre la porta e vede un'amica di Maria. 3. Luisa entra in[1] salotto. 4. Dove sono Maria e Giulia? 5. Maria scopa il pavimento e Giulia spolvera i mobili di ogni camera da letto. 6. Pulisci le camere ogni giorno, Maria? 7. Si, puliamo le camere ogni giorno e laviamo i pavimenti ogni settimana. 8. Quando cambiate i lenzuoli e le federe? 9. Cambiamo e laviamo i lenzuoli e le federe ogni due settimane. 10. Ogni anno laviamo anche le coperte. 11. Dove appendi i vestiti, Giulia? 12. Appendo sempre i vestiti in un armadio e conservo la biancheria in un cassetto. 13. Che cosa leggi, Roberto? Leggo un giornale. 14. Giulia, preferisci una penna stilografica o una biro? 15. Maria cambia la tovaglia e lava la biancheria. 16. Dove sono le tovaglie, i lenzuoli e le federe? 17. Maria

[1] Note the idiomatic use of *in*, e.g. in cucina—in the kitchen, in giardino—in the garden; in casa—in the house.

conserva la biancheria in un cassettone. 18. Dov'è il cassettone? C'è un cassettone in ogni camera da letto. 19. Luisa dorme in una camera con un balcone. 20. Roberto mette sei libri in uno scaffale.

B. *Translate into Italian:* 1. Where are Mary and Julia? Mary is in the kitchen and Julia is cleaning the bedrooms. 2. Mary dusts the bedrooms every day and washes the floors every week. 3. Mary, do you open the windows when you dust the furniture? 4. Yes, I always[1] open the windows when I sweep the floors and dust the furniture. 5. Julia cleans the windows every two weeks. 6. Louise, do you change the beds often? 7. Yes, I change the beds and wash the sheets and pillow-cases every week. 8. Louise sleeps with one pillow, two blankets and a quilt. 9. Mary and Julia also have one pillow, three blankets and a quilt. 10. Mary changes the tablecloth too, every week. 11. Do you wash the linen, Mary? 12. Yes, I wash the linen every week. 13. Mary keeps the sheets and blankets in a cupboard. 14. Julia puts the tablecloths and pillow-cases in a drawer. 15. Mary often cleans the study and dusts the furniture. 16. When Mary cleans the study, she dusts the desk, table and bookcases and puts the pens and pencils in a drawer. 17. When you write a letter do you prefer a fountain pen to (translate: or) a biro? 18. Robert writes two or three letters every week. 19. Where is the pencil, Robert? 20. I keep the pens, pencils and notepaper in a drawer.

C. Qualcuno suona il campanello? Chi è?—Is someone ringing the bell? Who is it? È l'amico di Roberto. Apri la porta.—It is Robert's friend. Open the door. Posso parlare con Roberto?—May I speak to Robert? Mi rincresce ma non è a (in) casa.—I am sorry but he is not at home. Quando ritornerà? Ritornerà tra qualche minuto.—When will he be back? He will be back in a few minutes. Parla italiano? Sì, un poco.—Do you speak Italian? Yes, a little. Comprende quando Roberto parla? Non troppo bene.—Do you understand when Robert speaks? Not too well. Roberto non parla lentamente? No, parla sempre in fretta.—Does Robert not speak slowly? No, he always speaks quickly. Vuol aspettare Roberto in salotto? Grazie tante. Prego.—Would you like to wait for Robert in the sitting-room? Thank you so much. Don't mention it. Preferisce leggere il giornale o una rivista?—Do you prefer (would you like) to read the paper or a magazine?

D. *Favorisca*

Favorisca—Please come in.
Favorisca il biglietto—Tickets, please.
Favorisca la patente—Your driving licence, please.

[1] In Italian adverbs always follow the verb they modify.

LESSON IV

Adjectives

Adjectives in Italian can be divided into two classes. To the first group belong those that have different endings for the masculine and the feminine, both in the singular and plural.

First Class

	Masculine		*Feminine*
Singular:	*o*	e.g. questo, questa = this	*a*
Plural:	*i*	questi, queste = these	*e*

To the second group belong those adjectives that have one form only for the masculine and feminine singular, and one for the masculine and feminine plural: singular ending *e*, plural *i*.

Second Class

	Masculine		*Feminine*
Singular:	*e*	e.g. intelligente = intelligent	*e*
Plural:	*i*	intelligenti = intelligent	*i*

lo scolaro intelligɛnte, la scolara intelligɛnte
the intelligent pupil (m. and f.)
gli scolari intelligɛnti, le scolare intelligɛnti
the intelligent pupils (m. and f.)

Adjectives must agree in gender and number with the nouns they qualify. If two or more nouns of different genders are qualified by one adjective, the adjective must be plural and masculine:

Questo teatro e questa chiɛsa sono modɛrni.
This theatre and this church are modern.

Note: Rules regarding the position of adjectives will be given in Lesson XIII. The sentences selected have their adjectives in the same place as in English.

Subject Pronouns

	Singular		*Plural*	
1st Person	io	I	noi	we
2nd ,,	tu	you	voi	you
3rd ,,	egli, ella	he, she	essi, esse	they (m.), they (f.)
	esso, essa	he, she, it		
3rd ,, Direct address (courtesy form)	lɛi	you	loro	you

The pronoun *tu* is used only in addressing relatives and intimate friends, while the more general and correct form of addressing people of importance, older people, and people with whom we are not familiar, is always *lɛi*, followed by the 3rd person singular of the verb, when speaking to one person, and *loro*, followed by the third person plural of the verb, when speaking to more than one person. We shall refer to this use of the third person as the courtesy form. During the Fascist regime an attempt was made to enforce the use of *voi* (common in some parts of Southern Italy) and to extend it to the whole of Italy. It is advisable to learn right from the start and to use in conversation the *tu* and the *lɛi* form, using *voi* only as the plural of the intimate *tu*. *Egli* and *ella*, used more in writing than in conversation, refer only to persons. *Esso* and *essa*, likewise used more in writing, can refer to both things and persons. The colloquial form, sometimes used also in familiar writing, is *lui* (he) and *lɛi* (she).

As we have stated in Lesson I, each person of the verb has such a distinctive ending in Italian as to render the use of pronoun subjects superfluous. They must, however, be used in the following cases:

(a) Whenever the pronoun is modified by an adverb: He also loves Italy—Anch'egli ama l'Italia.

(b) In order to emphasize contrast: I work, they rest—Io lavoro, essi riposano.

Vocabulary IV

città city, town
piazza square, market place
strada street, roadway
viale (m.) avenue
marciapiɛde (m.) pavement
pedone (m.) pedestrian
musɛo museum
chiɛsa church
banca bank
***a*lbero** tree
stazione (f.) station
monumento monument
uff*i*cio postale post office
albɛrgo hotel
teatro theatre
amico, -a friend
p*i*ccolo (adj.) small, little
largo (adj.) wide, broad
interessante (adj.) interesting
bɛllo (adj.) beautiful
grande (adj.) big, great
antico (adj.) old
modɛrno (adj.) modern
molto (adj.) much, many
no (adv.) no
ora (adv.) now
vicino a (prep.) near
vicino (adj.) near
vicino (adv.) near by
pɔi (adv.) then, after
lungo (prep.) along
lungo (adj.) long
a dɛstra to the right, on the right
a sinistra to the left, on the left
voltare to turn (trans. and intrans.; aux. **avere**)

camminare to walk (aux. **avere**) **domandare . . . a** to ask
arrivare . . . a to arrive **ricevere** to receive
attraversare to cross **visitare** to visit

Exercise 1

1. *Supply the subject pronouns in the following:*

1. ...... hanno.	6. ...... sei.	11. ...... suona.	16. ...... attraversate.
2. ...... pulisce.	7. ...... entro.	12. ...... abbiamo.	17. ...... apriamo.
3. ...... metti.	8. ...... volta.	13. ...... chiama.	18. ...... cammina.
4. ...... cambiano.	9. ...... ricevete.	14. ...... vediamo.	19. ...... scrivono.
5. ...... dormiamo.	10. ...... scopi.	15. ...... conservi.	20. ...... avete.

Exercise 2. *Translate into Italian keeping same order of words as in English:* 1. this book 2. a beautiful chair 3. an interesting museum 4. a big city 5. an old monument 6. a broad avenue 7. an old church 8. a small church 9. this bedroom 10. a little street 11. a large square 12. a broad pavement 13. a big town 14. two or three books 15. these gardens 16. a big bank 17. six beautiful houses 18. a big hotel 19. two big bookcases 20. this tree.

Exercise 3. *Translate into Italian both pronoun and verb:* 1. We cross. 2. They walk. 3. I turn. 4. He enters. 5. You[1] sleep. 6. She sees. 7. You have. 8. I live. They (*f.*) change. 10. We are writing. 11. She cleans. 12. We fear. 13. He rings. 14. You hang. 15. We are. 16. They (m.) read. 17. She dusts. 18. He writes. 19. You prefer. 20. We keep.

A. *Translate into English:* 1. Dove abitano Maria e Roberto? 2. Essi abitano in una piccola città. 3. La casa è in una larga strada. 4. Che cosa c'è in questa piazza? 5. Ci sono un interessante museo, una piccola chiesa e una grande banca. 6. È antica la chiesa? No, è moderna. 7. Vicino a questa chiesa c'è un largo viale con grandi alberi. 8. Ci sono interessanti monumenti in questa città? 9. Ci sono interessanti monumenti e belle chiese. 10. Maria attraversa la strada poi volta a sinistra. 11. Anche noi attraversiamo la strada ed entriamo in una banca. 12. Maria e Roberto camminano su un largo marciapiede. 13. Voltano a sinistra e arrivano a casa.[2] 14. L'ufficio postale è in una piccola piazza, vicino a un teatro. 15. Ci sono chiese in questa città? 16. Ci sono tre grandi chiese. 17. Giulia e Luisa camminano lungo un viale. 18. Esse attra-

[1] For practice translate *you* throughout the exercises by all four forms (*tu, lɛi, voi, loro*).

[2] 'A casa', note idiomatic use. Cf. a teatro, a scuola, etc.—*to, in* or *at* the theatre; *to, in* or *at* school.

versano la piazza e voltano a sinistra. 19. Un pedone attraversa la strada e domanda a Roberto: "Dov'è la stazione?" 20. Ecco la stazione. Il pedone cammina lungo il viale e vede la stazione.

B. *Translate into Italian:* 1. Mary and Julia live in a beautiful city. 2. The house where Julia and Mary live is in a large square. 3. There is a long avenue with big trees near this square. 4. Do you prefer to live in a large city or a small town? 5. I prefer to live in a small town. 6. Are there many interesting monuments in this town? 7. Yes, there are many interesting monuments, an old church and a museum. 8. The hotel, the station, the bank and the post-office are modern. 9. The streets of this city are beautiful. 10. Pedestrians walk along the pavement. 11. Mary crosses the road and enters a post-office. 12. Is this hotel big? 13. No, it is a small hotel: it has ten bedrooms. 14. Do you live in this hotel now? asks Mary. 15. No, here is the house where we live. 16. Robert walks along a broad avenue. 17. He arrives at a small square, crosses the road, turns left and enters a bank. 18. It is a small bank near an old museum. 19. There is a beautiful station in this city; it is large and modern. 20. Do you turn right or left? I turn left and he turns right and crosses the road.

C. Dove abita lei?—Where do you live? (addressed to one person). Dove abitano loro?—Where do you (plural) live?

Preferisce abitare in campagna o in città?—Do you prefer living in the country or in the city? Preferisco abitare in città ma non al centro.—I prefer living in the city but not in the centre.

Molte persone hanno una casa propria in Italia?—Do many people in Italy have their own houses? In Italia poche persone hanno una casa propria, molti abitano in appartamenti in affitto.—In Italy few people own their own houses, almost all live in rented flats. E loro?—And you? Abbiamo una casa nostra.—We have our own house.

Che cosa usano come riscaldamento?—What do you use for heating? In salotto c'è un caminetto ed in esso usiamo legna.—In the sitting-room there is a fireplace and in it we use wood. In quasi ogni altra stanza c'è il termosifone.—In almost every other room there is central heating.

Sono alti gli affitti in Italia?—Are rents high in Italy? Sì, sono alti e in Italia si paga l'affitto ogni mese.—Yes, they are high and in Italy rents are paid every month.

Come si dice 'a block of flats' in italiano? Si dice un casamento, ma più comunemente una casa.—How do you say 'a block of flats' in Italian? You say 'un casamento', but more commonly 'una casa'.

Quanti piani ci sono in una casa?—How many storeys are there in a block? Ci sono quattro o cinque piani e ci sono due appartamenti ad ogni piano.—There are four or five storeys and there are two flats on each.

Come si chiama una persona che abita uno di questi appartamenti in affitto?—What are the people who live in these rented flats called? Si chiamano inquilini.—They are called tenants.

D. *Avanti*

Avanti! (in response to a knock on the door)—Come in!
Avanti, andiamo!—Come on, let's go!

LESSON V

Prepositions

Every time the definite article is preceded by one of the prepositions *di, a, da, in, su, con,* and *per* it combines with them and generally becomes one single word.

		il	i	lo	gli	la	le	l'
di	of	del	dei	dello	degli	della	delle	dell'
a	to, at	al	ai	allo	agli	alla	alle	all'
da	by, from	dal	dai	dallo	dagli	dalla	dalle	dall'
in	in, into	nel	nei	nello	negli	nella	nelle	nell'
su	on	sul	sui	sullo	sugli	sulla	sulle	sull'
con	with	col	coi	(collo)	cogli	(colla)	(colle)	coll'
per	for	(pel)	(pei)	(pello)	(pegli)	(pella)	(pelle)	(pell')

The preposition *di* is used to denote possession: Il libro di Giulia—Julia's book; la penna d'Ɛlena—Helen's pen; le matite dello scolaro—the pupil's pencils.

In the case of *con* and *per*, modern usage prefers to keep the preposition and article separate, since ambiguity would arise in many cases if they were joined: *cɔllo* (neck), *cɔlla* (glue), *cɔlle* (hill), *pɛlle* (skin). The shortened forms: *de', a', da'*, are sometimes found in poetry.

Past Absolute

Past Absolute of Model Verbs

am-ai	I loved	tem-ei	I feared	dorm-ii	I slept
am-asti	you loved	tem-esti	you feared	dorm-isti	you slept
am-ò	he loved	tem-é	he feared	dorm-ì	he slept
am-ammo	we loved	tem-emmo	we feared	dorm-immo	we slept
am-aste	you loved	tem-este	you feared	dorm-iste	you slept
am-arono	they loved	tem-erono	they feared	dorm-irono	they slept

The endings of the past absolute, apart from the characteristic vowel maintained throughout the tense, are identical in the three conjugations; with the sole exception, however, of the 3rd person singular of the first conjugation that ends in *o* instead of in *a*.

In most verbs of the second conjugation there is a double form for the 1st and 3rd person singular and the 3rd plural in *ɛtti, ɛtte, ɛttero*. This form is equally correct and is also used.

Past Absolute of 'Ɛssere' and 'Avere'

fui	I was	ɛbbi	I had
fosti	you were	avesti	you had
fu	he was	ɛbbe	he had
fummo	we were	avemmo	we had
foste	you were	aveste	you had
furono	they were	ɛbbero	they had

Uses

The past absolute is called in Italian 'Passato Remoto' and is used to indicate simply an action or state in the past, without any reference to the present. It is the tense of the narrative, the story, otherwise used only to relate an action, but never to describe the circumstances:

Le truppe italiane entrarono in Roma. The Italian troops entered Rome.
Cesare fu un famoso generale. Caesar was a famous general.

This tense translates the English simple past (I went), and the emphatic past (I did go).[1]

In everyday Italian (spoken), modern usage prefers the perfect tense (passato prossimo), as we shall see later.

Vocabulary V

a**ngolo** corner
incr*o*cio crossing
sem*a*foro traffic lights
fermata stop, stopping place
tr*a*ffico traffic
metropolitano policeman
autom*ɔ*bile (f.) car, motorcar
tram (m.) tramcar
***a*utobus** (m.) bus
passegg*ɛ*ro passenger
luce (f.) light
conduc*ɛ*nte (m.) driver
fattorino conductor
biglietto ticket, card
n*ɔ*tte (f.) night
verde (adj.) green
rosso (adj.) red
giallo (adj.) yellow
affollato (adj.) crowded
i*ɛ*ri (adv.) yesterday
fa (adv.) ago
chi? (inter. pron.) who, whom?
chiedere . . . a to ask
guidare to drive, to guide
aspettare to wait, wait for
guardare to look at, look
dir*i*gere to direct, manage, conduct
pr*ɛ*ndere to take
sc*e*ndere . . . da to descend, come down, get off
***v*endere** to sell
distribuire* to distribute, give, issue

Exercise 1

1. *Repeat orally the past absolute of:* conservare, abitare, domandare, vendere, ricevere, aprire, pulire, distribuire, preferire.

2. *Translate into Italian with pronoun subject:* 1. We called. 2. They

[1] When the context indicates that the action was habitual, the Italian past descriptive tense must be used. See page 33.

feared. 3. I received. 4. He understood. 5. You cleaned. 6. They waited. 7. He distributed. 8. You sold. 9. We watched. 10. I drove. 11. She arrived. 12. They walked. 13. I sold. 14. They (f.) swept. 15. She dusted. 16. We preferred. 17. You feared. 18. They (m.) crossed. 19. She washed. 20. You slept.

Exercise 2

Translate into Italian: 1. in the garden 2. from the window 3. on the balcony 4. from the theatre 5. to the church 6. in the mirror 7. at the corner 8. from the house 9. of the picture 10. in the books 11. in the study 12. on the table 13. at the stop 14. on the sideboard 15. in the kitchen 16. on the divan 17. in the bathroom 18 in the hall 19. on the beds 20. in the newspapers.

A. *Translate into English:* 1. Tre giorni fa Maria ricevette una lettera da Luisa. 2. Anche Roberto e Giulia ricevettero due lettere. 3. Chi aprì la porta quando arrivarono le lettere? 4. Giulia aprì la porta e distribuì le lettere a Maria e a Roberto. 5. Dove dormisti ieri notte, Giulia? 6. Dormii sul divano nel salotto. 7. Un'amica dormì nella camera di Giulia. 8. Guidasti tu l'automobile ieri, Roberto? 9. Le strade di questa città sono affollate; il metropolitano dirige il traffico delle automobili, degli autobus e dei tram. 10. Maria aspetta il tram alla fermata nella piazza. 11. Anche Giulia e Luisa prendono il tram con Maria. 12. Maria chiede tre biglietti al fattorino. 13. "Dove scendono?" domanda il fattorino e distribuisce i biglietti ai passeggeri. 14. Il tram arriva alla fermata e Giulia e Luisa scendono. 15. Un semaforo ha tre luci: una rossa, una gialla, una verde. 16. I pedoni guardano il semaforo: la luce è rossa ed essi attraversano la strada. 17. All'incrocio di due strade c'è un semaforo: la luce è verde e i pedoni aspettano. 18. "Dov'è la fermata dell'autobus?" chiede Maria al conducente. "È all'angolo della strada." 19. Ieri Roberto e Maria e Giulia furono alla banca. 20. Roberto guidò l'automobile; quando arrivarono, Roberto entrò nella banca e Giulia e Maria aspettarono nell'automobile.

B. *Translate into Italian:* 1. Robert received a letter from a friend yesterday. 2. A year ago Louise sold a house with a little garden to this friend. 3. She prefers to live in a large flat. 4. "What are you looking at, Robert?" "I am watching the traffic." 5. At the crossing of two roads there are often traffic lights (say: there is a traffic light). 6. Every evening the streets of this city are crowded. 7. There is a stop at the corner of the square, where we wait for the bus. 8. We looked at the traffic lights, and when the lights changed we crossed the street. 9. Pedestrians cross the street when the light is red. 10. Every day Robert waits for the bus at the corner of the street. 11. He asks for a ticket, and gets off at the post office. 12. The driver drives the bus and the conductor issues the tickets. 13. When the bus arrives at a stop the conductor rings the bell and the passengers get off. 14. There is a policeman at cross-roads. 15. He directs the traffic when the streets are crowded. 16. When the traffic lights changed the bus turned to the left and the tram turned to the right. 17. "Do you prefer a tram or a bus, Robert?" "I prefer a bus." 18. Two or three passengers get off the bus at every stop. 19. Louise received a letter from a friend a week ago. 20. The passengers often read a paper in the bus.

C. Per piacere può indicarmi dov'è il teatro dell'Opera?—Could you please direct me to the Opera House? Con piacere, cammini lungo questa strada e all'incrocio volti a sinistra: lo vedrà alla fine della strada.—With pleasure, walk along this street and at the cross-roads turn to the left: you will see it at the end of the street.

Repeat similar questions, varying instructions to suit.

Qual'è la strada più breve per l'ospedale?—Which is the shortest way to the hospital? Prenda l'autobus numero dieci e scenda all'angolo della piazza vicino al monumento ai Caduti.—Take a number ten bus and get off at the corner of the square near the war memorial.

Repeat similar questions and corresponding answers.

Può dirmi quale autobus devo prendere per ritornare qui dalla stazione?—Could you tell me which bus to take to get back here from the station? Lo stesso numero.—The same number.

Può avvertirmi, per favore, quando arriviamo a Piazza Cavour?—Can you tell me, please, when we reach Piazza Cavour? Per favore, dov'è la fermata del 9?—Where does the number 9 bus stop, please? Per scendere a una fermata facoltativa, bisogna suonare il campanello.—One must ring the bell to get off at a request stop.

Repeat similar questions making suitable changes in the answer.

Quanto ci vuole per arrivarci?—How long will it take to get there? Le sono molto grato.—I am most grateful. Lei è molto gentile.—You are very kind. Devo cambiare?—Have I to change? Come si dice 'to board' un autobus? Si dice 'salire su' un autobus.—How does one say 'to board' a bus? One says 'salire su'. Quanto costerebbe un taxi dalla stazione all'albergo?—How much would a taxi cost from the station to the hotel?

Repeat question with necessary variations.

Ogni quanto tempo passa quest'autobus?—How often does this bus run? Passa ogni dieci minuti circa.—It runs roughly every ten minutes. Ci sono molti autobus per il centro della città?—Do many buses go to the city centre? Sì, i numeri 2, 3, 7, 9 e 10 passano ogni cinque minuti e arrivano al centro in dieci minuti.—Yes, numbers 2, 3, 7, 9 and 10 run every 5 minutes and take 10 minutes to reach the centre of the city.

D. *Figurati!* *Si figuri!* *Figuriamoci!*

Ti dispiace di accompagnarmi? Figurati!—Do you mind coming with me? Not at all!

Le sono molto grato. Si figuri!—I am most grateful to you. Don't mention it!

Figuratevi se ci va!—Can you imagine him going?

LESSON VI

Possessives

Masculine		*Feminine*		
Singular	*Plural*	*Singular*	*Plural*	
il mio	i miɛi	la mia	le mie	my, mine
il tuo	i tuɔi	la tua	le tue	your, yours
il suo	i suɔi	la sua	le sue	his, her, hers, its, your, yours
il nɔstro	i nɔstri	la nɔstra	le nɔstre	our, ours
il vɔstro	i vɔstri	la vɔstra	le vɔstre	your, yours
il loro	i loro	la loro	le loro	their, theirs your, yours
il prɔprio	i prɔprii	la prɔpria	le prɔprie	one's own (any person)

The possessives, both adjectives and pronouns, have the same endings as adjectives of the first class: c.f. *questo*, *questi*, *questa*, *queste*, with the exception of *loro* which never changes, and the irregular masc. plu. of *mio*, *tuo*, *suo*.

Two points of difference between English and Italian possessives must be stressed:

1. Like other adjectives, the possessives agree in number and gender with the noun they qualify, not as in English with the possessor to which they refer.

2. Unlike English, possessives are normally preceded in Italian by the definite article:

Essa vendé il suo libro. She sold her book.
Egli guida la sua automɔbile. He drives his car.
Ognuno ama la prɔpria patria. Everyone loves his own fatherland.

They follow the English construction, however, and omit the article with the names of relatives, when they are in the singular:

Amo mio padre e mia madre. I love my father and my mother.

In the plural, however, they require the article:

le mie sorɛlle my sisters.

The omission of the article (with the names of the relatives in the singular) does not occur in the following cases:

1. When the possessive adjective follows the noun:

il padre mio (not used colloquially) my father.

2. When the possessive adjective does not directly precede the noun, but is separated from it by another adjective:

la nɔstra cara sorɛlla our dear sister.

3. When the noun is modified by a suffix:

il suo fratellino his little brother.

4. With the five words: *babbo*—daddy, *papa*—daddy, *mamma*—mummy, *nɔnno*—grandfather, *nɔnna*—grandmother:

il nɔstro babbo our daddy.

5. With the possessive form *loro*:

il loro zio their uncle.

Since *suo* can refer equally well either to the subject or to another person, when 'his', 'her', etc., is not reflexive, *di lui* (of him), *di lɛi* (of her), are used to avoid ambiguity:

Maria aprì il suo libro. Mary opened her book.
Maria aprì il libro di lui. Mary opened his book.

Possessives can also be preceded by:

1. The indefinite article: un mio zio—an uncle of mine.
2. A demonstrative adjective: questa mia cugina—this cousin of mine.
3. A numeral: due miɛi fratɛlli—two brothers of mine.
4. A quantitative adjective: molti suɔi nipoti—many of her nɛphews.
5. The partitive: dei miɛi parɛnti—some of my relatives.

The English 'of' is not translated; we literally say 'two my brothers'. The possessives must be repeated before each noun to which they refer.

Titles

All titles whether referring to aristocracy or professions, when followed by a proper name, require the definite article, except in direct address:

il conte Bentivoglio Count Bentivoglio.

Titles ending in *ore*, such as *signore*, *dottore*, *monsignore*, drop the final *e* when followed by a proper name or another title:

il dottor Giorgi Dr Giorgi
il signor professore professor.

The use of professional and honorary[1] titles resembles the English use of "Doctor" and "Professor" so that, in direct address, one says:

(to a lawyer) "Come sta, avvocato?" "How are you, . . . ?"

[1] The most common honorary titles, in order of increasing importance, are Cavaliɛre, Commendatore and Grand' Ufficiale. The title of Onorevole is given to Parliamentary Deputies.

(to an engineer) "Quando parte, ingegnɛre?" "When are you leaving . . . ?"
(to an accountant) "Arrivederla, ragioniɛre" "Good-bye, . . ."
(to a Deputy) "Buon giorno, onorevole!" "Good morning, . . .!"
"Commendatore, che piacere vederla! ". . . what a pleasure to see you!"
"Da quanto tɛmpo non l'abbiamo vista, Cavaliɛre!" "What a long time since we last saw you, . . .!"

Some professional people, such as pharmacists and graduates in economic and commercial science, are addressed as "Dottore", and this title is always used, when the person addressed is not personally known, by employees and by the lower classes.

These titles are used in the same manner when writing letters (see Lesson XL):

Gentile Dottore Egrɛgio Professore Caro Ingegnɛre

Vocabulary VI

fam*i*glia family
genitore (m.) parent
padre (m.) father
madre (f.) mother
marito husband
f*i*glio son
f*i*glia daughter
fratɛllo brother
sorɛlla sister
m*o*glie (f.) wife
zio uncle
zia aunt
nɔnni grandparents
nɔnno grandfather
nɔnna grandmother
suɔcero father-in-law
cugino, -a cousin (m. & f.)
parɛnte (m. & f.) relative
signore (m.) gentleman, Mr, sir
signora lady, Mrs
signorina young lady, Miss
ragazzo boy
ragazza girl
scuɔla school
Francesco Francis
Filippo Philip
Vera Vera
mentre (conj.) while, as, whereas
comprɛndere to understand, consist of, comprehend
comprare to buy
parlare . . . con (aux. avere) to speak, talk to
ritornare a to come back
con*o*scere to know, be acquainted with

Exercise 1

Translate into Italian: ('your' to be translated in four ways) 1. my father 2. my little brother 3. your sisters 4. our aunt 5. your dear uncle 6. their cousins 7. his sister 8. her father-in-law 9. their dear relative 10. one's own grandmother 11. my daddy 12. our parents 13. an uncle of mine 14. three of his cousins 15. many of your relatives

16. this cousin of yours 17. his grandfather 18. my dear sister 19. some of my friends 20. her parents.

Exercise 2

Translate into Italian, inserting subject pronouns: 1. I understand 2. we spoke 3. he gets off 4. they feared 5. it consists of 6. he issued 7. we have 8. you are 9. he was 10. we are 11. they have 12. you were 13. he had 14. I cleaned 15. they asked 16. you had 17. he bought 18. they came back 19. we were 20. he crossed.

A. *Translate into English:* 1. Maria e Giulia sono sorelle; esse hanno un fratello, Roberto. 2. Conosce i loro genitori? Conosciamo la loro madre. 3. Ecco la sorella della madre di Maria, la signora Bruni. 4. Abita con la famiglia di Maria? 5. No, ma la sua casa è vicino al loro appartamento. 6. Filippo e Vera sono i cugini di Maria. 7. Essi sono il figlio e la figlia di sua zia. 8. Dov'è il marito della signora Bruni? 9. È in una libreria e compra un libro per suo figlio. 10. La moglie del signor Bruni è la sorella di tuo padre? domanda Luisa a Giulia. 11. No, è la sorella di mia madre. 12. Chi aspettano Filippo e Vera? aspettano il loro cugino. 13. Roberto e Maria comprano un giornale e ritornano a casa. 14. "Dove sono i nostri cugini?" domanda Maria. 15. Essi aspettano nel salotto e leggono un libro. 16. Con chi parla Filippo ora? parla con sua sorella. 17. Conoscete il loro nonno? Egli abita in questa strada. 18. Ieri ricevei una lettera da sua moglie. 19. Una settimana fa un mio parente, il signor Ansaldi, parlò con i genitori dei suoi cugini. 20. Luisa aspettò ieri sua cugina alla fermata dell'autobus. 21. Esse comprarono un giornale e poi ritornarono a casa.

B. *Translate into Italian:* 1. Philip is the son of Mr and Mrs Bruni and Vera is their daughter. 2. They are cousins of Mary, Julia and Robert. 3. The two boys are great friends. 4. Does Robert live with his aunt and uncle? 5. No, he lives with his own parents and his two sisters. 6. Vera sees Mary and Julia every day at school. 7. They take the bus at the stop near their school. 8. When they get off the bus, they look at the traffic lights and cross the street when the lights are red. 9. When the girls rang the bell yesterday, Miss Ansaldi opened the door. 10. Who is Miss Ansaldi? She is an old friend of the family. 11. Is she a relative? No, but she is a great friend of theirs. 12. Does she live with Vera's cousins? No, a year ago she bought a little flat near their house. 13. Often when Mary and Julia return home, their mother is in the sitting-room with Miss Ansaldi. 14. "Where is mummy?" the girls asked Miss Ansaldi. "She is in town with your daddy." 15. Does Mrs Bruni drive the car? Yes, but not in town. 16. Mary and Julia watch the traffic from the drawing-room window. 17. The streets of this city are always crowded. 18. Louise is a friend of Vera. She lives with her grandparents in an old house near the station. 19. Are they her mother's parents? 20. No, they are her father's parents, and they have a beautiful house with a garden.

C. La nostra famiglia è composta di cinque persone.—Our family is composed of five people. Di quante persone è composta la sua famiglia? —How many people are there in your family?

Repeat the question to several pupils varying the answers.

Quanti figli ci sono in media in una famiglia italiana?—How many children are there in an average Italian family? In una famiglia borghese ci sono generalmente due o tre figli ma il caso del figlio unico diviene sempre più frequente.—In a middle class family there are generally two or three children but the case of an only child is becoming ever more common. Le famiglie dei contadini sono numerose?—Sì, sono generalmente più numerose.—Are the families of the peasants bigger? Yes they are usually larger. La madre di una mia amica è dottoressa.—The mother of one of my friends is a doctor. E tua madre, che fa?—And your mother? What does she do? Non esercita nessuna professione—sul suo passaporto c'è scritto 'casalinga'.—She does not practise any profession—'housewife' is written on her passport. Le donne italiane continuano a lavorare dopo essersi sposate?—Do Italian women continue to work after they are married? Molto spesso sì, anche perché è facile in Italia trovare delle cameriere.—Very often yes, especially as it is easy to find maids in Italy. Tutta la famiglia si riunisce sempre per il pranzo, compresi il padre e figli che ritornano a casa da scuola.—The whole family meets for lunch including the father and children who come home from school. Lei è figlia unica?—Are you an only daughter? No ho due sorelle e un fratello.—No I have two sisters and a brother.

Repeat question with various answers.

D. *Proprio*

E proprio uno sciocco!—He really is a fool!

Proprio così!—Just so!

Hai parlato proprio con lui?—Did you really speak to *him*?

LESSON VII

Negative Sentences

A sentence is made negative in Italian by placing the adverb *non* in front of the verb:

Maria conosce Roma.	Mary knows Rome.
Maria non conosce Roma.	Mary does not know Rome.

Interrogative Negative

A negative sentence is made interrogative simply by the intonation of the voice in speaking, and by a question mark in writing:

Non ami le lingue? Do you not like languages?

Double Negative

Contrary to the English construction, negative sentences in Italian may contain two negative words. Such negative words used along with the negative adverb *non*, are:

non . . . nessuno	nobody, not anybody
non . . . mai	never
non . . . niɛnte nulla	nothing
non . . . affatto	not at all
non . . . né . . . né	neither . . . nor

Non conosco nessuno	I don't know anybody.
Non lɛggono mai.	They never read.
Non compriamo niɛnte.	We don't buy anything.
Non capite affatto.	You do not understand at all.
Non vediamo né Giorgio né Maria.	We see neither George nor Mary.

When, however, *nessuno*, *niɛnte*, *nulla*, as subjects, stand at the beginning of the sentence, *non* is omitted:

Nessuno aspettava alla fermata.	Nobody was waiting at the stop.
Niɛnte scoraggia gli audaci.	Nothing daunts the valiant.

Né . . . né—neither . . . nor, requires special attention. When this negative expression precedes the verb, *non* is omitted and the verb must be plural in Italian:

Né Maria né Giulia visitarono il museo.
Neither Mary nor Julia visited the museum.

The English word 'only' can be expressed in Italian by putting *non* before the verb and *che* after it:

Non ho che una sorɛlla. I have only one sister.

'Any' in Negative Sentences:

In a negative sentence the English word 'any' is not translated if it is followed by a plural: it is rendered by the adjective *nessun*, *nessuno*, *nessuna* and *nessun'* (same forms as the indefinite article) when followed by a singular noun:

Non compro libri. I do not buy any books.
Non compro nessun libro. I do not buy any book.

Vocabulary VII

nipoti grandchildren
dottore (m.) doctor
tɛmpo time, weather
professione (f.) profession
professore (m.) professor
ponte (m.) bridge
malato (n. & adj.) ill, sick
lìngua language, tongue
rivista magazine, review
cɔsa thing
cognato brother-in-law
cognata sister-in-law
nipote (m. & f.) nephew, niece
suɔcera mother-in-law
gɛnero son-in-law
nuora daughter-in-law
avvocato lawyer
ingegnɛre (m.) engineer

altro (adj.) other; (pron.) something else
studioso (adj.) studious
intelligɛnte (adj.) intelligent
famoso (adj.) famous
italiano (adj.) Italian
francese (adj.) French
tedesco (adj.) German
cɔmodo (adj.) comfortable
quale (inter. adj., & pron.) which?
vɛcchio (adj.) old
molto (adv.) very
costruire* to build, erect
incontrare to meet
esercitare to practise
studiare to study
curare to treat, cure
insegnare . . . a to teach

Exercise 1

Translate into Italian: 1. They never write. 2. He understands nothing. 3. They don't know anybody. 4. She reads nothing. 5. We don't understand at all. 6. I see neither Mary nor Julia. 7. We bought nothing. 8. Neither you nor I understood. 9. Have you only one brother? 10. Nobody spoke. 11. Did you not buy any books? 12. Nobody met the boy. 13. They did not sell anything. 14. We did not speak to anybody. 15. Neither Robert nor Francis arrived. 16. Have you not any books? 17. She bought only one pen. 18. No one entered. 19. They teach nothing. 20. We fear nobody.

Exercise 2

Translate into Italian and supply the other 5 persons of the tense, completing the sentence each time: 1. I am looking at nothing. 2. I did not receive anything. 3. I never read. 4. I did not understand at all. 5. I opened neither the door nor the window. 6. I am writing nothing. 7. I did not buy a book. 8. I never clean the house. 9. I issued no tickets. 10. I did not cross any street.

Exercise 3

Translate the following questions into Italian and write a short answer in sentence form: 1. Do you never read? 2. Have you no brothers? 3. Did you not buy anything? 4. Did neither Mary nor Julia arrive? 5. Do you not understand my Italian? 6. Do you not practise any profession? 7. Do you not speak any other language? 8. Have you only one sister? 9. Do your friends not read any books? 10. Do you not live in town?

A. *Translate into English:* 1. Il signor Mazzoni, il padre di Maria è ingegnere.[1] 2. Egli costruisce ponti, strade, case. 3. Che professione esercita suo padre? 4. Il nonno di Maria è vecchio e non esercita nessuna professione. 5. Chi curò il nonno quando fu malato un anno fa? 6. Il dottor Duranti curò il nonno e la nonna. 7. La nuora e il genero della signora Ansaldi parlano molte lingue. 8. Parla il francese lei, Giulia? 9. No, non parlo né il francese né il tedesco, ma un anno fa io e mia sorella studiammo l'italiano. 10. Chi insegnò la lingua italiana a Giulia e a Maria? 11. Maria e Giulia sono intelligenti e studiose e studiano ogni giorno con i loro cugini. 12. Chi costruì questa casa? domanda a Vera una sua amica. 13. Mio zio, l'ingegnere Mazzoni ed egli costruisce ora un grande teatro ed una bella chiesa. 14. Quali lingue studiano i suoi nipoti, signora Bruni? 15. Maria e Giulia studiano l'italiano ma Roberto non ama affatto le lingue; non conosce né il francese né il tedesco. 16. L'avvocato Ansaldi è malato e suo suocero chiama un dottore. 17. Dov'è sua suocera, professor Tonini? La mia cara suocera è nello studio e legge una rivista tedesca. 18. Quale ponte attraversaste quando ritornaste in città? 19. Non attraversammo nessun ponte; all'incrocio voltammo a destra e prendemmo la strada vicino alla chiesa. 20. L'ingegnere Mazzoni e il signor Bruni sono cognati.

B. *Translate into Italian*: 1. My brothers are studious, they read many books. 2. Robert's friends are not intelligent, they never read anything. 3. Do you know Mr and Mrs Boni? They are relatives of Robert.

[1] Note the idiomatic omission of the indefinite article which is, however, kept when the complement is qualified by an adjective: un bravo ingegnere—a good engineer.

4. What profession does Mr. Boni practise? 5. He teaches languages. He speaks English, French and Italian. 6. Dr Duranti is a friend of ours. His wife knows my mother. 7. Our lawyer is also a friend of the doctor and his family. 8. He is a famous lawyer. Do you know his sons? 9. One son is practising his father's profession. The other is an engineer and their sister is studying languages. 10. What does an engineer build? He erects bridges, roads and houses. 11. Who cures the sick (pl.)? Doctors cure the sick. 12. My aunt's children live in Italy. 13. Is this aunt your mother's sister? No, she is my father's sister. 14. My father writes often to his sister but he never receives any letter from my aunt. 15. She has a large family and hasn't any time to (per) write. 16. Which of your relatives do you prefer? I prefer my mother's sister and her husband. 17. They have five children and we see these cousins every week. 18. The boys are intelligent but not studious. 19. They prefer to look at magazines and they never read any books. 20. They live in a comfortable flat but they have not any garden.

C. Che cosa farai quando sarai grande?—What will you be (or do) when you grow up? Quando sarò grande farò l'avvocato.—When I grow up I am going to be a lawyer.

Repeat the question—e lei che cosa farà? and vary the answer—farò l'ingegnere, il dottore, l'insegnante etc.

Quale professione preferisce lei?—Which profession do you prefer.—Supply answers.

Purtroppo in Italia c'è molta disoccupazione e molti giovani dopo aver preso una laurea non trovano lavoro.—Unfortunately there is a lot of unemployment in Italy and many young people after having taken a degree cannot find a job. In questo paese c'è una mancanza di insegnanti specialmente di insegnanti di matematica e scienze.—In this country there is a shortage of teachers, particularly of mathematics and science. Anche in Italia c'è una mancanza di professori?—Is there also a shortage of teachers in Italy? Sì, ma molto meno che in Gran Bretagna; quasi tutti i professori danno lezioni private nel pomeriggio.—Yes, but much less than in Great Britain, and almost all of them give private lessons in the afternoons.

D. *Mica*

Non è mica stupido—He is by no means a fool.

Non ti piace mica?—You don't like it, do you?

LESSON VIII

Past Descriptive

Past Descriptive of Model Verbs

am-avo[1]	(I loved, was	tem-evo	(I feared,	dorm-ivo	(I slept,
am-avi	loving, used	tem-evi	was fearing,	dorm-ivi	was sleep-
am-ava	to love, etc.)	tem-eva	used to fear	dorm-iva	ing, used
am-avamo		tem-evamo	etc.)	dorm-ivamo	to sleep,
am-avate		tem-evate		dorm-ivate	etc.)
am-avano		tem-evano		dorm-ivano	

Apart from the characteristic vowel, the endings are indentical for all three conjugations.

Past Descriptive of 'Ɛssere' and 'Avere'

ɛro	(I was, was being,	avevo	(I had, was having,
ɛri	used to be, etc.)	avevi	used to have, etc.)
ɛra		aveva	
eravamo		avevamo	
eravate		avevate	
ɛrano		avevano	

Uses

Unlike the past absolute which corresponds to the English simple past tense (I lost) and is mainly a narrative tense, the past descriptive, called in Italian "Imperfetto", is primarily what its English name suggests, *the* past tense[2] for describing. It is therefore used to render:

1. A state in the past:

ɛra pɔvero he was poor

2. An action that was either continuous or habitual:

Egli leggeva per ore e ore.	He used to read for hours and hours.
Prendevo il tram ogni mattina.	I took the tram every morning.
Ripeteva sɛmpre la stessa cɔsa.	She would repeat the same thing again and again.

3. An incomplete action going on while something else happened or was happening:

Mentre egli scriveva il telɛfono suonò. While he was writing the telephone rang.

[1] Io amava, temeva, dormiva are now obsolete forms.

[2] The past descriptive tense is however sometimes used, where the past absolute might be expected, to recount past events in describing the background to a historical narrative: Nel 1492 moriva Lorenzo il Magnifico e Cristoforo Colombo scopriva l'Amɛrica.

Mentre egli leggeva Maria lavorava. — While he was reading Mary was working.

4. And in general the circumstances and details of an action that has taken place:

Il professore aprì il libro: egli leggeva lentamente e spiegava ogni parɔla.

The teacher opened the book: he read slowly and explained every word.

5. The past descriptive is also used in Italian to render the English past perfect when the action was still continuing:

La conoscevo da molto tɛmpo. I had known her for a long time.

It is often difficult for English-speaking students to distinguish the uses of the past descriptive and the past absolute in Italian. In English the past definite, the tense corresponding to the past absolute, is used both for description and narration, but in Italian a distinction must be made between the representation of an action, whether momentary or continuous, recurring habitually, and that of similar action which occurred on a single occasion only: the former requires the past descriptive, the latter the past absolute. The words 'usually', 'often' and the forms 'on certain days', 'used to . . .', 'was . . . -ing' are all clear indications of the need for the past descriptive in Italian; on the other hand the words 'once', 'instantly', 'on that occasion' call for the past absolute.

They often walked for several hours.
Spesso camminavano per molte ore.
Once they walked for several hours.
Una volta camminarono per molte ore.

Both these sentences describe a continuing action: the past descriptive should be used to translate the first, past absolute the second.

Every morning he went to the bar several times for a coffee.
Ogni mattina andava parecchie volte al bar a prendere il caffè.
That morning he went to the bar several times for a coffee.
Quella mattina andò parecchie volte al bar a prendere il caffè.

Both these sentences describe a repeated action: again the past descriptive should be used to translate the first, past the absolute the second.

Where the text does not contain any such indications, the writer's intention must be considered.

He bought and sold at the right moment.

This sentence may refer to the continuous application of a particular skill or to a single instance only, and the respective translations are:

Comprava e vendeva al momento giusto.
Comprò e vendɛtte al momento giusto.

'Some' or 'Any' in Affirmative Sentences

The English words 'some' or 'any' are rendered in Italian, in affirmative sentences, in several different ways:

1. The simplest way, the partitive construction—*di* followed by the definite article—is considered by purists a Gallicism. It is however constantly used in spoken and written Italian[1]:

Mi mostrò dei libri.	He showed me some books.
Ha delle cartoline.	He has some postcards.
Comprai degli utensili.	I bought some tools.

They can also be rendered by:

2. *Qualche*—some, any. *Qualche* is invariable and followed always by the singular even though expressing a collective idea:

Mi mostrò qualche libro.	He showed me some books.
Ha qualche cartolina.	He has some postcards.
Comprai qualche utensile.	I bought some tools.

3. *Alcuno*—some, any. This adjective is used always in the *plural* and agrees in gender with the noun it qualifies:

Mi mostrò alcuni libri.	He showed me some books.
Ha alcune cartoline.	He has some postcards.
Comprai alcuni utensili.	I bought some tools.

4. *Un po'*—some, a little. In all cases, dealing with an indefinite quantity or in the expression 'a little', *un po'* is used:

Comprai un po' di caffè.	I bought some coffee.
Regalò un po' di farina a Giulia.	She gave Julia a little flour.

Vocabulary VIII

galleria gallery, arcade
pittura painting, picture
scultura sculpture
guida guide, guide book
visitatore (m.) visitor
spettacolo show, play
commedia comedy, play
attore (m.) actor
attrice (f.) actress
negozio shop
oggetto object, article
bravo, -a (adj.) good, fine, clever
divertente (adj.) amusing
pittore (m.) painter
opera work, composition
arte (f.) art, skill
meraviglioso (adj.) marvellous, wonderful
quanto (adj., pron., & adv.) how much, how many
chiuso (adj.) closed
tra (prep.) between, among

[1] The partitive construction is also used when "some" or "any" are only implied: Delle ragnatele le sfiorarono il viso—Cobwebs brushed her face.

vetrina shop window, glass case, show case
statua statue
esposizione (f.) exhibition
bene (adv.) well
spiegare to explain, unfold, display, spread out
desiderare to desire, wish, want
finire* to finish, end
accompagnare to accompany, escort
invitare to invite, request
ammirare to admire
applaudire* to applaud, cheer
passare to spend (time) (aux. avere); to pass by (aux. essere)
mostrare . . . a to show

Exercise 1

Repeat orally the past descriptive of: accompagnare, invitare, visitare, spiegare; conoscere, scrivere, vendere, ricevere; pulire, finire, costruire, preferire.

Exercise 2

Translate into Italian inserting the appropriate subject pronouns: 1. I was calling. 2. He used to sleep. 3. We were opening. 4. You were changing. 5. They used to live. 6. We were washing. 7. I used to see. 8. They (f.) were crossing. 9. He used to watch. 10. You were asking. 11. They were driving. 12. He was distributing. 13. She used to know. 14. They (f.) were speaking. 15. He used to study. 16. We were explaining. 17. They were applauding. 18. He used to read. 19. She was writing. 20. I was walking.

Exercise 3

Translate into Italian: 1. He had some pencils. 2. Have you any books? 3. I bought some pictures. 4. He was reading some newspapers. 5. Had they any tickets? 6. Have you a little ink? 7. They had no carpet. 8. She was buying some magazines. 9. Have you any sisters? 10. We had neither blankets nor a quilt. 11. He was writing some letters. 12. She was cleaning some rooms. 13. They were putting away some sheets. 14. Did you buy some paper? 15. They had not any paper. 16. Has he any furniture? 17. We have not any tablecloth. 18. Neither the magazine nor the newspaper arrived. 19. Did you cross any roads? 20. There are no trees in the garden.

A. *Translate into English:* 1. Alcuni nostri amici arrivarono tre giorni fa per visitare la città. 2. Il padre è un famoso pittore e desiderava conoscere i musei le gallerie della nostra città. 3. Roberto conosce bene la città e accompagnò il signor Marini e suo figlio a visitare la galleria e le chiese. 4. Nella galleria una guida accompagnava i visitatori e spiegava i quadri, le statue e le altre opere d'arte. 5. Il signor Marini preferisce la pittura antica alla pittura moderna e ammirò i meravigliosi quadri di molti famosi pittori. 6. C'è anche una sala di pitture e sculture moderne. 7. Mentre gli altri visitavano i musei e le chiese, la signora Mazzoni accompagnò la sua amica a vedere dei tappeti. 8. Poi esse ammirarono dei vestiti nelle vetrine del negozio vicino. 9. Non erano affatto cari. 10. Mentre aspettavano l'autobus alla fermata vicino al semaforo, Roberto passò nella sua automobile. 11. La signora Mazzoni chiamò suo figlio e le signore ritornarono a casa in automobile. 12. Ieri sera l'ingegnere Mazzoni invitò i suoi amici a teatro. 13. C'era una divertente commedia e gli attori e le attrici erano bravi. 14. I nostri amici applaudivano spesso gli attori. 15. E voi non applaudiste affatto? 16. Quando lo spettacolo finì Roberto accompagnò a casa i suoi amici e i suoi cugini. 17. I signori Marini desiderano anche vedere il famoso museo della città. 18. "Non avete una guida?" domandò la signora. 19. C'erano tre guide della città nello scaffale di Roberto ed una era molto buona. 20. Maria aprì il libro e mostrò alla signora la strada per il museo.

B. *Translate into Italian:* 1. Two weeks ago Mr and Mrs Mazzoni invited to their home for three or four days a dear friend and his family. 2. When they arrived at the house Mrs Mazzoni showed Mr and Mrs Marini their bedroom. 3. In three days they visited the art gallery, the museum, one of the churches and one of the theatres. 4. There was an exhibition of the works of a famous painter and the gallery was crowded. 5. There are some sculptures also in the gallery but these rooms were closed. 6. Many visitors were walking through the large rooms and looking at the works of art. 7. Mr Mazzoni used to know this painter well, but he does not admire his art and never bought any of his paintings. 8. The art gallery was near a little shop where they wanted to buy something for Mary and Julia. 9. They looked in the windows and went into the shop but they did not buy anything. 10. While the ladies were talking Mr Marini bought a newspaper to see what there was at the theatre. 11. In one of the theatres there was an amusing play and he invited the Mazzonis. 12. The theatre is large but it was crowded. 13. It is always crowded when the actors are good and the play is amusing. 14. "Do you know any of the actors?" Mr Marini asked. We only know one actor well, Robert's friend. 15. The actors were fine and when the play ended we applauded. 16. As we waited for the bus at the corner of the square, we spoke about the play. 17. How many churches are there in this city? There are ten churches and some are modern. 18. In the old church there are many interesting statues and also some famous paintings. 19. What did Robert buy at the entrance of the museum? He bought a guide. 20. While we were walking from one room to another we read the guide and admired the works of art.

C. Come si chiamano i diversi posti in un teatro?—What are the different seats in a theatre called? I posti migliori sono le poltrone di platea e i palchi di prima, seconda e terza fila.—The best seats are the orchestra stalls and the first, second and third tier boxes. I posti meno costosi sono le poltroncine e i posti di galleria.—The less expensive seats are the upper tiers and the gallery. Si possono prenotare i biglietti in anticipo?—Can seats be booked in advance? All'opera la gente fa spesso un abbonamento per parecchie recite e va a teatro in abito da sera. —People often buy a series of tickets for the opera and go in evening dress. Quando cominciano gli spettacoli? Cominciano e finiscono più tardi che in questo paese.—When do shows begin? They begin and finish later than in this country. Gli spettacoli al cinema sono continuati e non finiscono mai prima di mezzanotte.—Cinema performances are continuous and never finish before midnight. Preferisci la prosa o l'opera?—Do you prefer a play to the opera? Per alcuni spettacoli si danno biglietti gratuiti a spettatori che si impegnano ad applaudire.—For some shows free tickets are given to the spectators who undertake to applaud. Questi spettatori si chiamano con un vocabolo francese 'la claque'.—These spectators are called by the French word 'la claque'. Gli spettatori che ricevono dei biglietti di favore e vanno al teatro senza pagare si chiamano 'portoghesi'.—Spectators who receive complimentary tickets and get into the theatre free are called 'portoghesi'. Come si chiama la persona che controlla i biglietti e ci conduce a posto?—What do you call the person who checks the tickets and takes you to your seat? Si chiama 'maschera'. —She is called the 'maschera'.

D. *Ma che* (also spelt *macchè*)

Te l'hanno regalato? Ma che! l'ho comprato.—Did they give it to you? Certainly not! I bought it.

LESSON IX

Plural of Nouns

Nouns and Adjectives in -ca, -ga, -cia and -gia

Nouns ending in the singular in *ca* and *ga* form their plural in *che* and *ghe* if they are feminine and in *chi* and *ghi* if they are masculine:

amaca, amache	hammock
sega, seghe	saw
duca, duchi	duke
collɛga, collɛghi	colleague

Exception: Bɛlga, Bɛlgi (m.)—the Belgians.

Nouns ending in *cia* and *gia* form their plural in *e*; they keep the *i* if it is accented, they omit it if it is unaccented:

bugia, bugie	lie
provincia, province	province
lɔggia, lɔgge	loggia

The unaccented *i* is sometimes kept to avoid confusion between words which would otherwise have been identically spelt:

audacia—courage, audacie—daring deeds	to distinguish it from the adjective *audace*—daring
camicia—shirt, camicie	to distinguish it from *camice*—surplice

also acacia, acacie—acacia, quɛrcia, quɛrcie—oak, and valigia, valigie—suitcase.

Adjectives in *ca* and *ga* and in *cia* and *gia* follow the same rules as nouns of the same type:

carica, cariche	laden
lunga, lunghe	long
liscia, lisce	smooth
egrɛgia, egrɛge	distinguished

Nouns and Adjectives in -io

Nouns and adjectives ending in *io* form their plural in *ii* when the *i* of *io* is stressed; when the *i* is unstressed the double *i* of the plural contracts to one:

zio, zii	uncle
natio, natii	native

studio, studi	study
ampio, ampi	wide, spacious

but: tɛmpio, tɛmpii—temple to distinguish it from tɛmpo, tɛmpi—time
ɔdio, ɔdii—hatred to distinguish it from ɔde, ɔdi—ode

Nouns and Adjectives in -co and -go

Nouns and adjectives in *co* and *go* consisting of two syllables form their plural in *chi* and *ghi*:

fuɔco, fuɔchi	fire
bianco, bianchi	white
luɔgo, luɔghi	place
largo, larghi	wide

Exceptions: pɔrco, pɔrci—pig; and greco, greci—Greek.

Nouns and adjectives in *co* and *go* of more than two syllables make their plural in *chi* and *ghi* if the *co* and *go* are preceded by a consonant:

fuggiasco, fuggiaschi	fugitive, runaway
vigliacco, vigliacchi	coward
albɛrgo, albɛrghi	hotel
solingo, solinghi	lonely

If however the *co* and *go* are preceded by a vowel they form their plural in *ci* and *gi*:

amico, amici	friend
magnifico, magnifici	magnificent
psicɔlogo, psicɔlogi	psychologist

There are exceptions both among nouns and adjectives of this category; here, for reference, are the commonest:

abbaco, abbachi	ready reckoner	catalogo, cataloghi	catalogue
antico, antichi	old	dialogo, dialoghi	dialogue
aprico, aprichi	sunny	epilogo, epilòghi	epilogue
caduco, caduchi	transient	impiɛgo, impiɛghi	employment, job
carico, carichi	load, laden	monologo, monologhi	monologue
opaco, opachi	opaque	ɔbbligo, ɔbblighi	obligation, duty
pudico, pudichi	modest	pedagɔgo, pedagɔghi	tutor, pedagogue
ubbriaco, ubbriachi	drunk	prɔlogo, prɔloghi	prologue
strascico, strascichi	trail		

First Conjugation Verbs in -ca, -ga and -cia, -gia

In order to keep the same sound which the *c* and *g* have in the infinitive, verbs ending in *care* and *gare* insert an *h* before *e* and *i*:

cercare—cerco, cerchi . . . cerchiamo, cercherò, etc. to try, look for
spiegare—spiɛgo, spiɛghi . . . spieghiamo, spiegherò, etc. to explain, unfold

Verbs in *ciare* and *giare* drop the *i* as unnecessary whenever it precedes *e* and *i*:

> **cominciare—comincio, cominci . . . comincerò, etc.** to begin
> **mangiare—mangio, mangi . . . mangerò, etc.** to eat

Vocabulary IX

collega (m.s.f.) colleague
bottega little shop
farmacia chemist's shop
quɛrcia oak
mɛdico doctor
chirurgo surgeon
psichiatra (m.) psychiatrist
val*i*gia suitcase
bag*a*glio luggage
pɔrtico porch; pl. colonnade
parco park, grounds
bɔsco wood
pacco parcel
vigliacco coward
ɔdio hatred
prov*i*ncia province
fuɔco fire
lɔggia loggia
luɔgo place
numeroso (adj.) numerous
pɔco (adj. & adv.) little; **pɔchi** few
magn*i*fico (adj.) magnificent
bianco (adj.) white
***a*mpio** (adj.) wide, ample, roomy
c*a*rico (n. & adj.) load, laden
c*a*rico di laden with
ricco (adj.) rich
stanco (adj.) tired
egrɛgio (adj.) distinguished
sotto (prep.) under
soltanto (adv.) only
perché (conj. & adv.) because, why?
portare to carry, to take, to wear
cercare to look for
cercare di to try
trovare to find
mandare to send

Exercise 1

Give the plural of the following nouns: la provincia; l'amaca; il collega; la bugia; lo zio; il parco; l'ufficio; il fuoco; il medico; la farmacia; il bagaglio; la bottega; la loggia; l'amico; il luogo; l'albergo; l'amica; l'armadio; il carico; la collega; lo psicologo; la camicia; la quercia; il portico.

Exercise 2

Translate into Italian: on the loggias; in the shops; to the hotels; of the sons; from the crossings; into the parks; by the Belgians (m.); in the hammocks; by the old dukes; into these places; in the little mirrors; from the magnificent hotels; of the huge oaks; in the large wardrobes; in the vast provinces; of the long colonnades; in the spacious galleries; from the magnificent monuments; of the broad avenues; in the old museums.

Exercise 3

Translate into Italian: (a) these large hotels; our dear friends; some little shops; five magnificent oaks; some of their suitcases; four of my friends; three small provinces; many of our surgeons; my distinguished colleagues; some magnificent churches;

(b) 1. They never invite friends. 2. No one admires cowards. 3. We only visited old churches. 4. He does not send any parcels. 5. We never go into the woods. 6. We sent neither parcels nor letters. 7. Do you never visit other provinces? 8. Did no one admire the old colonnade? 9. They explained their old hatreds. 10. The cars were laden with cases.

A. *Translate into English:* 1. Nelle vetrine delle botteghe vicino alla nostra casa ci sono molte belle cose. 2. Noi non entriamo mai nei grandi negozi; preferiamo le piccole botteghe. 3. Alcune nostre amiche trovarono dei magnifici vestiti nei negozi sotto i portici. 4. Portasti i pacchi all'ufficio postale, Giulia? 5. Sì, mio fratello e mia sorella erano stanchi e i due uffici postali non sono vicini alla nostra casa. 6. La nostra città è ricca di ampi parchi e magnifici giardini. 7. Noi attraversiamo sempre il parco quando ritorniamo a casa e spesso, mentre camminiamo lungo un viale di antiche quercie, leggiamo i giornali. 8. Due colleghi dell'ingegnere Mazzoni invitarono Maria e Giulia a casa loro per tre settimane. 9. Portarono molti bagagli? No, non avevano che poche valigie. 10. Ci sono molti negozi in questa città? 11. No, ci sono pochi negozi e soltanto due farmacie. 12. Quanti medici ci sono? 13. Ci sono tre chirurghi e cinque medici ma due sono psichiatri. 14. Maria e Giulia ebbero due magnifiche camere con larghi balconi. 15. Nelle camere c'erano ampi armadi con grandi specchi. 16. Esse desideravano comprare qualche cosa per i loro genitori e i colleghi dell'ingegnere Mazzoni accompagnarono le due ragazze in molti negozi. 17. In una piccola bottega Giulia trovò due antichi cassettoni. 18. Maria non comprò che dei libri perché non trovò niente altro. 19. Quando tornarono a casa trovarono nella loro camera due pacchi con i libri. 20. La libreria mandò un ragazzo con i pacchi.

B. *Translate into Italian:* 1. In a large city there are many stores and numerous little shops. 2. I often see cars laden with luggage and suitcases at the entrance to the station. 3. In the town where our cousins live there are four banks, two post offices and two chemist's shops. 4. We go into a post office when we want to send letters and parcels to our friends. 5. In the city where I used to live there were some old houses with long colonnades. 6. Were there many doctors in the town where you used to live? Yes, but there were only two surgeons. 7. These surgeons had many distinguished colleagues in their profession. 8. Which profession does Mr Bruni's brother practise? Mr Bruni and his brother are famous psychiatrists. 9. Our city is also famous for its parks and gardens and old squares with their magnificent houses. 10. At the corner of the street where we live there is a magnificent store where they sell beautiful furniture. 11. Two or three weeks ago we were wanting to buy some furniture for our bedrooms. 12. Our house is large and old and we were looking for antique furniture. 13. We bought three wardrobes, two chests of drawers and some chairs. 14. We also bought some old mirrors and three or four pictures. 15. In another shop in town we bought some sheets and blankets. The sheets were white, the blankets green. 16. Who brought these parcels from the shop? They send a boy when the parcels are big. 17. While we were buying these things our friends were looking at other shop windows. 18. There were some magnificent articles in one shop. 19. We did not buy anything because they were dear. 20. Some of the rooms of our house are very wide with large windows.

C. Molte signore quando sono in vacanza in Italia desiderano andare dal parrucchiere.—Many ladies when they are on holiday in Italy want to go to the hairdresser. Come si domanda un appuntamento?—How does one make an appointment? Si può telefonare e chiedere: Potrei avere un appuntamento per domani mattina?—One can phone and ask, "Could I make an appointment for tomorrow morning?" Se il parrucchiere domanda: Cosa deve fare signora? si risponde: shampoo e messa in piega, oppure: shampoo, taglio e messa in piega, oppure: desidererei fare una permanente.—If the hairdresser asks "What do you want done, madam?" one answers "Shampoo and set" or "Shampoo, trim and set" or "I should like a perm." Vorrei una messa in piega semplice con un'onda (due onde) qui e riccioli di dietro.—I should like an ordinary set with one (two waves) wave here and curls at the back. Desidera i capelli un po' cotonati?—Would you like your hair back-combed? Quando si paga si dà sempre una mancia alla persona che ha lavato i capelli e a quella che li ha messi in piega.—When paying their bill people always give a tip both to the person who has washed their hair and to the person who has set it. I prezzi sono quasi gli stessi.—The prices are almost the same. Quanto costa un taglio? Circa seicento lire.—How much is a trim (or haircut)? About 600 lire. E una messa in piega? Circa 1,500 lire.—And a set? About 1,500 lire. Quanto si dà di mancia? Cento o duecento lire.—What tip does one give? 100 or 200 lire.

D. *Come mai*

Come mai non mi avete avvertito?—How is it that you didn't warn me?

LESSON X

Future Tense

Future of Model Verbs

amer-ò	I shall love, etc.	temer-ò	I shall fear, etc.	dormir-ò	I shall sleep, etc.
amer-ai		temer-ai		dormir-ai	
amer-à		temer-à		dormir-à	
amer-emo		temer-emo		dormir-emo	
amer-ete		temer-ete		dormir-ete	
amer-anno		temer-anno		dormir-anno	

The endings of the future tense (futuro) are identical for all conjugations. It is important to notice that: (a) The stem of the future tense is obtained by removing *only* the final *e* of the infinitive ending. (b) In the first conjugation the characteristic vowel *a* becomes *e* in all regular verbs.

Future of 'Essere' and 'Avere'

sarò	I shall be, etc.	avrò	I shall have etc.
sarai		avrai	
sarà		avrà	
saremo		avremo	
sarete		avrete	
saranno		avranno	

Uses

The future tense is used in Italian, as in English, to indicate an action that is going to happen in the future. Unlike English, where we use the present tense, the future tense is used in Italian in subordinate clauses introduced by *when* and *if* where the future is implied. It is also used to denote possibility or probability:

Quando i miei amici arriveranno, aprirò la porta.
When my friends arrive, I shall open the door.

Se saremo in ritardo, prenderemo l'autobus.
If we are late, we shall take the bus.

Sarà vero. It may be true.
Avrà molti amici. He may have many friends.

Plural of Nouns (*continued*)—Invariable Nouns

The following groups do not change in the plural:

1. All nouns ending in an accented vowel:

la città, le città city, town
la virtù, le virtù virtue

il falò, i falò	**bonfire**
il lunedì, i lunedì	**Monday.**

2. All nouns ending in a consonant:

il tram, i tram	**tram**
lo spɔrt, gli spɔrt	**sport.**

3. Nouns ending in an unaccented *i* or *ie*:

la tɛsi, le tɛsi	**thesis**
l'analisi, **le analisi**	**analysis**
la sɛrie, le sɛrie	**series.**

Exceptions: superficie—surface, which has two plural forms—superficie and superfici; and moglie, mogli—wife.

4. The following nouns in *a*: bɔia (m.)—executioner; sɔsia (m. & f.)—double; paria (m.)—outcast; vaglia (m.)—money order; cinema (m.) cinema; procaccia (m.)—rural postman.

5. Some nouns of a scientific nature ending in *o*:

la radio, le radio	radio
la dinamo, le dinamo	dynamo.

Vocabulary X

università university
tɛsi (f.) thesis
c*i*nema (m.) cinema
film (m.) film
bar (m.) bar
caffè (m.) café, coffee
v*a*glia (m.) money order
r*a*dio (f.) radio
sɛrie (f.) series
cat*a*logo catalogue
di*a*logo dialogue
an*a*lisi (f.) analysis
impiɛgo job
virtù (f.) virtue
appuntamento appointment, date
autorimessa[1] garage
post*e*ggio parking place

spɔrt (m.) sport
centro centre; **in centro** in town
document*a*rio documentary
programma (m.) programme
pɔsto place, seat
taxi (m.) taxi
nuɔvo (adj.) new
puntuale (adj.) punctual
domani (adv.) tomorrow
fra (prep.) in, within
prima di (prep.) before
Umberto Hubert
frequentare to frequent, attend
restare to stay
ascoltare to listen to
avere fretta to be in a hurry
ɛssere in ritardo to be late

Exercise 1

Repeat orally the future tense of: restare, conoscere, finire, pulire, mandare, comprendere, applaudire, essere, visitare, vendere, costruire, avere.

[1] In everyday spoken Italian the word 'garage' is much more commonly used.

Exercise 2

Translate into Italian supplying subject pronouns: (a) 1. You will send. 2. We were writing. 3. You are finishing. 4. I shall buy. 5. You sold. 6. We shall clean. 7. She was explaining. 8. He will construct. 9. We have. 10. They were. 11. We shall accompany. 12. He carried. 13. We used to buy. 14. You will attend. 15. She applauded. 16. They will sell. 17. He was distributing. 18. I shall study. 19. They were taking. 20. She will write.

(b) 1. They asked, they will ask. 2. They finished, they will finish. 3. They bought, they will buy. 4. They sold, they will sell. 5. They cleaned, they will clean. 6. They invited, they will invite. 7. They built, they will build. 8. They accompanied, they will accompany. 9. They carried, they will carry. 10. They applauded, they will applaud.

Exercise 3

Translate into Italian: these universities; many long films; our cinemas; two money orders; many buses; four catalogues; their wives; some dialogues; many bars; every series; some marvellous virtues; the old trams; two large banks; some interesting analyses; these theses; three new hotels; some old churches; many sports; two large cafés; some wide surfaces.

A. *Translate into English*: 1. Roberto e sua cugina hanno un appuntamento per domani con degli amici vicino ad uno dei cinema del centro. 2. Se arriveranno prima dei loro amici aspetteranno in uno dei caffè vicini. 3. Ci sono due film e un documentario in programma ma Roberto desidera vedere soltanto i film. 4. Sono puntuali i vostri amici? 5. Sì, sono sempre puntuali ma se saranno in ritardo prenderanno un taxi. 6. Il posteggio dei taxi è vicino alla loro casa. 7. Roberto metterà l'automobile in uno dei posteggi vicino al cinema. 8. Spesso se il programma è interessante i cinema sono affollati e non troviamo posto nei posteggi vicini. 9. Maria preferisce ascoltare la radio e resterà a casa. 10. C'è in programma una interessante commedia e i dialoghi sono divertenti. 11. Giulia frequenta l'università e fra un anno, quando finirà i suoi studi, cercherà un impiego. 12. Giulia ha fretta perché desidera finire la sua tesi. 13. Le sue amiche finiranno le loro tesi fra qualche settimana. 14. Cercheranno anche esse degli impieghi quando finiranno gli studi? 15. No, una insegnerà lingue e l'altra ritornerà a casa. 16. Qualche giorno fa ricevemmo i cataloghi di due grandi negozi di mobili. 17. Desideravamo comprare un nuovo divano e due poltrone e due grandi specchi e mandammo due vaglia. 18. Dov'è la vostra autorimessa? 19. Queste case sono antiche e non hanno autorimesse; noi costruiremo la nostra nel giardino. 20. Desidero prendere un caffè; ci sono dei bar in questa strada?

B. *Translate into Italian:* 1. Every large city has nine or ten cinemas and three or four theatres. 2. Numerous cinemas have cafés and many theatres have bars. 3. We often accompany our cousins and their friends to the theatre. 4. If they are not in a hurry tomorrow evening, we shall have (take) coffee when the play finishes. 5. The show is always good and the theatre is crowded every night. 6. If we are late for the theatre this evening we shall take a taxi. 7. Some of our friends have their own cars but prefer to take a bus or a taxi. 8. Often there is no room in the parking places near a theatre. 9. There are some good plays on the radio but I prefer to see the actors and actresses. 10. Is there a good university in your town? Yes, and there are two other famous universities in the two nearby provinces. 11. My sister will finish her studies within a year and she will teach French and German. 12. Will she teach in town? Yes, she will look for a job in one of the schools in this city and she will live at home. 13. Mr Bruni and Mr Ansaldi accompany their wives to the theatre every week. 14. I receive numerous catalogues from bookshops and I read many books in French for my thesis. 15. Do you understand every word? No, but the study of this language is interesting. 16. When I finish reading this book I shall write my thesis. 17. These French books may be interesting but I prefer to read books in my own language. 18. Neither Hubert nor his friend will understand these mistakes. 19. What will you study now? We shall not study anything. We are looking for a job. 20. Are you in a hurry? Yes, I have an appointment and if I don't take a taxi I shall be late.

C. Dov'è un telefono pubblico?—Where is there a public telephone? C'è un telefono in quasi ogni bar.—There is a phone in almost every bar. Vorrei telefonare: posso avere un gettone per favore?—I should like to phone: can I please have a token? Quanto costa?—How much is it? Come funziona questo apparecchio?—How does this machine work? Vuole chiamare lei il numero per me?—Would you get the number for me? Si inserisce il gettone nella fessura, poi si ascolta per vedere se la linea è libera, poi si fa il numero e se la linea non è occupata si aspetta.—One inserts the token into the slot, then one listens to see if the line is free, then one dials the number and if the line is not engaged, one waits. Altrimenti si mette giù il ricevitore e si richiama il numero dopo qualche minuto.—Otherwise one replaces the receiver and calls the number again after a few minutes. Quando la persona risponde si preme il bottone e il gettone cade nell'apparecchio.—When the person answers one presses the button and the token falls into the machine. Che cosa si dice?—What does one say? Si dice: Pronto, chi parla?—One says, Hello, who is speaking? Potrei parlare con la signorina XY?—Could I speak to Miss XY? Non c'è? A che ora ritornerà a casa?—Is she not in? When will she be back? Può prendere il mio numero di telefono?—Can you take my phone number? Può dirle che ho telefonato e la richiamerò alle quattro?—Will you tell her that I phoned and shall ring her again at 4 o'clock? Grazie.—Thank you. Arrivederla.—Goodbye. Se si vuol telefonare che cosa si fa prima?—If one wishes to phone what does one do first? E dopo?—And next? E poi?—And then? etc.

D. *Senz'altro, senza meno*

Verrò senz'altro—I shall certainly come.
I shall come without fail.

LESSON XI

Conjunctive Pronouns

Personal pronouns, besides the forms used as subjects, have distinctive forms used as direct and indirect objects of verbs. These forms are called in English 'Conjunctive Pronouns' because they are closely connected with the verb in the relation of object and may never stand alone.

Conjunctive Direct Objects

Singular				
1st	mi	me	egli mi vede	he sees me
2nd	ti	you	egli ti vede	he sees you
3rd	lo	him, it	egli lo vede	he sees him, it
	la	her, it, you[1]	egli la vede	he sees her, it, you[1]
Plural				
1st	ci	us	egli ci vede	he sees us
2nd	vi,	you	egli vi vede	he sees you
3rd	li	them (m.), you[1]	egli li vede	he sees them (m.), you[1]
	le	them (f.), you[1]	egli le vede	he sees them (f.), you[1]

Conjunctive Indirect Objects

Singular				
1st	mi	to me	egli mi scrive	he writes to me
2nd	ti	to you	egli ti scrive	he writes to you
3rd	gli	to him, to it	egli gli scrive	he writes to him
	le	to her, to it, to you[1]	egli le scrive	he writes to her, to you[1]
Plural				
1st	ci	to us	egli ci scrive	he writes to us
2nd	vi	to you	egli vi scrive	he writes to you
3rd	loro	to them (m. & f.), to you[1]	egli scrive loro	he writes to them, to you[1]

From the preceding two tables, it can be seen that the two forms differ from one another only in the third person singular and plural. *Lo* and *la* generally elide before a vowel; when standing for *it* they follow, of course, the gender of the Italian noun they are replacing:

Conosci Maria? Sì, la conosco.
Do you know Mary? Yes, I know her.
Comprò il libro? Sì, lo comprò.
Did he buy the book? Yes, he bought it.

[1] Used in direct address. See p. 77.

Position of Conjunctive Pronouns

Unlike English, conjunctive pronouns always precede the verb in Italian, except the form *loro* which always follows it. We shall see later that there are a few forms of the verb to which this rule does not apply.

Direct and Indirect Conjunctive Pronouns in the Same Sentence

When both types of pronoun occur in a sentence:

(a) They precede the verb in the following order:
1. Indirect object. 2. Direct object. 3. Verb.

(b) The final *i* of the first and second person singular and plural of the indirect object changes to *e* before *lo*, *la*, *li*, *le*, and *ne*,[1] giving *me lo*, *te lo*, *ce lo*, *ve lo*, etc., *me la*, *te la*, etc.

Egli me lo manda.	He sends it, him to me.
Ella te la lɛgge.	She reads it to you.
Essi ce lo vendono.	They sell it to us.
Noi ve la leggeremo.	We shall read it to you.
Tu me la scrivi.	You write it to me.
Io te lo spiegherò.	I shall explain it to you.
Voi ce li mandaste.	You sent them to us.
Io ve le vendei.	I sold them to you.

(c) The third person *gli* and *le* become *glie* before *lo*, *la*, *li*, *le* and *ne*,[1] and combine with them in one single word: *glielo*, *gliela*, *glieli*, *gliele*, *gliene*.

Egli glielo manda.	He sends it, to him, to her, to you.[2]
Noi gliela leggeremo.	We shall read it to him, to her, to you.
Ella glieli vende.	She sells them to him, to her, to you.
Io gliele spiegai.	I explained them to him, to her, to you.

(d) *Loro* remains unchanged and in its usual position after the verb.

Egli lo manda loro.	He sends it to them, to you.[2]
Io lo spiegherò loro.	I shall explain it to them, to you.
Ella lo vendé loro.	She sold it to them, to you.

Vocabulary XI

trɛno train

trɛno dirɛtto, esprɛsso express train

sala d'aspɛtto waiting room

sportɛllo carriage door, office window

finestrino window (of a train)

vettura coach

vagone (m.) **lɛtto** sleeping car sleeper.

carrɔzza ristorante dining car

scompartimento compartment

[1] See Lesson XV.
[2] Used in direct address. See p. 77.

binario rails, platform
facchino porter
viaggio journey, travel
impiegato clerk
vacanza holiday
lunedì (m.) Monday
persona person, pl. people
cestino da viaggio packed lunch
carretto trolley
minuto minute
limonata lemonade
aranciata orangeade
panini imbottiti sandwiches
baule (m.) trunk
qualche volta sometimes
già (adv.) already
prenotare to book, reserve
partire to leave, set out
viaggiare (aux. avere) to travel
consegnare to hand in, give, deliver
mangiare to eat

Exercise 1

Translate into Italian: 1. We met them. 2. He invited us. 3. They know you. 4. I always see her. 5. They were applauding it (f.). 6. He never understood me. 7. Did he call you? 8. You will understand him. 9. I bought it (m.). 10. He received us. 11. We accompanied them (f.). 12. They received him. 13. He called you. 14. We cleaned them (m.). 15. I preferred it (f.). 16. She keeps it (m.). 17. They used to love her. 18. He did not open it (f.). 19. They waited for you. 20. He distributed them (m.).

Exercise 2

Translate into Italian: 1. He sent a letter to her. 2. Will you write to me? 3. They send parcels to him. 4. I shall sell the car to you. 5. They often speak to us. 6. We sometimes write to them. 7. They brought books to him. 8. I shall explain the programme to you. 9. They never spoke to me. 10. Who brought the parcel to her? 11. I shall teach Italian to you. 12. She will read the book to them. 13. He often asks me. 14. We often buy him books. 15. Will you bring me a pencil? 16. We explained the picture to her. 17. She teaches them Italian. 18. He never sent me any letters. 19. He sometimes speaks to them. 20. They never explain anything to you.

Exercise 3

Translate into Italian: 1. We shall read it to you. 2. I explained them (m.) to him. 3. He sent it (m.) to me. 4. You taught it (m.) to her. 5. She brought it (f.) to us. 6. I shall sell it (m.) to you. 7. He distributed them (m.) to them. 8. I shall write it (m.) to him. 9. We shall bring them (f.) to you. 10. We sold them (f.) to her. 11. I often play it to him. 12. He changed it (m.) for me. 13. They wash them (f.) for us. 14. She explained it (m.) to him. 15. We did not bring it (f.) to them. 16. They send them (m.) to her. 17. Will she explain it (f.) to you? 18. You taught it (m.) to him. 19. He sent them (m.) to them. 20. They never sold it (m.) to us.

A. *Translate into English:* 1. Fra qualche giorno partiremo per le vacanze. 2. Desideriamo vedere i nostri zii e resteremo tre settimane con loro. 3. Molte persone viaggiano il (on) lunedì e se non sarete puntuali non troverete posto. 4. Noi abbiamo già i posti; mio fratello li prenotò due settimane fa. 5. Sono dei posti d'angolo in uno scompartimento vicino alla carrozza ristorante. 6. Mangerete al vagone ristorante? 7. No, prenderemo dei cestini da viaggio in qualche stazione e compreremo delle limonate o delle aranciate. 8. In alcune stazioni ci sono dei carretti con limonate, aranciate e panini imbottiti. 9. È lungo il viaggio? Sì, è lungo ma il nostro è un treno diretto e arriveremo la sera. 10. Ieri fummo alla stazione per portare i nostri bagagli. 11. Un facchino li portò allo sportello e un impiegato ci domandò dove desideravamo mandare i due bauli. 12. Glielo spiegammo e glieli consegnammo. 13. La sala d'aspetto era affollata e numerose persone aspettavano vicino allo sportello dei biglietti. 14. Alcuni facchini attraversavano i binari, carichi di bagagli; Roberto li chiamò. 15. Porta il vagone letto questo treno? No, non lo porta. 16. Se saremo stanche dormiremo un poco. 17. Mentre ritornavamo a casa comprammo dei giornali. 18. Un ragazzo me li porta sempre a casa ma desideravo vedere quali film c'erano nei cinema vicino alla stazione. 19. Mio zio e i miei cugini ci aspetteranno alla stazione. 20. Noi saremo al finestrino e quando il treno arriverà nella stazione, scenderemo e li cercheremo.

B. *Translate into Italian* :1. When we visit our friends, sometimes father takes (portare) us in the car and sometimes we travel by (in) train. 2. I never take much luggage because we only stay with them for two or three weeks. 3. When we travel by train we prefer the corner seats in the compartment, and if it is a long journey we always reserve a (the) sleeper. 4. When there is no dining car on the (in) train we buy packed lunches and eat in the compartment. 5. Sometimes I buy sandwiches and lemonade or orangeade from trolleys in the station. 6. I also buy newspapers and magazines and read them on the (in) journey. 7. Some friends of ours were waiting for us in the waiting room. 8. "Are we late?" I asked the porter when we arrived at the station. "Yes, your train leaves in a few minutes." 9. We arrived at the platform where the train was and went into our compartment. 10. There were two people already in the compartment and they had many suitcases. 11. We sent our brother to the waiting room to call our friends and asked him also to buy some magazines. 12. We looked at (our) magazines, ate (our) sandwiches and then we slept a little because we were tired. 13. The train was a little late, but when we arrived our friends were waiting for us and called a porter, as we were getting off the train. 14. We always book rooms in an hotel in the centre because it is handy for theatres and shops. 15. When we left we asked the hotel porter to take our luggage to the station. 16. Our friends accompanied us to the station. 17. They bought us many magazines for the journey. 18. The station was crowded; many people were leaving with our train. 19. Our friends are kind. When we arrive home we shall write to them. 20. We shall also invite them to our house for a week or two.

C. Quanto costa un biglietto di andata e ritorno?—How much does a return ticket cost? Un biglietto di andata e ritorno costa generalmente meno di due biglietti semplici.—A return ticket generally costs less than two single tickets. C'è un treno diretto per XX o dobbiamo cambiare? —Is there a through train to XX or have we to change? Se non c'è una linea diretta per andare in un posto che cosa dobbiamo fare?—If there is not a through line to a place what must we do? Quando non c'è una linea diretta per andare in qualche posto bisogna trovare una coincidenza. —When there is no through line to a place, it is necessary to find a connection. Ci sono dei ribassi qualche volta sulle ferrovie italiane?—Are there ever reductions on the Italian railways? Ci sono dei ribassi in occasione di Fiere, partite di football e manifestazioni culturali come il Maggio fiorentino.—There are reductions for Fairs, football matches and cultural exhibitions such as the Florentine May Festival. Quante classi ci sono sulle ferrovie?—How many classes are there on the railways? Ci sono due classi.—There are two classes. In Italia non esistono vagoni letto di seconda classe.—There is no such thing as 2nd class sleepers in Italy. Si paga un supplemento sui Pullman?—Does one pay extra on Pullman carriages? Sì, sui treni Pullman si paga sempre un supplemento. —Yes, there is always an extra payment on Pullman trains. Ci sono dei controllori sui treni?—Are there inspectors on the trains? Sì, i controllori vengono spesso a controllare i biglietti ma non li ritirano mai.—Yes, inspectors check the tickets often, but never collect them. Come si passa da un binario all'altro?—How does one get from one platform to the other? Per passare da un binario all'altro in una stazione italiana si va attraverso un sottopassaggio.—To get from one platform to another in an Italian station, one crosses by a subway. Ci sono dei ristoranti nelle stazioni?—Are there restaurants in the stations? Ci sono sempre dei ristoranti nelle stazioni e sono aperti sino a tardi, a volte tutta la notte.—There are always restaurants in the stations and they are open till late, at times all night. È libero questo posto?—Is this seat free? No, è occupato.—No, it is occupied. I facchini in Italia non sono pagati dalle

Ferrovie dello Stato ed il loro compenso è costituito da quello che ricevono dai viaggiatori.—Porters in Italy are not paid by the Railways and they earn only what they receive from the travellers. C'è una tariffa fissa per ogni valigia?—Is there a fixed charge for each case? Si, 150 lire per un collo solo, e 100 lire per ogni collo successivo—Yes, 150 lire for the first article and 100 lire for each additional article. È vero che di martedì e di venerdì viaggia meno gente?—Is it true that fewer people travel on Tuesdays and Fridays? C'è un proverbio che dice: "Né di Venere né di Marte né si sposa né si parte".—There is a proverb which says "One should not marry nor travel on Fridays or Tuesdays."

D. *Ma come?*

Ma come? Accetti l'invito e poi non vai?—What's this? You accept the invitation and then you don't go?

LESSON XII

Past Participle and Compound Tenses

Besides the simple tenses already learned, the indicative mood consists of four compound tenses. These are formed by the four simple tenses of the auxiliary verbs *Essere* and *Avere*, followed by the past participle of the verb in question.

In all regular verbs the past participle is obtained by adding the following endings to the stem of the verb:

Past Participle

1st Conj.		2nd Conj.		3rd Conj.	
Am-*ato*	loved	Tem-*uto*	feared	Dorm-*ito*	slept[1]

The names of the compound tenses are:

Present Perfect (Passato Prossimo): Ho amato—I have loved.
Past Perfect (Trapassato Prossimo): Avevo amato—I had loved.
Second Past Perfect (Trapassato Remoto): Ebbi amato—I had loved.
Future Perfect (Futuro Anteriore): Avrò amato—I shall have loved.

Use of Auxiliary Verbs

Avere is used as the auxiliary:

(1) With transitive verbs (verbs in which the action passes from the subject to the object and which can become passive).
(2) With a few intransitive verbs.[2]
(3) With the verb *avere* itself:

Io ho comprato un libro.	I have bought a book.
Essa ha viaggiato con un'amica.	She has travelled with a friend.
Noi abbiamo avuto una lettera.	We have had a letter.

Essere is used as the auxiliary:

(1) With the majority of intransitive verbs
(2) With the passive form
(3) With reflexive verbs
(4) With *essere* itself:

[1] Past participles have inflections like adjectives of the first group (*o*, *i*, *a*, *e*) and can be used as adjectives.

[2] The intransitive verbs requiring *avere* and those that can be conjugated equally with either *avere* or *essere* will have the appropriate auxiliary in brackets in the vocabulary.

Sono già arrivate?	Have they already arrived?
Mi sono guardato nello spεcchio.	I have looked at myself in the mirror.
Sono stato malato.	I have been ill.

Agreement

In the verbs conjugated with *avere*, the past participle does not agree with the object if the latter follows the verb:

Ho ammirato dei magnifici quadri.	I admired some beautiful paintings.

It *can* agree if the object precedes the verb:

I quadri che ho {ammirato. / ammirati.	The pictures which I admired.

It *must* agree if the object is a personal pronoun:

Hai ammirato i quadri?	Sì, li ho ammirati.
Did you admire the paintings?	Yes, I admired them.

In the verbs conjugated with *εssere* the past participle *always* agrees with the subject:

Essi sono stati alla stazione.	They have been to the station.
Maria è arrivata?	Has Mary arrived?
Esse sono amate da tutti.	They are loved by everyone.
Ci siamo guardati nello spεcchio.	We looked at ourselves in the mirror.

Present Perfect *Present Perfect of Model Verbs*

ho amato	I have loved,[1] etc.	ho temuto	I have feared, etc.	ho dormito	I have slept, etc.
hai amato		hai temuto		hai dormito	
ha amato		ha temuto		ha dormito	
abbiamo amato		abbiamo temuto		abbiamo dormito	
avete amato		avete temuto		avete dormito	
hanno amato		hanno temuto		hanno dormito	

Present Perfect of Εssere and Avere

sono stato	I have been, etc.	ho avuto	I have had, etc.
sεi stato		hai avuto	
è stato		ha avuto	
siamo stati		abbiamo avuto	
siεte stati		avete avuto	
sono stati		hanno avuto	

[1] This tense is used also to translate: I have been buying, travelling, looking, etc.—Ho comprato, viaggiato, guardato.

Uses

The present perfect (passato prossimo) indicates an action or state in the fairly recent past or an action that, though past, bears some reference to the present:

Ho studiato l'italiano per molti mesi.
I have studied Italian for many months (and may still be doing so).

Modern Italian, especially colloquial, prefers the present perfect to the past absolute:

Due settimane fa siamo andate in campagna.
Two weeks ago we went to the country.

Vocabulary XII

pensione (f.) boarding house, pension
pomeriggio afternoon
tavolino small table
spiaggia beach, sea-side
ombrellone (m.) parasol, large umbrella
sole (m.) sun
sabbia sand
sɛdia a sdraio deck chair
mare (m.) sea
onda wave
barca boat
cartolina post card
dɔpo (prep. & adv.) after
che (conj.) that
fresco (adj.) cool, fresh
stesso (adj.) same
tutto all; **tutto il** the whole
agitato (adj.) (of sea) rough, (man) worried
calmo (adj.) calm
usare to use
nuotare to swim (aux. **avere**)
remare to row (aux. **avere**)
passeggiare to go for a walk (aux. **avere**)
spedire* to forward, send, dispatch
ballare to dance (aux. **avere**)
cenare to dine (aux. **avere**)

Exercise 1

Translate into Italian: 1. We have bought. 2. She has been ill. 3. They have booked. 4. We have dined. 5. You have swum. 6. They (f.) have returned. 7. I have explained. 8. You have finished. 9. She has set out (left). 10. They have applauded. 11. They (m.) have entered. 12. I have feared. 13. We have understood. 14. He has crossed. 15. You (f.) have arrived. 16. They have seen. 17. She has received. 18. We have changed. 19. They have distributed. 20. You have spent.

Exercise 2

Translate into Italian: 1. Have you bought any books? We have bought them. 2. Has she been ill? She and her sister have been ill.

3. Have you driven this car? I have not driven it. 4. Have they returned home? They have returned yesterday. 5. Have you explained the mistake? I have explained it. 6. Have they understood the book? They have understood it. 7. Do you know her? I have met her. 8. Has he visited the church? No, he has never visited it. 9. Has she invited you to her home? She has invited me often. 10. Has he not arrived? Yes, he and his brother have arrived yesterday. 11. Have they changed their clothes? Yes they have changed them. 12. Have you seen her? Yes I have seen her three days ago. 13. Has Mary cleaned her bedroom? Yes, she has cleaned it this morning. 14. Have you washed the sheets, Julia? No, I shall wash them to-morrow. 15. Has John sold his car? Yes, he sold it yesterday.

Exercise 3

Translate into Italian: 1. I have sent it (f.) to him. 2. We have explained it (m.) to them. 3. She has handed them (m.) to her. 4. You have forwarded it (f.) to us. 5. He has often taught it (f.) to you. 6. He has distributed them (m.) to them. 7. They have brought them (f.) to her. 8. He has sold it (f.) to him. 9. Has she explained it (f.) to you? 10. I have sold them (f.) to him. 11. We brought it (f.) to them. 12. Have you sent them (m.) to us?

A. *Translate into English:* 1. Ieri abbiamo ricevuto una lettera dalla nostra amica Silvia. 2. Essa ci parla delle sue vacanze e ci scrive che le ha passate in un magnifico posto al mare. 3. Silvia e la sua famiglia avevano delle camere in una piccola pensione vicino alla spiaggia. 4. Silvia e sua sorella sono restate nello stesso posto tutte le vacanze ma i loro genitori sono partiti dopo tre settimane. 5. Essi sono ritornati in città perché il padre di Silvia è avvocato ed esercita la sua professione. 6. Essa mi scrive che ha remato e nuotato ogni mattina e ha ballato con i suoi amici ogni sera. 7. Nella stessa pensione c'erano molti ragazzi e ragazze e nel pomeriggio spesso passeggiavano nei vicini boschi. 8. Nel giardino della pensione c'erano molti tavolini con ombrelloni e la sera qualche volta cenavano al fresco. 9. Era calmo il mare? Sì, ma qualche volta era agitato e c'erano molte onde. 10. Silvia ha incontrato dei nostri amici sulla spiaggia e li ha invitati alla sua pensione. 11. Anche noi partiremo per il mare tra due settimane. 12. Ritorneremo nello stesso posto dove siamo stati tre anni fa. 13. La spiaggia era bella e la pensione dove abitavamo non era affatto cara. 14. Spesso il pomeriggio passeggiavamo o restavamo sulla spiaggia sulle sedie a sdraio. 15. Remavate spesso? Mia sorella non rema mai ma io prendevo spesso la barca quando il mare era calmo. 16. Quando il mare è agitato poche persone nuotano. 17. Quando c'è molto sole portiamo gli ombrelloni e li mettiamo sulla spiaggia. 18. Avete già prenotato i biglietti per il viaggio? 19. Sì, abbiamo domandato all'impiegato di prenotare per noi dei posti d'angolo. 20. Quando saremo al mare scriveremo ai nostri parenti ed ai nostri amici e manderemo loro delle belle cartoline.

B. *Translate into Italian:* 1. Some friends of mine have bought a little house near the sea. 2. Their parents have invited us to their house for a holiday. 3. Our friends love the sea-side and have always wanted to live near the sea. 4. When the sea is calm and there are not many waves we take their boat: two of my friends row. 5. In the afternoon, if the sea is rough, we often go for a walk along the beach or in the nearby woods. 6. In the garden of their house my friends have little tables with large umbrellas and deck chairs. 7. Our friend's mother has been ill and often she stays at home: we spend the morning in the garden and I read newspapers and magazines to her. 8. This morning I sent a postcard to my parents; they will receive it to-morrow. 9. In their letter they ask me: "Have you been to the beach every day?" 10. They also ask me if we have been swimming and rowing and if the sea has been rough or calm. 11. We have only been one week in this place and already we know everyone. 12. This morning we met some friends of yours in one of the little shops. 13. They have been on holiday and return to town to-morrow. 14. We want to send some books to our father and they will take them to him. 15. They have booked tables in the large hotel near the beach where we shall all dine and dance this evening. 16. We have danced every night this week and Mrs Rossi has invited us to her house on Monday night. 17. They have invited many people and Mrs Rossi has bought a magnificent dress. 18. She showed it to us this morning. 19. We have met many people this year and will write to them after the holidays. 20. Are your holidays finished? We have already forwarded one of our trunks and return home in a few days.

C. Dove passa le vacanze lei generalmente? In questo paese?—Where do you generally spend your holidays? In this country? Sì, passo generalmente le vacanze con i miei genitori in un magnifico posto al mare.—I generally spend my holidays with my parents in a magnificent seaside resort. È stato mai all'estero in vacanza?—Have you ever been abroad on holiday? Io no, ma un numero sempre maggiore di persone va ora a passare le vacanze all'estero.—I have not, but an ever increasing number of people are spending their holidays abroad now. Quali stagioni dell'anno sono le migliori per andare all'estero?—Which are the best seasons of the year for going abroad? La primavera e l'autunno sono le stagioni migliori e molte persone visitano l'Italia specialmente in primavera.—Spring and autumn are the best seasons and many people visit Italy in spring especially. D'estate però specialmente in luglio e agosto fa troppo caldo per noi.—It is too hot for us however in summer especially in July and August. Parla italiano lei?—Do you speak Italian? Ho studiato un po' l'italiano e posso capire quasi tutto, se mi parlano lentamente.—I have studied Italian a little and can understand almost everything if people speak to me slowly. Preferisco conoscere la lingua del paese dove passo le mie vacanze.—I prefer to know the language of the country where I spend my holidays. Mi corregga, per favore, se sbaglio.—Please correct me if I make a mistake. Sono io stesso sorpreso di poter seguire una conversazione, ma mi piacerebbe poter parlare un po' di più.—I myself am surprised at being able to follow a conversation but it would please me better to be able to speak a bit more.

D. *Altro che*!

Allora, ti è piaciuta? Altro che!—You liked her, then? Indeed I did!

Altro che ballo! Mettiti a studiare, piuttosto!—Dance, indeed! Go and study, rather!

LESSON XIII

Position of Adjectives

The position of an adjective varies in Italian depending on the type of adjective[1] and whether it stands alone or is modified by an adverb.

The following always follow the noun:

1. adjectives denoting nationality and religion:

una signora italiana	an Italian lady
una chiesa Anglicana	an Anglican church

2. adjectives of colour:

un fazzoletto rosso	a red handkerchief

3. adjectives denoting shape:

una scatola quadrata	a square box

4. all adjectives modified by an adverb:

una casa abbastanza grande	a pretty big house

Many adjectives can either precede or follow the noun according to the sense implied in the sentence; if they precede, they have a lighter touch and their tone is more descriptive; if they follow, the distinction conveyed by the adjective is more emphatic and stresses that aspect of the noun in particular.

Un lungo manto le copriva le spalle.	A long cloak covered her shoulders.
Quest'anno sono di mɔda i vestiti corti.	The fashion this year is for short clothes.

The following adjectives, because of their descriptive character, generally precede the noun: *giovane*—young, *vεcchio*—old, *núovo*—new, *antico*—old, *lungo*—long, *largo*—wide, *grande*—big, *piccolo*—little, *brεve*—short, *bεllo*—beautiful, lovely, *brutto*—ugly, *buɔno*—good, *cattivo*—bad.

Meaning of Adjectives Determined by Position

Some adjectives change their meaning completely according to their position:

Cεrto means 'certain' if it precedes the noun, and 'sure', 'reliable', if it follows it:

una cεrta notizia	certain news
una notizia cεrta	reliable news

[1] Cardinal numbers always precede the noun. Ordinals precede or follow. See Lesson XXVIII.

Nuɔvo, meaning 'new' when preceding or following the noun, can also mean 'another' when it precedes the noun:

un nuɔvo vestito another dress
un vestito nuɔvo a new dress

Divɛrso, vario mean 'several' if they precede the noun, and 'different' if they follow it:

divɛrse, varie riviste several magazines
idee divɛrse different ideas

Pɔvero means 'unfortunate' if it precedes the noun, and 'poor' (not rich) if it follows it:

una pɔvera donna an unfortunate woman
una donna pɔvera a poor woman

Irregular Forms Determined by Position

Bɛllo, perfectly regular when following a noun, has forms similar to those of the definite article when preceding it: *bɛl, bɛi, bɛllo, bɛgli, bɛll' bɛlla, bɛlle*

un libro *bɛllo* a beautiful book, *but*: un *bɛl* libro (il)
due libri *bɛlli* two beautiful books, *but*: due *bɛi* libri (i)
uno spɛcchio *bɛllo* a beautiful mirror *and* un bɛllo spɛcchio (lo)
due spɛcchi *bɛlli* two beautiful mirrors, *but*: due *bɛgli* spɛcchi (gli)
un'amica *bɛlla* a beautiful friend, *but*: una *bɛll*'amica (*l'*)
una casa *bɛlla* a beautiful house *and* una *bɛlla* casa (*la*)
due case *bɛlle* two beautiful houses *and* due *bɛlle* case (*le*)

Buɔno in the same way is regular when it follows a noun but has forms similar to the indefinite article when preceding a singular noun: *buɔn, buɔno, buɔna, buɔn'*:

un libro *buɔno* a good book, *but*: un *buɔn* libro (*un*)
uno sconto *buɔno* a good discount *and* un *buɔno* sconto (*uno*)
una madre *buɔna* a good mother *and* una *buɔna* madre (una)
un'amica *buɔna* a good friend, *but*: una *buɔn*'amica (*un'*)

Santo—saint, holy, and *grande*—great, big, in the masculine become *san* and *gran*[1] before a singular noun beginning with a consonant other than *s* impure, *z*, etc.

San Paolo Saint Paul gran maɛstro great master

Santo elides, taking an apostrophe before a vowel in both genders:

Sant'Antonio Saint Antony Sant'Anna Saint Anne

[1] *Gran* is sometimes used in the feminine singular and in the masculine plural: una gran casa—a big house; i gran signori—the important people.

When there are two adjectives which require different positions, the one precedes, the other follows the noun:

una grande tavola rotonda	a large, round table
due bɛi tappeti cinesi	two beautiful Chinese carpets
una brutta stɔffa marrone	an ugly brown material

But if they both usually precede the noun they are coupled by the conjunction 'and':

con grandi e bɛlle stanze with beautiful large rooms

Plural of Nouns (*continued*)

1. Some nouns in Italian are of common gender, that is they have the same ending for masculine and feminine; their gender is shown by means of the article:

il ciclista, la ciclista	the cyclist
il violinista, la violinista	the violinist
l'omicida, la omicida	the murderer
il parɛnte, la parɛnte	the relative

If they end in *a* in the singular, they form the masculine plural in *i* and the feminine plural in *e*; if they end in *e* in the singular, they form the plural, both masculine and feminine, in *i:*

i ciclisti	le cicliste
i parɛnti	le parɛnti

2. Certain masculine nouns ending in *o* in the singular form their plural in *a*, changing their gender to the feminine:

un centinaio	alcune centinaia	about one, some hundreds
un migliaio	molte migliaia	about one, many thousands
un miglio	due miglia	one, two miles
un paio	molte paia	one, many pairs
un uɔvo	tre uɔva	one, three eggs

To this category belong nouns which, besides their feminine plural in *a,* have also a regular plural in *i*, often with a different meaning:

braccio	arm	bracci	of a chandelier
		braccia	of the human body
dito	finger	diti	singly
		dita	all together
riso	rice	risi	different kinds of rice
	laugh	risa	laughter
frutto	fruit	frutti	of work
		frutta	of trees

ginɔcchio knee	ginɔcchi	
	ginɔcchia	(more common)
lenzuɔlo sheet	lenzuɔli	(equally common)
	lenzuɔla	
mɛmbro member	mɛmbri	of parliament, of a society
	mɛmbra	of the body
labbro lip	labbri	of a wound
	labbra	of the mouth
muro wall	muri	of a room
	mura	of a city

The following nouns have irregular plurals:

uɔmo, uɔmini men bue, buɔi oxen Dio, dɛi gods

Vocabulary XIII

arredamento furnishing
stɔffa material, fabric
broccato brocade
cotone (m.) cotton
seta silk
lana wool
disegno design, pattern
tɛnda curtain
tendina small curtain, screen
colore (m.) colour
caminetto fireplace, mantelpiece
marmo marble
fotografia photograph
fiore (m.) flower
interɛsse (m.) interest
vaso vase
violinista (m. & f.) violinist
porcellana porcelain, china

rè (m.) king
candelabro chandelier
parete (f.) wall (of a room)
cristallo crystal
caro (adj.) dear, expensive
nero (adj.) black
grigio (adj.) grey
marrone (adj.) brown
azzurro (adj.) blue
celɛste (adj.) pale blue
rɔsa (adj. inv.) pink
rotondo (adj.) round
ovale (adj.) oval
scorso (adj.) last
cinese (adj.) Chinese
Anna Anne
recentemente (adv.) recently
di sɔlito usually, generally.

Exercise 1

Give the plural of the following nouns in Italian, supplying the definite article: violinist (f.), relative (m.), pair, mile, arm (body), thousand, hammock, hundred, chemist's shop, laugh, suitcase, luggage, wood, wardrobe, uncle, friend (m.), friend (f.), hotel, ox, man, king, god, Greek, tram, park, wall (city), finger, egg.

Exercise 2

Translate into Italian: 1. last week. 2. a French newspaper. 3. a young girl. 4. a new book. 5. a square garden. 6. an ancient monument. 7. a brown suitcase. 8. the same week. 9. an Italian lawyer.

10. modern flats. 11. rich relations. 12. all the people. 13. wide squares. 14. a few coaches. 15. these white houses. 16. some small parcels. 17. many intelligent people. 18. fresh fruit. 19. a famous violinist (m.). 20. large sheets. 21. numerous theatres. 22. a grey carpet. 23. crowded streets. 24. expensive hotels.

Exercise 3

Translate into Italian: 1. a lovely garden. 2. the beautiful carnations. 3. a beautiful mirror. 4. the beautiful bookcases. 5. a beautiful hotel. 6. the beautiful trees. 7. a lovely house. 8. a beautiful car. 9. some beautiful chairs. 10. a good carpet. 11. a good wardrobe. 12. a good friend (f.). 13. a good psychiatrist. 14. a good suitcase. 15. a big park. 16. a large study. 17. a large bus. 18. two large hammocks. 19. a great king. 20. Saint Robert. 21. a holy man. 22. Saint Louise.

A. *Translate into English:* 1. La settimana scorsa la signora Bruni ha comprato una rivista di arredamento. 2. È una magnifica rivista con molte fotografie di belle case e di bei mobili. 3. La signora Bruni le ha guardate con grande interesse perché desidera cambiare l'arredamento del suo salotto. 4. Una delle fotografie mostra il salotto della casa di una famosa attrice francese. 5. È un salotto moderno con un gran divano e poltrone e qualche bel mobile antico. 6. Alle finestre ci sono delle tende di un magnifico broccato giallo. 7. Il broccato è una stoffa di seta o di cotone e i broccati italiani e francesi sono sempre stati famosi. 8. Al centro del soffitto c'è un candelabro di cristallo a sei bracci. 9. Su un tavolino rotondo vicino al divano c'è un gran vaso cinese verde con dei bei fiori. 10. Recentemente abbiamo veduto nel salotto di un nostro amico un cassettone antico e un divano e delle poltrone moderni. 11. Nello stesso salotto c'era un meraviglioso caminetto di marmo antico. 12. Di che colore sono i tappeti? Il tappeto grande è marrone; il tappeto piccolo è verde con un disegno grigio e rosso: sono degli antichi tappeti cinesi. 13. Nella stessa rivista c'era la fotografia di una bella camera da letto moderna. 14. La coperta dei letti e le tende erano di una stoffa di cotone celeste a fiori rosa. 15. Anche le tendine bianche avevano un disegno di piccoli fiori. 16. Recentemente abbiamo ricevuto due cataloghi di stoffe da arredamento di seta, di lana e di cotone. 17. C'erano anche delle stoffe per biancheria da letto nel catalogo: alcune persone preferiscono le lenzuola e le federe rosa, celesti o anche nere. 18. Preferite le tavole da pranzo quadrate, rotonde o ovali? 19. Una tavola da pranzo rotonda è comoda. 20. Maria ha comprato ieri dei bei garofani rossi per la signora Anna, la madre di Silvia e glieli ha mandati perché oggi è Sant'Anna.

B. *Translate into Italian:* 1. In Dr Duranti's waiting-room there is a large round table laden with magazines and newspapers. 2. Some of the magazines are old but the doctor keeps them because some people have not seen them. 3. Which magazine do you prefer? I prefer magazines of household furnishing with coloured (a colori) photographs. 4. A few days ago I was looking at a magazine where there were photographs of two old English houses with their large beautiful grounds. 5. In the magazine there were not photographs of every room but only of the hall and dining-room of one house and of the drawing-room and staircase of the other. 6. All the dining-room furniture was antique: the large oval table and huge sideboard were magnificent. 7. On the floor there were some small Chinese rugs and on the mantelpiece two beautiful old vases. 8. The long curtains were (say, of) brown brocade, the chandelier was (of) crystal and there was a china lamp on a little round table near the fireplace. 9. In the other photograph the divan and the armchairs in the drawing-room were modern; some of the paintings were modern also. 10. One fairly big bookcase and some other pieces of furniture in the same room were antique. 11. Among these was a magnificent showcase with little china statues, crystal vases and many other interesting objects. 12. In some modern houses the four walls of a room are not always (say, of) the same colour. 13. Sometimes two walls are red and the other two grey or yellow: or one wall is red and the other three grey. 14. In some rooms all the walls are white and the ceiling is pale blue or pink or red, and the curtains and cushions are red, green or blue. 15. Many modern kitchens have white walls and ceilings, a green floor, table and cupboards: and green and white cotton curtains on the windows. 16. We have always preferred cotton material for bathroom and kitchen curtains because we wash them often. 17. Many modern materials with checked (a quadri) or floral (a fiori) designs are not at all dear and are very fashionable in small houses and flats. 18. Recently we bought some magnificent silk material for curtains and a bedspread for one of the bedrooms. 19. In the same catalogue where we had seen this material there were also, among the bed-linen, beautiful coloured materials for sheets and pillow cases. 20. Do you like striped (a strisce) bed-linen?

C. In Italia c'è lo stesso entusiasmo verso l'arredamento moderno?—Is there the same enthusiasm for modern furnishing in Italy? C'è come qui la tendenza ad avere le pareti dipinte in colori diversi o tappezzate con differenti carte da parato?—Is it the fashion, as it is here, to have the walls painted different colours or papered with different wallpapers? Non tanto come in questo paese.—Not so much as in this country. Le carte da parato sono usate nell'arredamento molto di meno.—Wallpapers are much less used in interior decorating. La gente non è abituata in generale a dipingere da sè le stanze o a tappezzarle.—People are not so accustomed to doing their own papering and painting. Non ci sono mobili in serie? —Is there no standard production furniture? Tranne una fabbrica o due di mobili che producono mobilia di un certo tipo, non esistono mobili in serie, eccetto per gli uffici.—Apart from one or two furniture factories which manufacture a particular type of furniture, standard ranges of furniture do not exist—except for offices. Esiste un artigianato in Italia?—Is there good craftsmanship in Italy? L'artigianato in Italia è molto più sviluppato che qui.—Craftsmanship is much more developed in Italy than it is here. Che cosa producono gli artigiani?—What do the craftsmen make? Producono mobili, vasi, tappeti, stoffe, scarpe, borsette, insomma oggetti di arredamento e di abbigliamento che mostrano e riflettono il gusto e la capacità degli operai.—They make furniture, vases, carpets, materials, shoes, hand-bags, in short articles of furnishing and of clothing that display and reflect the taste and the ability of the craftsmen.

D. *Come no*

Hai imbucato la lεttera? Come no!—Did you post the letter? Of course I did!

LESSON XIV

Past Perfect; Second Past Perfect; Future Perfect

Past Perfect of Model Verbs

avevo amato	I had loved, etc.	avevo temuto	I had feared, etc.	avevo dormito	I had slept, etc.
avevi amato		avevi temuto		avevi dormito	
aveva amato		aveva temuto		aveva dormito	
avevamo amato		avevamo temuto		avevamo dormito	
avevate amato		avevate temuto		avevate dormito	
avevano amato		avevano temuto		avevano dormito	

Past Perfect of Ɛssere and *Avere*

ɛro stato	I had been, etc.	avevo avuto	I had had, etc.
ɛri stato		avevi avuto	
ɛra stato		aveva avuto	
eravamo stati		avevamo avuto	
eravate stati		avevate avuto	
ɛrano stati		avevano avuto	

Second Past Perfect of Model Verbs

ɛbbi amato	I had loved, etc.	ɛbbi temuto	I had feared, etc.	ɛbbi dormito	I had slept, etc.
avesti amato		avesti temuto		avesti dormito	
ɛbbe amato		ɛbbe temuto		ɛbbe dormito	
avemmo amato		avemmo temuto		avemmo dormito	
aveste amato		aveste temuto		aveste dormito	
ɛbbero amato		ɛbbero temuto		ɛbbero dormito	

Second Past Perfect of Ɛssere and *Avere*

fui stato	I had been, etc.	ɛbbi avuto	I had had, etc.
fosti stato		avesti avuto	
fu stato		ɛbbe avuto	
fummo stati		avemmo avuto	
foste stati		aveste avuto	
furono stati		ɛbbero avuto	

Uses

The English pluperfect is translated into Italian either by the past perfect, formed by the past descriptive of the auxiliary verb *Avere* or

Ɛssere and the past participle of the main verb, to denote an habitual past action, or by the second past perfect, formed by the past absolute of the auxiliary verb and the past participle of the main verb, to denote one particular single past action; thus these two tenses reflect the characteristics of their respective auxiliary verb tenses.

The past perfect is used in a main clause, or in a dependent clause introduced by *quando*, *ogni vɔlta che*, etc., with the main clause verb in the past descriptive or the past perfect:

L'aveva sɛmpre amato.
She had always loved him.
Quando aveva finito di lavorare andava a casa.
When he had finished work he went home.
Ogni vɔlta che era andato a farle visita l'aveva trovata a casa.
Every time he had visited her he had found her at home.

The second past perfect is used only in subordinate clauses introduced by *quando*, *appena*[1] (*che*), *dopo che*, *subito che*, etc., with the main clause verb in the past absolute:

Quando ɛbbe finito di lavorare andò a casa.
He went home when he had finished work.
Appena Maria ɛbbe suonato il campanɛllo, la cameriɛra aprì la pɔrta.
As soon as Mary rang the bell the maid opened the door.
Quando ɛbbi comprato i guanti ritornai a casa.
When I had bought the gloves I returned home.
Dopo che i nɔstri amici furono partiti, pulimmo il salɔtto.
When our friends had left we cleaned the sitting-room.

Future Perfect of Model Verbs

avrò amato	I shall have loved, etc.	avrò temuto	I shall have feared, etc.	avrò dormito	I shall have slept, etc.
avrai amato		avrai temuto		avrai dormito	
avrà amato		avrà temuto		avrà dormito	
avremo amato		avremo temuto		avremo dormito	
avrete amato		avrete temuto		avrete dormito	
avranno amato		avranno temuto		avranno dormito	

Future Perfect of Ɛssere and *Avere*

sarò stato	I shall have been, etc.	avrò avuto	I shall have had, etc.
sarai stato		avrai avuto	
sarà stato		avrà avuto	
saremo stati		avremo avuto	
sarete stati		avrete avuto	
saranno stati		avranno avuto	

[1] When *appena* means 'just', it requires the past perfect and follows the auxiliary verb: Aveva appena chiuso la pɔrta quando il campanɛllo suonò.

Uses

The rules given for the use of the simple future apply equally to the future perfect:

Quando avrò finito, partirò.	When I have finished, I shall set out.
Sarà stato malato.	He probably has been ill.

Adverbs

Adverbs of manner are commonly formed by adding 'mente' to the feminine form of the adjective:

magnifico	magnificamente	magnificent	magnificently

Adjectives ending in *re* and *le* drop the *e* if the final syllable is preceded by a vowel:

	gentile	gentilmente	kind	kindly
but:	mɔlle	mollemente	soft	softly

Some adverbs have forms similar to adjectives; as adverbs they are invariable; as adjectives they have the usual endings: *o, a, i, e*:

molto	(adv.)	very	molto	(adj.)	much, many
pɔco	„	little	pɔco	„	little, few (pl.)
trɔppo	„	too, too much	trɔppo	„	too much, too many
parecchio	„	much, very much	parecchio	„	several (pl).; quite a lot (time); considerable (distance)
quanto	„	how, how much	quanto	„	how much, how many, as much as
tanto	„	so much	tanto	„	so much, so many, so great

The position of adverbs modifying verbs is usually after the verb, but it is subject to variation according to different shades of meaning:

La vedo spesso.	I often see her.
Spesso la vedo preoccupata.	I often see her worried.

Irregular Verbs—First Conjugation

There are four irregular verbs in the first conjugation, namely: *andare*—to go; *stare*—to stay, to be; *dare*—to give; *fare*—to do, to make. The irregularity occurs in several forms but we shall confine ourselves, for this lesson, to the present indicative.

vado I go, etc.	sto I am, stay, etc.	do I give, etc.	faccio I do, make, etc.
vai	stai	dai	fai
va	sta	dà	fa
andiamo	stiamo	diamo	facciamo
andate	state	date	fate
vanno	stanno	danno	fanno

Vocabulary XIV

commesso shop assistant
cappɔtto coat, top coat
modɛllo model, model clothes
scarpa shoe
borsetta handbag
vestito a giacca suit
cam*i*cia shirt
imperme*a*bile (m.) raincoat
calzino sock
pigiama (m.) pyjamas (a pair of)
guanto glove
cam*i*cia da nɔtte nightdress
camicetta blouse
gɔnna skirt
cappɛllo hat
fazzoletto handkerchief, scarf, headsquare
calza stocking
gentile (adj.) kind, courteous
elegante (adj.) elegant, smart
diritto (adj.) straight
adatto (adj.) suitable
prima (adv.) before, first, first of all
s*e*mplice (adj.) simple
stretto (adj.) narrow, tight
provare to try on, try (a)
pagare to pay
salutare to greet, say goodbye
raccontare to tell, relate

Exercise 1

Repeat orally: (a) *the past perfect, second past perfect and future perfect of the following verbs:* portare, mandare, mangiare, vèndere, ricevere, vedere, preferire, applaudire, pulire.

(*b*) *The present of:* andare, fare, stare, dare.

Exercise 2

Translate into Italian: 1. They had spent. 2. We had been. 3. As soon as they had gone away. 4. You had entered. 5. When I had forwarded. 6. It will have arrived. 7. You had worn. 8. He had never shown. 9. After she had spoken. 10. They (f.) will have been ill. 11. As soon as it had rung. 12. He will have departed. 13. They (f.) had arrived. 14. When they had sent them (m.) to us. 15. We had explained it (m.) to them. 16. As soon as you had returned. 17. After they had listened. 18. We had not seen her at all. 19. They will not have sold it (m.). 20. He had often driven it (f.).

Exercise 3

Translate into Italian: 1. Many clothes are too dear. 2. Some hotels are very modern. 3. There are too many books on that bookshelf. 4. Few people understand modern art. 5. She had so many friends. 6. I understand German a little. 7. He escorted us courteously to the tram stop. 8. They built it (m.) very near the station. 9. We sold it (f.) to him recently. 10. He swam magnificently. 11. I was a little late. 12. They talk too often.

A. *Translate into English:* 1. Qualche settimana fa Maria entrò in un negozio e domandò alla commessa di mostrarle un vestito rosso. 2. Essa l'aveva veduto la stessa mattina in vetrina. 3. Era un bel vestito di seta rossa e Maria aveva avuto dalla madre un cappotto di lana dello stesso colore qualche giorno prima. 4. La commessa guardò nella vetrina e negli armadi ma non trovò il vestito. 5. Chiamò l'altra commessa ed essa le spiegò che aveva venduto il vestito la mattina ad una signora francese. 6. "Desidera vedere lo stesso modello in qualche altro colore?"—le domandò la commessa. 7. Maria guardò i vestiti ma quando la commessa glieli ebbe mostrati tutti, le spiegò che aveva già un cappotto rosso e che aveva anche comprato un paio di scarpe e una borsetta nere. 8. Nello stesso negozio c'erano dei bei vestiti a giacca con delle camicette bianche. 9. Erano semplici ma eleganti con una gonna stretta e diritta. 10. Maria provò anche un bell'impermeabile ma era giallo ed essa non ama questo colore. 11. Nella vetrina vicina c'erano dei bei cappelli. Giulia li ammirò ma Maria non porta mai cappelli. 12. Una signora elegante ha sempre un bel cappello, dei bei guanti, una bella borsetta e delle belle calze e scarpe. 13. Maria e Giulia entrarono poi in un gran negozio di biancheria. 14. Giulia desiderava comprare dei fazzoletti bianchi di cotone, tre paia di calzini di lana e un buon pigiama per Roberto e delle camicie da notte per la mamma. 15. Quando il commesso le ebbe consegnato il pigiama, le camicie da notte, i fazzoletti e i calzini in una gran scatola quadrata, Giulia pagò e domandò a Maria se desiderava prendere un caffè. 16. C'era un piccolo bar all'angolo della strada ed esse entrarono e domandarono due caffè; ad un tavolo c'era la signora Ascenzi ed esse la salutarono e le domandarono dove aveva passato le sue vacanze. 17. Essa era stata a Parigi due settimane e aveva incontrato dei nostri amici. 18. Ci raccontò che a Parigi aveva comprato dei bei vestiti e una magnifica borsetta. 19. Che cosa portava? Era molto elegante; aveva un vestito a giacca di lana grigia con scarpe, cappello, borsa e guanti marrone. 20. "Chi avete incontrato stamattina?"—domandò loro la madre quando ritornarono a casa.

B. *Translate into Italian*: 1. My sister and I had not bought any clothes last year. 2. We had always bought our clothes in a large shop where we know all the assistants but a week ago we found a new shop where clothes are not very expensive. 3. They always have elegant models in all their windows. 4. We do not often buy model clothes as they are expensive and we are not rich. 5. Did you not buy some new shoes recently? No, I tried on two or three pairs, but I did not buy them. 6. How much do they cost? If they are smart they are usually very dear. 7. Ladies generally wear hats but young girls often prefer to wear woollen or silk squares. 8. Two weeks ago my brother received a parcel from my aunt. She had sent him some black socks and white handkerchiefs, and a beautiful (pair of) pyjamas. 9. He has recently bought a new grey suit and a very smart top coat, and two white cotton shirts. 10. Do you wear pyjamas, Mary? 11. I have sometimes worn them but I prefer a silk or cotton nightdress. 12. As soon as I entered the shop I met Julia's aunt: we were admiring the same model. 13. Neither her aunt nor I bought it because it was too large, but the material and the colour were beautiful. 14. After I had seen some other suits, the assistant brought me a very expensive model in grey wool. 15. I tried it on and I bought it because I had always wanted a grey suit. 16. This suit had two skirts. 17. Straight skirts are very elegant but sometimes they are not very convenient. 18. My handbag and my gloves are black and my new blouse is red. 19. I like a little (di) colour with grey but not too much. 20. As soon as we returned home, we opened all our parcels and showed our mother the new suit and the new shoes.

C. I negozi italiani sono simili ai negozi in questo paese?—Are Italian shops the same as those in this country? Sono molto più specializzati.—They are much more specialized. Ci sono in Italia negozi che hanno succursali in tutte le grandi città?—Are there chain-stores in Italy with branches in all the large cities? I negozi più popolari in tutte le città sono la Rinascente, Standa ed Upim e in alcuni di questi negozi ci sono reparti di commestibili, frutta e verdura come in alcuni grandi magazzini in Gran Bretagna.—The most popular shops in all the cities are the Rinascente, Standa and Upim and in some of these shops there are departments for foodstuffs, fruit and vegetables as there are in some large stores in Britain. Che cosa si dice alla commessa o al commesso?—What does one say to the assistant? Per chiedere qualche cosa in un negozio si dice al commesso—"Vorrei vedere delle cravatte di seta, dei guanti da sera, delle sciarpe, dei sottabiti ricamati."—To ask a shop assistant for something one says, "I should like to see some silk ties, some evening gloves, some scarves, some embroidered slips." Vuole mostrarmi quello che ha?—Would you show me what you have? Che misura? La mia misura di guanti è sei e mezzo.—What size? My size in gloves is six and a half. In che altri colori li ha?—What other colours do you have? Li preferirei di camoscio, di cinghiale.—I should prefer chamois, peccary. Sono lavabili?—Are they washable? Se si tratta di una stoffa si chiede:—If it is a question of material one asks: "Quanto costa al metro?"—How much does it cost per metre? (one metre is a little more than a yard). Quanti metri crede che occorrono per fare un vestito?—How many metres do you think I'll need to make a dress? Posso vederla alla luce?—May I see it in the light? Posso avere un campione?—May I have a sample? Le piace questo? Mi piace molto ma è troppo caro.—Do you like this one? I like it very much but it is too dear. Può metterlo da parte sino a questo pomeriggio?—Can you put it aside till this afternoon?

D. *Ɛcco*!

Allora, le vuɔle tutte e due? Ɛcco!—You want both of them, then? Exactly!

Ɛcco fatto!—That's done then!

E pɔi se n'è andato, ɛcco tutto!—And then he went away, and that's all there is to it!

LESSON XV

Imperative Mood

The imperative mood (modo imperativo) expresses a wish or a command that something be done. It has two tenses, the present and the future.

Imperative Mood of Model Verbs

Present

Singular						
2nd	ama	love	tɛmi	fear, etc.	dɔrmi	sleep, etc.
3rd	ami (courtesy form)		tɛma		dɔrma	
Plural						
1st	amiamo	let us love	temiamo		dormiamo	
2nd	amate	love	temete		dormite	
3rd	amino (courtesy form)		tɛmano		dɔrmano	

In the present, with the exception of 2nd person singular of the first conjugation, which has a form of its own, all the other persons are borrowed from the present indicative or, in the case of the courtesy form, from the present subjunctive (3rd person singular and plural). The use of the subjunctive renders the courtesy form more of an exhortation than a forthright command. The future imperative is used when the command given is not to be carried out immediately but after some time or habitually in the future. The forms of the future imperative (2nd person singular and plural) are identical with those of the simple future.

Imperative of 'Ɛssere' and 'Avere'

Present

Singular				
2nd	sii	be	abbi	have
3rd	sia*	be	abbia*	have
Plural				
1st	siamo	let us be	abbiamo	let us have
2nd	siate	be	abbiate	have
3rd	siano*	be	abbiano*	have

*Courtesy form

Imperative of 'Andare', 'Stare', 'Dare' and 'Fare'

Present

Singular								
2nd	va'	go, etc.	sta'	be, stay, etc.	da'	give, etc.	fa'	do, make etc.
3rd	vada*		stia*		dia*		faccia*	

*Courtesy form

Plural

1st	andiamo	stiamo	diamo	facciamo
2nd	andate	state	date	fate
3rd	vadano*	stiano*	diano*	facciano*

*Courtesy form

Uses

The imperative mood is used to express:

1. *an order*: In the present: Impara—Learn!; Guarda—Look!
   In the future: Resterete qui—You will stay here.
2. *an entreaty*: Mi aiuti—Help me!
3. *an exhortation*: Siate buoni—Be good!
4. *advice*: Studiate—Study!

Conjunctive Pronouns (*continued*)

The general rule that pronouns always precede the verb, does not apply when the verb form is: (a) the *Infinitive*, (b) the *Imperative* (except 3rd persons), (c) the *Gerund* and (d) the *Participle*.[1] The pronouns follow these forms and—with the exception of *loro*—are joined to them to form one single word. In the case of compound forms pronouns follow the auxiliaries.

(a) Desideriamo vederlo. We wish to see him.
Preferisce scrivergli. He prefers to write to him.
(b) Scrivimi prεsto. Write to me soon.
but: Mi scriva prεsto (courtesy form). Write to me soon.
Conservali. Keep them.
but: Li conservi (courtesy form). Keep them.
(c) Guardandola. Looking at her.
Avεndola guardata. Having looked at her.
(d) Finitala. Having finished it.
Avεndolo finito. Having finished it.
Parlando loro. Talking to them.

This also applies when both direct and indirect pronouns occur in the same sentence; they follow the above forms in their usual order:

(a) Desidero scriverglielo. I wish to write it to him.
Preferisco regalarglielo. I prefer to give it to him.
(b) Mandamelo. Send it to me.
but: Me lo mandi (courtesy form). Send it to me.
(c) Leggεndotela. Reading it to you.
Avεndotela letta. Having read it to you.

[1] See Lessons 29 and 30 respectively.

(d) Insegnatocelo.	Having taught it to us.
Avεndocelo insegnato.	Having taught it to us.
Scrivεndone loro.	Writing of it to them.

Note carefully that:

(1) The infinitive drops the final *e* before the pronoun:

Spero di comprarlo. I hope to buy it.

(2) All pronouns (*gli* being the only exception) double their initial consonant when combined with the following monosyllabic imperatives:

da' (give), *di'* (tell), *fa'* (do, make), *sta'* (be, stay), *va'* (go)

resulting in such forms as *dimmi, falle, vacci,* etc.

(3) *Ɛcco* combines with the pronouns in a single word:

εccolo (here he is), εccomi (here I am), εccoli (here they are) etc.

Courtesy Form in Direct Address

Just as the third person is used as the courtesy form of the subject pronouns, so the following third persons are used for the courtesy form of the object:

Direct Object

Singular			
la	you (m. & f.) e.g.	La vedo spesso.	I see you often.
Plural			
li	you (m.)	Li vedo spesso.	I see you (m.) often.
le	you (f.)	Le vedo spesso.	I see you (f.) often.

Indirect Object

Singular			
le	to you m. & f.) e.g.	Le manderò.	I shall send to you (m. & f.)
Plural			
loro	to you (m. & f.) e.g.	Mando loro.	I send to you (m. & f.)

Conjunctive Adverbs: ci, vi, ne

ci, vi		here, to here there, to there
ne	pron.	of it, of them
	adv.	from there

Besides the use of *ci* (us) and *vi* (you) as conjunctive pronouns we must learn their use as conjunctive adverbs, expressing motion towards or rest in a place already mentioned. *Ne* likewise is used both as conjunctive pronoun and a conjunctive adverb. The pronoun *ne* must never be omitted in Italian when the noun is not repeated and there is a numeral or an adjective of quantity after the verb. The position of *ci, vi* and *ne* as adverbs is governed by the identical rules given for their use as pronouns:

Ritornerai in ufficio? Sì, ci ritornerò nel pomeriggio.

Are you going back to the office? Yes I shall go back there in the afternoon.

Spɛro di ritornarci.

I hope to return there.

Conosci questa piazza? Sì, ci abito.

Do you know this square? Yes, I live here.

Sɛi stato in chiɛsa? Sì, ne ritorno.

Have you been to church? Yes, I am on my way back from there.

Hai delle matite? Sì, ne ho tre.

Have you any pencils? Yes, I have three (of them).

C'è del caffè? No, non ce n'è.

Is there any coffee? No, there is not any.

Vocabulary XV

carta da lɛttere notepaper
foglietto sheet of notepaper
busta envelope
francobollo stamp
affrancatura postage
buca delle lɛttere letter box
telɛfono pubblico public telephone
cabina telefɔnica telephone box
tabaccaio tobacconist
indirizzo address
mittɛnte (m. & f.) sender
raccomandata registered letter
esprɛsso express letter
telegramma (m.) telegram
ricevuta receipt
firma signature
pɔsta mail, post office
postino postman
vaglia postale (m.) postal order
vaglia telegrafico (m.) (by wire)
intreccio plot
govɛrno government
Gran Bretagna Great Britain
Italia Italy
ɔggi (adv.) today
assiɛme (adv.) together
quasi (adv.) almost
telefonare to telephone
imbucare to post
firmare to sign
riscuɔtere to cash
rispondere . . . a to answer (aux. avere)
andare . . . a + infin. = to go to do something
costare to cost
consigliare a qualcuno di to advise

Exercise 1

(a) *Repeat orally the present imperative of:* fare, stare, dare, andare, comprare, vedere, partire, spedire.

(b) *Translate into Italian:* 1. We make. 2. They finish. 3. He cashes. 4. I go. 5. You give. 6. You try. 7. She pays. 8. We stay. 9. They make. 10. I sign. 11. He telephones. 12. They arrive. 13. We go. 14. She opens. 15. They give. 16. You make. 17. You (s) give. 18. They go. 19. You stay. 20. We give. 21. Stay! 22. Go! 23. Give! 24. Make! 25. Tell! 26. Listen! 27. Let us cross. 28. Answer! 29. Let us come back. 30. Open!

Exercise 2

Translate into Italian: 1. We shall pay. 2. They have arrived. 3. We had signed. 4. You will have had. 5. I (f.) have been. 6. You are making. 7. We used to write often. 8. She will have been. 9. They had changed. 10. You are giving. 11. They will be late. 12. We went.

Exercise 3

Translate into Italian: 1. I want to give it (f.) to them. 2. We prefer to make them (m.). Here they are. 3. He was wanting to send them (f.) to us. 4. Where is the post office? We are returning from there. 5. Do you not want to go there? Tell me. 6. I shall accompany you there. Here we are. 7. Where is the parcel? Give me it. 8. Here it is. I want to send it registered. 9. Where is the letter? Do you wish to send it also to her? 10. These roses are beautiful; I shall buy ten (of them).

A. *Translate into English:* 1. Ieri ho comprato della carta da lettere: dieci foglietti e buste celesti. 2. Oggi scriverò molte lettere e risponderò a tutti i miei amici. 3. In una delle lettere metterò un vaglia postale e l'impiegato della Posta mi ha consigliato di spedirla raccomandata. 4. Quando entro nell'Ufficio postale vado allo sportello delle raccomandate e dei telegrammi e do le lettere all'impiegato. 5. Gliele dai tutte assieme? No, prima gliene consegno due e gli chiedo di spedirle raccomandate. 6. Poi gli domando quanto costa l'affrancatura per una lettera espresso e gli do le altre. 7. Quante volte al[1] giorno arriva la posta? 8. Il postino va all'Ufficio postale due volte al giorno, prende la posta e ce la distribuisce. 9. Dov'è una cabina telefonica? Eccone una all'angolo della strada. 10. In Italia ci sono cabine telefoniche soltanto negli uffici postali e negli alberghi, ma in quasi ogni bar e caffè c'è un telefono pubblico. 11. Dove comprate i francobolli? Li compriamo all'Ufficio postale ma in Italia anche i tabaccai li vendono. 12. I vecchi vanno ogni mese all'Ufficio postale per riscuotere la loro pensione. 13. Vai a casa ora? No, ne ritorno. 14. "Dove sta e che cosa fa suo fratello?" mi chiede un amico. 15. "Abita in città e frequenta l'Università," gli rispondo. 16. Avete veduto la nuova commedia a teatro? 17. No, non

[1] Note the idiomatic use: *cf.* tre volte alla settimana, al mese—three times a week, a month.

ci sono stato ma mia sorella l'ha veduta e me ne ha raccontato l'intreccio. 18. Perché non ci vai stasera? Noi ci andiamo con degli amici. 19. Hai comprato i francobolli? Ne ho comprati sette. 20. Vado ora dal (to the) tabaccaio. Ci vado anche io, perché non facciamo la strada assieme?[1]

B. *Translate into Italian:* 1. There is a pillar box at the corner of the street where we live. It is very handy. 2. We post all our letters and cards there, but we go to the post office when we want to send parcels. 3. If we receive a registered letter or a parcel from the postman we sign a receipt and give it to him. 4. When letters and parcels are registered they bear the name of the sender. 5. Postmen deliver (distribuire) letters and parcels twice a (al) day. The post is usually very punctual. 6. At the entrance to the post office there are five or six telephone booths. 7. In Italy there is usually a public telephone in every bar. 8. I sent an express letter from the post office and my friend received it the same evening. 9. I have never sent an express letter. If I am in a hurry I prefer to send a telegram. 10. When we are on holiday the post office forwards the mail to our new address. 11. In Britain we buy all our stamps at (all') the post office, but when we were on holiday in Italy we bought them also at (dai) the tobacconists. 12. We were returning to the hotel one day when we met an English lady. 13. She did not understand Italian at all and she asked us to accompany her to the post office. 14. The post had brought her, that morning, a money order from her husband. 15. As soon as she received it she asked the clerk in the hotel where the post office was. 16. "How much is the postage for a registered letter?" asked an old lady at one of the counters. 17. At another counter there was a poor old (man). 18. "What do you wish, sir?" an assistant asked him. 19. "Which counter is it for pensions?" asked the old man. 20. The Government gives a pension to the old (pl.) and they go every month to the post office to cash it.

C. Di che colore sono le cassette postali in Italia?—What colour are the letter boxes in Italy? Generalmente sono dipinte in rosso e sono sempre fissate al muro.—They are generally painted red and are always fixed to the wall. Quante distribuzioni della posta ci sono?—How many deliveries are there? Due o tre al giorno, secondo le città.—Two or three per day according to the towns. In Italia si usano molto più gli espressi e per spedire una lettera espresso basta comprare un francobollo espresso, applicarlo sulla busta e imbucare la lettera in una speciale cassetta.—In Italy they make more use of express letters and to send an express letter it is sufficient to buy an express stamp, put it on the envelope and post

[1] Idiomatic—walk there together.

the letter in a special box. Che cosa significa "stampe"?—What does the word 'stampe' indicate? 'Stampe' vuol dire 'printed matter'.—'Stampe' means 'printed matter'. Giornali e stampati sono imbucati in queste cassette speciali su cui c'è scritto 'Stampe'.—Newspapers and printed matter are posted in these special boxes on which is written 'Stampe'. Per favore, faccia seguire questa lettera al nuovo indirizzo!—Please forward this letter to the new address. È sufficiente l'affrancatura su questa lettera?—Is the postage on this letter sufficient? Che francobollo devo mettere su una lettera per l'Inghilterra? Un francobollo da 90 lire. E per l'interno? Un francobollo da 40.—What stamp should I put on a letter for England? A 90 lire stamp. And for this country (Italy)? A forty lire stamp.

D. *Tutt'altro*

È tutt'altro che stupido—He is far from being a fool

Ma tu l'hai incoraggiato? Tutt'altro!—Did you encourage him, then? On the contrary!

LESSON XVI

Conditional Mood

Unlike the indicative mood which is purely factual, the conditional mood (modo condizionale) is potential, expressing what should or would happen under certain circumstances. It has two tenses: one simple, the present, the other compound, the perfect.

Conditional Present of Model Verbs

amer-ɛi I should love, etc.	temer-ɛi I should fear, etc.	dormir-ɛi I should sleep, etc.
amer-esti	temer-esti	dormir-esti
amer-ɛbbe	temer-ɛbbe	dormir-ɛbbe
amer-emmo	temer-emmo	dormir-emmo
amer-este	temer-este	dormir-este
amer-ɛbbero	temer-ɛbbero	dormir-ɛbbero

The endings of the present conditional are identical for all conjugations. As in the future, the stem is obtained by removing the final *e* of the infinitive, and similarly in the first conjugation the characteristic vowel *a* changes to *e* in all regular verbs.

Conditional Present of 'Ɛssere' and 'Avere'

sarɛi I should be, etc.	avrɛi I should have, etc.
saresti	avresti
sarɛbbe	avrɛbbe
saremmo	avremmo
sareste	avreste
sarɛbbero	avrɛbbero

Conditional Perfect of Model Verbs

avrɛi amato I should have loved, etc.	avrɛi temuto I should have feared, etc.	avrɛi dormito I should have slept, etc.
avresti amato	avresti temuto	avresti dormito
avrɛbbe amato	avrɛbbe temuto	avrɛbbe dormito
avremmo amato	avremmo temuto	avremmo dormito
avreste amato	avreste temuto	avreste dormito
avrɛbbero amato	avrɛbbero temuto	avrɛbbero dormito

Conditional Perfect of 'Ɛssere' and 'Avere'

sarɛi stato I should have been, etc.	avrɛi avuto I should have had, etc.
saresti stato	avresti avuto

sarɛbbe stato
saremmo stati
sareste stati
sarɛbbero stati

avrɛbbe avuto
avremmo avuto
avreste avuto
avrɛbbero avuto

Uses

1. In subordinate clauses to express future time, when in the principal clause there is a past tense of verbs of saying, thinking, believing, etc.:

Pensavano che avrɛbbe capito. They thought he would understand.
Credevo che sarɛbbe venuta. I thought she would come.

Note the use of the conditional perfect in Italian compared with the simple conditional in English.

2. In the conclusion of a conditional sentence. (For fuller treatment, see p. 155).

3. Frequently in what really is the conclusion though the entire *if* clause has been suppressed:

Il facchino la porterɛbbe.
The porter would carry it (understood: if you asked him).

4. With verbs expressing wish, desire or preference:

Vorrɛi chiɛderle un favore. I would like to ask you a favour.
Potrɛi aiutarla? Can I help you?

5. To express an intention or make an observation without the finality implied by the indicative mood:

Pensɛrɛi di partire domani.
I am thinking of leaving tomorrow.

Preferiresti prima il pesce o la carne? Non saprɛi.
Would you prefer the fish or the meat first? I do not know.

6. To quote someone else's opinion:

Secondo loro egli sarɛbbe malato. According to them he is ill.

7. In rhetorical questions or exclamations:

Chi l'avrɛbbe pensato?
Who would have imagined it?

Che cɔsa non farɛbbe per conoscerlo!
What would he not do to meet him!

Would and Should

When the English 'would' expresses repeated action, it must be translated by the Italian past descriptive—see example on page 33.

Where 'would' implies determination, it is translated by such verbs as *insistere, ostinarsi a, volere, rifiutare di:*

Lo pregai e lo ripregai ma non volle venire.
I begged and begged him but he would not come.

Malgrado i miei consigli si ostinò ad andare.
He would go in spite of my plea.

There is also an idiomatic use of 'would' which must be rendered by an equally idiomatic Italian form:

Non saresti tu se non lo raccontassi a tutti.
You would tell everyone.

Where 'should' denotes obligation, the Italian verb *dovere* must be used:

Dovresti andare a vederla perché sta male.
You should go and see her because she is ill.

Suffixes

Whereas in English adjectives must be employed along with nouns to express such qualities as greatness, smallness, prettiness, ugliness, etc. this can be done in Italian by means of suffixes which alter the sense of the noun. Adjectives and adverbs may be similarly modified. Adjectives so altered are sometimes used as nouns.

Suffixes in Most Common Use

Augmentatives (accrescitivi)	Diminutives (diminutivi)	Terms of endearment (vezzeggiativi)	Terms of disparagement (dispregiativi)
one a	**etto a**	**ino a**	**accio a**
	ello a	**uccio a** (when applied to proper names)	**uccio a** (when applied to common nouns)
	ino a		

The final vowel is dropped before suffixes are added. When adding a suffix the gender of the original noun is kept, though in the case of *one*, even feminine nouns tend to become masculine:

libro	book	un librone	a large book
signore	gentleman	un signorone	a very wealthy man
dɔnna	woman	un donnone or una donnona	a huge woman
vɛcchio	old	un vecchietto	a little old man
giovane	young	un giovanetto	a youth
asino	ass	un asinɛllo	a donkey
cattivo	bad	cattivɛllo	rather naughty (naughty boy)
caro	dear	carino	pretty (adj.)
cappɛllo	hat	cappellino	smart little hat

pɔco (adv.)	little	pochino	very little
Giovanni	John	Giovannino	Johnny, dear little John
Maria	Mary	Mariuccia	little Mary
un ragazzo	a boy	un ragazzaccio	a bad boy
pɔvero	poor	poveraccio	poor wretch
dɔnna	woman	una donnuccia	a silly little woman

Other suffixes in less common use are:

-astro, -onzolo	disparagement	poetastro	worthless poet
		giallastro	yellowish
		mediconzolo	quack
-otto, -occio	more than one shade of meaning but mostly solidity	contadinɔtto	sturdy little peasant
		grassɔccio	pretty plump
-iccio, -ino	tending towards	rossiccio	reddish
		verdino	greenish

Certain suffixes have entirely altered the meaning of some words:

cavallo horse cavalletto easel (and not little horse)

N.B. Because of the shades of meanings that most suffixes can have. it is advisable for foreigners to use only those they have heard or seen used.

Vocabulary XVI

ristorante (m.) restaurant
pranzo dinner, lunch
camieriɛre (m.) waiter
lista menu
porzione (f.) helping, portion
piatto plate, dish, course
conto bill
m*a*ncia tip
vino wine
bott*i*glia bottle
minɛstra soup
brɔdo broth, clear soup
pasta asciutta macaroni
burro butter
pesce (m.) fish
carne (f.) meat
contorno side-dish
insalata salad
dolce (m.) sweet, cake
gɛnte (f.) people
fuɔri . . . di (prep. & adv.) outside
a prɛzzo fisso table d'hôte dinner
alla carta à la carte
***s*ubito** (adv.) immediately, at once
tardi (adv.) late
come (adv.) how, as
primo (adj.) first
secondo (adj.) second
sufficiɛnte (adj.) sufficient
***l*ibero** (adj.) free
avere appetito to have an appetite
avere fame to be hungry
avere sete to be thirsty
fare fresco to be cool
ordinare to order
lasciare to leave

pensare to think, to consider, to believe
riconoscere to recognize
credere to believe
cominciare . . . a to begin
grazie (f. pl., interj.) thanks, thank you

Exercise 1

(a) *Translate into English supplying the adjective implied by the suffix:* 1. una casetta 2. una insalatina 3. un camerone 4. una letteraccia 5. un ragazzino 6. un pranzetto 7. un alberello 8. un fazzoletto bellino 9. una stoffa giallastra 10. una scarpina 11. un vestituccio. 12. una piazzetta 13. uno scolaro bravino 14. una statuetta 15. una stradina 16. una stoffetta 17. una parolaccia 18. una ragazza carina 19. una chiesetta 20. una parolona.

(b) *Translate into Italian rendering the adjectives by means of suffixes:* 1. a little lounge 2. a small mirror 3. a bad book 4. a pretty little house 5. a low wall 6. a small blanket 7. some bad paper 8. a cheap little dress 9. a nice little letter 10. a naughty boy 11. a small window 12. little Robert 13. a small square 14. a pretty little church 15. an old uncomfortable hotel 16. a bad poet 17. a big dinner 18. a little carpet 19. dear little Helen 20. a little tree.

Exercise 2

Translate into Italian: 1. I should advise. 2. They would leave. 3. No one would believe. 4. You would think. 5. He would forward. 6. They would have set out. 7. He would not telephone. 8. What would you prefer? 9. He would greet no one. 10. Would you wish it (m.)? 11. Who would have believed it? 12. He would never be famous. 13. I should never fear. 14. What would he not try! 15. She would never sell it (f.) 16. According to others, he is rich. 17. He would have had nothing. 18. They would understand. 19. Would you not cheer? 20. We should prefer. 21. He should order. 22. You should recognize. 23. He would not forward it. 24. She should telephone.

Exercise 3

Translate into Italian: 1. Would he not send it (f.) to them? 2. No one would give it (m.) to us. 3. I should love to teach it (f.) to her. 4. He would not return from there. 5. They would never speak of it to me. 6. He would never explain anything to us. 7. Who would read it (m.) to her? 8. She would not send any to me. 9. I am considering leaving them (f.) to her. 10. Who would bring it (m.) to you (4 ways). 11. He would never read it (m.) to them. 12. They would not explain it (m.) to you (4 ways). 13. We should like to read it (f.) to her. 14. Would you send some to him? 15. Would you hand them (m.) to me? 16. She would not relate it (m.) to you (4 ways). 17. Would they not write it (m.) to him? 18. I should send some to him. 19. He would take none of it. 20. It would be amusing.

A. *Translate into English:* 1. Un amico di Roberto ci ha invitati a pranzo due sere fa. 2. Ci aveva dato appuntamento in un ristorante del centro. 3. Avrebbe desiderato prenotare una tavola d'angolo vicino alla finestra ma questo ristorante è sempre affollato e non c'erano tavole d'angolo libere. 4. Sul marciapiede fuori del ristorante c'erano parecchie tavole. 5. "Non preferirebbero cenare fuori?" ci domandò il cameriere. 6. No, c'è molto traffico nella strada e comincia a fare fresco. 7. L'amico di Roberto chiamò il cameriere e gli domandò la lista. 8. Il cameriere gliela portò e gli domandò: "Preferisce vino rosso o bianco?" 9. Roberto non prende mai vino ma il suo amico aveva sete e ordinò una bottiglia di un vinello bianco molto buono. 10. "Che cosa prendono le signore?" domandò il cameriere. "Desiderano una minestrina o preferirebbero un buon piatto di pasta asciutta?" 11. "Che cosa ci consiglierebbe?" domandò Roberto "il pranzo a prezzo fisso o alla carta?" 12. "Il pranzo a prezzo fisso è buono e non è caro ma consiglierei loro di ordinare alla carta." 13. Roberto e il suo amico avevano fame e ordinarono pasta asciutta al burro ma noi non avevamo molto appetito e ordinammo una minestrina. 14. Per secondo piatto il cameriere ci consigliò di prendere pesce perche era molto fresco. 15. Roberto preferì mangiare carne e ordinò due contorni e un'insalata. 16. "Le signorine non hanno molto appetito, ma c'è un dolce molto buono; ne desidererebbero una porzione?" domandò il cameriere. 17. "No, grazie, noi preferiremmo della frutta fresca. "Ci sarebbe della buona frutta?" domandò l'amico di Roberto. 18. Io pensai che saremmo arrivati tardi a casa e preferii ordinare subito il caffè. 19. Quando avemmo finito il pranzo, l'amico di Roberto domandò il conto e pagò. 20. Pensavamo che l'amico di Roberto ci avrebbe accompagnati a casa ma egli aveva fretta e ci salutò fuori del ristorante.

B. *Translate into Italian:* 1. Many people dine in restaurants (say: at, followed by the sing.) every day. 2. We dined one evening last week in a small but very smart restaurant in the centre of the town (say: of the centre). 3 My brother's friend Robert had invited us to dinner before (prima di and infinitive) going to the theatre. 4. Robert would have liked to reserve a table near the windows but they were all reserved already. 5. We did not think that the waiter would recognize us because we had only been there two or three times before. As soon as we arrived he greeted us and showed us our table. 6. The waiter showed the menu to

Robert and the two young men (giovanotti) studied it while we admired the restaurant. 7. Outside the restaurant there were several tables where people dine when the weather is good. 8. "Would you not prefer to dine outside?" the waiter asked, when Robert was ordering our first course. 9. No, there is always so much traffic in the streets and it is (use: fare) already cool this evening. 10. The table d'hôte dinner is good and it is not dear but I should advise you to order à la carte. 11. We ordered soup for our first course; Robert and my brother ordered a good helping of macaroni and butter. 12. "What do you wish as a second course?" the waiter asked. "I should advise fish because it is fresh every day." 13. Mary and I ordered fish but Robert and John were hungry and ordered meat with a side-dish and salad. 14. Robert does not often take wine but he ordered a bottle for his friends. 15. "What wine would you advise, waiter?" "I should advise this sweet white wine. It is very good." 16. As we dined we spoke about the play. Robert had already seen it some years ago and thought we would find it interesting. 17. We had all seen some of the actors when they were young. Who would have believed that they would be famous one day? 18. Some people were ordering sweets and coffee but we only wished for some fresh fruit. 19. We asked the waiter to bring the bill and we paid it immediately because, according to Robert, we would arrive late at the theatre. 20. We left a good tip for the waiter. Poor wretch! his wife is ill and he has five children.

C. Molte persone, quando sono all'estero, non sanno che cosa siano i vari piatti nella lista.—Many people when they are abroad do not know what the dishes on the menu are. È buona la cucina italiana?—Is Italian cooking good? La cucina italiana è molto saporita ma molti stranieri la trovano un po' pesante per l'uso dell'olio, della cipolla e dell'aglio.—Italian cooking is very tasty but many foreigners find it a little heavy because they use oil, onion and garlic. Quali sono le specialità più conosciute della cucina italiana?—What are the best known specialities of Italian cooking? Ogni città ha le sue specialità.—Every city has its own. Bologna ad esempio è famosa per le sue tagliatelle alla bolognese che sono un tipo di pasta fatta in casa con un sugo di carne.—Bologna for example is famous for its 'tagliatelle alla bolognese' which is a sort of home-made macaroni and meat sauce. E per la mortadella, un salame fatto con carne di maiale.—And for 'mortadella' a sausage made of pork. Milano è famosa per il risotto alla milanese—riso cotto con cipolla e brodo.—Milan is famous for its 'risotto alla milanese'—rice cooked with onions and broth: 'le cotolette alla milanese'—carne passata nell'uovo e nella mollica di pane e poi fritta—meat dipped in egg and bread crumbs and then fried: e per il 'panettone', un dolce che si mangia specie a Natale—and for its 'panettone', a cake eaten especially at Christmas time. Napoli per gli spaghetti al pomodoro—Naples for spaghetti in tomato sauce. Genova per i maccheroni col pesto, una salsa fatta con olio, basilico e aglio—Genoa for its macaroni and strong sauce made of oil, basil and garlic. E il minestrone che cosa è? È una minestra con molte verdure e legumi.—And what is 'minestrone'? It is a thick broth with many vegetables. Quali sono i vini più famosi in Italia?—Which are the best known Italian wines? Sono i vini del Chianti nella Toscana.—There are the Chianti wines of Tuscany. I vini dei Castelli vicino a Roma—the Castelli wines in the neighbourhood of Rome. Il vino Marsala in Sicilia—Sicilian Marsala. Che cosa si dice quando si beve?—What does one say (what is the toast) when one drinks? Si dice 'salute'.—One says 'your health'.

D. *Pure*

Posso telefonare? Faccia pure!—May I telephone? Do, by all means!

LESSON XVII

Disjunctive Pronouns

Personal pronouns, in addition to the forms already studied as subject and object (direct and indirect), have other forms the particular uses of which are detailed below. Since these are not connected so strongly with the verb as the conjunctive personal pronouns, they are called disjunctive pronouns.

Disjunctive Pronouns

Singular		
1st	me	me
2nd	te	you
3rd	lui, lɛi	him, her
	esso, essa	him, it; her, it
	lɛi	you (courtesy form)
	sé	himself, herself, itself
Plura		
1st	noi	us
2nd	voi	you
3rd	loro, essi, esse	them (m. & f.)
	loro	you (courtesy form)
	sé	themselves (m. & f.)

Uses

Disjunctive forms must be used:

1. Whenever a pronoun is governed by a preposition:

Mi parlò male *di* lui.	He spoke badly of him to me.
Viaggiò *con* lɛi.	He travelled with her.
Imparai tutto *da* me	I learned all by myself.
Ricevei una lɛttera *da* loro.	I received a letter from them.

Such prepositions as: *su*, *sopra*—on, above; *sotto*—under; *fra*—between, among; *entro*, *dentro*—within; *fuɔri*—without; *diɛtro*—behind; *dopo*—after; *prima*—before; *contro*—against; *sɛnza*—without; *lungo*—along; require an additional preposition *di* before a disjunctive pronoun:

contro di me	against me
sotto di lui	under him
dopo di lɛi	after you

2. When it is a question of special emphasis on direct or indirect objects. Compare and contrast the following sentences:

A *me* non mandò nulla.	He did not send anything to *me*. (though he might have to someone else)
Non mi mandò nulla.	He did not send me anything.
Egli ama *lɛi*.	He loves *her*. (not someone else)
Egli la ama.	He loves her.

3. Whenever there are two or more direct or indirect objects in a sentence:

Scriverò a lui e a lɛi.	I shall write to him and to her.
Salutò voi e noi.	He greeted you and us.

4. In the third persons only—*lui*, *lɛi* and *loro* instead of *egli*, *ella*, etc., when the subject is to be emphasized. Emphasis is further secured by placing the pronoun after the verb. Often these pronouns are preceded by such emphatic conjunctions as *neanche*, *nemmeno*—not even, *anche*—also, *tanto quanto*—as much as, *più*—more, *tanto . . . che . . .*—both . . . and . . . :

Lo ha domandato *lui*.	It was he who asked for it.
Me lo spiegò *lɛi*.	She herself explained it to me.
Non parlò nemmeno *lui*.	Not even he spoke, he did not speak either.
L'hanno capito anche *loro*.	They too understood.
Tanto *lui* che *lɛi* arrivarono tardi.	He and she both arrived late.
Scrive più *lui* degli altri.	He writes more than the others.

For the use of these forms after *come*—as, *che*—than, *più*—more, etc. in the second term of a comparison, see Lesson XXI.

5. As complements of the verb 'to be':

Se fossi *te*[1] partirɛi subito.	If I were you I would go at once.
Fu *lui* ad aprire la lɛttera.	He was the one who opened the letter.

In such phrases as: *it is I*, *it is you*, *it is he*, notice that the disjunctive form is used only in the 3rd person singular and plural, whereas the subject pronouns are used in the 1st and 2nd persons singular and plural:

	è lui	it is he;	*è lɛi*	it is she;	*sono loro*	it is they.
but:	*sono io*	it is I;	*sɛi tu*	it is you;	*siamo noi*	it is we

similarly: *c'ɛrano anche loro* they were there also
but: *c'ɛri anche tu* you too were there.

6. In exclamations, after some adjectives:

Felice te!	Happy you!
Pɔvero me!	Wretch that I am.

[1] The idiomatic se fossi *in* te, *in* lui, is more frequently used.

Dovere, Potere, Volere

The three verbs *dovere*—to be obliged, *potere*—to be able, and *volere*—to want, to wish, to be willing, belonging to the second conjugation, are irregular in certain tenses. We shall confine ourselves for this lesson to the present indicative using, of the other tenses, only the regular ones.

Present Indicative

dɛvo	I must, I am obliged, I have to, etc.	pɔsso.	I can, may, am able, etc.	vɔglio	I wish, want, will, etc.
dɛvi		puɔi		vuɔi	
dɛve		può		vuɔle	
dobbiamo		possiamo		vogliamo	
dovete		potete		volete	
dɛvono		pɔssono		vɔgliono	

Vocabulary XVII

trattoria restaurant (modest)
osteria inn, pub
colazione (f.) lunch, breakfast
specialità speciality
tagliatelle (f.pl.) home made macaroni
sugo (tomato) sauce
zuppa soup
zuppa inglese trifle
cotoletta alla milanese cutlet coated in egg and breadcrumbs and fried
pane (m.) bread
salame (m.) salami
form*a*ggio cheese
mattina morning
latte (m.) milk
nome (m.) name
caffè (m.) **e latte** white coffee
marmellata marmalade, jam
passeggiata walk (**fare una . . .**)
terrazza terrace
idɛa idea
giornata day (duration)
casalingo (adj.) home made, homely.
arrɔsto (n. & adj.) roast, roasted
fritto (n. & adj.) fried
contɛnto (adj.) (**di**) glad
purtrɔppo (adv.) unfortunately
sino a (conj.) until
apɛrto (adj.) open, opened
all'apɛrto in the open air
all'ɛstero abroad
seguire to follow
assaggiare to sample, taste
cons*i*stere to consist of

Exercise 1

Translate into Italian using prepositions and disjunctive pronouns: 1. of you (pl.) 2. to them 3. with me 4. from him 5. for you (courtesy form) 6. on it (f.) 7. by him 8. in it (m.) 9. by himself 10. of us 11. with you (s.) 12. to me 13. from them 14. into it (f.) 15. for you (courtesy form) 16. to them (m.) 17. by him 18. with her 19. on it (m.) 20. by herself.

Exercise 2

Translate into Italian using conjunctive or disjunctive pronouns as required: 1. Not even she. 2. He teaches him and her. 3. It is I. 4. Happy you! 5. He works as much as she does. 6. We know her (unemphatic). 7. They want it (m.). 8. It was he. 9. He looked at him not at her. 10. He sent it (m.) to me and to her. 11. He himself was going. 12. They give it (f.) to her. 13. They learned it (m.) by themselves. 14. I also learned it (f.). 15. Here I am. 16. They showed it to him not to me. 17. He bought some. 18. We were reading it (m.) to them. 19. He was speaking of it to me and to you (s.). 20. Even he would not eat it (m.).

Exercise 3

Translate into Italian: 1. We wish. 2. They used to be able. 3. He must. 4. You can. 5. She wishes. 6. You are able. 7. They were wanting. 8. We can. 9. You must. 10. I want. 11. He has to. 12. He can. 13. We must. 14. You (courtesy form) wish. 15. I am able. 16. You are obliged to. 17. They wish. 18. We have to. 19. I must. 20. You were wanting.

A. *Translate into English:* 1. Oggi è una bella giornata. Maria apre la finestra e vede che c'è un bel sole. 2. Essa domanda a Giulia: "Vogliamo telefonare a Luisa e domandarle se vuole fare una passeggiata con noi?" 3. Giulia va al telefono e chiama Luisa. 4. "Vuoi fare una passeggiata con noi?" le domanda. 5. "Sarei molto contenta di fare una passeggiata con te e Maria"—risponde Luisa—"ma purtroppo non posso." 6. Mia madre deve andare in città e ha domandato a me e a Filippo se potevamo restare a casa con il fratellino e la sorellina sino a quando essa ritorna. 7. "Io e Maria non abbiamo fretta e possiamo aspettarvi se volete" risponde Giulia. 8. Io preferirei portare dei panini, ma Roberto e Maria hanno sempre molto appetito al mare e né a lui né a lei i panini sarebbero sufficienti. 9. Roberto, Maria e Giulia vanno a casa di Luisa e Filippo; Luisa va con loro in automobile, Filippo li seguirà in treno con un suo amico. 10. Tanto lui che il suo amico arriveranno dopo di loro. 11. Quali sono le specialità della trattoria? 12. Il pesce fritto e la zuppa di pesce ma anche le loro tagliatelle al sugo sono famose. 13. Le tagliatelle sono dei maccheroni casalinghi. 14. Nella stessa trattoria fanno molto bene l'arrosto e le cotolette alla milanese. 15. Nel viale della stazione c'è anche un'osteria dove siamo andati qualche volta. 16. Quando vi andiamo mangiamo sempre all'aperto e ordiniamo pane casalingo, salame, formaggio, frutta fresca e una bottiglia di buon vino. 17. L'amico di Filippo vuole assaggiare le famose tagliatelle al sugo; io e Maria preferiamo una zuppa di pesce e chiediamo al cameriere di portarci del pane nero. 18. Sulla terrazza ci sono molti tavolini con tovaglie di cotone a disegni bianchi e rossi e bianchi e azzurri e molta gente mangia all'aperto sotto gli ombrelloni. 19. Alla tavola vicina alla nostra due inglesi anno ordinato uova fritte al burro, salame e vino. Quando ordinano 'white coffee' il cameriere non capisce perché in Italia o lo chiamano caffè e latte e lo prendono solo alla prima colazione o lo chiamano 'cappuccino' e lo prendono in un bar. 20. La prima colazione consiste generalmente di latte o latte e caffè, panini, burro e marmellata.

B. *Translate into Italian:* 1. Mary and Louise go abroad for their holidays every year but this is the first time that they have been in Italy. 2. They have an Italian maid at home: she always speaks to them in Italian and they understand it well. 3. They did not want to stay in the hotel where their friends are staying and booked rooms in a nearby pension. 4. "What does breakfast consist of in Italy?" they asked the waitress the first morning. 5. Breakfast consists of rolls, butter, marmalade, fruit and black or white coffee. 6. "Do you wish breakfast in your room?" the waitress asked them "or would you prefer to have breakfast on the terrace when it is sunny?" 7. They understood every word and ordered breakfast in their room because they were in a hurry. 8. May we use the telephone? We must phone Robert's sister. She leaves tomorrow but he will remain for a second week. 9. They want to speak to her not to him. "Is it you, Vera?" Mary asks when a girl answers in English. 10. Would you like to go for a walk (fare una passeggiata) with us? We shall take (portare) sandwiches and fruit and eat in the open. 11. The girls spent the whole morning on the beach but in the afternoon they returned to town as Vera wanted to show them a little restaurant. 12. She explained to them that these little restaurants were called in Italian 'trattorie'. The cuisine is generally very good and it is not dear. 13. She taught them the names of some very good dishes: cotolette alla milanese, pasta asciutta and tagliatelle al burro o al sugo. 14. There were many people in the trattoria when Vera and her friends entered and waiters were carrying tagliatelle to one table, trifle to another, roast and salads to others. 15. We should like to visit the art gallery; is it open every day? 16. I have never been there but Robert goes there often. 17. He would accompany you and also show you the museum. 18. If you wish to go to a theatre one evening, you can telephone him and he will book seats for you. 19. "Do you want to go and (a) see the shops tomorrow?" Mary asked Louise—"or would you prefer to wait a day or two?" 20. I should prefer to stay at home tomorrow; I must write to Philip.

C. Molta gente in Italia fa la spesa al mercato e non nei negozi perché lì la roba costa meno.—Many people in Italy do their shopping at the market and not in the shops as goods there cost less. C'è un mercato in ogni città italiana?—Is there a market in every Italian town? In molte città in Italia c'è un mercato centrale dove si possono comprare tutti i generi commestibili che si vogliono.—In many towns in Italy there is a central market where every kind of foodstuffs can be bought. Come sono disposti i varii banchi?—How are the various stalls arranged? Il mercato è diviso in varie sezioni.—The market is divided into different sections. Macellai, pollivendoli, pescivendoli, fruttivendoli.—Butchers, poulterers, fishvendors, fruiterers. "Che cosa è questo?" e "quanto costa?" sono le domande più frequenti in ogni mercato.—What is this and how much does it cost are the questions most frequently asked at any market. Anche i salumieri hanno i loro banchi con salami di ogni qualità dalla rosea e larga mortadella al salame di Milano e di Verona.—There are also delicatessen stalls with every quality of sausage from the huge rose coloured one of Bologna to that of Milan and Verona. Dove si può comprare il formaggio?—Where can one buy cheese? I salumai vendono anche ogni tipo di formaggio dai formaggi freschi ai formaggi molli come il Belpaese e a quelli forti come il Gorgonzola e a quelli usati per cucina come il Parmigiano.—The grocers sell cheese also, every kind from fresh ones to soft ones like Belpaese, to strong ones like Gorgonzola and those used for cooking like Parmesan. Quanta gente al mercato! —What a lot of people were at the market! Che carne preferisce lei e cotta in che modo?—What meat do you like best and how do you like it cooked? Quale pesce le piace di più?—What fish do you like best? Qual'è la sua frutta preferita?—Which is your favourite fruit? Che frutta c'è d'inverno? E in primavera? E d'estate? E in autunno? —What fruit is there in Winter? And in Spring, Summer, Autumn?

Carne Meat

vitɛllo veal
manzo beef
maiale pork
agnɛllo lamb
montone mutton

Pollame Poultry

polli chickens
tacchini turkeys
anatre ducks

Cacciagione Game-birds

fagiani pheasants
starne partridges
beccacce wood-cocks

Pesce Fish

merluzzo cod
sɔgliola sole
triglia red mullet
aragosta lobster
scampi crayfish
cɔzze mussels
vɔngole cockles
ɔstriche oysters

Frutta Fruit

arancio orange
manderino mandarin
pera pear
mela apple

susina plum
uva grapes
melone (m.) melon
ciliɛgia cherry
albicɔcca apricot
fr*a*gola strawberry
pɛsca peach
lampone (m.) raspberry
fico fig

Verdure e Legumi Vegetables
patate potatoes
cavolfiori cauliflowers
c*a*voli cabbages
rape turnips
carciɔfi artichokes
spinaci spinach
pisɛlli peas
fagiolini beans
cicɔria chicory (endive)
carɔte carrots
barbabiɛtole beetroots
sɛdano celery
pomodɔri tomatoes
cetriɔli cucumbers
ravanɛlli radishes
cipolle onions
***a*glio** garlic
prezzɛmolo parsley
ɛrbe arom*a*tiche sweet herbs
lattuga lettuce
finɔcchio fennel
peperone capsicum

D. *Tale e quale*
Cɔpialo tale e quale—Copy it just as it is.

LESSON XVIII

Negative Imperative or Prohibition

The imperative is made negative by putting *non* before every form of the verb, except the 2nd person singular in the present tense, where *non* is followed by the infinitive:

Scriva (courtesy form)	Write.	Non scriva.	Do not write.
Restiamo.	Let us remain.	Non restiamo.	Let us not remain.
but: Lεggi.	Read.	Non lεggere.	Do not read

Position of Pronouns

As was stated in Lesson XV, in the 2nd person singular and in the 1st and 2nd persons plural of the affirmative imperative the conjunctive pronouns follow the verb and, with the exception of *loro*, combine with the verb to form one word. When the same forms are negative, however, and always with the courtesy form, the pronouns precede the verb:

Vendilo.	Sell it.	Non lo vendere.	Don't sell it.
Lo venda.	Sell it.	Non lo venda.	Don't sell it.
Vendiamolo.	Let us sell it.	Non lo vendiamo.	Let us not sell it.
Vendetelo.	Sell it.	Non lo vendete.	Don't sell it.
Lo vendano.	Sell it.	Non lo vendano.	Don't sell it.

Demonstrative Adjectives, Pronouns and Adverbs

Demonstrative Adjectives and Pronouns

Questo, -a, -i, -e,	this, these
Codesto, -a, -i, -e	that, those
Quello, -a, -i, -e	that, those

Whereas in English there are two demonstrative adjectives and pronouns, in Italian there are three: 'that' being translated in two different ways according to the position of the persons who speak or listen.

Questo—this—indicates a person or a thing near the person speaking:

Questa casa è modεrna. This house is modern.

Codesto—that—indicates a person or thing near the person spoken to:

Codesto vestito è elegante. That dress is elegant.

Quello—that—indicates a person or thing distant from both the person speaking and the person spoken to:

Quelle signorine sono bɛlle.—Those young ladies are beautiful.

Demonstrative adjectives agree in number and gender with the noun they qualify. *Codesto* has no exact English equivalent. Its use which is rather more literary, is confined now almost solely to Tuscany. *Quello* has forms identical to *bɛllo* (see Lesson XIII, p. 62) and like the plural *bɛlli*, *quelli* is only used when standing alone.

Questo and *quello*, as pronouns, together with the indefinite pronoun *altro*, take the apparently plural forms *questi*, *quegli*, *altri*, referring to a singular masculine person:

Questi non era altri che il Prof. Rossi.
This was no other than Prof. Rossi.

The demonstrative pronouns *questo*, *quello* are also used to render respectively 'the latter' and 'the former', agreeing in number and gender with the persons or objects referred to, except in the case of singular masculine persons when the above rule must be observed.

Maria e Luisa vanno all'ɛstero, questa in Francia, quella in Belgio.

Mary and Louise are going abroad, the latter to France and the former to Belgium.

Roberto e Giovanni sono all'università: questi studia lɛgge, quegli medicina.

Robert and John are at the University: the latter is studying law and the former medicine.

The following demonstrative pronouns are only applied to persons:

costui (m.s.), costɛi (.f.s.), costoro (m. & f. plu.)	this man, woman these men, women
colui (m.s.), colɛi (f.s.), coloro (m. & f. plu.)	that man, woman those men, women

An idea of disparagement is associated with *costui*, *costɛi*, *costoro*:

Non parlerɛi mai con costoro—I would never speak to these people.

Ciò (inv.) means 'this', 'that', 'what' when applied to an abstraction:

Ciò che mi dispiace . . . —What I do not like . . .

Demonstrative Adverbs

Qui or *qua*	here (near the person speaking)
Costì or *costà*	there (near the person spoken to)
Colà, *lì* or *là*	there (distant from both)

Vocabulary XVIII

mese (m.)	**month**	**coltɛllo**	**knife**
posata	cutlery	**forchetta**	**fork**

cucchiaino (da tè, da caffè) tea-spoon, coffee-spoon
cucchiaio spoon
bicchiere (m.) glass
tazza cup
tovagliolo napkin
vassoio tray
piattino saucer
caffettiera coffee-pot
lattiera milk-jug
teiera tea-pot
zuccheriera sugar-basin
zucchero sugar
dentro (adv.) inside, within
apparecchiare to set the table
sparecchiare to clear the table
preparare to prepare
cucinare to cook
aiutare (qualcuno a fare qualchecosa) to help (somebody to do something)
asciugare to dry
stirare to iron
aver bisogno . . . di to need
bussare to knock (aux. **avere**)

Exercise 1

Translate into Italian giving, whenever possible, four forms of the imperative (keep: conserva, conservi, conservate, conservino): 1. Keep. 2. Let us change. 3. Ask. 4. Sleep. 5. Do not telephone. 6. Let us take. 7. Sign. 8. Do not sell. 9. Leave. 10. Do not applaud. 11. Call. 12. Let us not open. 13. Learn. 14. Be punctual. 15. Do not be in a hurry. 16. Look. 17. Do not buy. 18. Write. 19. Let us eat. 20. Help.

Exercise 2

(a) *Translate into Italian, giving four forms of the imperative whenever possible:* 1. Send it (m.) to him. 2. Let us show them (m.) to her. 3. Do not write it (f.) to me. 4. Teach it (f.) to them. 5. Let us carry it (m.) to him. 6. Sell it (f.) to us. 7. Leave it (m.) to them. 8. Do not forward them (f.) to us. 9. Let us explain it (m.) to him. 10. Take them (m.) to her.

(b) *Translate into Italian giving the 2nd person singular and plural and the courtesy forms of the imperative present:* 1. Give it to him (Daglielo, dateglielo, glielo dia, glielo diano). 2. Give me. 3. Give it to us. 4. Don't give it to her. 5. Go there with your sister. 6. Do three of them. 7. Give it (f.) to me. 8. Don't go there alone. 9. Make me some. 10. Give them (f.) to them. 11. Be kind. 12. Stay with us. 13. Make a little of it. 14. Do it immediately. 15. Do it for me.

Exercise 3

Translate into Italian: 1. Julia, bring those books here. 2. I shall take this tram here. 3. That mirror is beautiful. 4. I prefer those there. 5. These ladies live here. 6. John, write those addresses on those envelopes. 7. Waitress, may I book this table here? 8. There is a tram stop there. 9. These table napkins are clean. 10. Where shall I put the tea-pot? Put it here.

A. *Translate into English:* 1. La nostra cuoca è partita la settimana scorsa; era molto stanca ed è andata a passare un mese con sua madre. 2. Anche la cameriera è in vacanza e tanto lei che la cuoca ritorneranno fra tre settimane. 3. La mattina mia madre ci chiama: "Maria, Giulia, fate i vostri letti, scopate e spolverate la vostra camera." 4. "Che cosa vuoi per colazione, Mamma,"—domanda Giulia—"tè o caffè?" 5. Prendi questa tovaglia rosa e le tazze e i piattini di porcellana celeste: i cucchiaini devono essere là nella credenza; guarda nel primo cassetto a sinistra. 6. Maria apparecchia e mette sulla tavola tre tazze, tre piattini, tre piatti, tre cucchiaini, la lattiera, la zuccheriera, la teiera e la caffettiera. 7. "Dove sono i tovaglioli?" domanda la mamma. Giulia, prendine tre là, nell'armadio; la biancheria è nel secondo cassetto. 8. Fammi anche un'aranciata e mettila in quel bicchiere di cristallo su un vassoio. 9. Maria desidera un'aranciata anche lei; "fanne una anche per me"—essa chiede a Giulia. 10. La mamma dà una tazza di caffelatte a Maria e una di caffè nero a Giulia e domanda a Giulia di passarle lo zucchero e la marmellata. 11. Non mettere tanto burro sul pane, Maria, ce n'è poco e dobbiamo comprarne dell'altro stamattina. 12. "Dove devo mettere questa tovaglia?"—domanda Giulia alla mamma. Piegala e mettila con i tovaglioli lì in un cassetto della credenza. 13. La cameriera ha lavato molta biancheria prima di partire e noi dobbiamo stirarla. 14. Maria, stira quella biancheria da letto perché ne abbiamo bisogno. 15. "Qualcuno ha suonato il campanello; devo andare ad aprire la porta?"—domanda Maria. 16. No, non ci andare; Giulia è nell'ingresso ed aprirà la porta. 17. È Elena. "Possiamo invitarla a colazione, mamma?" domanda Giulia. 18. "Non la invitate oggi"—risponde la signora Bruni—"non ci sono né la cuoca né la cameriera e dobbiamo fare tutto noi." 19. Elena ci aiuterebbe ad apparecchiare e sparecchiare la tavola e a lavare ed asciugare piatti, bicchieri e posate. 20. Allora invitatela e mettete un altro posto a tavola.

B. *Translate into Italian:* 1. We have a young Italian maid, Elena; she is willing to learn and tries (di) to understand, but mother has always to show her what she must do. 2. Set the table for breakfast, Elena. We shall be four at table. The knives, forks and spoons are in this drawer. 3. Our breakfast usually consists of white coffee with rolls and butter and marmalade. 4. Elena sets for four: four cups, saucers, plates, knives and teaspoons. 5. She cannot find the table napkins and calls mother. 6. "Look in the sideboard drawer," answers mother from the kitchen where she is preparing the coffee. 7. We use these large cups for breakfast, not those small (ones). Elena goes into the kitchen and returns with the coffee-pot. 8. She has left the sugar-bowl in the kitchen but we never put sugar in our coffee. 9. Clear the table Mary and Louise, while I show Elena what she has to do in the bedrooms. 10. The girls carry everything into the kitchen. Mary washes the dishes and Louise dries them and puts them in the cupboard. 11. The bell rings; Elena, please open the door. 12. "Will you iron these sheets and those tablecloths, please, Elena?" asks mother. 13. When Elena has finished she goes into the kitchen to prepare lunch. 14. "Would you prefer an Italian dish today, madam?" she asks. "Yesterday I received some 'tagliatelle' from home and I can make a good tomato sauce." 15. Then prepare only a salad for the second course and we shall take our coffee in the garden. 16. Girls, help to set the table for lunch; bring six glasses from the kitchen; they are in that cupboard, near the window. 17. After lunch the girls go out for a walk; Elena washes the dishes, forks, knives and spoons. 18. Do not set the table for tea, Elena. We shall take it in the garden; put five cups, saucers, plates and teaspoons on a tray and bring it into the garden. 19. Girls, help Elena! Put the teapot, milk-jug and sugar-bowl on this little table near me. 20. You can go to bed when you wish, this evening Elena. You must be tired and we are dining out to-night.

C. Bambini lavatevi le mani.—Wash your hands, children. Suona il gong, la colazione è pronta.—Sound the gong, lunch is ready. Posso prendere questa sedia?—May I have this chair? Per favore non aspetti altrimenti tutto si raffredda.—Please don't wait otherwise everything will get cold. Vuoi un altro panino?—Would you like another roll? Metti via quel giornale! è ineducato di leggere a tavola.—Put away the magazine: it is rude to read at table. Prenda ancora un po' di patate o di verdura. Please help yourselves to more potatoes and vegetables. Vuole passarmi il sale per favore?—Please pass the salt. Ne prenda ancora un po'.—Have a little more. Mi dispiace ma non posso finirlo: non ho molto appetito.—I am sorry I cannot finish it: I am not very hungry. Me ne ha dato troppo.—You have given me too much. C'è un po' di ghiaccio per l'acqua?—Is there any ice for the water? Mi dispiace di aver versato il caffè e fatto una macchia!—I am sorry I have spilled my coffee and made a stain! Non importa, son cose che succedono. Vado a prendere uno straccio.—Never mind, it cannot be helped. I shall fetch a cloth. È stato un pranzo squisito: mi è piaciuto molto.—It has been a delightful meal: I have enjoyed it immensely. Il conto per favore.—The bill please. (Can we have the bill?) Può cambiare 10 mila lire?—Can you change a 10,000 lire note? Tenga pure il resto.—Do keep the change.

D. *Neanche per sogno*!

Hai intenzione di sposarla? Neanche per sogno!—Are you going to marry her? Not on your life!

LESSON XIX

Relative Pronouns

Relative pronouns (pronomi relativi) are so called because they establish a relationship between two clauses, joining them together to form one sentence. They can be used as subjects of verbs, direct or indirect objects of verbs and after prepositions.

Relative Pronouns

1. *Che*	who, whom, that, which	4. *Chi, colui che*	He who, him who
2. Il *quale* la *quale* i *quali* le *quali*	who, whom, that, which	*colɛi che* *coloro che*	she who they who
3. *cui*—whom, which (after preps.) il *cui*, i *cui*, la *cui*, le *cui*	 whose	5. *Quello che* *quel che* *ciò che*	that which

Uses

1. *Che*—who, that, etc. is invariable and is used as the subject and the direct object of a verb:

La ragazza che è arrivata.	The girl who has arrived.
La penna che vedi.	The pen which you see.

2. *Il quale*, etc.—who, which, etc., agrees always in number and gender with the noun to which it refers. It is also used as subject, as direct object of a verb (though very rarely in modern Italian) and when preceded by a preposition:

L'uɔmo il quale lavora è onɛsto.	The man who works is honest.
I giornali dei quali ti parlai.	The newspapers of which I spoke to you.
La ragazza alla quale scrivo.	The girl to whom I write.
Il trɛno col quale partii.	The train in which I left.
L'automɔbile dalla quale scende.	The car from which he comes out.
La casa nella quale abito.	The house in which I live.

3. *Cui*—whom, which, etc. is invariable and is used only when it is governed by a preposition:

I giornali di cui ti parlai.	The newspapers about which I spoke to you.
La ragazza a cui scrivo.	The girl to whom I write.

Il trɛno con cui partii. The train in which I left.
L'automɔbile da cui scende. The car from which he comes out.
La casa in cui abito. The house in which I live.

It is sometimes used (though rarely) without a preposition as an indirect object:

Il fanciullo cui donasti il libro. The child to whom you gave the book.

Il cui, i cui; la cui, le cui—whose

Cui preceded by *il, i,* if the noun following is masculine, and by *la, le* when the noun following is feminine, translates 'whose':

Lo scrittore *il cui* libro ɛra stato premiato.
The writer whose book had been awarded a prize.

Il pittore, *i cui* quadri sono famosi.
The painter whose pictures are famous.

Ho incontrato Roberto, *la cui* sorɛlla tu conosci.
I met Robert whose sister you know.

Arrivai ad una casa *le cui* finɛstre ɛrano chiuse.
I reached a house the windows of which were closed.

4. *Chi*—he who, etc., is invariable. Besides its use in interrogative sentences, *chi* is used to translate such expressions as: he who, she who, especially in proverbs and generalizations. They can also be translated by *colui che* (m.), *colɛi che* (f.), *coloro che* (pl. m. & f.):

Chi va piano va sano e va lontano.
He who goes slowly goes well and far.

Coloro che hanno studiato saranno promɔssi.
Those who have studied will be promoted.

Perdona chi ti offɛnde.
Forgive those who offend you.

5. *Quello che, quel che, ciò che*—that which, what, are used when referring to things and not persons:

Ricɔrda ciò che ti insegnai. Remember what I taught you.
Guarda quello che ho comprato. Look what I bought.

Unlike the English construction, where the relative pronoun is often understood, in Italian the relative pronoun may never be omitted:

Il vestito che comprai. The dress I bought.

In such sentences as *It is I who, it is they who*, etc., the pronoun *che* must always be used:

Sono io che l'ho veduto. It is I who saw it.
È lui che l'ha mandato. It is he who sent it.

Interrogative Pronouns and Adjectives summarized

The relative pronouns and adjectives *chi*, *che*, *che cosa*, *quale* (without the article) and the pronouns and adjectives of quantity *quanto*, *quanti* can also be used as interrogative pronouns and adjectives.

Chi? — who? (pronouns)

Chi sei?	Who are you?
Chi l'avrebbe mai immaginato?	Who would ever have imagined it?
A chi andranno l'onore e la gloria?	Who will get the honour and the glory?

Che? che cosa?—what? (pronoun and adjective)

Che fai?	What are you doing?
Che cosa dici?	What are you saying?
Di che parlerai?	What will you talk about?
Che libro hai scelto?	Which book did you choose?

Quale? (without article)—which? (pronoun and adjective)

Quale preferisci?	Which one do you prefer?
Quale albergo mi consigli?	Which hotel do you recommend?

Quanto? quanti?—how much? how many? (pronoun and adjective)

Quanto costa?	How much is it?
Di quanto spazio hai bisogno?	How much space do you need?
Quanti ne hai visti?	How many of them did you see?
Quanti invitati verranno?	How many guests will come?

N.B. *Che*, *quanto*, *quale* can also be used as exclamations.

Che disastro!	What a disaster!
Quanta premura!	What haste!

Sapere

Sapere—to know, is another irregular verb of the 2nd conjugation. Only regular tenses will occur in this lesson apart from the present indicative here given

Present Tense

sɔ	I know	sappiamo	we know
sai	you know	sapete	you know
sa	he, she, it knows	sanno	they know

Sapere and *Conoscere*—To know

Sapere—To know, to be aware of a thing or a fact, to know how (can):

Sa che cɔsa significa?	Do you know what it means?
Sa parlare italiano?	Can you speak Italian?

Conoscere—To know, to be acquainted with:

Conosce tutti.	He knows everybody.
Conosciamo quello scrittore.	We know that writer.
Conosce qualche buɔn ristorante?	Do you know any good restaurant?

Vocabulary XIX

cartoleria, cartol*a*io stationery, stationer
drogheria, droghiɛre grocer's shop, grocer
latteria, latt*a*io dairy, milkman
salumeria, salum*a*io Italian warehouse, man
tabaccheria, tabacc*a*io tobacconist
farmacia, farmacista chemist
pasticceria, pasticciɛre cake shop, pastrycook
panetteria, forn*a*io baker's shop, baker
medicina medicine
frutti*v*endolo fruiterer
pesci*v*endolo fishmonger
macelleria, macell*a*io butcher's shop, butcher
foc*a*ccia yeast bun
ed*i*cola, giornal*a*io paper stall, newsvendor
provviste (f. pl.) provisions
fornitore (m.) tradesman
paniɛre (m.) basket
n*u*mero number
verdura vegetables, greens
legume (m.) vegetable (pulse)
patata potato
denaro money
sale (m.) salt
pepe (m.) pepper
frigor*i*fero refrigerator
pɛzzo piece
salato (adj.) savoury, salty
chiuso (adj.) closed
l*i*bero (adj.) free
freddo (adj.) cold
per favore please
fare la spesa to go shopping
sapere di to taste of

Exercise 1

Translate into Italian, giving when possible two forms: 1. The cup which is on the table. 2. The forks which Helen is cleaning. 3. The books of which I spoke. 4. The room in which I sleep. 5. The girl to whom I phoned. 6. The train in which I travelled. 7. The newspaper I am reading. 8. The baker whose bread we prefer. 9. The butcher from whom we buy meat. 10. The little shop in which he works. 11. The grocer's shop which is near the bank. 12. The provisions for which I phoned. 13. The stationer from whom we buy our postcards. 14. The fruiterer whose vegetables are dear. 15. The friend to whom I sent that letter. 16. This restaurant whose cakes are famous. 17. The assistant who greeted us. 18. The waiter to whom I paid the bill. 19. The lady whose phone I used. 20. The bus I take every morning.

Exercise 2

Translate into Italian: 1. He who sleeps doesn't catch (pigliare) fishes. 2. It is he who knows how to phone. 3. You must understand what you learn. 4. On the table is a vase behind which there is a mirror. 5. It is

I who ordered it. 6. In that corner there is a desk above which there is a lamp. 7. I know the lawyer's daughter who is studying Italian. 8. Here is the house behind which there is a huge garden. 9. Tell me what you are doing. 10. Those are the paintings among which we found a famous picture.

Exercise 3

Translate into Italian (using *sapere*—to know): 1. We wish. 2. They can. 3. We know. 4. He must. 5. I can. 6. You know. 7. We are obliged to. 8. She wishes. 9. You (s) know. 10. We are able. 11. They have to. 12. I wish. 13. She knows. 14. You wish. 15. You must. 16. He can. 17. I do not know. 18. We can. 19. You must. 20. They know.

A. *Translate into English:* 1. Oggi la mamma non può andare a fare la spesa e manda la cameriera. 2. Essa le consegna del denaro e una lista di tutto quello che deve comprare. 3. La macelleria è il negozio più vicino, all'angolo di questa strada. Compri un bel pezzo di carne per fare il brodo. 4. Il fruttivendolo è lì vicino ed ha sempre verdura fresca; abbiamo bisogno di insalata, frutta, legumi e patate. 5. Non compri il pane; ce n'è ancora di quello che abbiamo comprato ieri mattina. 6. Se desiderate di mangiare del pesce, il pescivendolo ha ogni mattina del bel pesce fresco che sa di mare. 7. Mentre Giulia entra in una tabaccheria per comprare i francobolli, la cameriera va nella vicina salumeria, nella cui vetrina c'è un formaggio italiano che mia madre preferisce a tutti gli altri. 8. Quando ha comprato il formaggio entra nella drogheria, ordina tutte le provviste per la settimana, poi mette le cose di cui abbiamo bisogno oggi nel paniere e chiede al droghiere di mandare le altre a casa. 9. Nella vetrina della panetteria ci sono delle focaccie; Giulia entra e chiede al fornaio: "Mi dà una di quelle focaccie che sono in vetrina?" 10. "Quale desidera, signorina?"—domanda il fornaio; "queste sono dolci, quelle salate." 11. "Mentre io compro la carta da lettere in questa cartoleria, vuole andare all'edicola e vedere se è arrivata quella rivista di cui la mamma parlava stamattina?"—chiede Giulia alla cameriera. 12. Non dimentichi il giornale, quello in cui ci sono i programmi dei cinema. 13. Ecco la nostra latteria; c'è poca gente in questo momento e il lattaio ci dà le tre bottiglie di latte che prendiamo ogni giorno. 14. "Hai comprato quelle medicine che il dottore ha ordinato a Maria?"—chiede la mamma a Giulia, quando ritornano a casa. 15. No, il farmacista non ne aveva nessuna ma mi ha dato una lista delle farmacie che saranno aperte domani e nelle quali potremo trovarle. 16. Il campanello suona: è il ragazzo del droghiere con le provviste; Giulia guarda nel paniere per vedere se c'è tutto ciò che ha ordinato e paga il conto. 17. Poi porta il paniere in cucina e mette il caffè, il tè, lo zucchero, la pasta, il formaggio, il salame e la marmellata nell'armadio; il burro, il latte, la carne, il pesce e la frutta nel frigorifero. 18. Il commesso della drogheria ha dimenticato il pepe di cui abbiamo bisogno stasera e il burro che ha mandato non è fresco. 19. Giulia prende un libretto in cui ci sono tutti i numeri di telefono dei fornitori e cerca quello del droghiere. 20. "Vuole mandare il ragazzo con dell'altro burro?"—essa gli chiede—"quello che ci ha mandato non è buono. Ci mandi anche del pepe per favore."

B. *Translate into Italian:* 1. My sister and I do not live in the centre of the city because there is so much traffic, but we always go there to do our shopping. 2. When we go shopping we always take (portare) a basket, because we often have to leave the car in a car park. 3. Yesterday morning I was free and my sister asked me if I wanted to go shopping with her. 4. We looked into the refrigerator and in all the cupboards to see what we needed because we wanted to make a list of the provisions we had to buy. 5. We also phoned the grocer who sends us tea, coffee, butter and sugar every week. We had paid our bill at the end of the month and he had not sent us our receipt. 6. That grocer does not sell wine but there is an Italian grocer in town where we can buy good red and white wines, French and Italian cheeses, Italian and German salami. 7. "What do you wish to-day ladies?" an assistant asked us. "We want some cheese, black and white pepper, some (say: un po') of that salame, some macaroni and two bottles of wine." 8. "Which wine do you prefer?" "Last week we bought a bottle of white wine which was very good. If you have the same, give me two bottles, please." 9. The assistant asked us if we wanted to take everything we had bought with us. 10. My sister had been able to leave the car outside the shop and while I was paying the bill, the assistant carried the box with the provisions we had bought to the car. 11. There was a paper stall near by and I bought a paper to see which films there were in town. 12. While my sister was turning the car, I looked at the list to see what we had still to buy. 13. We still had to buy fish, meat, fruit and vegetables, order another bottle of milk and ask the baker to send some rolls every day. 14. The other baker whose rolls we prefer, unfortunately sold his shop recently. 15. In Italy the bakers who make bread do not sell cakes. When we were there on holiday we used to buy cakes from a 'pasticceria'. 16. Elena, our maid, who has been ill, had finished the medicine which the doctor had ordered so we went into a chemist's to get her another bottle. 17. "Will you buy the meat while I wait here?" I asked my sister. "I never know what to buy from the butcher, but that roast you bought last week was very good." 18. "We can phone the dairy and the fishmonger and order the milk and the fish." 19. We had hardly arrived home when the bell rang. It was the fishmonger's boy who brought the fish we had ordered by phone. 20. We did not go to the cinema because we were tired and preferred to stay at home and listen to an interesting programme on (alla) the radio.

C. Molte salumerie specialmente nelle città in cui ci sono molti turisti hanno anche dei panini e confezionano dei sandwiches quando c'è qualcuno che li domanda.—Many delicatessen shops, especially in towns where there are lots of tourists, keep rolls also and make up sandwiches for anyone who asks. Spesso hanno anche vino sfuso.—They often have uncorked wine also. Si domanda: "Vorrei un etto di prosciutto (crudo o cotto), non troppo grasso."—One asks: "I should like a quarter of ham (raw or boiled) not too fat . . ." di salame, di mortadella; quanto costa all'etto? allora me ne dia solo 50 grammi—of salami, of (Bologna) sausage; how much is it the quarter? Well then give me only 2 ounces. Ha dei panini freschi? Può farmi due panini?—Have you any fresh rolls? Can you make me two sandwiches? Uno con salame e l'altro con formaggio—one with salami the other with cheese. Che formaggio ha? Vorrei un formaggio grasso, non troppo forte: Bel Paese. Fontina. —What kind of cheese do you have? I'd like a rich cheese that is not too strong. Me ne tagli una fetta sottile—un etto e mezzo.—Cut me a thin slice—about 6 ounces. Faccia tutto un pacchetto.—Put everything into one parcel. Poi vorrei mezzo litro di vino bianco o rosso, secco.—Then I should like half a litre of dry wine, white or red. Dov'è un fruttivendolo?—Where is there a fruiterer? Mi dia mezzo chilo di queste pesche. Quanto costano al chilo?—Give me a pound of these peaches. How much do they cost the kilo (=2 lbs.)? Vorrei un po' di uva—per piacere.—I should like a few grapes, please. Questa frutta è un po' acerba, non è abbastanza matura, è troppo matura, è guasta.—This fruit is a bit sour, it is not ripe enough, it is too ripe, it is spoilt.

D. *Neanche per scherzo*

Non lo dire neanche per scherzo (per ridere)—Don't say it even in fun.

LESSON XX

Cardinal Numerals

11	undici	26	ventisɛi	100	cɛnto
12	dodici	27	ventisɛtte	101	cɛnto uno
13	trɛdici	28	ventɔtto	105	cɛnto cinque
14	quattɔrdici	29	ventinɔve	160	cɛnto sessanta
15	quindici	30	trɛnta	200	duecɛnto
16	sedici	31	trentuno	300	trecɛnto
17	diciassɛtte	32	trentadue	900	novecɛnto
18	diciɔtto	33	trentatrè	1000	mille
19	diciannɔve	38	trentɔtto	1100	mille cɛnto
20	venti	40	quaranta	1200	mille duecɛnto
21	ventuno	50	cinquanta	1800	mille ottocɛnto
22	ventidue	60	sessanta	1900	mille novecɛnto
23	ventitrè	70	settanta	2000	due mila
24	ventiquattro	80	ottanta	100.000	cɛnto mila
25	venticinque	90	novanta	1.000.000	un milione

1. *Venti*, *trɛnta*, etc., drop their final vowel before combining with *uno* or *otto*:

quarantuno 41 sessantɔtto 68

2. *Ventitrè*, *quarantatrè*, etc., require the accent on the final *e*.
3. *Cɛnto* (invariable) and *mille* (pl. mila) must never be preceded by the indefinite article:

cɛnto cinquanta one hundred and fifty
mille chilometri one thousand kilometres

4. *Milione* (m.) is a noun and must be separated from the noun to which it refers by the preposition *di*:

Tre milioni di ascoltatori. Three million listeners.

5. Unlike English the conjunction *and* is omitted in compound numbers. Dates are written as one word:

trecentocinquanta three hundred and fifty
millenovecentocinquantacinque nineteen fifty-five

6. From eleven hundred upwards the numbers are translated: one thousand one hundred, one thousand two hundred, etc., and, especially for lengthy numbers, not referring to money or dates, it is advisable to write them separately:

mille trecɛnto persone thirteen hundred people.

I mesi dell'anno The months of the year		I giorni della settimana The days of the week		Le stagioni The seasons	
gennaio	January	lunedì	Monday	invεrno	winter
febbraio	February	martedì	Tuesday	primavεra	spring
marzo	March	mercoledì	Wednesday	estate	summer
aprile	April	giovedì	Thursday	autunno	autumn
maggio	May	venerdì	Friday		
giugno	June	sabato	Saturday		
luglio	July	domεnica	Sunday		
agosto	August				
settεmbre	September				
ottobre	October				
novεmbre	November				
dicεmbre	December				

The months, days and seasons are spelt with small letters.

Note: in spring, in autumn—*in primavεra, in autunno*; but: in summer, in winter— *d'estate, d'invεrno*, and: in the morning, in the afternoon, in the evening—*di mattina, di pomeriggio, di sera.*

Use of Cardinals

The cardinals are used in Italian to render:

1. *Dates*, except for the first day of the month, when the ordinal *primo* is used as in English. The preposition *on* is never translated; the preposition *of* is seldom translated. The numeral is always preceded by the definite article *il*, *giorno*, *mese* and *anno* being understood. The article is omitted in modern Italian when writing the date in a letter heading:

il due gennaio on January the 2nd; the 2nd of January
il 1º maggio on May the 1st; the 1st of May
Roma, 31 ottobre 1955 Rome, 31st October 1955
il 1955 (millenovecentocinquantacinque) 1955
nel 1948 (nel millenovecentoquarantɔtto) in 1948

Useful Phrases to Note

Quanti ne abbiamo del mese? È il cinque.
What is the date? It is the 5th.

Che giorno è ɔggi?
What day is it to-day?

In che giorno sεi libero?
What day are you free?

Da quanti giorni piove? Da tre giorni.
How long has it been raining? For three days.

A Natale, a Pasqua, a Capodanno.
At Christmas, at Easter, on New Year's day.

2. The cardinals are used with *εssere* to express time. The numeral is preceded by the feminine article agreeing with *ora* (hour), *ore* (hours) understood. Except for 1 o'clock, midday, and midnight, the verb will therefore be plural.

Che ora è?	What time is it?
È l'una (il tocco).	It is one o'clock.
È mεzzogiorno, mεzzanɔtte.	It is midday, midnight.
Sono le due.	It is two o'clock.
Sono le tre e un quarto.	It is a quarter past three.
Sono le quattro meno cinque.	It is five to four.
Sono le cinque e diεci.	It is ten past five.
Sono le sεi e mεzzo. e mεzza.	It is half past six.
Va bene il tuo orolɔgio?	Is your watch right?
Il mio orolɔgio va indiεtro.	My watch is slow.
Questo orolɔgio va avanti.	This watch is fast.

Official times for trains, ships, etc. arriving and departing are calculated from midnight to midnight:

Il trεno parte alle diciassεtte e trεnta. The train leaves at 5.30 p.m.

Note the following expressions of time:

lì per lì	then and there
su due piεdi	instantly
a tamburo battεnte	at once
di punto in bianco	suddenly
improvvisamente	suddenly
ad un tratto	suddenly
a pɔco, a pɔco	little by little
con l'andar del tεmpo	as time went by
quasi sεmpre	almost always
ogni tanto	every now and again
di quando in quando	every now and then
a lungo	for a long time
d'ora in pɔi	from now on
prima o pɔi	sooner or later
ben prεsto	pretty soon
in brεve	shortly
fra breve	very soon
fra pɔco	soon
pɔco fa	a little while ago
diurno	by day, daily, during the day
notturno	by night
quotidiano	daily

settimanale	weekly
mensile	monthly
annuale	yearly

3. The cardinals are used with *avere* to express age:

Quanti anni hai? Che età hai?	How old are you?
Ho diciassette anni.	I shall be seventeen.
Compirò 18 anni il mese prossimo.	I will be 18 next month.

Circa—about, can be used to express an approximate number of years, months, etc.:

Circa venticinque persone.—About twenty-five people.

Approximation is also rendered by the addition of the suffix *ina* to the numerals ten, twenty, thirty, up to ninety, including fifteen. These must be preceded by the indefinite article:

Una quindicina di giorni.	About fifteen days.
Una decina di anni.	About ten years.
È sulla quarantina.	He is about forty.

The noun *dozzina* can mean either exactly twelve or approximately twelve:

Una dozzina di uova.	A dozen eggs.
Una dozzina di persone.	About twelve people.

Other approximate expressions are: *un centinaio*—about a hundred; *un migliaio*—about a thousand; *alcune centinaia*—several hundred; *alcune migliaia*—several thousand.

Vocabulary XX

basilica basilica
tomba tomb, grave
cupola dome, cupola
facciata front, façade
colonna column, pillar
colonnato colonnade
obelisco obelisk
rovina ruin
architetto architect
distanza distance, range
informazione (f.) (often pl.) information
mezzo half, middle, means
interno interior
all'interno inside; (adj.) inner, inland
fontana fountain
lavoro work, toil, task
metro metre, tape-measure
popolazione (f.) population
abitante (m. & f.) inhabitant, resident
forestiere (m.) visitor, stranger, guest
classe (f.) class, rank
lira lira (Italian money); lyre
Londra London
prossimo (adj.) next, nearest
principale (adj.) principal, chief
impossibile (adj.) impossible
alto (adj.) high, tall
enorme (adj.) huge, enormous
barocco (adj.) baroque (style)
difficile (adj.) difficult
esatto (adj.) exact, precise
seguente (adj.) following

certamente (adv.) certainly
ancora (adv.) still, yet, again
verso (prep.) towards, against
davanti (prep.) in front of
demolire* to demolish
disegnare to design, draw
morire to die
continuare to continue
contare to count, reckon
contare . . . su to rely on
cominciare to begin (aux. **avere**)

Exercise 1

Translate into Italian: 1. 5th October, 1938. 2. On the 12th March, 1945. 3. April 21st, 1870. 4. What is the date to-day? 5. It is the 1st May, 1955. 6. 3rd June, 1560. 7. 25th August, 1729. 8. 13th February, 1681. 9. In 1453, in the month of July. 10. What was the date yesterday? 11. It was the 8th December. 12. What day is it to-day? 13. It is Sunday, the 2nd of January. 14. In 1939; in the month of November. 15. In 1495; in the month of September. 16. How many days are there in a month? 17. In spring, in summer, in autumn, in winter. 18. These are the four seasons of the year. 19. How many days are there in a week? There are seven. 20. What day did he leave? 21. He left on the 6th of July. 22. When does the summer begin? It begins on . . . 23. When does winter begin? It begins on . . . 24. There are twelve months in a year. 25. Seven of the months have 31 days.

Exercise 2

Translate into Italian: 1. What time is it? 2. It is a quarter past five. 3. It is half past seven. 4. It is twenty to four. 5. It is a quarter to eight. 6. What time is it now? 7. It is seven forty-five. 8. It is five minutes to eleven. 9. It is midday, . . . midnight. 10. It is one o'clock. 11. My watch is slow; it is five to one. 12. What time was it when you returned? 13. It was 9.30 p.m. 14. Is your watch fast? Yes it is always fast. 15. It is eighteen minutes to eleven. 16. At what hour does the train leave? 17. It leaves at 9.30 p.m. (say: 21.30) 18. Our train leaves at 5.35 p.m. 19. My train leaves at 8.15 p.m. 20. His train leaves at 6.45 p.m. 21. Every day a train leaves London at 11 a.m. 22. It arrives in Rome the following day about two in the afternoon. 23. Our train was late; it did not arrive till 3 p.m. 24. Sometimes in winter trains are very late. 25. Are you punctual? Yes when my watch is not slow.

Exercise 3

Translate into Italian: 1. How old is she? 2. She is fifteen. 3. How old is her brother? 4. He will be about thirty. 5. No, he is only twenty-five. 6. Her cousin will stay at the seaside for about three weeks. 7. When will your mother come back? 8. She has gone shopping and will be back in a little while. 9. She will return in about ten minutes. 10. When will you finish that book? 11. In a couple of weeks. 12. We shall wait for him only five minutes. 13. He will be 21 soon. 14. We looked at him for a long time. 15. I wrote to her a little while ago. 16. I receive two weekly magazines and one monthly. 17. The papers we read every day are called dailies. 18. He works every now and then. 19. Give us our daily bread. 20. From now on I shall pay the bill myself. 21. John almost always buys the tickets. 22. The driver suddenly stopped the bus. 23. As time went by he began to love Italy. 24. Little by little she learnt French. 25. I shall find that address sooner or later.

A. *Translate into English:* 1. In primavera Roma è molto bella e questa è la stagione in cui migliaia di forestieri ci vanno per visitarne i magnifici monumenti e le chiese meravigliose. 2. Noi visiteremo certamente le quattro Basiliche: San Pietro, San Giovanni, San Paolo, e Santa Maria Maggiore e una dozzina delle altre chiese principali. Sarebbe impossibile visitarle tutte perché resteremo a Roma solamente una decina di giorni. 3. San Pietro fu costruito nello stesso posto in cui c'era la tomba di San Pietro e in cui Costantino aveva costruito una Basilica nel 319. 4. Il Papa Giulio secondo demolì la chiesa costruita nel 1452 e il 18 aprile 1506 Bramante cominciò per suo ordine a costruire la nuova chiesa. 5. Michelangelo ne disegnò la magnifica cupola e quando egli morì nel 1564, Vignola ed altri architetti continuarono il lavoro. 6. La facciata della chiesa è barocca ed è alta 46 metri e lunga 115; la porta a destra è la Porta Santa ed è aperta solamente nell'anno Santo; quella a sinistra, bellissima, è moderna ed è opera dello scultore Manzù. 7. La magnifica piazza davanti a San Pietro fu costruita tra il 1566 e il 1567 da Bernini per ordine del Papa. 8. La piazza è ovale e ha un portico a quattro colonne (four columns deep) con 284 enormi colonne e 140 statue di santi. 9. C'è una distanza di 240 metri tra i due colonnati e di 340 metri dalla scala della Basilica sino alla fine del colonnato. 10. Nel mezzo della piazza c'è un obelisco di 41 metri che Caligola portò a Roma da Heliopolis e a destra e a sinistra due magnifiche fontane. 11. Roma ha una popolazione di circa due milioni e mezzo di abitanti ma sarebbe difficile contare tutti i forestieri che la visitano specialmente in primavera e in autunno. 12. La nuova stazione di Roma è molto moderna: centinaia di treni diretti ed espressi arrivano ogni giorno in questa stazione e portano migliaia di forestieri che desiderano visitare Roma. 13. Ci sono molte trattorie che hanno un pranzo a prezzo fisso? Sì, la lista del giorno è sempre in vetrina e in questi posti la colazione può costare dalle 1200 alle 1500 lire. 14. Quanto costa l'affrancatura di una lettera? Un francobollo per l'Inghilterra costa 90 lire e per l'interno, 40. 15. Con che treno arriverete? Non sappiamo l'ora esatta ma arriveremo di pomeriggio. 16. C'è un treno che parte da Londra alle 11 di mattina e arriva a Roma il giorno seguente alle 14 circa. 17. Tre anni fa una camera a due letti in un buon albergo costava dalle 2500 alle 3500 lire per notte. 18. Anche il viaggio costa molto; da Londra a Roma costa dalle 25.000 alle 35.000 lire circa. 19. Sai se i teatri sono cari? e quanto costa l'ingresso nei musei e il biglietto su un autobus? 20. Una poltrona a teatro costa dalle 2000 alle 3000 lire e in un buon cinema dalle 800 alle 1200 lire; l'ingresso in un museo dalle 200 alle 250 e in un autobus o in un tram il biglietto costa 50 lire.

B. *Translate into Italian:* 1. In 1950 some friends of ours spent eleven days in Rome at the end of the Holy Year. 2. In the Holy Year Rome was crowded and there were often eighty thousand people inside the Basilica of St Peter. 3. On the days when the Pope speaks from the balcony (say: which is) above the main entrance of St Peter's there are thousands of people in the square. 4. We are going to Rome for about ten days in the spring and some friends have given us a little guide which they bought five years ago. 5. I have already learned the names of the four principal Basilicas and even know the numbers of the buses we shall take. 6. One day we shall take a bus along the "Via Appia" which was constructed in 312 B.C. (Avanti Cristo). It is a very famous road and along it much (say: a great part) of Rome's traffic used to pass. 7. To-day we can still see among the trees the ruins of ancient tombs and monuments along this narrow roadway which was once so important. 8. Do you know how much a bus or tram ticket costs? It costs fifty lire. 9. How much does a double bedroom cost today in Rome per night? From four to five thousand lire. 10. My brother will accompany us on holiday and we shall have lunch and dinner in the small restaurants for which Rome is famous. 11. The cooking is generally very good. The lunch or dinner costs from one thousand two hundred to one thousand five hundred lire. 12. Among other things, I have seen that the postage on (di) a letter to England costs ninety lire. 13. I have found in an old book that the population of Rome in 1911 was 538,634 (say: inhabitants) where nowadays it is about 2 millions and a half. 14. Our friends left London one Friday at 11 a.m. and arrived in Rome the following day about 2 p.m. We shall try to do the same. 15. In the middle of the square in front of St Peter's and St Mary Major there are obelisks which have been there for hundreds of years. 16. St Peter's Basilica, (the) work of many famous architects and artists from 1506 to 1626 is constructed in the same place in which Constantine had built a Basilica in 319, above the tomb of St Peter. 17. Michelangelo designed the magnificent cupola 119 metres high which is constructed on four columns. 18. He was 71 in 1546 when the Pope summoned him to Rome to finish the work which Bramante had begun in 1506—the magnificent new Basilica of St Peter.

19. Michelangelo was 89 when he died in 1564. 20. Admission (l'ingresso to a museum costs from 200 to 250 lire; on Sundays (say: the Sunday) admission is free.

C. In tutte le grandi città d'Italia i negozi sono aperti ogni giorno sino a tardi.—In all the large cities of Italy shops are open daily till a late hour. Quando chiudono i negozi?—When do the shops close? D'estate chiudono alle otto o otto e mezzo: d'inverno alle sette.—They close at eight or half past eight in summer and at seven in winter. Sono aperti i negozi la domenica?—Do shops open on Sundays? La domenica mattina le panetterie, alcune drogherie e tutti i caffè sono aperti in Italia.—On Sunday mornings bakers, a few grocers and all cafés are open. E gli uffici sono aperti?—What about offices? No, ma i cinema e i teatri sono aperti sino a tardi anche la domenica.—No, but cinemas and theatres are open too on Sundays till late. A Roma, Firenze, Venezia e Milano quali sono le strade in cui ci sono i migliori negozi?—Which streets in Rome, Florence, Venice and Milan have the best shops? In Roma i più bei negozi sono in Via Condotti e al Corso Umberto, ma per trovare roba più a buon mercato è meglio andare a Via Nazionale o nel quartiere dei Prati.—The best shops in Rome are in the Via Condotti and the Corso Umberto, but to find cheaper wares it is better to go to the Via Nazionale or the Prati quarter of the city. E quali sono le strade in cui ci sono i più bei negozi in Firenze?—And where are the best shops in Florence? In Firenze i migliori negozi sono in Via Tornabuoni e in Via Calzaiuoli.—The best shops in Florence are in . . . A Venezia i negozi più belli sono nella famosa Piazza San Marco, non è vero?—Aren't the finest shops in Venice in the famous St Mark's Square? Anche in Milano, con tutte le sue industrie, si trovano bellissimi negozi?—Do you also find gorgeous shops in Milan, with all its industries? Sì, una delle strade più conosciute è Via Manzoni.—Yes, one of its best known streets is the Via Manzoni. Che cosa comprano i turisti principalmente in Italia?—What do tourists mainly buy in Italy? Comprano oggetti di cuoio, di paglia, ceramiche, riproduzioni artistiche, oggetti-ricordo, fazzoletti di seta pura e alcuni comprano anche vestiti, scarpe, guanti, ecc.—They buy leather goods, things made of straw, pottery, art prints, souvenirs, pure silk scarves and some tourists also buy clothes, shoes, gloves, etc.

D. *Che*

Che, mi presteresti la macchina?—Look, would you lend me the car?

LESSON XXI

Comparison of Adjectives

In Italian as in English, qualifying adjectives have three degrees of comparison: (1) positive; (2) comparative; (3) superlative. As in English, variations in adjectives are rendered either by adverbs or by the use of suffixes.

Positive	*Comparative*	*Superlative*
bɛllo beautiful	(a) più bɛllo (superiority) (more beautiful)	il più bɛllo (relative) (the most beautiful)
	(b) meno bɛllo (inferiority) (less beautiful)	il meno bɛllo (relative) (the least beautiful)
	(c) tanto bɛllo quanto[1] (equality)	bellissimo (absolute) (very beautiful)
	così bɛllo come (as beautiful as)	

Positive

Positive (positivo) denotes the simple quality possessed by a person or a thing without reference to any other person or thing.

Comparative

The comparative (comparativo) denotes a greater degree (maggioranza —superiority), a lesser degree (minoranza—inferiority) or an equal degree (eguaglianza—equality) of the quality possessed by one person or thing compared with another.

The comparative of superiority or inferiority is formed by placing the adverbs *più*[2]—more or *meno*—less, before the adjective. *Than* is expressed by either *di* or *che*.

Than is *di* in front of numerals, pronouns or nouns:

L'ho pagato più di mille lire.
I have paid more than 1000 lire for it.

Essa è più giovane di me.
She is younger than I am.

[1] *Tanto . . . quanto* preceding two nouns or pronouns can also mean 'both'; e.g. *Tanto lui quanto lɛi*—both he and she; as adjectives they agree with the noun they qualify; e.g. Tante ragazze quanti ragazzi—as many girls as boys. Note the correlatives *tale . . . quale* which agree with the nouns they qualify; e.g. Ho lasciato i libri quali li ho trovati—I left the books as I found them.

[2] *Più* is always invariable whether it is an adverb or the comparative of the adjective *molti*—many. See p. 124

Questa chiesa è più antica di quella.
This church is older than that one.

Maria è più alta di Giulia.
Mary is taller than Julia.

Luisa è meno diligente di Roberto.
Louise is less diligent than Robert.

When the comparison is between two nouns or pronouns that are subjects or objects of the same verb, *than* is expressed by *che*:

È più cotone che seta. It is more cotton than silk.
Ama più me che te. He loves me more than you.

Than is *che* before adjectives, adverbs, prepositions, participles, infinitives:

La stanza è più lunga che larga.
The room is longer than it is wide.

Ho studiato più ɔggi che iɛri.
I have studied more today than yesterday.

È più bɛllo in primavɛra che in autunno.
It is more beautiful in spring than in autumn.

Egli è più temuto che amato.
He is more feared than loved.

È meno facile ascoltare che parlare.
It is less easy to listen than to speak.

Than is *che non* or *di quel che* before an inflected verb; the first requires the subjunctive, the second the indicative:

È più diligɛnte che non sembri.
She is more diligent than she seems.

Capisce più di quel che tu credi.
He understands more than you think.

The *comparative of equality* is formed by placing *tanto*—as, so, or *così*—as, so, before the adjective and *quanto*—as or *come*—as, after the adjective. *Tanto* and *così* are frequently omitted:

Il dottore non è tanto ricco quanto l'avvocato.
The doctor is not so rich as the lawyer.

La ragazza è così intelligente come il fratɛllo.
The girl is as intelligent as her brother.

Silvia è studiosa come intelligɛnte.
Silvia is as studious as she is intelligent.

Superlative

Superlative (superlativo) denotes the highest degree of the quality in relative superlative) or a very high degree of some quality when no comparison is being made (*superlativo assoluto*—absolute superlative).

The relative superlative is formed by placing the definite article before the comparative *più* or *meno*. If the superlative follows a noun that already has a definite article no other is used:

Questa è la più bɛlla chiɛsa della città.
This is the most beautiful church in the town.
È il libro meno interessante della libreria.
This is the least interesting book in the library.

Note that 'in' after a relative superlative is always *di*.

The *absolute superlative* is formed in several ways:

1. By adding *issimo* to the positive after the final vowel is dropped:

cortese, cortesissimo very kind

2. By using some adverbs such as *molto, assai, estremamente*:

molto bɛllo very beautiful
assai elegante very smart

3. By repeating the adjective, though this is much less common, the adjective here having the force of an adverb:

Camminava lɛnto lɛnto. He walked very slowly.

4. By means of prefixes, which however should be used with the same caution as suffixes; the most common are: ***extra, arci, ultra, sopra, stra***:

sopraffino	first quality	straricco	very rich
arcicontɛnto	very happy	stravɛcchio	very old

5. With other adjectives:

stanco mɔrto	dead tired	piɛno zeppo	crammed full
ubriaco fradicio	dead drunk	vɛcchio decrɛpito	terribly old

Vocabulary XXI

calzoleria shoe shop, bootmaker's
misura measurement
cent*i*metro centimetre, tape-measure
sarto, -a, tailor, dressmaker
colletto collar
velluto velvet
flanɛlla flannel
pantaloni (m.) trousers
cravatta tie
mɔda fashion; **di mɔda** fashionable
assortimento selection, assortment
aiuto help

ascensore (m.) lift
scellino shilling
periodo period, time
al pian terreno on the ground floor
vivace (adj.) gay, lively
pesante (adj.) heavy
fɔrte (adj.) strong
ultimo (adj.) last, latest, top
sportivo (adj. & n.) sports, sporting
colorato (adj.) coloured
riconoscente (adj.) grateful
oscuro (adj.) dark
pallido (adj.) pale
specialmente (adv.) especially
forse (adv.) perhaps
naturalmente (adv.) naturally, of course
fare le commissioni to go shopping
osservare observe, remark
servire to serve, be of use, attend to
offrire to offer

Exercise 1

Translate into Italian: 1. He is less intelligent than Vera. 2. She is more studious than I. 3. It costs more than 750 lire. 4. More boys than girls. 5. The church is more modern than beautiful. 6. This is cheaper than that. 7. More in the cup than in the cream jug. 8. Less easy than we think. 9. As many visitors as inhabitants. 10. He is as rich as his brother. 11. More magazines than books. 12. It will cost more than 50.000 lire. 13. You are less tired than I. 14. Blankets are heavier than sheets. 15. The carpet is longer than broad. 16. Try to be kinder than him. 17. He is less ill than we feared. 18. I received more letters from him than from you. 19. She is not so clever as her brother. 20. As many saucers as plates.

Exercise 2

Translate into Italian: 1. The newest theatre in town. 2. She always reads very interesting books. 3. A most courteous assistant. 4. She bought some very smart clothes. 5. That is the ugliest painting in the gallery. 6. A very big mistake. 7. He invited two very dear friends. 8. The oldest house in the street. 9. A most famous violinist. 10. The sweetest wine in the shop. 11. They visited two very interesting museums. 12. He is the richest man in town. 13. They are extremely amusing. 14. The simplest designs. 15. Send me the most recent reviews. 16. They were very drunk. 17. He is very old. 18. They used to be very rich. 19. He was very calm. 20. She wore a very wide skirt.

A. *Translate into English:* 1. Sabato scorso siamo andate a fare delle commissioni in città. 2. Entrammo prima in una calzoleria nella cui vetrina Luisa aveva veduto un bellissimo paio di scarpe. 3. Il commesso ci mostrò le scarpe e Luisa le provò ma erano troppo strette. 4. "Non avrebbe la misura più grande?"—domandò Luisa. "Io porto il 38."

5. No signorina, ma abbiamo un grandissimo assortimento e ci sono altri due modelli elegantissimi che sono anche meno cari. Li provi. 6. "Quanto costano?"—domandò Maria. "Queste settemila e cinquecento, quelle seimila lire; io le consiglio queste perché sono fortissime e nello stesso tempo molto eleganti." 7. Quando Luisa ebbe comprato le scarpe entrammo in un grandissimo negozio di stoffe che è vicino alla calzoleria. 8. "In che cosa posso servirle?"—domandò il commesso. 9. Gli chiedemmo di mostrarci dei broccati di seta pesante. 10. Che colore preferirebbe? Il bianco e il nero sono sempre di moda ed elegantissimi ma forse per lei sarebbe più adatto un colore vivace come il rosso o il verde o molto pallido come il rosa o il celeste. 11. Il commesso ci portò una stoffa di un rosa pallidissimo e un broccato rosso assai vivace. 12. Giulia consigliò a Maria di prendere il broccato rosso che era più alto (wide) della seta e meno caro. 13. Vicino al negozio incontrammo un amico di Roberto che, gentilissimo come sempre, ci offrì di accompagnarci a casa. 14. "Io abito lontano dalla sua casa ed è già molto tardi"—osservò Luisa. 15. Accompagni le mie cugine che sono più stanche di me ed hanno un appuntamento con la loro sarta. 16. La sarta abita in un appartamento vicino a casa nostra. 17. Il suo appartamento è all'ultimo piano della casa ma c'è l'ascensore. 18. Nella stessa casa in cui abita la sarta, al pian terreno, c'è il sarto di Roberto. 19. Roberto gli ha ordinato un paio di pantaloni di flanella grigia ed una giacca sportiva marrone assai elegante ed ha anche comprato due bellissime cravatte nel negozio più elegante della città. 20. Siamo molto riconoscenti all'amico di Roberto che ci ha accompagnato a casa, perché col suo aiuto non siamo arrivate in ritardo per la colazione.

B. *Translate into Italian:* 1. Often on Saturdays I have an appointment with one of my oldest friends; we have coffee and then we usually do some shopping. 2. Last week we had an appointment at ten o'clock, because at this time of the year the shops are more crowded. 3. We did not spend (restare) more than twenty minutes in the little café. 4. Usually there are more women than men there but last Saturday there were as many men as women. 5. Mary was wanting some very heavy velvet to make an evening coat, (say: of) the same colour as her dress but a little darker. 6. Very gay colours are fashionable this year; they are more suitable for younger people. 7. "Do you want to look at our materials which have just arrived?" asked the assistant. "The colours are not too strong and the prices are cheaper than last year." 8. All the assistants in that shop, from the oldest to the youngest, are most helpful. 9. I wanted to buy some new curtains for our drawing-room. In winter we use heavier curtains and I had seen some magnificent brocade in the window. 10. "We only have dress materials (stoffe per . . .) on the ground floor," explained the assistant. "Take the lift in that corner; furnishing materials are on the top floor." 11. The assistant showed us a dark red brocade with a most beautiful design but it was not as heavy as I wanted and it was more cotton than silk. 12. In that shop they have all the latest designs and the biggest selection in town. 13. I bought 13 yards (say: 12 metres) of a very pale green brocade 48 inches wide (say: 120 centimetres high). Some fabrics are 54 inches wide (say: 140 centimetres high). 14. When I had left my friends I phoned my brother; his tailor had sent him his new suit and he wanted my help to buy some new shirts and collars and one or two smarter ties. 15. When I went into the shop Robert was already there. He had given his measurement to the assistant who was showing him their smartest shirts. 16. Their shirts were all much dearer than those we had bought six months ago.. 17. The assistant remarked that they sold more coloured shirts than white (ones) but that doctors, lawyers and older people (anziano) preferred to wear white shirts. 18. Robert wanted a grey woollen shirt too to wear with his sports jacket and flannel trousers but the one they showed us was too dark and they did not have any in a paler grey. 19. I looked also at some handkerchiefs; the white ones were more expensive than the coloured cotton ones. 20. I wanted to buy a dozen for a friend who will be twenty-one next month.

C. In Italia poche signore comprano i loro vestiti già confezionati. La maggior parte di esse li fanno fare da una sarta o, se sono vestiti a giacca, da un sarto.—Few women in Italy buy ready-made clothes. The majority of them have them made by a dressmaker or a tailor in the case of suits. Ci sono molte sarte?—Are there many dressmakers? Sì, e la fattura di un abito non costa tanto quanto qui.—Yes, and the cost of dress-making is not so expensive as it is here. Che cosa si dice alla sarta?—What does one say to the dressmaker? Vorrei fare un vestito semplice da mattina, da pomeriggio o da sera.—I should like to have a morning, an afternoon or an evening dress made. "Diritto o con la gonna larga?"—domanda la sarta e prende intanto le misure.—"With a straight or wide skirt?" the dressmaker asks, and meanwhile takes one's measurements. La cliente domanda "Quando posso venire per la prima prova?"—The customer asks, "When shall I come for the first fitting?" Ecco qualche frase di cui forse la cliente avrà bisogno.—Here are some phrases that the customer will perhaps need. È un po' stretto—it is a little tight; un po' largo qui—a bit wide here; mi pare che faccia un difetto nelle spalle—it seems to me that there is something wrong with the shoulders; è più lungo davanti che di dietro—it is longer at the front than at the back; potrebbe restringerlo?—could you take it in?; allargarlo—let it out; accorciarlo—shorten it; allungarlo un po'—lengthen it a little. Potrebbe darmi un ritaglio di stoffa? Mi occorrono delle scarpe, dei guanti, un cappello e una borsetta e voglio comprarli subito.—Could you give me a scrap of the material? I need shoes, gloves, a hat and a handbag and I wish to buy them at once. Quando si entra in una calzoleria che cosa si dice?—When one goes into a shoe shop what does one say? Si dice "Vorrei comprare un paio di scarpe col tacco alto".—One says, "I should like to buy a pair of shoes with high heels." "Che numero calza?" domanda il commesso.—"What size?" the assistant asks. Le misure italiane sono diverse da quelle inglesi—Italian sizes are different from English ones. Vanno dal 33, 34, che sono misure molto piccole al 40 o 41.—They range from 33, 34 which are very small sizes to 40 or 41. Queste scarpe sono strette.—These shoes are tight. Mi fanno male in punta.—They hurt my toes. Ha il numero più grande?—Have you a larger size? Potrebbe metterle in forma?—Could you stretch them on the last? Le vorrei più scollate.—I should like them with lower fronts.

D. *Ma*

Ma che cosa dici?—What on earth are you saying?
Ma sta un po' zitto!—Be quiet, for goodness' sake!
Ma si!—Yes, of course!
Ma no!—Of course not!
Ma che fai?—Whatever are you doing?

LESSON XXII

Comparison of Adjectives (*Continued*), Adverbs

Irregular Comparison

As well as the regular forms of the comparative and superlative formed by *più*, *il più*, etc., some adjectives have another form derived from the original Latin. They are both in use.

Positive	Comparative	Relative Superlative	Absolute Superlative
buɔno—good	migliore—better	il migliore—the best	ɔttimo—very good
cattivo—bad	peggiore—worse	il peggiore—the worst	pɛssimo—very bad
alto—high	superiore—higher	il suprɛmo—the highest	suprɛmo—very high
basso—low	inferiore—lower	l'infimo—the lowest	infimo—very low
grande—big	maggiore—bigger	il maggiore—the biggest	massimo—very big
piccolo—small	minore—smaller	il minore—the smallest	minimo—very small

The two forms of comparison differ sometimes in meaning and their use can only be learned by experience. In general, the irregular forms have a wider and looser meaning than the regular. Contrary to the rule, the relative superlative of *alto*, and *basso* is formed by placing the article before the absolute superlative *suprɛmo* and *infimo* and not before the comparative *superiore* and *inferiore*. *Maggiore* and *minore* are frequently used to express comparative age.

The plural adjective *molti* has the following forms: *più* (comp.)—more, *i più* (rel. sup.)—the majority, most people; *moltissimi* (absolute sup.)—very many.

Acre—acrid, *integro*—whole, honest, *cɛlebre*—famous and *salubre*—healthy, become in the absolute superlative *acɛrrimo*, *integɛrrimo*, *celebɛrrimo*, *salubɛrrimo*.

Comparison of Adverbs

The comparative and superlative degrees of adverbs are formed in the same way as those of adjectives.

Positive	Comparative	Relative Superlative	Absolute Superlative
velocemente (quickly)	più velocemente (more quickly)	il più velocemente (most quickly)	molto velocemente (very quickly)

tardi (late)	più tardi (later)	il più tardi (latest)	tardissimo; molto tardi } very late
prɛsto (early)	più prɛsto (earlier)	il più prɛsto (earliest)	prestissimo; molto prɛsto } very early

The absolute superlative of adverbs ending in *mente* can also be formed by adding *mente* to the feminine singular superlative of the corresponding adjective. Such forms, however, are rarely used:

veloce velocissima velocissimamente

Irregular Comparison

Positive	Comparative	Relative Superlative	Absolute Superlative
bɛne (well)	mɛglio (better)	il mɛglio (best)	ottimamente (very well)
male (bad)	pɛggio (worse)	il pɛggio (worst)	pessimamente (very badly)
molto (very; much)	più (more)	il più (most)	moltissimo (very much)
pɔco (little)	meno (less)	il meno (least)	pochissimo (very little)

The four adverbs *mɛglio*, *pɛggio*, *più* and *meno* can also be used as nouns as in the following examples:

di male in pɛggio—from bad to worse; *alla mɛglio*—as best one can, somehow; *fa del suo mɛglio*—he does his best; *guardare dall'alto in basso*—to look down upon (disparagingly); *di più*—more; *parlare del più e del meno*—to talk about this and that; *il più è fatto*—it is nearly finished; *lavora il meno possibile*—he works as little as possible.[1]

Vocabulary XXII

clima (m.) climate
montagna mountain
sci (m. inv.) ski (vb. **sciare**)
alpinismo mountaineering
Alpi (f. pl.) the Alps (adj. **alpino**)
rifugio mountain inn
scalatore (m.) climber
scalata a climb (vb. **scalare**)
cima top, summit
bellezza beauty
natura nature (adj. **naturale**)
squadra team
neve (f.) snow (adj. **nevoso**)
lago lake
rɔccia rock (adj. **roccioso**)
filovia cable railway
pista ski track, trail
canottaggio rowing
nuɔto swimming
cɔsta coast, shore, rib
bambini little children
acqua water

[1] *Possibile* following the relative superlative renders as . . . as possible.

per*i*colo danger
ciɛlo sky
sviluppo development, expansion
campo field, course
***a*rbitro** referee, umpire
fase (f.) stage
grado grade, degree, rank
Fr*a*ncia France
Romani the Romans
Firɛnze Florence
spettatore (m.) spectator
paese (m.) country, village
corsa race
quartiɛre (m.) quarter, district
costume (m.) costume, custom
c*a*lcio football
st*a*dio playing ground
partita match
piɛde (m.) foot (**a piɛdi** on foot)
intorno (adv.) } around
intorno a (prep.) } around

sɛnza (prep.) without
leggɛro (adj.) light, slight, frivolous
copɛrto (adj.) covered
circostante (adj.) surrounding
rosato (adj.) pinkish
popolare (adj.) popular
differɛnte (adj.) different
medioevale (adj.) mediaeval
favorito (adj.) favourite
ingiusto (adj.) unjust
caratter*i*stico (adj.) characteristic
sentire to feel or hear
dimenticare to forget
giocare to play
partecipare to take part in (aux. **avere**)
fischiare to hiss
criticare to criticize
diventare to become

Exercise 1

Translate into Italian: 1. He spoke slowly. 2. Better late than never. 3. We spoke of this and that. 4. Try to arrive earlier than him. 5. Tell her as kindly as possible. 6. This bridge was constructed more recently than that one. 7. She always arrives most punctually. 8. She used to speak very little. 9. Robert, you must learn to answer more courteously. 10. She sang very well. 11. They arrived very late. 12. He speaks Italian better than his sister. 13. Send it to me as quickly as possible. 14. The girls will be here shortly. 15. Wait as long as possible.

Exercise 2

Translate into English, noticing the different uses of the two forms of comparison: 1. Maria è più buona di Olga. 2. Questa stoffa è migliore di quella. 3. Egli abita in un appartamento migliore del nostro. 4. Questo ragazzo è più cattivo di quel che credi. 5. L'impiegato peggiore. 6. Il peggiore giornale. 7. Una cattivissima figlia. 8. Un pessimo chirurgo. 9. L'uomo più alto. 10. Una casa altissima. 11. Il piano superiore. 12. Questo vino è superiore a quello. 13. L'arbitro supremo. 14. L'albero più basso. 15. Va al piano inferiore. 16. Un uomo bassissimo. 17. Questo candelabro è molto inferiore a quello. 18. Di infimo grado.

19. Ilpacco più grande. 20. La sorella maggiore. 21. Un appartamento grandissimo. 22. Il massimo grado. 23. La bottiglia più piccola. 24. La minore distanza. 25. La mia camera è più piccola della tua. 26. Un negozio piccolissimo. 27. Senza il minimo sbaglio. 28. Un disegno piccolissimo.

Exercise 3

Translate into Italian: 1. The majority. 2. The most honest. 3. Very healthy climate. 4. Very many steps. 5. Very acrid. 6. Very famous painters. 7. It is going from bad to worse. 8. The eldest daughter. 9. He looks down upon me. 10. They do as little as possible. 11. We talked about this and that. 12. She does her best. 13. He works more now. 14. The lowest degree. 15. It is nearly finished.

A. *Translate into English*: 1. Il clima in Italia è molto migliore che in Gran Bretagna ma alcuni sport all'aperto non sono così popolari come in questo paese. 2. Il più popolare di essi è forse il calcio, che gli Italiani amano molto sia come giocatori che come spettatori. 3. Il gioco del calcio è antichissimo e ogni anno a Firenze giocano una partita in costume medioevale. 4. Spesso la domenica e nei giorni in cui ci sono partite interessanti, c'è un traffico molto maggiore nelle strade vicine allo stadio e molti, quando gli autobus e i tram sono molto affollati, preferiscono andare e ritornare a piedi. 5. All'interno dello stadio gli spettatori seguono con grande interesse la partita. 6. Se tutto va bene essi applaudiscono ma se, secondo loro, l'arbitro è stato ingiusto verso la squadra favorita, fischiano tanto che quelli che abitano vicino a uno stadio possono quasi seguire le diverse fasi della partita. 7. Le corse di automobili e le corse di cavalli sono tanto popolari in Italia quanto in Gran Bretagna. 8. Una corsa di cavalli molto caratteristica è quella che ha luogo due volte all'anno a Siena, chiamata il Palio. 9. Ad essa partecipano in costume i diversi quartieri della città chiamati le contrade e la corsa ha luogo nella piazza principale della città. 10. Il canottaggio e il nuoto sono anch'essi popolari e i bambini imparano molto presto a nuotare perché le spiagge scendono dolcemente in mare e anche i più piccoli possono giocare nell'acqua senza pericolo. 11. In Italia solo i ricchi giocano al golf perché ci sono pochissimi campi di golf e perché sono quasi sempre lontani dalla città e soltanto coloro che hanno una automobile possono andarci. 12. Non ogni classe di persone gioca al tennis come in Gran Bretagna e anche questo è uno sport per persone ricche. 13. Cortina d'Ampezzo e Sestrière sono tra i centri più famosi per lo sci, che ha avuto sempre maggiore sviluppo in Italia in questi ultimi anni. 14. Cortina d'Ampezzo è d'estate un centro di alpinismo e alcuni scalatori italiani sono diventati famosi per le loro scalate nelle montagne attorno a Cortina. 15. Le montagne attorno a Cortina chiamate Dolomiti, sono famose in tutto il mondo per la loro meravigliosa bellezza e per il colore rosato delle loro roccie. 16. Da Cortina, per mezzo di una filovia, gli sciatori possono arrivare in pochi minuti sulla cima del Faloria dove c'è un rifugio e di dove parte la nuova pista di sci. 17. Tutti quelli che hanno scalato le Dolomiti non dimenticheranno mai la meravigliosa bellezza di queste montagne. 18. Lo spettacolo delle cime coperte di neve contro il cielo azzurro, dei laghi di un azzurro profondo e dei piccoli rifugi lontani sulle montagne è uno dei più belli del mondo. 19. Nei numerosi rifugi delle Dolomiti gli scalatori e gli sciatori possono passare la notte prima di una scalata e trovare brave guide. 20. A volte le scalate sulle Alpi sono piene di pericoli e spesso per il cattivo tempo gli scalatori non possono né continuare la scalata né scendere, e devono passare la notte 'in parete'.

B. *Translate into Italian:* 1. Italy is one of the best countries for all lovers of outdoor sports at every season of the year. 2. Very many people go there every year, both in summer and in winter, for climbing its wonderful mountains and for skiing. 3. The best season for mountaineering in the Alps is summer when the mountain inns (or refuges) are open and climbers can spend the night there. 4. Climbers when they reach (say: arrive at) the summit forget how tired they are, so great is the beauty of nature all around. 5. Sometimes climbers cannot continue their climb and they often have to spend the night 'in parete' on the rock where they are. 6. The snow on the highest summits of the Alps, the lakes with their deep blue water and the woods full of flowers are among some of the greatest beauties of nature. 7. Cortina d'Ampezzo is a centre for mountaineers in summer too, and the surrounding mountains called the Dolomites are famous for the pinkish colour of their rocks. 8. In winter Cortina is a popular centre for skiing. There is a cable-railway by means of which those who wish to ski, arrive at the top of the mountain from which the ski-track starts. 9. Rowing and swimming are very popular sports in Italy. The beaches all along the coast are crowded in summer and they slope so gently to the sea that even very young children can play in the water without danger. 10. Car and horse races are as popular in France and in Italy as they are in our country and thousands of spectators go to watch them. 11. A very famous horse race called the Palio takes (say: has) place every year in Siena, when all the different parts of the city called 'le contrade' take part in the race in mediaeval costume in the main square. 12. Sometimes we read that the ancient Romans used to play football but even if this is not true there is certainly no more popular sport in Italy today. 13. All the large towns have their sports grounds which are packed with spectators on Sundays and on days on which there are important matches. 14. Some spectators go there by car, others use trains or buses and the traffic in all the streets surrounding the ground is so great that many people prefer to go on foot. 15. Once the match starts the spectators follow the different stages of the game with the greatest interest. 16. They cheer when their favourite side does (andare) well, or hiss if, according to them, the umpire has been unjust. 17. In Italy only the rich play golf and tennis whereas people of all classes can play both golf and tennis in this country. 18. Our golf courses are often quite near the centre of the town, but in Italy for the most part they are far away, and only those who have car(s) can play golf. 19. Many people in this country criticise those who play tennis, golf or football on Sundays, but this has always been the custom abroad. 20. Among the names of sportsmen famous throughout the world, many are those of Italians.

C. Dove posso rivolgermi per avere delle informazioni?—Where can I apply for information? Per informazioni si rivolga all'apposito sportello alla stazione o all'agenzia turistica.—For information apply to the appropriate booking office at the station or to the tourist agency. Dove posso trovare un paio di scarpe da montagna?—Where can I get a pair of climbing boots? una piccozza—an ice-axe, una buona corda—a stout rope, un bastone—a stick (alpenstock), un sacco da montagna—a rucksack. C'è un negozio di articoli sportivi qui vicino.—There is a sports outfitter near by. È un'ascensione difficile questa?—Is this one a difficult climb? Sì, è necessario prendere una guida.—Yes, one must have a guide. Quanto dura l'ascensione?—How long does the climb take? Quanti letti ci sono in quel rifugio?—How many beds does that shelter have? Quali sono le tariffe delle guide?—How much does it cost for a guide? Ci sono dei crepacci nel ghiacciaio?—Are there crevasses in the glacier? Sì, ci sono dei crepacci pericolosi in quel ghiacciaio; bisogna attraversarlo in cordata, con una guida sicura.—Yes, there are dangerous crevasses in that glacier; it must be crossed roped together with a reliable guide. Gioca a tennis, a golf lei?—Do you play tennis, golf? Vuol fare una partita?—Would you like to play a game? Non ho la racchetta, le mazze da golf con me.—I have not my racquet, golf clubs with me. Non faccio molto sport.—I do not play much in the way of games. Dove ci si spoglia quando si è al mare?—Where do people undress at the seaside? Su quasi ogni spiaggia in Italia ci sono delle cabine per spogliarsi e rivestirsi, dove si lasciano i propri vestiti, gli ombrelloni e le sedie a sdraio.—On almost every beach in Italy there are huts for undressing and dressing where people leave their clothes, their large umbrellas and deckchairs. Esse sono raggruppate in stabilimenti balneari e si possono prendere in fitto per alcune ore, per una giornata o per una settimana o per un mese o due.—In bathing establishments they are grouped together and can be hired by the hour, day, week or for a month or two. In ogni stabilimento c'è un bagnino che bada agli ombrelloni, alle sedie a sdraio, dà in affitto le barche e i sandolini e sorveglia i bagnanti perché non si spingano troppo a largo.—In all baths there is an attendant who looks after the umbrellas and deck-chairs, hires out the boats and dinghies and watches that bathers do not go too far out. La bagnina bada ai costumi e alla pulizia delle cabine.—The attendant looks after the costumes and the cleaning of the huts.

D. *Sfido*

Non l'avevo visto da molti anni. Sfido che non lo riconoscevo—I hadn't seen him for years. No wonder I didn't recognize him.

LESSON XXIII

The Subjunctive Mood

The subjunctive mood (modo congiuntivo), used in Italian much more than in English or French, expresses an action or a state not as a fact, but as possible, probable, uncertain or expedient and, most frequently, depending on another action or state expressed or understood. It is therefore used especially in subordinate clauses which depend on principal clauses—hence the name *congiuntivo*, the mood which joins two actions or states, when one wishes to convey an impression, an opinion or some conception of the mind, but never a fact.

As a result of the relationship between the two clauses, the tense of the subjunctive is regulated strictly in accordance with the tense used in the clause on which the subjunctive depends.

The subjunctive mood has four tenses; two simple: the present and the imperfect; two compound: the perfect and the past perfect, formed respectively by adding the past participle of the verb to the present and imperfect of the auxiliaries essere and avere.

Present Subjunctive of Model Verbs

che io	am-i	tεm-a	dɔrm-a
che tu	am-i	tεm-a	dɔrm-a
che egli	am-i	tεm-a	dɔrm-a
che noi	am-iamo	tem-iamo	dorm-iamo
che voi	am-iate	tem-iate	dorm-iate
che essi	am-ino	tεm-ano	dɔrm-ano

The endings of the 1st, 2nd, and 3rd persons singular are the same: *i* in the 1st conjugation and *a* in the 2nd and 3rd conjugations. The endings of the 1st and 2nd persons plural are the same in all three conjugations; the 3rd person plural differs, each keeping the characteristic vowel of the singular (am-ino, tem-ano, dorm-ano).

Present Subjunctive of 'Ɛssere' and 'Avere'

che io	sia	abbia
che tu	sia	abbia
che egli	sia	abbia
che noi	siamo	abbiamo
che voi	siate	abbiate
che essi	siano	abbiano

Perfect of Model Verbs and 'Essere' and 'Avere'

che io	abbia amato	temuto	dormito
	sia stato	abbia avuto, etc.	

Uses

Although the subjunctive is used chiefly in subordinate clauses, it is used in the following principal clauses:

(a) to express a command in the 1st person plural and in the 3rd person singular and plural:

Stia, stiano attenti.	Be careful, pay attention.
Andiamo via.	Let us go away.

(b) to express a wish or a curse:

Dio vi guardi!	May God protect you!
Cresca sana e felice!	May she grow healthy and happy!
Vadano alla malora!	Bad luck to them!

In subordinate clauses the subjunctive is used:

1. When the principal clause contains a verb expressing hope, fear, opinion, command, wish, either in the active or passive voice, provided that the subjects of the two clauses are different. If the subject is the same the verb goes in the infinitive:

Spero che egli scriva.
I hope he will write.

Temerà che essi non arrivino.
He is probably afraid that they will not come.

Non credi che esse siano ricche?
Do you not believe they are rich?

Comanda che egli parta.
Order him to leave.

Non desideriamo che Ella accetti.
We do not wish you to accept.

Dicono che tu sia intelligente.
They say you are intelligent.

Credono che egli sia povero.
They believe that he is poor.

Raccontano che egli l'abbia pagato un milione.
They say he paid a million for it.

but: Credo d'essere in ritardo.
I believe I am late.

Desidera di comprarlo subito.
He wants to buy it at once.

2. When the principal clause contains an impersonal verb: see Lesson XXV.

Sequence of Tenses

If the verb of the principal clause refers to the present or the future it is followed in the subordinate clause by the present subjunctive, when the two actions are contemporaneous, or by the perfect subjunctive, when the action expressed in the subordinate clause is past in relation to the principal verb:

Penso che dɔrma.
I think he is asleep.

Penso che abbia dormito troppo.
I think he has slept too much.

Penserà che tu parta.
He will think that you are leaving.

Penserà che tu sia partito.
He will think that you have left.

Avrà creduto che tu sia ricco.
She will have thought that you are rich.

Digli che vɛnga.
Tell him to come.

Vocabulary XXIII

ricevimento reception, party
compleanno birthday
invito invitation
invitato guest
macedonia di frutta fruit salad
farina flour
sapore (m.) flavour, taste
regalo gift, present
data date
ballo ball, dance, dancing
giɔco game, play, sport
giɔco di società parlour game
società society, community, partnership
sciarada charade
mɔdo way, manner, means
rɛsto rest, remainder, change (money)
serata evening
evening party
evening performance
mucchio heap, stack, pile
ɔspite (m. & f.) guest, host, hostess
rispɔsta answer
impegno engagement
prɛndere l'impegno to undertake
chilo kilo (2·25 lbs.)
abbastanza (adv.) enough, somewhat, fairly
inoltre (adv.) besides
accettare to accept, approve, agree to.

Exercise 1

Repeat orally the present and the perfect subjunctive of the following verbs: contare, arrivare, temere, vedere, finire, partire, essere.

Exercise 2

Supply the required form (both tenses when possible) of the subjunctive of the verb given in the infinitive and translate into English: 1. (Restare) Pensa che sua sorella . . . a casa. 2. (Essere) Temo che essi . . . spesso in ritardo. 3. (Pagare) Credi che egli . . . sempre il conto. 4. (Accettare) Egli crede che essi non . . . l'invito. 5. (Essere) Vera spera che sua cugina . . . libera. 6. (Mandare) Essa domanderà al droghiere che . . . le provviste in tempo. 7. (Essere) Temiamo che tutti i negozi . . . chiusi. 8. (Parlare) Sai se esse . . . bene l'italiano? 9. (Imparare) Suo padre vuole che Filippo . . . molte lingue. 10. (Avere) Temiamo che molti invitati . . . degli altri impegni.

Exercise 3

Translate into Italian: 1. I think there is a heap of letters on your table. 2. She does not believe he has tried. 3. He hopes she will write. 4. His mother wants him to return to school. 5. We are afraid he will leave. 6. I am glad you have arrived. 7. I think his birthday is next week. 8. She fears that the guests have not received the invitation. 9. We hope that all the gifts will be different. 10. Do you think that the flavour is good?

A. *Translate into English:* 1. La settimana prossima a casa Bruni ci sarà un ricevimento per il compleanno di Giulia. 2. Maria e Giulia scrivono gli indirizzi sugli inviti e mandano la cameriera ad imbucarli. 3. Esse temono che gli inviti non arrivino in tempo e che le loro amiche abbiano già qualche altro impegno per quella data. 4. "Credi che Vera e Luisa saranno libere il giorno prima?"—domanda Maria;—"Spero che esse ci aiutino a preparare i dolci e a mettere i fiori nei vasi." 5. "C'è abbastanza zucchero in casa?"—chiede la cameriera—"Se vogliono fare degli altri dolci bisogna che ne ordinino un chilo o due." 6. "Ordinatene di più se volete fare anche una macedonia di frutta"—osserva la signora Bruni. 7. Credo di avere ordinato la farina e il burro e spero che il droghiere mandi le uova in tempo. 8. "Credi che le uova di quel droghiere siano abbastanza fresche?"—domanda Giulia. 9. "Pensi che il mio vestito rosso sia adatto per il ricevimento?"—domanda Maria. "Se credi che non sia adatto posso domandare alla sarta di fare subito quello nuovo che porterò al ricevimento per il compleanno di Luisa." 10. L'invito al ricevimento è per le nove di sera; Maria e Giulia amano molto il ballo ed hanno invitato anche molti amici di Roberto. 11. Alle dieci e mezza ci sarà una cena fredda e poi per quelli che non amano il ballo, ci saranno dei giochi di società o delle sciarade. 12. Il gioco delle sciarade è molto divertente e Maria pensa che sia un modo intelligente di passare il resto della serata. 13. Maria e Giulia sperano che Filippo sia libero e accetti l'invito perché egli è molto bravo in questo gioco. 14. Giulia guarda la lista degli inviti e conta le persone: 20 ragazze e 19 ragazzi. 15. Ci devono essere tanti ragazzi quante ragazze per ballare e per molti dei giochi. 16. "Temo che sia difficile trovare un altro ragazzo, abbiamo già invitato tutti i miei amici"—risponde Roberto. 17. "Spero che tutti accettino l'invito; io sono sempre contenta di aiutare la mamma"—osserva Maria. 18. Una di voi deve contare i bicchieri e i piatti per vedere se ce ne sono abbastanza. 19. "Credo che ce ne siano abbastanza" —risponde Maria—"ma posso sempre telefonare alla zia e chiederle di darcene una dozzina." 20. Maria e Giulia sperano che tutte le persone che hanno invitato rispondano presto e accettino l'invito.

B. *Translate into Italian:* 1. On the 3rd of next month it will be Vera's birthday, and as usual there will be a party in the Bruni's house. 2. They sent the invitations two weeks ago and have already received many replies. 3. I hope we have not forgotten any of our friends, I cannot find the list of invitations. 4. Let us write another list and count the names. I think we invited 12 boys and 12 girls; there must be as many boys as girls for the games. 5. Vera and Philip very much hope that all their friends will accept their invitation. 6. At this time of year, however, some of their friends have other engagements. 7. "Did you send invitations to Mary and Julia?" asks Philip. No, Mother prefers to invite them by telephone because she wants to know if they are free. 8. I am glad that we have bought so many small gifts. I think we shall need them for the games. 9. I think that Vera always invites Philip's friends to her party because her brother always invites her friends to his (party). 10. Vera's mother is phoning the grocer; she had already sent him a long list, but she had forgotten one or two things she needed. 11. She wants the grocer to send the provisions as soon as possible. 12. "Do you think my white dress will be suitable for my party?" Vera asked her mother, "or must I buy a new one?" 13. I think you have worn the white dress a lot (say: many times) and you will receive invitations to other parties after your one. 14. Often the same people are (say: go) at the same parties and I prefer you not always to wear the same dress. 15. We hope that Miss Ansaldi will be free the day before (di) the party; we want her to help us to make the trifle, fruit salad and some of the sweets. 16. Vera wants her cousins Mary and Julia to help her to lay the table and put flowers in all the vases. 17. The invitation to the party is for 7.30 in the evening and for those who do not like dancing there will be parlour games. **18.** We think that one of the most amusing games is (that of) charades. **19.** It can be quite an intelligent way of spending an hour; we shall put a pile of old clothes in the cupboard in the hall and our guests will take what they need for the charade. **20.** We shall have a cold supper at about 9 o'clock; there will be cold meat, salad, sandwiches, fruit salad, sweets and trifle.

C. Quanti sensi abbiamo?—How many senses have we? Abbiamo cinque sensi—la vista, l'udito, l'olfatto, il gusto e il tatto.—We have five senses—sight, hearing, smell, taste and touch. Da che organi dipendono i sensi?—On what organs do our senses depend? La vista dagli occhi—sight on the eyes. L'udito dagli orecchi—hearing on the ears. L'olfatto dal naso—smell on the nose. E il gusto dalla lingua e dal palato—and taste on the tongue and palate. E il tatto da che organi dipende?—And what about touch? Il tatto è diffuso in tutto il corpo ma noi tocchiamo gli oggetti principalmente con le mani.—The sense of touch is distributed throughout the body, but we touch things mainly with our hands. Che facciamo con gli occhi?—What do we do with our eyes? Con gli occhi guardiamo, vediamo, fissiamo, esaminiamo, osserviamo, ammiriamo gli oggetti.—With our eyes we look at, see, gaze at, examine, observe, and admire things. E con gli orecchi?—And with our ears? Udiamo, sentiamo i rumori, i suoni; ascoltiamo un discorso, una musica, una canzone.—We hear, are conscious of noises and sounds; we listen to talking, music and songs. Che facciamo con il naso?—What do we do with our noses? Con il naso odoriamo i profumi, gli odori, e gli animali fiutano.—With our noses we smell perfumes and smells, and animals sniff with theirs. E come funziona il gusto?—And how does taste work? Quando mettiamo un cibo in bocca ne gustiamo il sapore. —When we put food in our mouths we relish the taste of it. Che cosa facciamo con le mani?—What do we do with our hands? Con le mani tocchiamo gli oggetti e sentiamo se la loro superficie è ruvida o liscia, calda o fredda, soffice, morbida o dura.—We touch things with our hands and feel if their surface is rough or smooth, hot or cold, yielding, soft or hard. Come si chiama chi non vede? Cieco.—How do we describe people who cannot see? Blind. Chi non sente?—Those who do not hear? Sordo—deaf. Chi non può parlare è muto.—A person who cannot speak is dumb. Si dice che una persona non ha tatto quando dice delle cose a sproposito offendendo senza volerlo la persona con cui parla. —We say a person has no tact when he blunders unwittingly in conversation thereby offending the person without meaning to do so. Che cosa usiamo per vedere meglio?—What do we use in order to see better? Per vedere molti portano gli occhiali.—Many people wear glasses in order to see. Chi sono i miopi?—Who are shortsighted? Quelli che non vedono bene da lontano.—Those who do not see well at a distance. E i presbiti?—And the longsighted? Quelli che non vedono bene da vicino.—Those who do not see well close up. A teatro per vedere che cosa si adopera? Si usa il binocolo.—To see well at the theatre what do we use? Opera glasses. E gli astronomi, cosa usano per guardare le stelle?—And what do astronomers use to look at the stars? I telescopi—Telescopes. In Italiano si dice "Non c'è peggior sordo di chi non vuol sentire."—There is an Italian saying that no one is deafer than he who does not wish to hear Di qualunque cosa si gusti con i cinque sensi si può chiedere—Ti piace?—Whatever one apprehends with the five senses can be discussed in terms of "Do you like it?"

D. *To'*! or *Toh*! (apocopation of togli)

To'! Prɛndi questo libro e mettilo sullo scaffale—Here! Take this book and put it on the shelf.

Toh! Guarda chi si vede!—Heavens! Look who is here!

LESSON XXIV

Subjunctive Mood (*Continued*)

Imperfect Subjunctive of Model Verbs

che io	am-assi	tem-essi	dorm-issi
che tu	am-assi	tem-essi	dorm-issi
che egli	am-asse	tem-esse	dorm-isse
che noi	am-assimo	tem-essimo	dorm-issimo
che voi	am-aste	tem-este	dorm-iste
che essi	am-assero	tem-essero	dorm-issero

Bearing in mind the characteristic vowel of each conjugation (*a, e, i*), the endings of the imperfect subjunctive are alike in all three conjugations.

Imperfect Subjunctive of 'Ɛssere' and 'Avere'

che io	fossi	avessi
che tu	fossi	avessi
che egli	fosse	avesse
che noi	fossimo	avessimo
che voi	foste	aveste
che essi	fossero	avessero

Compound Tenses: Past Perfect of Model Verbs and of 'Ɛssere' and 'Avere'

Past Perfect: che io avessi amato   temuto   dormito
fossi stato   avessi avuto, etc.

Sequence of Tenses

If the verb of the main clause, or the clause on which the subjunctive depends, refers to the past or implies doubt (expressed by a conditional tense), it is followed in the subordinate clause by the imperfect subjunctive, when the two actions are contemporaneous, or by the past perfect subjunctive when the action of the subordinate clause is past in relation to that verb.

Temεvano che non venisse.
They feared that he was not coming.

Temεvano che non fosse venuto.
They feared that he had not come.

Pensò che partisse.
She thought that he was leaving.

Pensò che fosse partito.
She thought that he had left.

Temerɛi che non lo trovassero.
I should fear that they would not find him.

Non avrɛi creduto che lo desiderasse.
I should not have thought that he wanted it.

but: Desideravo vederlo. I wanted to see him.
Potrɛi conservarlo? Could I keep it?

The following table summarizes the division of tenses.

Tenses referring to the Present and Future	Tenses referring to the Past and With Doubt
Present Indicative	Imperfect Indicative
Future Indicative	Past Absolute
Future Perfect Indicative	Past Perfect Indicative
Imperative	Present Conditional
	Perfect Conditional

The present perfect, because of its connections with the present is treated, mostly, as a present tense.

Sometimes a present tense is found in the principal clause and a past tense in the dependent clause:

Non ti pare che gli antichi vivessero meglio di noi?
Don't you think that long ago people lived better than we do?

This happens when the dependent action has no connection with the present, having taken place at a much earlier time.

Compound Nouns

The plural forms of compound words vary according to the elements of which the words are composed; they may be divided into the following groups.

1. Compound words comprising an adjective (first) and a noun (second), or two adjectives, form the plural by changing only the second part.

il francobollo, i francobolli = the postage stamp(s)
il bassorilievo, i bassorilievi = the bas-relief(s)
il pianoforte, i pianoforti = the piano(s)

2. Compound words comprising a noun (first) and an adjective (second) form the plural by changing both parts.

l'acquaforte, le acqueforti = the etching(s)
il caposaldo, i capisaldi = the stronghold(s)

3. Compound words comprising two nouns: if both the nouns are of the same gender, the plural is formed by changing only the second;

il capolavoro, i capolavori = the masterpiece(s)
il pomodoro, i pomodori = the tomato(es);

if the nouns are of different genders, only the first changes.

il capostazione, i capistazione = the station master(s)

4a. Compound words comprising a verb and a plural noun are invariable.

il cambiavalute, i cambiavalute = the money-changer(s)
il portalettere, i portalettere = the postman (postmen)

4b. Compound words comprising a verb, or an invariable part of speech (adverb or preposition), and a single masculine noun, form the plural by changing only the noun.

il passaporto, i passaporti = the passport(s)
il dopopranzo, i dopopranzi = the afternoon(s)
il sottaceto, i sottaceti = the pickle(s)

this group also contains, as an exception, compound words containing mano, mani = hand(s)

l'asciugamano, gli asciugamani = the towel(s)

4c. Compound words comprising a verb, or an invariable part of speech (adverb or preposition), and a single feminine noun, are invariable when the gender of the compound word is masculine:

il cavalcavia, i cavalcavia = the over-bridge(s)
il retroterra, i retroterra = the rear area(s)

when the gender of the compound word is feminine, the noun forms the feminine plural.

la retroguardia, le retroguardie = the rearguard(s)

5. Compound words comprising two verbs, or a verb and an adverb, are invariable.

il dormiveglia, i dormiveglia = dozing (half asleep, half awake)

Vocabulary XXIV

pɔrto port
***i*sola** island
ind*u*stria industry (adj: **industriale**)
eruzione (f.) eruption
confettura jam
pomodɔro tomato
costruzioni navali (f.plu.) shipbuilding
corallo coral
tartaruga tortoiseshell
gɔlfo bay, gulf
vulcano volcano
villa villa
distruzione (f.) destruction
aranceto orange grove
lava lava
strato layer
cɛnere (f.) ashes, cinders
lapilli (m. plu.) small fragments of lava
sɛcolo century
archeɔlogo archaeologist
vita life
edi*fi*cio building
detto saying
capolavoro masterpiece
manoscritto manuscript
cons*i*glio advice

movimento movement
canzone (f.) song
artista (m. & f.) artist
influɛnza influence, influenza
architettura architecture
vitalità vitality
N*a*poli Naples (adj. **napoletano**)
Virg*i*lio Virgil
Gr*e*cia Greece
Ercolano Herculaneum
Pompei Pompeii
Ves*u*vio Vesuvius
Camp*a*nia Campania
fɛsta festival
dɔnna woman
infɛrno hell, inferno
sibilla sibyl
collina hill, height
Rinascimento Renaissance
Paesto Paestum
commerciale (adj.) commercial
rumoroso (adj.) noisy
nazionale (adj.) national
fɛrtile (adj.) fertile (n. **fertilità**)
compɔsto composed
protetto protected
in isc*a*tola tinned
dopo Cristo A.D.
a picco abruptly
descr*i*vere to describe
dominare to dominate
sɔrgere to rise, stand
ricostruire* to reconstruct
odiare to hate (n. **odio**)
perm*e*ttere to allow
cantare to sing
Enea (m.) Aeneas
Eneide (f.) the Aeneid

Exercise 1

Repeat orally the imperfect and past perfect subjunctive of the following verbs: conservare, accettare, vedere, finire, attraversare, servire, disegnare demolire, sapere, asciugare, bussare, credere.

Exercise 2

Supply required form (*both tenses when possible*) *of the subjunctive of verbs given in infinitive and translate into English:* 1. (finire) Essi temevano che il babbo . . . troppo tardi. 2. (osservare) Sperava che egli . . . il suo vestito. 3. (essere) Pensavi che il velluto . . . di moda? 4. (portare) Domandò che il ragazzo . . . i pantaloni a casa. 5. (avere) Credevate che essi . . . un assortimento più grande? 6. (visitare) Avrei preferito che essi . . . la chiesa prima. 7. (demolire) Temeva che . . . la basilica. 8. (disegnare) Volevo che egli . . . la facciata del museo. 9. (essere) Pensavo che . . . impossibile continuare il lavoro. 10. (essere) Egli non sapeva che il negozio . . . chiuso.

Exercise 3

Translate into Italian: 1. Were you afraid that she had not understood? 2. He ordered that he should leave at once. 3. Did you think that they had not received the parcel? 4. She did not believe he had come back. 5. Did you want him to write to me? 6. He did not wish them to pay the bill. 7. We were glad that you did not need his help. 8. Were you afraid she had bought the book? 9. I thought they had knocked at the door. 10. I wanted them to play with me.

Exercise 4

Form the plural of the following nouns: melagrana (f.) = pomegranate; retrovia (m.) = rear area; cantastorie (m.) = story teller; capobanda (m.) = ringleader; chiaroscuro (m.) = chiaroscuro; biancospino (m.) = hawthorn; purosangue (m.) = thoroughbred; sordomuto (m.) = deafmute; acquaforte (f.) = etching; caposaldo (m.) = stronghold; cacciavite (m.) = screwdriver (vite (f.) = screw); sottaceto (m.) = pickle; terracotta (f.) = terracotta; salvagente (m.) = lifebelt; guardaroba (m.) = cloakroom; scioglilingua (m.) = tongue-twister; lungotevere (m.) = street along the banks of the river Tiber; capoluogo (m.) = county town; battimano (m.) = handclap.

A. *Translate into English:* 1. Napoli è una delle città più belle d'Italia e tutti conoscono il detto popolare "Vedi Napoli e poi muori". 2. Essa sorge sul golfo dello stesso nome—uno dei più belli del mondo—dominato dal Vesuvio, il vulcano che tante volte ha portato la distruzione nei paeselli che sorgono ai suoi piedi. 3. Le campagne circostanti però devono alla lava del Vesuvio la loro meravigliosa fertilità. 4. Nel golfo di Napoli sorgono dal mare azzurrissimo le incantevoli isole di Capri, Ischia e Procida dove ogni anno migliaia di forestieri passano le loro vacanze. 5. Le coste della Campania sono alte e rocciose e i bellissimi paesi di Positano, Sorrento e Lavello sorgono sulla roccia che scende a picco nel mare di un azzurro meraviglioso. 6. Napoli fu anticamente città greca, poi romana e il museo nazionale conserva magnifiche statue e vasi, capolavori di questi periodi. 7. Chi desidera avere un'idea della vita nei tempi romani deve visitare Pompei, Ercolano e Stabia che nel 79 D.C. una eruzione del Vesuvio coprì di molti strati di lava, cenere o lapilli. 8. Gli archeologi hanno ricostruito dagli oggetti, i vasi, i mobili e le tombe trovate in queste città la vita dei suoi abitanti. 9. Nei Campi Flegrei, vicino alla città di Napoli, gli antichi credevano fosse l'ingresso dell'Inferno, e Virgilio ne parla nell'Eneide, quando Enea scende nell'Inferno per vedere suo padre. 10. A Cuma secondo gli antichi abitava la Sibilla che con i suoi consigli aiutava la gente che aveva dei problemi. 11. Le principali industrie di Napoli sono le costruzioni navali, l'industria dei pomodori e delle confetture in iscatola, della pasta e, lungo la costa, del corallo e della tartaruga. 12. Ogni anno le canzoni composte per la Festa di Piedigrotta a Napoli, canzoni che cantano la bellezza della città o delle donne amate o odiate, diventano famose in tutto il mondo. 13. I Napoletani amano tutti cantare e al teatro San Carlo, uno dei più importanti d'Italia, c'è ogni anno una famosa stagione d'opera. 14. Un'altra specialità napoletana, famosa quasi quanto le sue canzoni, è la pizza napoletana che deve essere assaggiata a Napoli. 15. Molti posti nella città come Santa Lucia, il Vomero, Posillipo, Marechiaro sono diventati famosi per le canzoni che ne cantano la bellezza. 16. Sulla collina del Vomero vi sono bellissime ville con meravigliosi giardini e aranceti. 17. Molti pensano che i Napoletani amino soltanto 'il dolce far niente' ma molti di essi sono industriosi e lavorano molto. 18. Essi amano il sole e il clima dolce della loro città che permette loro di passare molte ore della loro giornata all'aperto. 19. Nelle strade di Napoli spesso strette e rumorose c'è sempre un gran movimento mentre molti, seduti dinanzi alla porta della loro casa o sui balconi, guardano il traffico o parlano con i vicini. 20. Quando guardiamo le chiese e i palazzi vediamo che il Rinascimento ebbe meno influenza su gli edifici e sull'architettura di questa città che in altre città italiane.

B. *Translate into Italian:* 1. Naples, principal city of Campania, is with her large port one of the great industrial centres of Italy. 2. Tinned tomatoes, jams, shipbuilding and, along the coast, coral and tortoiseshell are among the industries for which Naples is noted. 3. But first let us describe the natural beauty of the city which is one of the most beautiful in the whole of Italy. 4. The city overlooks (sorge su) the magnificent bay of Naples, protected by the enchanting islands of Ischia, Procida and Capri. 5. Inland is a rich plain dominated by the volcano Vesuvius which is about 4,000 feet high. 6. Built on the smaller heights of Posillipo and Vomero there are some beautiful villas whose gardens and orange groves are very fertile because of the lava from Vesuvius. 7. Vesuvius has sometimes brought ruin to thousands of people but it has also at the same time preserved in Pompeii and Herculaneum under layers of ashes and lapilli, houses, furniture, vases and tombs of the first century A.D. 8. Archaeologists can reconstruct the lives of the inhabitants of these ancient towns with their villas, public buildings, streets and squares. 9. The earliest (primi) inhabitants of Pompeii and Herculaneum were Greeks and Vesuvius has preserved in their houses, vases, objects and pictures in which we see the Greek influence. 10. In the National Museum of Naples there are masterpieces of ancient sculpture, while Greek and Roman manuscripts found in Pompeii and Herculaneum are in the museums of many countries. 11. In yet another town, Paestum, near Naples, there are three Greek temples very well preserved and in no way inferior to those which we can still admire in Greece. 12. There are other interesting ruins at Cuma where, according to the ancients, the Sibyl helped people with her advice: and the ruins of some famous villas in one of which are the ashes of Virgil. 13. In Naples however, perhaps more than in other Italian cities visitors can feel the great vitality of the people and even to watch them in the noisy streets helps us to understand them. 14. The climate of

Naples from April to December is excellent and the people spend many hours of the day in the open. The narrow streets are always full of movement and life. 15. They say that the Neapolitans love doing nothing (dolce far niente) but they can also be very industrious. 16. Neapolitans love to sing especially arias (romanze) from famous operas, and from the poor people to (sino a) the greatest Italian artistes at the famous San Carlo theatre, they all sing. 17. Songs composed each year for the festival of Piedigrotta will be famous for that year not only in Italy but in distant lands. 18. The commercial centre of the town with its narrow old streets comprises most of mediaeval Naples. 19. Among other buildings of the same period are the Castel dell'Uovo and the Castel Nuovo. 20. The Renaissance had less influence on the architecture and buildings in Naples than in other famous Italian cities.

C. Come è stata chiamata l'Italia?—What has Italy been called? L'Italia è stata chiamata da scrittori e poeti il giardino d'Europa.—Italy has been called the Garden of Europe by writers and poets. Che forma ha l'Italia?—What shape is Italy? L'Italia è una penisola a forma di uno stivale.—Italy is a peninsula shaped like a boot. Che mare bagna le sue coste?—What sea bathes its coasts? Il mare Mediterraneo che prende diversi nomi: Mar Tirreno a Ovest, mar Ionio a Sud, mare Adriatico a Est.—The Mediterranean which takes on several names: the Tyrrhenian sea to the west, the Ionian sea to the south, the Adriatic to the east. Come chiamarono i Romani il mare Mediterraneo?—What did the Romans call the Mediterranean?—Lo chiamarono Mare Nostrum.—They called it "Our Sea". Quante catene di monti ci sono in Italia?—How many ranges of mountains are there in Italy? Due catene di monti ne costituiscono il confine e la spina dorsale: le Alpi e gli Appennini.—Two mountain ranges constitute its boundary and its back-bone: the Alps and the Apennines. Quali sono i monti più importanti nelle Alpi?—Which are the most important of the Alps? Le Alpi comprendono alcuni tra i monti più alti e maestosi d'Europa, quali il Monte Bianco, il Cervino, il Monte Rosa e il gruppo delle Dolomiti.—The Alps include some of the highest and most majestic mountains in Europe such as Mont Blanc, the Matterhorn, Mount Rosa and the Dolomite group. Dove sono gli Appennini? Gli Appennini staccandosi dal golfo Ligure dividono l'Italia longitudinalmente in tutta la sua lunghezza proseguendo anche nell'isola di Sicilia una volta attaccata al continente.—Where are the Apennines? The Apennines stretching from the gulf of Liguria divide Italy lengthwise throughout continuing even into the island of Sicily which at one time was part of the mainland. Quali altre isole importanti ha l'Italia?—What other important islands belong to Italy? Altre isole sono la Sardegna, la Corsica (che appartiene politicamente alla Francia), le isole dell'arcipelago Toscano tra cui Elba, ora meta di molti turisti, e famose per la loro bellezza, Capri e Ischia nel golfo di Napoli.—Other important islands are Sardinia, Corsica (which belongs to France), the islands of the Tuscan archipelago among which is Elba, now a tourist centre, and famous for their beauty Capri and Ischia in the bay of Naples. L'Italia ha molti fiumi?—Has Italy many rivers? L'Italia è più ricca di fiumi nel Nord che nel Sud.—Italy has more rivers in the north than in the south. Tra i laghi più conosciuti ci sono il lago Maggiore, il lago di Lugano, il lago di Como, il lago d'Iseo e il lago di Garda, ma nelle Alpi ci sono anche laghetti di incantevole bellezza come i laghi di Carezza e di Misurina.—Among the best known lakes are Lake Maggiore, Lake Lugano, Lake Como, Lake Iseo, Lake Garda, but in the Alps there are also many little lakes enchanting in their beauty such as Carezza and Misurina.

D. *Be*'! or *Beh*! (apocopation of bene)

Perché non sei venuto? Be', mi è stato impossibile.
Why didn't you come? Well, I just couldn't.
Beh, che te ne pare?—Well, what do you think?

LESSON XXV

Impersonal Verbs

In English, impersonal verbs are defined merely as verbs which take 'it' for their subject, and are followed, except in expressions concerning the weather, by a personal pronoun object which in personal verbs would be the subject. In English all such verbs are 3rd person singular:

It grieves *me* to hear this = *I* am grieved to hear this.

Impersonal verbs in Italian are more complicated, but fall into three groups.

1. Verbs referring to the weather:

Piɔve—it rains (piɔvere); nevica—it is snowing (nevicare); tuona—there is thunder (tuonare); lampeggia—there is lightning (lampeggiare); grandina—it hails (grandinare); gela—it freezes (gelare); tira vɛnto—it is windy (tirare).

These can be conjugated with *ɛssere* or *avere*, the latter especially to stress duration of action.

Expressions such as: fa freddo—it is cold; faceva caldo—it was hot; farà bɛl tɛmpo—it will be fine; fa nɔtte—night is approaching; fa giorno—day is breaking; etc., are impersonal and are conjugated always with *avere*.

2. The verb *ɛssere* (3rd pers. sing.) followed by an adjective:

è necessario—it is necessary; è probabile—it is likely; è facile—it is likely.

These impersonal expressions are normally followed in Italian by a clause, whose verb must be in the subjunctive mood, if the person for whom it would be useful, likely, etc., is mentioned:

Sarɛbbe utile che egli scrivesse.	It would be useful for him to write.
È probabile che tu lo trovi.	It is likely that you will find it.
È facile che noi partiamo.	It is likely that we shall leave.

But they are followed immediately by the infinitive in Italian if they are followed immediately by the infinitive in English:

Sarà difficile vederlo.	It will be difficult to see him.
Sarɛbbe inutile scrivere.	It would be useless to write.

3. Verbs expressing necessity, need, opportunity, conjecture, etc., though frequently personal in English are often impersonal in Italian and are followed either by a dependent clause whose verb is in the subjunctive or by an infinitive as in the preceding group.

These verbs are conjugated with *ɛssere*:

bisogna (bisognare) }
occorre (occorrere) } it is necessary
conviɛne (convenire) it is fitting
pare (parere) }
sembra (sembrare) } it seems, appears
accade (accadere) }
succɛde (succɛdere) } it happens, occurs
avviene (avvenire) }
impɔrta (importare) it matters
basta (bastare) it is enough.

Bisognerɛbbe che tu ci andassi.
You would need to go.

Occorreva che egli scrivesse.
He had to write.

Pare che sia stato premiato.
It appears that he has been rewarded.

Non impɔrta che egli lo paghi subito.
It does not matter if he pays for it at once.

Bisogna pulirlo.
It is necessary to clean it.

Occorreva studiarli.
It was necessary to study them.

These same verbs, and a few others such as *piacere*—to please, *dispiacere*—to displease, *rincrescere*—to regret, always in the 3rd person singular have sometimes an indirect object expressing the person to whom it appears, happens, etc. They follow the same rules:

Ti impɔrta che egli lo venda?
Does it matter to you if he sells it?

Gli pareva che avessero capito.
It seemed to him that they had understood.

Mi basta che essa lo pɛnsi.
It is enough for me that she thinks it.

Mi bastava guardarlo.
It was enough for me to look at it.

Mi piace vederlo.
I am glad to see him.

Mi rincresce che tu parta.
I am sorry you are leaving.

Gli dispiaceva che essi non venissero.
He was sorry that they would not come.

Note: These same verbs can be used personally as in English with a subject in the 3rd person plural as well as singular:

Ci occorrono dei guanti.	We need gloves.
Molte cose accadono inaspettatamente.	Many things happen unexpectedly.
Essi parevano stanchi.	They seemed tired.
Vi sɛrvono delle scarpe?	Do you need shoes?
A che gli sɛrve?	What does he need it for?

Vocabulary XXV

temperatura temperature
temporale (m.) storm (adj. secular)
n*e*bbia fog, haze, mist
piɔggia rain (adj. **piovoso**)
gr*a*ndine (f.) hail
n*u*vola cloud (adj. **nuv*o*loso**)
pianura plain, open plain
monte (m.) mountain, bulk
raccɔlto crop, harvest
argomento subject, theme, topic
vɛrbo verb
conversazione (f.) conversation, talk
zɛro zero
mite (adj.) mild, gentle, moderate
violɛnto (adj.) violent
fitto (adj.) thick, dense
soffocante (adj.) suffocating, stifling, oppressive
moderato (adj.) moderate
piac*e*vole (adj.) pleasant, agreeable
brɛve (adj.) short, brief
tra brɛve shortly
sereno (adj.) clear, cloudless
frequɛnte (adj.) frequent
di frequɛnte frequently
però (adv.) however, but, yet
eccɛtto (adv.) except
specialmente (adv.) especially
coprire to cover
rovinare to ruin
soffiare to blow, blow out
rɛndere to make
diluviare to pour with rain

Exercise 1

Translate into Italian. 1. It has been fine all week. 2. Is it very hot? No there is a light wind. 3. Do you think it will rain tomorrow? 4. It is not raining today because it is too windy. 5. It had been snowing all day. 6. In summer there is often thunder and lightning. 7. It often freezes when night is approaching. 8. It is hotter in Italy in summer than in England. 9. Our climate is fairly moderate but it is often cold. 10. When it rains the sky is frequently very cloudy.

Exercise 2

Translate into Italian: 1. It will be necessary to study a great deal. 2. It will not be easy for us to write at once. 3. It was difficult for him to forget it. 4. It is likely that they will arrive in time. 5. It is amusing to look at old magazines. 6. It will be interesting (di) to meet them. 7. It was not possible for her to attend the university. 8. It is pleasant to visit beautiful cities. 9. Would it be prudent to leave so soon? 10. It is wonderful that she has returned so soon.

Exercise 3

Translate into Italian: (a) 1. You must study more. 2. It is fitting that you depart at once. 3. It seems that he understands. 4. It will be necessary to change them. 5. I often happen to meet him. 6. It seemed that he knew us. 7. It would be useful if they took him home. 8. Is it essential for you to stay here? 9. It frequently happened that he arrived late. 10. It does not matter that he is not intelligent.

(b) 1. It seems to me that she likes dancing. 2. It was enough for me to see it. 3. It does not matter to me if you leave her. 4. Does it suit you that he is arriving tonight? 5. It suits him (di) to travel by train. 6. I think (di) I know her. 7. It is enough for me that she has understood. 8. Did it matter to him that she was ill? 9. I am sorry (di) I am late. 10. I am sorry she is not at home.

(c) 1. We need some handkerchiefs. 2. Does she seem intelligent to you? 3. I do not like her clothes. 4. We like charades. 5. Do you like modern paintings? 6. They seem very kind. 7. What is this used for? 8. Mistakes happen frequently. 9. She seemed so good. 10. He needed new gloves.

A. *Translate into English:* 1. In Italia il clima è migliore che in Gran Bretagna. 2. Non piove tanto quanto in Inghilterra e la temperatura è più mite. 3. In alcuni luoghi non nevica quasi mai e d'estate per lunghi periodi non piove affatto. 4. Vi sono però a volte violenti temporali: lampeggia, tuona e grandina violentemente. 5. Molto spesso se non piove i raccolti sono poveri, se grandina, la grandine rovina i raccolti. 6. Il cielo è quasi sempre sereno e le nuvole o la nebbia non coprono quasi mai il suo bell'azzurro. 7. Le pioggie sono molto più frequenti d'inverno che d'estate e solo la neve che copre le cime dei monti resta tutto l'inverno. 8. In Italia la gente non pensa che il tempo sia un argomento di conversazione così interessante come in Inghilterra. 9. Quando fa quasi sempre bel tempo è difficile trovare qualche cosa da dire sull'argomento eccetto "Che bella giornata." 10. Nelle Alpi però, specialmente d'inverno, fa molto freddo e la temperatura scende spesso molti gradi sotto zero. 11. In alcune città dell'interno il clima è peggiore che in Inghilterra. 12. D'inverno a Milano e in tutta la pianura del Po c'è molto spesso una fitta nebbia e fa molto freddo. 13. D'estate fa un caldo soffocante e la temperatura arriva sino a 38, 39 gradi, 102 della scala Fahrenheit. 14. Lungo le coste invece, il clima, tanto d'estate che d'inverno, è più moderato e più piacevole che nell'interno. 15. Le stagioni migliori per andare in Italia, specialmente per le persone a cui non piace il caldo, sono la primavera e l'autunno. 16. In questi periodi è meglio andare in posti meno conosciuti perché gli alberghi migliori sono quasi sempre molto affollati. 17. Gli alberghi fanno anche prezzi differenti nella stagione bassa e nella stagione alta ma tanto nell'una che nell'altra la cucina è ottima. 18. Spesso quando siamo in Inghilterra guardiamo nei giornali le temperature massime e minime in Italia per vedere se fa più freddo o più caldo. 19. Fa freddo, fa caldo, piove, diluvia, tira vento, grandina, lampeggia, tuona, c'è molta nebbia, sono i verbi che usiamo quando parliamo del tempo. 20. Quando nevica ci piace di guardare la neve che scende fitta fitta e copre di un bianco lenzuolo le strade, gli alberi e le case.

B. *Translate into Italian:* 1. In Britain, where there is so much sport, the weather is a very important topic of conversation. 2. It seems to us that our climate is never either too hot or too cold, even if the weather often changes. 3. It is colder in (the) hill(s) and in mountain(s) than in (the) plain(s), but even in winter it is never as cold as in the Alps as we do not have any mountains as high as them. 4. In the Alps in winter the temperature is often several degrees below zero. 5. Warm winds from the sea make the climate of many of our towns mild and even in the interior it is never very cold in England. 6. Dense clouds often cover the sky: in summer the sun would be too strong without these clouds and in winter they are like a blanket which helps to keep us warm. 7. While the heat can be stifling sometimes in London we never have violent storms such as there are in Italy. 8. Too much rain ruins the crops, but they are also poor if it does not rain at all. 9. We think that the best seasons of the year to go to Italy are spring and autumn and thousands of visitors go there every year at those times. 10. My sister who likes French and Italian cooking wishes to go to Italy for her holidays and it is likely that we shall go there together next summer. 11. When we go abroad for our holidays we should like to stay longer and we are always sorry to return home. 12. In English schools summer holidays are shorter than in Italy and when we leave, it always seems to us that the time has passed too quickly. 13. Usually in November it is cold and here its often thick fog but this year even the winter has been mild. 14. Last week it snowed a little; usually it does not snow before January. We do not often have a 'white Christmas'. 15. Yesterday there was lightning and a violent wind was blowing and there was very little traffic on (per) the roads. 16. Some friends had invited us to their home. Their house is (a) 6 miles from the main road and we must always go there by (in) car. 17. My sister drove the car and at times it was necessary for her to go very slowly because it was very windy and it poured with rain. 18. In the afternoon however it was sunny and our friends asked us if we wanted to go for a walk on the hills. 19. When we returned home we had (prendere) a cup of tea near the fire (say: near the fireplace) and the main topic of conversation was the weather and the crops. 20. Rain, snow, hail, clouds and winds are much more important for our friends than for us who live in town.

C. Gli stranieri si meravigliano molto quando vengono in Inghilterra a vedere come la maggior parte delle case in un paese che essi considerano molto più freddo dell'Italia non abbiano termosifone.—When foreigners arrive in England they marvel to see the majority of houses in a country which they consider much colder than Italy, without central heating. In Italia nelle città quasi tutte le case ora hanno il termosifone e, se c'è un caminetto nel salotto, vi si brucia solo legna. Almost all houses in Italian towns now have central heating, and if there is a fire-place in the sitting-room wood only is burned. È per questo che gli stranieri sentono maggiormente la differenza del clima.—It is for this reason too that foreigners notice the difference in climate all the more. Che tempaccio!—What beastly weather! E quello che più sorprende e annoia gli stranieri sono gli improvvisi rovesci d'acqua che in Italia si verificano solo in marzo, il mese pazzo, l'unico in cui i continui cambiamenti di tempo e di temperatura somiglino al tempo mutabile e incostante che dà tanta materia e varietà di espressioni alle conversazioni britanniche.—And another thing that surprises and annoys foreigners are the sudden downpours of rain that in Italy happen only in March, the mad month when alone constant changes of weather and temperature are like the changeable and unreliable weather which provides so many and varied expressions in conversation in Britain. Che freddo!—how cold! che caldo!—how hot! opprimente—depressing; soffocante—suffocating; umido—damp; che pioggia dirotta!—what a downpour!; fitta—dense; insistente—persistent; un vento freddo —a cold wind; tagliente—cutting; penetrante—piercing; un vento caldo e umido—a clammy (warm and damp) wind; nevischio—sleet; una nebbia fitta—a dense fog; una caligine—a thick mist; raffiche di vento—gusts of wind; una grandinata violenta—a violent hail-storm; una nevicata—a snow-storm; una gelata—frost; la bruma—thick mist; fango—mud;

strade fangose—muddy streets; infangarsi—to be spattered with mud; scivolare—to slide, slip.

D. *Non mancarci altro*

Pɔsso lavarlo io? Non ci mancherɛbbe altro!

Can I wash it for you? Certainly not! (it would be taking advantage of your kindness).

LESSON XXVI

The Subjunctive Mood (*Continued*)

The subjunctive mood is also used in a number of dependent clauses, other than the noun clauses we have already explained. Every such clause, whether introduced by the relative *che* or by certain conjunctions, continues to denote something uncertain or indeterminate, or to reflect an opinion or an attitude of mind, or to supply certain circumstances such as aim, manner, concession, etc. which have a bearing on the main statement, restricting its general application and thereby lessening its matter-of-factness.

Among such subordinate clauses are those denoting:

1. *Aim or purpose*, introduced by: *affinché, acciocché, perché*—in order that:

   Lo chiamò perché aiutasse nel lavoro.
   She called him in order that he might help in the work.

2. *Concession*, introduced by: *benché, quantunque, sebbɛne, per quanto*—although; *nonostante che, malgrado che*—in spite of the fact that:

   Sebbɛne fosse in ritardo camminava lentamente.
   Although he was late he was walking slowly.

3. *Manner*, introduced by *comunque*—however, *quasi*—as if, *come se*—as if, *sɛnza che*—without:

   Comunque risponda gli sarò sempre riconoscɛnte.
   However he answers, I shall always be grateful to him.

   Egli mi guardava come se mi conoscesse.
   He looked at me as if he knew me.

   Essa mandò l'invito sɛnza che sua sorɛlla lo sapesse.
   She sent the invitation without her sister knowing.

4. *Time*, but only when introduced by: *prima che*—before and *finché*—until (referring to the future):

   Preparò il pranzo prima che arrivassero.
   She prepared the lunch before they arrived.

   L'aspetteremo finché arrivi.
   We shall wait for her until she arrives.

5. *Condition*, introduced by: *dato che*—given; *se pure*—even if; *quando*

—when[1]; *purché*—provided that; *a meno che non*—unless; *tranne che*—except; *nel caso che*—in case:

Vi aiuterò purché siate discreti.
I shall help you provided that you are discreet.

Lo comprerò domani a meno che non l'abbiano venduto.
I'll buy it tomorrow unless they have already sold it.

The subjunctive is also used:

6. in clauses following a comparative, when the implied negative must be expressed[2]:

Ritornò più presto che non lo aspettassimo.
He returned sooner than we expected.

7. in clauses introduced by: *chiunque*—whoever; *dovunque*—wherever; *qualunque*—whichever, *qualunque cosa*—whatever, *qualsiasi*—whichever:

Chiunque arrivi non sono in casa. Whoever comes, I am not at home.

8. in clauses expressing an indirect question, or an indirect statement when the verb of the main clause is negative or interrogative:

Domandò se il dottore fosse ritornato.
He asked if the doctor had returned.

Non sapevo che egli fosse malato.
I did not know that he was ill.

Ti spiegò dove fossero andati?
Did he explain to you where they had gone?

9. in relative clauses which:

(a) restrict the application of the noun:

Aiuta ogni persona che ne abbia bisogno.
He helps everyone who needs it.

(b) in relative clauses following a relative superlative and the words: *primo*—first, *ultimo*—last, *unico*, *solo*—only:

È la più bella donna che conosca.
She is the most beautiful woman I know.

È l'unico che mi abbia aiutato.
He is the only one who has helped me.

(c) in relative clauses depending on a negation such as: *niente*, *nulla*—nothing; *nessuno*—no-one:

Non c'è nessuno che mi capisca. There is no-one who understands me.

[1] When *quando* means purely "when" and not "at such time as", it is followed by the indicative.

[2] Note other idiomatic uses of *Non*: A meno che non approviate—unless you approve; Sin a quando tu non abbia imparato—until you have learned.

Subjunctive and Conditional Moods in Conditional Sentences

When the possibility of an action being fulfilled is subject to a condition referring to the future, it can be expressed in Italian either by the simple future in both clauses (see Lesson X), or by the imperfect subjunctive in the conditional clause and the conditional in the conclusion clause:

Se saremo in ritardo prenderemo l'autobus.
If we are late we shall take the bus.
Se fossimo in ritardo prenderemmo l'autobus.
If we were late we should take the bus.

When the condition is more closely related to the present and contrary to the actual state of affairs, then only the imperfect subjunctive can be used in the conditional clause and the conditional in the conclusion clause:

Se avesse l'automɔbile l'accompagnerɛbbe a casa.
If he had his car he would drive you home.

When the conditional clause refers to the past, past perfect subjunctive and conditional perfect are used.[1]

Se fosse restata a casa sarɛbbe guarita più prɛsto.
If she had stayed at home she would have recovered sooner.

Vocabulary XXVI

raffreddore (m.) cold, chill (**raffreddato** chilled)
malattia illness, sickness, disease
cambiamento change
ch*i*mico (n. & adj.) chemist, chemical
ricerca research, investigation
or*i*gine (f.) origin, cause
umanità humanity, mankind
tosse (f.) cough
bronchite (f.) bronchitis
fɛbbre (f.) fever
contagioso (adj.) infectious, contagious
improvviso (adj.) sudden, unexpected
all'improvviso suddenly
noioso (adj.) annoying, boring
d*e*bole (adj.) weak
prudɛnte (adj.) prudent, careful
***u*mido** (adj.) damp, wet
completamente (adv.) completely
via (n. & adv.) road, away
tossire* to cough
starnutare to sneeze (aux. **avere**)
affl*i*ggere to afflict, distress
abituare to accustom
sopportare to bear, endure
salire to rise, go up
guarire* to recover, cure
prɛndere to catch
stare mɛglio to feel better, to be better
stare bɛne to be well
stare male to be unwell
raccomandare to recommend

[1] Occasionally a mixture of these tenses may be required, when the conclusion clause refers to the present, e.g. Se avesse risparmiato, oggi sarebbe ricco. If he had saved, he would be rich today.

Exercise 1

Repeat orally all the four tenses of the subjunctive mood of: abituare, starnutare, sopportare, credere, vedere, avere, essere, guarire, sentire, tossire.

Exercise 2

Translate into Italian: 1. We departed before she arrived. 2. She entered the room without our seeing her. 3. Although she had not a temperature she was not well. 4. She bought the medicine at once in order that he might recover as soon as possible. 5. You do not need to stay (restare) in bed, provided that you remain indoors (a casa). 6. I shall wait until they return. 7. Let us go into the study so that we may read. 8. Even if it rings, do not answer the 'phone. 9. Unless you wear warmer clothes you will catch cold. 10. She posted the letter before I had seen it.

Exercise 3

Translate into Italian: 1. This is the most interesting book that I have ever studied. 2. There was no one to help her. 3. Whoever calls (telefonare), I am not at home. 4. She is the best friend I have ever had. 5. May God advise us! 6. Mary recovered sooner than we hoped. 7. If they knew my address they would send the letter to me. 8. It is the worst film we have ever seen. 9. If I had known that you were ill I should have telephoned at once. 10. It is the only illness she ever had.

A. *Translate into English:* 1. D'inverno, quando fa freddo, è facile prendere dei raffreddori. 2. A teatro, in chiesa, in autobus abbiamo spesso vicino a noi una persona che è raffreddata e che tossisce e starnuta. 3. Il raffreddore, benché sia una malattia molto leggera, è molto contagioso e la gente che ha un raffreddore dovrebbe restare a casa affinché gli altri non lo prendano. 4. Quest'inverno credo che gli improvvisi cambiamenti di temperatura più che il freddo siano stati la causa di molte influenze e raffreddori. 5. Benché dottori e chimici abbiano studiato a lungo per trovare la natura del raffreddore, non conosciamo ancora l'origine di questa malattia che ci sembra una delle più noiose che affliggano l'umanità. 6. In un clima umido e freddo la gente dovrebbe abituare i propri figli a sopportare freddo, pioggia, vento e cambiamenti improvvisi di temperatura in modo che siano più forti. 7. Nella casa in cui abitiamo, al secondo piano, c'è lo studio di un dottore, e, benché egli lavori dalla mattina alla sera, accade spesso che non arrivi a visitare tutti i suoi malati. 8. Un mese fa mia madre lo chiamò perché visitasse mia sorella; essa aveva una leggera temperatura e un po' di tosse e mia madre temeva che avesse una bronchite. 9. Il dottore la visitò, le ordinò delle medicine e le raccomandò di restare a letto finché la temperatura scendesse. 10. Egli consigliò anche a mia madre, senza che mia sorella lo sentisse, di non mandarla al mare la prossima estate. 11. Il dottore sa che a mia sorella piace molto il mare e che se avesse sentito quello che egli consigliava a mia madre non sarebbe stata contenta. 12. Benché mia sorella prendesse le medicine la sera stessa, la febbre salì di tre gradi. 13. La mattina seguente però la febbre non era più così alta e per quanto mia sorella fosse molto debole e non avesse fame, il giorno dopo era completamente sfebbrata e stava molto meglio. 14. Il dottore le consigliò di restare a casa qualche giorno e di ritornare a scuola la settimana seguente, purché mio fratello l'accompagnasse in automobile. 15. Prima che il dottore andasse via, mia madre gli domandò se credeva che mia sorella fosse completamente guarita. 16. La signorina sta certamente meglio, ma è necessario che sia prudente e che non prenda un altro raffreddore. 17. "Vuoi che telefoni a Luisa per domandarle se può andare lei a provare il tuo vestito?"—domandò Maria. 18. È l'unica che abbia le tue stesse misure e se provasse il vestito la sarta lo finirebbe presto. 19. Forse sarebbe meglio che tu le telefonassi subito a meno che la sarta non preferisca mandare una delle ragazze a provartelo a casa. 20. Mia sorella guarì più presto che non pensassimo.

B. *Translate into Italian:* 1. Although last summer was the best we have had for (da) many years, doctors have had many sick people this winter. 2. In winter, especially when the temperature is very low, it often happens that we catch colds. 3. Notwithstanding the researches of doctors and chemists on colds, they do not yet know their cause. 4. Our doctor believes that the frequent change of temperature is the main cause of colds (even) though our climate is fairly moderate. 5. Any person who has a cold ought to stay at home so as not to give it to others. 6. It often happens that in trams and buses we are next to people who cough and sneeze. 7. If my sister and I were not so strong we would often catch colds. 8. Last week mother phoned the doctor because my brother seemed very tired and had a bad (forte) cough. 9. He had a slight temperature and mother was afraid that it might be bronchitis. 10. Dr Duranti who has always treated our family found that he had influenza and explained to him that he must stay in bed till his temperature came down. 11. If you had no temperature there would be no need to stay in bed, but we must be prudent. 12. Mother asked him if he would come back, but he did not think it necessary. 13. If the temperature does not come down tomorrow, phone me. 14. The doctor was very pleased that it was not bronchitis because the last time he had had it, he had been very ill. 15. As soon as he tasted the medicine Robert remarked that it was the worst medicine he had ever had. 16. My brother recovered sooner than we expected this time. 17. Within two days there was neither fever nor cough (non aveva né . . . né) so mother rang Dr Duranti to ask if he could go for a walk. 18. Dr Duranti advised him to wait a few days; he preferred to see him before allowing him to go for a walk. 19. "How do you feel now (stare)?"—Dr Duranti asked him the following day. 20. It seems that you are quite well now (guarire), but do not try to do too much. You are weaker than you think after a few days in bed.

C. 'Mens sana in corpore sano' dicevano i Romani e certo la salute è uno dei beni più preziosi.—The Romans used to say 'A healthy mind in a healthy body' and health is certainly one of the most priceless gifts. Quando ci si ammala che cosa si fa?—When one falls ill what does one do? Quando ci ammaliamo chiamiamo il dottore.—When we fall ill we call the doctor. In Italia tutti i medici dal medico generico allo specialista, dal chirurgo allo psichiatra si chiamano dottori, e se hanno la libera docenza o insegnano all'Università, professori.—In Italy all doctors from general practitioners to specialists, from surgeons to psychiatrists are called doctors, and if they have a teaching qualification or teach at a university, they are called professors. C'è un 'National Health Service' in Italia come in questo paese?—Is there a National Health Service in Italy as there is in this country? In Italia non c'è un N.H.S. come in Gran Bretagna ma i poveri sono ricoverati e curati gratuitamente all'ospedale e c'è una Cassa Mutua Malattia per gli impiegati e lavoratori che pagano le contribuzioni.—In Italy there is no N.H.S. as in Britain but the poor are given shelter and cared for in hospitals without charge, and there is a Mutual Sickness Fund for employees and workers who pay contributions. Ogni ospedale ha un Posto di Pronto Soccorso per incidenti e disgrazie dove ci sono sempre un medico e un chirurgo di turno.—Every hospital has a First Aid station for accidents and casualties where there is always a rota of doctors and surgeons on duty. In questo reparto si prestano i primi soccorsi alle persone che sono restate vittime di investimenti, di ustioni, di cadute che hanno procurato fratture o ferite ecc.—In this department they give immediate attention to people who have been victims of collisions, of falls, those who have fractures or wounds, burns, etc. I pazienti vengono medicati, fasciati e, se si tratta di una frattura e non è necessaria una radiografia, vengono ingessati.—The patients are treated, bandaged and in the case of a fracture, where X-ray is not necessary, put in plaster. Ci sono sempre una o due infermiere di guardia ed esse aiutano e preparano il paziente.—There are always one or two nurses on duty and they help and prepare the patient. Domandano: Come si sente? Dove le fa male? Soffre molto? e con la loro gentilezza e la loro presenza confortano i pazienti e li aiutano a sopportare il dolore.—They ask—How do you feel? Where is the pain? Are you suffering a great deal? and with their kindness and their very presence they comfort the patients and help them to bear their pain.

D. *Magari*

Magari potessi venire!—Oh, if only I could come!

La invito e pɔi magari non viɛne—I invite her and then quite likely she won't come.

Dovessi magari andarci a piɛdi, ma ci arriverò—I'll get there even if I have to walk all the way.

LESSON XXVII

Uses of the Definite Article
Passive Voice of Verbs

The use of the definite article in Italian differs from its use in English. Italian frequently employs the definite article where it is not used in English and conversely it is omitted in Italian in certain cases where it is used in English. The definite article is used in Italian:

1. before possessives—with certain exceptions:

il mio libro my book

2. before common and abstract nouns used in a general sense and nouns representing an entire category of persons:

I cani sono fedeli.	Dogs are faithful.
La virtù è ricompensata.	Virtue is rewarded.
I Francesi sono lɔgici.	French people are logical.

3. before numbers expressing time:

È l'una.	It is one o'clock.
Sono le due.	It is two o'clock.

4. before dates or expressions of time:

nel 1956	in 1956
il mese scorso	last month

5. before days of the week to express every (ogni):

il lunedì every Monday

6. before nouns preceded by such expressions as: *ambidue*, *entrambi*, *tutti e due*—both, *tutti e tre*—all three, etc.:

tutti e due i ragazzi both boys

7. before nouns denoting part of the body or objects belonging to the subject:

Si lavò le mani.	He washed his hands.
Si mise il cappɛllo.	He put on his hat.

8. Before surnames when not preceded by a Christian name:

Il Leopardi fu un poeta italiano molto famoso.
Leopardi was a very famous Italian poet.

9. before titles, except in direct address:

Il dottor Bruni Dr Bruni

10. before the names of continents, countries, provinces and large islands, with certain exceptions:[1]

l'Italia Italy l'Inghilterra England
la Sardegna Sardinia

After the preposition *in* the article is omitted provided the noun is feminine, ends in *a* and is not qualified by an adjective:

In Francia in France
but: nella Russia moderna in modern Russia.
and nell'Italia meridionale in Southern Italy.

When the preposition and the noun which follows it are together equivalent to an adjective of nationality:

il sole d'Italia	the sun of Italy.
gli abitanti degli Stati Uniti.	the inhabitants of the United States.

The adjectives *italiano, francese*, etc., when referring to the language, are preceded by the definite article except after *parlare*:

Egli capisce l'italiano.	He understands Italian.
Non parlano francese.	They do not speak French.

The definite article must be omitted in Italian:

1. before a noun in apposition to another noun:

Vittorio Emmanuele, rè d'Italia.
Victor Emmanuel, the king of Italy.

2. before an ordinal used with any proper name or with *canto, volume, capitolo, paragrafo* quoted with reference:

Pio nɔno Pius the ninth
Capitolo tɛrzo, paragrafo primo third chapter, the first paragraph

3. before the relative superlative of an adjective qualifying a noun already preceded by the definite article:

L'alunno più intelligɛnte della classe.
The cleverest pupil in the class.

Passive Voice of Verbs

Transitive verbs form their passive voice in Italian in the same way as in English, that is by using the required mood, tense and person of the auxiliary verb *ɛssere* with the past participle of the given verb. The past participle agrees with the subject, and in the compound tenses of *ɛssere* both participles agree with the subject:

Il quadro ɛra stato ammirato da tutti.
The picture had been admired by all.

[1] Names of towns are never preceded by the definite article except to denote a football team or to specify a particular period or aspect:

Il Bari	Bari football team
La Roma dei Papi	Papal Rome
La Parigi di cinquanta anni fa	Paris of fifty years ago.

La in La Spezia, L'Aquila, L'Aia must not be considered separate articles but part of the name of these towns.

Sometimes instead of the auxiliary *ɛssere*, *venire* (to come) is used:

I malati vennero portati all'ospedale.
The sick were taken to the hospital.

A construction regarded as passive in Italian is the use of the pronoun particle *si* (called in Italian *particella passivante*—particle which makes the verb passive) with the 3rd person singular and plural of a verb, depending on the number of the noun following:

Si parla italiano.	Italian is spoken.
Si raccontavano molte stɔrie.	Many stories were told.

This pronoun particle used when no agent is expressed, must not be confused with the reflexive *si*, being an entirely different part of speech. When used with an intransitive verb, it is always followed by the 3rd person singular and is then the equivalent of the English, *one*, *people*, *they* (French, *on*):

Se si partisse subito si arriverɛbbe in tɛmpo.
If one left immediately one would arrive in time.

Note that adjectives following *si* must always be plural:

Si è felici.	One is happy.
Si arriva stanchi.	One arrives tired.

Vocabulary XXVII

regione (f.) region
paes*a*ggio landscape, scenery
vigneto vineyard
valle (f.) valley
esɛmpio example
cortɛo (m.) procession
duɔmo cathedral
mondo world (adj. **mondiale**)
campana bell
luɔgo place (**l. di nascita** birthplace)
fioritura blossoming (**fiorire** to flourish, blossom)
vittɔria victory
lɔtta struggle
crudeltà cruelty (adj. **crudele**)
letteratura literature
campanile (m.) belfry, bell-tower
scultore (m.) sculptor
alba dawn
affresco fresco (painting)
palazzo palace
guɛrra war
or*e*fice (m.) goldsmith, jeweller
mescolanza blend, mixture
Toscana Tuscany
fiorentino (adj.) Florentine
copɛrto (adj.) covered; (n.) place at table
indifferɛnte (adj.) indifferent
meridionale (adj.) southern
straniɛro (adj. & n.) foreign, foreigner
durante (prep.) during
Parigi (f.) Paris
Accadɛmia Academy
Vaticano Vatican
Cappɛlla Sistina Sistine Chapel

Battistero Baptistery
Padova Padua
apprezzare to appreciate
commemorare to commemorate
ricordare to remember, remind
decorare to decorate
commissionare to commission
ornare to adorn, ornament

Exercise 1

Translate into Italian: 1. Her flat is on the second floor. 2. French people love good cooking. 3. Mary tried on her new dress. 4. Pirandello was an Italian writer. 5. Shop assistants must always be courteous. 6. Professor Vivaldi was on holiday. 7. Both the boys were intelligent. 8. Last month Robert returned from Italy. 9. Next week we shall be free. 10. When it is four o'clock in France it is only three o'clock in England. 11. Vera, Julia's dearest friend, is my cousin. 12. Robert is the cleverest boy in the school. 13. Every Monday we go to the theatre. 14. Almost every person learns French at school. 15. Last year we spent our holiday in France and in Southern Italy.

Exercise 2

Translate into Italian: (a) 1. The house was bought by Mr Bruni. 2. The boy had been cured by Dr Duranti. 3. The bill had been paid by my father. 4. The furniture has been dusted by Mary. 5. The car was driven by Robert. 6. The bridge was constructed in three months. 7. The invitations will be sent by post. 8. The glasses have been washed by the maid. 9. The picture was not finished. 10. The blankets have already been washed.

(b) 1. Is there a direct train or does one have to change? 2. How long (quanto tempo) before must one book the seats? 3. It is not far away if one crosses the bridge. 4. All seats must be booked in this theatre. 5. Many bottles were opened. 6. Tonight all glasses must be cleaned. 7. A new bridge is being built. 8. In this hotel dinner is at 7 (one dines). 9. They think that he is very rich. 10. One learns better when one is young. 11. When one is well one is happy. 12. From here one sees the coast.

Exercise 3

Translate into Italian: 1. Let us visit Tuscany. 2. Although there are many vineyards. 3. We wish you to appreciate. 4. It happens that I meet her every summer. 5. We rang her in order that she might help us. 6. We shall visit Florence whatever happens. 7. I will accompany you provided you get the tickets. 8. If we had had more money we would have stayed longer. 9. There is no city that I admire more. 10. It is necessary for him to study.

A. *Translate into English*: 1. Firenze è una delle più belle città d'Italia; i suoi monumenti, i suoi palazzi, il magnifico Duomo col campanile di Giotto, i meravigliosi quadri che si trovano nelle sue gallerie, le sue chiese e gli splendidi affreschi che le ornano, ne fanno una delle città più visitate del mondo. 2. Coloro che non hanno ammirato il David e le statue non finite di Michelangelo nell'Accademia e quelle del Giorno e della Notte e dell'Alba e della Sera nelle tombe dei Medici, non conoscono i maggiori capolavori della scultura italiana del cinquecento. 3. Spesso nei quadri dei pittori più celebri di quel tempo si ammirano, dietro Madonne e Santi, bellissimi paesaggi italiani. 4. Quando si guardano tutti questi capolavori, è difficile credere che nello stesso tempo in cui arte e letteratura fiorivano così meravigliosamente, ci fossero delle lotte così crudeli tra città e città e spesso anche tra gli abitanti della stessa città. 5. Gli abitanti di Firenze furono a lungo in lotta fra di loro e queste lotte interne sono ricordate da Dante Alighieri nella Divina Commedia. 6. Siena, Arezzo, Pisa, Lucca furono tutte città famose nel Medio Evo e benché parecchi secoli siano passati, esse ricordano e commemorano ancora le guerre e le vittorie di quel tempo lontano. 7. Il corteo del Carroccio e quello del Palio, in costumi medioevali a Siena richiamano ogni anno molti visitatori. 8. Dalle colline intorno a Firenze si può ammirare la città con le cupole di Santa Maria Novella e Santa Maria del Fiore e il celebre campanile di Giotto. 9. Famosissime e conosciute in tutto il mondo sono le porte del Battistero nella piazza del Duomo, opera del Ghiberti. 10. La Toscana fu la terra natale (birth place) di moltissimi pittori e scultori; basterà ricordare i nomi di Giotto, Fra Angelico, Masaccio, Verrocchio, Botticelli e del Ghirlandaio. 11. Michelangelo, Raffaello e Leonardo da Vinci sono conosciuti in tutto il mondo; essi sono tanto grandi che ci sembra meraviglioso che l'Italia sia stata la terra natale di tanti grandi artisti. 12. In Roma Michelangelo affrescò la Cappella Sistina e Raffaello le Stanze che hanno conservato il suo nome. 13. Si racconta che quando ebbe finito il Mosè, Michelangelo stesso domandasse alla statua perché non parlasse. 14. L'ultima Cena, uno dei maggiori capolavori di Leonardo da Vinci, è stata molto rovinata dal tempo. 15. Agli affreschi della Cappella Sistina, commissionatigli dal Papa, Michelangelo lavorò lunghi anni. 16. Tutti i ponti sull'Arno, opera di celebri architetti furono rovinati dai Tedeschi durante l'ultima guerra mondiale. 17. Soltanto uno ne resta, il Ponte Vecchio, famoso per le sue botteghe di orefici. 18. Il popolo fiorentino, benché abbia sempre intorno a sé tutte queste meravigliose opere d'arte, non è indifferente ad esse ma le apprezza e le ammira. 19. Non bisogna dimenticare che toscani furono l'Alighieri, il Petrarca, il Boccaccio, il Poliziano e in tempi più moderni il Carducci. 20. Firenze ebbe un periodo di grande fioritura delle arti e della letteratura al tempo dei Medici e specialmente di Lorenzo il Magnifico.

B. *Translate into Italian:* 1. Tuscany is one of the most beautiful regions of Italy. 2. The hills covered with vineyards, the pleasant valleys, the woods near the sea, are nature's works of art. 3. Nowhere (say: in no place) in the world perhaps is art more appreciated by the people who see such wonderful examples of it all around them. 4. It is said that in Siena the shops were closed and the bells sounded when Duccio's 'Vergine in Trono' was carried in procession to the cathedral. 5. The people of Siena commemorate every year their victory over the Florentines in 1249. 6. It would take (say: be) too long to describe the Carroccio procession and the Palio at Siena, in medieval costumes. 7. Even the name of the principal city of Tuscany, Fiorenza—today Firenze—reminds us (of) this blossoming of all the arts—sculpture, painting and literature. 8. Florence certainly was the birthplace of the greatest artists that have ever been known. 9. Although many of Giotto's paintings are in Padua and Assisi, his marble belfry of Santa Maria del Fiore is one of Florence's greatest works of art. 10. The story of Florentine art can be followed in the works of Masaccio, Fra Angelico, Verrocchio, Botticelli, Ghirlandaio and many others. 11. But the best period of Florentine art began in 1500. The names of Leonardo da Vinci, Michelangelo and Raffaello are known to all. 12. Leonardo's 'Last Supper' and 'The Gioconda' are among his most famous works. 13. In Florence we can see and admire Michelangelo's David and the wonderful statues of Day and Night, Evening and Dawn in the Medici tombs. 14. In Rome his 'Pietà' and his 'Mosè' have been admired by thousands of visitors and have been an example to the best artists from (di) every part of the world. 15. Famous throughout the world (in tutto) also are his frescoes in the Sistine Chapel commissioned (say: to him) by the Pope. 16. Raphael too was summoned by the same Pope to decorate the rooms which were called after (dal) his name 'Stanze di Raffaello'. 17. In the second world war some of the famous palaces in Florence and all the bridges across (sull') the Arno except one, the famous Ponte Vecchio, were ruined. 18. On this bridge, for centuries there have stood the same little goldsmiths' shops. 19. The inhabitants of Florence, although they live beside all these masterpieces, are not all indifferent to them. 20. Florence is beautiful at all seasons of the year. Many people, however, prefer to go there in spring when there is 'Il Maggio Musicale'.

C. Quali animali si trovano in Italia? In Italia ci sono quasi gli stessi animali selvatici che ci sono in Gran Bretagna con l'eccezione di qualche raro lupo che appare negli inverni molto duri negli Appennini, di alcuni cinghiali in Sardegna e in Basilicata e di stambecchi e camosci nelle Alpi. —What animals are found in Italy? Almost the same wild ones as in Britain with the exception of some rare wolves that appear in very hard winters in the Apennines, some wild boars in Sardinia and Basilicata and some wild goats and chamois in the Alps. Quali sono gli animali selvatici più comuni? Essi sono la volpe, lo scoiattolo, la faina, il ghiro, la lepre, la marmotta.—What are the commonest wild animals? They are the fox, the squirrel, the marten, the dormouse, the hare and the marmot. Quali sono gli animali domestici? Tra gli animali domestici ci sono il bue, la pecora, la capra, il cavallo, l'asino, il mulo, il cane, il gatto, il coniglio. —Which are the domestic animals? Among such are the ox, the sheep, the goat, the horse, the donkey, the mule, the dog, the cat and the rabbit. Amano molto gli animali gli Italiani? Si dice che gli Italiani non amino gli animali tanto quanto gli Inglesi. È certamente vero che nelle case italiane si trovano più spesso canarini e pappagallini che cani e gatti. —Are Italians very fond of animals? It is said that they are not so fond of animals as the English. It is certainly true that in the homes of Italians canaries and budgerigars are more often found than dogs and cats. E quali sono gli uccelli più comuni? In generale c'è una minore varietà di uccelli che in questo paese e la gente non li conosce altrettanto bene.—And which are the commonest birds? Generally speaking there is a smaller variety of birds than is found in this country and the people are not so familiar with them as we are. Passeri, fringuelli, usignoli, pettirossi, allodole, merli, rondini sono gli uccelli più comuni che tutti conoscono.—Sparrows, chaffinches, nightingales, robins, larks, blackbirds and swallows are the commonest birds that everyone knows. E quali sono i nomi di altri uccelli? Le beccacce, le pernici, le quaglie, i fagiani sono gli uccelli di cui si va a caccia.—And what other birds are there? Woodcock, partridges, quails and pheasants are game birds. Nelle Alpi si vedono a volte anche le aquile.—Sometimes eagles, too, are seen in the Alps. Quali alberi si trovano in Italia? Gli alberi più comuni sono i pioppi, le querce, i frassini, gli olmi, i lecci, le betulle, gli ippocastani, i pini, i cipressi, i salici.—Which trees are found in Italy? The commonest are poplars, oak trees, ash trees, elms, ilex, birches, horse chestnuts, pines, cypresses and willow trees. Quante specie di alberi da frutta si trovano in Italia?—How many kinds of fruit trees are there in Italy? Vi è una grande varietà di alberi da frutta—aranci, mandarini, limoni crescono in tutte le zone temperate e così pure ciliegi, fichi, mandorli, ulivi, albicocchi, peschi, noci, susini, gelsi, peri e meli.—There is a large variety of fruit trees—orange trees, mandarins and lemon trees grow in all the temperate zones as well as cherry trees, fig trees, almond trees, olive trees, apricot trees, peach trees, nut trees, plum trees, mulberry trees, pear trees and apple trees. Crescono facilmente i fiori in Italia? Sì ma non durano molto specie quando fa caldo.—Do flowers grow easily in Italy? Yes but they do not last long especially when it is hot. Molta meno gente però ha l'occasione e l'inclinazione di occuparsi di giardinaggio come qui. —Far fewer people however have the chance or the inclination to take up gardening as they do here. Tra i fiori più comuni ci sono rose, garofani, gelsomini, viole, gigli, gardenie, e fiori di pisello.—Among the best known flowers are roses, carnations, jasmin, violets, lilies, gardenias and sweet peas.

D. *E con questo?*

Si, l'ho licenziato. E con questo?—Yes, I've sacked him. So what?

LESSON XXVIII

Ordinal Numerals

1st	primo	20th	ventεsimo
2nd	secondo	21st	ventunεsimo or ventεsimo primo
3rd	tεrzo	22nd	ventiduεsimo or . . .
4th	quarto	23rd	ventitreεsimo or . . .
5th	quinto	30th	trentεsimo
6th	sεsto	40th	quarantεsimo
7th	sεttimo	50th	cinquantεsimo
8th	ottavo	101st	centunεsimo or centεsimo primo
9th	nɔno	112th	centododicεsimo etc.
10th	dεcimo	200th	duocentεsimo
11th	undicεsimo or dεcimo primo	1000th	millεsimo
12th	dodicεsimo or dεcimo secondo	1504th	millecinquecentoquattrεsimo or . . . millεsimo cinquecentesimo-quarto
19th	diciannovεsimo or dεcimo nɔno	1.000.000th	milionεsimo

Note: 1. The ordinal numerals, with the exception of the first ten which have their own distinctive forms, are obtained by adding the ending *-εsimo* to the corresponding cardinal from which the final vowel has been dropped.

2. Cardinals ending in *-trè*: ventitrè, trentatrè, etc., lose the grave accent but retain the final vowel thus becoming: ventitreεsimo—23rd, trentatreεsimo—33rd, etc.

3. From eleventh onwards there are two forms:

tredicεsimo; dεcimo tεrzo 13th

4. The ordinals are adjectives of the first group and as such they agree in gender and number with the noun they refer to:

primo	prima
primi	prime

5. Ordinals always come after proper names:

Giulio secondo Julius the second

and generally after the century:

il sεcolo dεcimo nɔno 19th century
(the form in *εsimo* can also precede: il diciannovεsimo sεcolo);

they precede common nouns except quoting a reference:

la tɛrza fila	the third row
but: capitolo primo, paragrafo tɛrzo	1st chapter, third paragraph.

Use of Ordinals

Ordinals are used:

1. after the proper names of popes, kings and rulers:

Pio nɔno	Pius the ninth
Carlo quinto	Charles the fifth

2. to enumerate the centuries:

il sɛcolo dɛcimo sɛsto	the sixteenth century

From the thirteenth century onwards, however, the commonest method of naming the century is by the cardinal preceded by the definite article. Mille is never expressed but merely understood:

il duecɛnto	the thirteenth century
il novecɛnto	the twentieth century

3. to specify the number of a chapter, verse, volume, etc.:

quarto volume	volume four
tredicɛsimo canto	canto thirteen
sɛsto capitolo	chapter six

4. to express the denominator of fractions when they have the value of nouns:

tre quinti	three-fifths
cinque ottavi	five-eighths

Note: un quarto—one-quarter or one-fourth.

Expressions to note: *il doppio*—the double; *la metà*—the half; *un paio*—a pair; *una cɔppia*—a couple; *un trimɛstre*—a term (three months) and such distributive expressions as: *a due a due*, *a tre a tre*—two by two, three by three, in threes; *due, tre, quattro alla vɔlta*—two, three, four at a time; *tre, quattro, cinque per uno*—three, four, five each.

Reflexive Verbs

A reflexive verb is one in which the object of the action is the subject itself. The reflexive pronouns used as objects of such verbs have, except in the 3rd person singular and plural, forms similar to those of the conjunctive pronouns, namely *mi, ti, si, ci, vi, si*; as already stated reflexive verbs are conjugated with the auxiliary *ɛssere.*

Present Indicative of Reflexive Verbs

Guardarsi		*Vedersi*		*Vestirsi*	
io mi guardo	I look at myself, etc.	vedo	I see myself, etc.	vesto	I dress myself, etc.
tu ti guardi		vedi		vesti	
egli si guarda		vede		veste	
noi ci guardiamo		vediamo		vestiamo	
voi vi guardate		vedete		vestite	
essi si guardano		vedono		vestono	

The position of the pronouns is governed by the rules already given:

Le ragazze si sono vestite. The girls have dressed.
Affrettatevi! Make haste!

In Italian these verbs are much commoner than in English. They are divided into two groups:

1. Reflexive verbs proper such as: *vestirsi*—to dress oneself; *lavarsi*—to wash oneself; *pettinarsi*—to comb one's hair; *chinarsi*—to bend, stoop; *specchiarsi*—to look at oneself, to be reflected, mirrored.

2. Verbs grammatically reflexive in form though not in meaning such as *pentirsi*—to repent; *vergognarsi*[1]—to be ashamed; *vantarsi*—to boast; *lagnarsi*—to complain; *rallegrarsi*—to rejoice; *chiamarsi*—to be called; *annoiarsi*—to be bored; *scusarsi*—to apologize; *divertirsi*—to enjoy oneself; *gloriarsi*—to boast; *arricchirsi*—to become rich; *meravigliarsi*—to be surprised.

Vocabulary XXVIII

matɛria subject, matter, substance
tipo type
istituto tɛcnico technical college
licɛo grammar school
importanza importance
matematica mathematics
sciɛnza science (adj. **scientifico**)
facoltà faculty, power
ingegneria engineering
legge (f.) law
sistɛma (m.) system
gruppo group
sezione (f.) section, form
mɛrito merit
istruzione (f.) instruction, education
livɛllo level
disciplina discipline (adj. **disciplinato**, v. **disciplinare**)
punizione (f.) punishment
esame (m.) examination
inizio beginning
ammissione (f.) admission, entrance
licɛnza leave, permission
latino Latin
promozione (f.) promotion
orario periods, hours of lessons
distinzione (f.) distinction
riforma reform

Reflexive verbs expressing emotions require the subjunctive in dependent clauses when the two subjects are different:

Mi meraviglio che egli sia riuscito. I am surprised that he has succeeded.

spagnuɔlo Spanish, Spaniard
alunno pupil
insegnante (m. & f.) teacher
cɔmpito task, homework
voto mark
registro register, book
pagɛlla report, certificate
intervallo interval
elementare (adj.) elementary
mɛdio (adj.) secondary, middle, average
comune (adj.) common
scuɔla magistrale normal school for training elementary teachers
cl*a*ssico (adj.) classic, classical
letter*a*rio (adj.) literary
r*i*gido (adj.) severe, stiff
obbligatɔrio (adj.) obligatory, compulsory (v. **obbligare**)
radicale (adj.) radical
corporale (adj.) corporal
indisciplinato (adj.) undisciplined, unruly
ammonito (adj.) admonished (v. **ammonire**)
sospeso (adj.) suspended
orale (adj.) oral
promɔsso promoted
bocciato failed, rejected (v. **bocciare**)
fless*i*bile (adj.) flexible, pliable
pr*a*tico (adj.) practical
limitato limited
privato (adj.) private
scritto written
div*i*dere to divide
durare to last
derivare to derive, originate
ripɛtere to repeat
confrontare to confront
interrogare to question
poco tempo fa quite recently
in via di attuazione in progress

Exercise 1

Translate the following numerals into Italian: 14th, 19th, 21st, 33rd, 40th, 92nd, 100th, 150th, 500th, 1000th, 1,000,000th, 20th, 51st, 16th, 48th, 76th, 2000th, 15th, 62nd, 101st.

Exercise 2

Translate into Italian: 1. the double. 2. Louis 15th. 3. the 17th century. 4. three at a time. 5. four-fifths. 6. five each. 7. in the sixth chapter. 8. four by four. 9. chapter 3 paragraph 10. 10. three-quarters. 11. a pair. 12. all three. 13. half. 14. a couple. 15. one each. 16. a dozen. 17. about ten. 18. May 18th. 19. the second row. 20. Charles the fifth.

Exercise 3

(a) *Translate:* 1. We are ashamed. 2. I have washed. 3. She will have dressed. 4. They boast of it. 5. You complain. 6. We (f.) have rejoiced. 7. He has repented. 8. They are called. 9. She will enjoy herself. 10. Rejoice! 11. He apologised. 12. We would be ashamed. 13. That he may have repented. 14. We have enjoyed ourselves. 15.

Although she had apologised. 16. They will be bored. 17. Amuse yourself. 18. You had boasted of it. 19. I was complaining. 20. Let us dress! 21. Look at yourself! 22. He used to be called. 23. Be ashamed of yourselves! 24. Did you enjoy yourself (f.)? 25. Hurry up! 26. Do not boast. 27. Be proud. 28. He stayed. 29. She looked at herself in the mirror. 30. They became rich during the war.

(b) *Translate into English:* 1. Lavati, vestiti, pettinati. 2. Affrettati, è ora di andare a scuola. 3. Roberto si prepara. 4. Il professore si lagna che gli alunni arrivino in ritardo. 5. Come ti chiami? Mi chiamo Roberto Duranti. 6. Egli si vanta di essere il primo della classe. 7. Si pentirà di essere stata pigra. 8. Va a lavarti le mani. 9. Si scusa di non aver finito i compiti. 10. Non se ne lagnano. 11. Affrettatevi, mettetevi il cappotto e il cappello e andate a scuola. 12. Vi annoiate? 13. No, non ci siamo annoiati, ci siamo divertiti molto. 14. Si dovrebbe vergognare. 15. Se ne sono pentiti.

A. *Translate into English:* 1. In Italia si comincia ad andare a scuola a sei anni, in Gran Bretagna a cinque. 2. Le scuole italiane si dividono in scuole elementari, scuole medie inferiori e superiori; le prime durano quattro o cinque anni, le seconde circa otto. 3. Benché ci siano diversi tipi di scuole medie, i primi tre anni sono comuni a quasi tutte perché vi si studiano le stesse materie. 4. Le scuole medie superiori si dividono in tre tipi principali: scuole magistrali, istituti tecnici e licei classici o scientifici. 5. Nelle prime si preparano i maestri per le scuole elementari; nei secondi si dà maggiore importanza alla matematica e alle materie scientifiche e gli alunni che le frequentano vanno generalmente alle Facoltà di Matematica, Ingegneria, Scienze; nei terzi si studiano di più le materie letterarie e da essi si va generalmente alle Facoltà di Lettere o di Legge. 6. Le scuole italiane hanno un sistema molto più rigido delle scuole inglesi: gli alunni di una classe non sono divisi in gruppi ed hanno tutti le stesse materie di studio e gli stessi professori durante i tre trimestri dell'anno scolastico. 7. Ogni classe ha diverse sezioni: per esempio: II A, II B, III C, IV D, ma gli alunni sono distribuiti nelle diverse sezioni senza alcuna distinzione di merito. 8. Sino a poco tempo fa soltanto l'istruzione elementare era obbligatoria e benché da ciò derivasse un basso livello di istruzione generale, nelle scuole medie si trovavano solamente alunni che volevano studiare o i cui genitori volevano che studiassero. 9. Questo è importante per la disciplina della classe perché spesso nelle nostre scuole gli alunni più indisciplinati sono quelli che sono obbligati a studiare per legge. 10. Anche le punizioni disciplinari sono diverse; in Italia non ci sono punizioni corporali; se un alunno è indisciplinato, è ammonito dal Preside o sospeso dalle lezioni per uno o più giorni. 11. Il sistema degli esami è molto diverso; alla fine delle scuole elementari e alla fine delle scuole medie vi sono esami che si chiamano di ammissione e di licenza. 12. Gli esami sono scritti e orali per alcune materie come italiano, latino, greco e lingue moderne e orali per gli altri. 13. Se un alunno va (fa) bene durante l'anno nelle classi in cui non ci sono esami è promosso, se non va bene è bocciato e deve fare un esame a settembre, prima dell'inizio del nuovo anno scolastico. 14. Se è bocciato anche agli esami di settembre, ripete l'anno (la classe). 15. In Italia si dà forse troppa importanza alla promozione da una classe all'altra. 16. Quando si confrontano i due sistemi di scuole, si trova che il sistema inglese è molto più flessibile, più pratico e più moderno. 17. Nelle scuole italiane non si fa tanto sport quanto nelle scuole inglesi anche perché gli orari sono più limitati. 18. In Italia non c'è tanta distinzione tra scuole pubbliche e private e le scuole pubbliche hanno quasi sempre professori migliori. 19. Gli Italiani trovano molto divertente che nella Gran Bretagna le scuole private si chiamino pubbliche. 20. Le lingue che si studiano nelle scuole medie sono il francese, l'inglese, lo spagnuolo e il tedesco ma esse sono insegnate solo nei primi anni delle scuole medie. 21. I professori spiegano le lezioni, interrogano e danno parecchi compiti da fare a casa. 22. Gli insegnanti delle scuole elementari si chiamano maestri, quelli delle scuole medie e dell'Università, professori. 23. Quando il maestro o il professore ha interrogato un alunno, gli dà un voto che scrive nel registro. 24. Alla fine di ogni trimestre gli alunni ricevono una pagella in cui ci sono i voti che hanno avuto in ogni materia. 25. Il voto minimo necessario per avere la promozione è il 6. 26. I periodi di vacanze nelle scuole italiane sono diversi da quelli delle scuole inglesi. 27. Si va a scuola ogni giorno della settimana e il sabato non è vacanza. 28. A Natale ci sono circa 10 giorni di vacanze, a Pasqua una settimana ma le vacanze d'estate durano circa tre mesi per gli alunni che non hanno esami. 29. A metà giugno fa già caldo, perciò le scuole generalmente si chiudono il 30 maggio e si riaprono al principio di ottobre. 30. Gli alunni, eccetto per le lezioni di scienze e disegno, stanno sempre nella stessa classe e sono i professori che vanno da una classe all'altra. Tra le lezioni ci sono sempre cinque minuti di intervallo.

B. *Translate into Italian:* 1. While children start school in Great Britain at five years they must be six before going to school in Italy. 2. For the first four or five years in Italy they attend the elementary school. 3. The teachers in these schools are called masters and mistresses while in the higher schools and universities they are called professors. 4. There are (a few) different types of secondary schools although the subjects studied for the first three years are common to almost all of them. 5. The principal types of secondary schools are the following: scuole magistrali, technical or scientific colleges and grammar schools. 6. In the first of these they prepare teachers for elementary schools, the only type of school which was, until recently compulsory in Italy. 7. From this it followed that the general education of those who left school at eleven years was of (aveva) a low level. 8. The pupils however who continued their education at secondary schools did so either because they themselves liked studying or because their parents wished them to study. 9. A radical reform of education is now in progress in Italy and education will be compulsory until the age of 14. 10. There is no corporal punishment in Italian schools. If a pupil is troublesome he is warned by the Principal once or even twice. 11. The worst punishment is to be suspended from lessons for a day or two. 12. In the technical schools a great (deal of) importance is given to mathematics and science and from these schools students generally go to a University to study engineering, mathematics or science. 13. Students in the Faculty of Letters or Law in a University have all attended a grammar school, where they have studied Latin, Greek, modern languages and literature. 14. In our schools almost all the pupils are promoted from one class to another at the end of the scholastic year even if they are not very clever. 15. In Italy however the system of promotion is much more rigid and if a pupil does not do well, he is failed. 16. When that happens (accade) he has to do an exam. in September, before the beginning of the new school year. 17. Any pupil who has failed (a) this exam, has to repeat the same class for another year. 18. Although classes in Italy have different sections called A, B, C, D etc. this is not as in almost all our schools a distinction of merit. 19. All these groups study the same subject with the same professors during the three terms. It often happens that the best pupil is in a section C or D. 20. Some schools in this country now have the same system so that the less intelligent pupils do not feel (refl.) inferior to the others. 21. As in Britain so in Italy there are private and corporation schools but in Italy there is not so great a difference between them, except that the better teachers are generally found in the corporation schools. 22. In Italy all schools are open on Saturdays also. 23. There are oral exams only in some subjects, but in Latin, Greek, Mathematics and all modern languages there are written and oral exams. 24. The marks given by a teacher when he questions pupils are from 1 to 10 and not from 1 to 100 as in our schools. 25. The average mark of all these marks is written on a report card which pupils get at the end of each term. 26. In order to be promoted a minimum of 6 marks (say: a minimum mark of 6) is required in every subject. 27. In Italy the pupils almost always stay in the same class but they have an interval of 5 minutes between each period (ora). 28. There are about ten days holiday at Christmas, a week at Easter while the summer holidays begin about the 15th of June, when the schools close (reflex.) for the three hottest months. 29. Because they have fewer periods (ore di lezione) there is not so much time for sport as in our schools. 30. Home exercises are given every day and sometimes even during holidays.

C. Ti senti stanco quando ti svegli la mattina?—Do you feel tired when you waken in the morning? Quando mi sveglio la mattina mi sembra sempre di non aver dormito abbastanza.—When I wake in the morning I never seem to have had enough sleep. Mi rincresce allora di non essermi coricato più presto e di essermi addormentato tardi.—I am sorry then that I had not gone to bed sooner and that I was late in going to sleep. Che cosa fai quando ti svegli?—What do you do when you waken? Mi alzo con un sospiro, mi infilo la vestaglia e le pantofole, vado nel bagno, mi lavo, mi pettino, poi ritorno nella mia camera e mi vesto.—I get up with a sigh, slip on my dressing gown and slippers, go to the bathroom, wash, comb my hair, then go back to my bedroom and dress. Ti alzi sempre appena la sveglia suona? No, spesso la mia mamma deve chiamarmi due o tre volte.—Do you always get up as soon as the alarm rings? No, often mother has to call me two or three times. Dopo esserti vestito che cosa fai?—After dressing what do you do? Mi faccio coraggio e vado a fare colazione.—I take courage and go and have breakfast. A che ora fate colazione? Non c'è un'ora fissa perché abbiamo tutti fretta e ognuno fa colazione appena è pronto.—When do you have breakfast? There is no fixed time because we are all in a hurry and everyone has breakfast as soon as he is ready. Ognuno si serve di pane, burro e marmellata e la mamma ci versa il caffè latte. "Vuoi un'altra tazza di caffè?", essa domanda a mio padre.—Everyone helps himself to bread, butter and marmalade and mother pours out the coffee. "Do you want another cup of coffee?" she asks father. Ci sono in Italia asili infantili?—Are there kindergarten schools in Italy? Sì, i bambini più piccoli vanno spesso all'asilo infantile.—Yes the youngest children often go to a kindergarten. Cosa fanno?—What do they do? Giocano e imparano a fare dei piccoli lavori.—They play and learn to do little tasks. I bambini passano tutta la giornata o solamente la mattina all'asilo? Ci vanno solo per poche ore la mattina.—Do children spend the whole day at the kindergarten or only the morning? They go there only for a few hours in the morning. Ci sono delle scuole serali in Italia?—Are there any night-schools in Italy? Sì, ma non tante come in Gran Bretagna.—Yes, but not so many as in Great Britain. Esse sono organizzate per permettere agli operai occupati durante il giorno di continuare gli studi.—They are organised to allow workers who are occupied during the day to continue their studies. Che materie si insegnano nelle scuole serali? Si insegnano tutte le materie che si studiano a una scuola.—

What subjects are taught in night-schools? All the subjects that are studied at school are taught in night-schools.

D. *Chi me lo* (*te lo* etc.) *fa fare*?

Vuəle uscire con questo tempaccio, ma chi glielo fa fare?

He wants to go out in this bad weather, but why should he? (literally —but who is compelling him to do so?)

LESSON XXIX

Present Participle – Gerund

English verb forms ending in *ing*—Present Participle and Gerund—have three distinct functions, namely those of: (1) verb; (2) noun; (3) adjective, and, according to these, they must be translated into Italian in three different ways.

1. Verbal Function—Gerundio

When they have a verbal function they are translated by the Italian 'gerundio'.[1]

Gerundio of Model Verbs, 'Avere' and 'Ɛssere'

Simple				
am-ando	tem-ɛndo	dorm-ɛndo	avɛndo	essɛndo
loving	fearing	sleeping	having	being
Compound				
avɛndo amato	avɛndo temuto	avɛndo dormito	avɛndo avuto	essɛndo stato
having loved	having feared	having slept	having had	having been

The gerundio is formed by adding the endings *ando*, *ɛndo*, *ɛndo* to the stem of each conjugation respectively, for the simple tense. The compound tense (gerundio composto) is formed by the gerundio of *ɛssere* or *avere* as required together with the past participle of the given verb. The gerundio is invariable.

The gerundio is therefore used:

(a) When the English form is equivalent to a clause of time, cause or condition:

Guardandolo vide che era cambiato.
Looking (when she looked) at him she saw that he had changed.
Usandolo bɛne lo conserverete a lungo.
Using (if you use) it carefully you will keep it for a long time.
Leggɛndolo tanto spesso lo conosce a memɔria.
Reading it so (as she reads it) often she knows it by heart.

Whenever a compound form is found in such clauses the compound gerundio is used:

Avɛndolo amato tanto   Having loved him so much

[1] We prefer to keep the Italian names of these verb forms to try and avoid confusion with the corresponding English names which are applied to different forms.

(b) When the English form is preceded by such prepositions as: *though*, *by*, *in*, *on*, etc.

Studiando assiduamente imparò la lingua.
By studying assiduously he learnt the language.

Arrivando vedemmo che era partito.
On arriving we saw that he had left.

Leggɛndo la lɛttera vi trovò uno sbaglio.
In reading the letter he found a mistake.

(c) To translate the progressive construction which is rendered in Italian with *stare* and less frequently *andare*.

Egli stava leggɛndo.	He was reading.
Essa andava scrivɛndo.	She was writing.

2. Noun Function—Infinitive

When the English forms have the function of a subject, an object or a predicate they are translated by the Italian infinitive. The infinitive as a subject or object can be preceded by the definite article:

Il parlare in pubblico richiede prontezza di spirito.
Public speaking requires a ready wit.

Preferisco scrivergli.
I prefer writing to him.

Questo è domandare trɔppo.
This is asking too much.

In this noun function the infinitive can likewise be governed by prepositions:

sɛnza dire una parɔla	without saying a word
prima di partire	before leaving
invece di cambiare	instead of changing

Dɔpo—after, requires the perfect infinitive:

dɔpo averlo visto	after having seen him

The infinitive can sometimes be preceded by the definite article:

tra il pescare e il remare	between fishing and rowing

When they are qualified in English by a possessive adjective, and the person to whom this adjective refers is also the subject or the object of the sentence, the Italian infinitive is still used but the English possessive adjective is omitted or replaced by the Italian definite article:

L'ɛssere solo lo rende infelice.	His being alone makes him unhappy.
Odiavo di ɛssere solo.	I hated my being alone.

But when different persons are concerned, a subordinate clause with the verb in the subjunctive must be employed:

Mi sorprendeva che fossero venuti. I was surprised at their coming.

Where the main clause verb is transitive, '*il fatto che*' must be inserted:

Odio il fatto che egli sia solo. I hate his being alone.

Sometimes a noun can be used:

Solo una malattia potrεbbe rimandare la mia venuta.
Only illness could postpone my coming.

Experience alone can help the student to decide where a noun may be employed, but when this form is preceded in English by the definite article a noun must be used in Italian:

L'imballaggio dei libri The packing of the books.

3. Adjectival Function—Participio Presente

When the English form has an adjectival function it is translated by the Italian 'Participio Presente'.

'Participio Presente' of Model Verbs, Avere and Ɛssere

am-ante	tem-εnte	dorm-εnte	avεnte	(ente)[1]
loving	fearing	sleeping	having	being

The 'participio presente' is formed by adding the endings *ante*, *εnte*, *εnte* to the stem of each conjugation respectively. In their capacity as adjectives they make their plural in *i*.

The 'participio presente' is therefore used:

(a) When its function is purely adjectival:

la lezione seguεnte the following lesson

(b) When it is the equivalent of a relative clause:

la scatola contenεnte la collana
the box containing the necklace or which contained the necklace.

The 'participio presente' should be used with some caution since even in Italian it is used only where it has been established by use and wont. In doubtful cases it will therefore be much safer to expand it into a relative clause:

Ascoltammo gli uccεlli che cantavano sui rami.
We listened to the birds singing on the branches.

The Italian present participle has in some instances acquired the function of a noun:

[1] The present participle of the verb *to be* is used only as a noun: gli εnti pubblici —public bodies.

gli amanti	the lovers
gli studɛnti	the students
i conoscɛnti	the acquaintances
i cantanti	the singers

Vocabulary XXIX

regina queen
rep*u*bblica republic
Venɛzia Venice
veneziano (adj.) Venetian
Vɛneto (n. & adj.) (region)
Adri*a*tico Adriatic
laguna lagoon
invasione (f.) invasion
parte (f.) part, side
g*o*ndola gondola
gondoliɛre (m.) gondolier
vaporetto steamer
stile (m.) style
in piɛdi standing
remo oar
capello hair
mɔtto motto
piɛtra stone
mos*a*ico mosaic
pescatore (m.) fisherman
colombo pigeon
sospiro sigh
prigione (f.) prison, gaol
prigioniɛro prisoner
canale (m.) canal, channel
vetro glass
merletto lace
collana necklace
braccialetto bracelet
terraferma mainland
ombra shade, shadow

palo pole, stake, post
capo head, chief
dɔge (m.) doge
commɛrcio commerce, trade
Oriɛnte (m.) East (adj. **orientale**)
ɛpoca epoch, period, age
pennɛllo brush
splendore (m.) splendour, magnificence
barb*a*rico (adj.) barbaric, barbarous
b*a*rbaro barbarian
scuro (adj.) dark, deep in colour
***u*tile** (adj.) useful
biondo (adj.) fair, blond
tizianesco (adj.) as depicted by Titian
dinnanzi (adv.) in front, before
fondare to build
fuggire to flee, run away
pescare to fish
unire* to unite, join
scivolare to slip, slide, glide
legare to bind, tie
cadere to fall, drop
dip*i*ngere to paint
recitare to perform, play, act
raccɔgliere to pick up, to gather
scintillare to sparkle
detto (adj.) called

Exercise 1

Translate into Italian: 1. Having tied the gondola to the pole, they entered one of the famous palaces. 2. While crossing St Mark's Square we met a group of Italians from our hotel. 3. Studying the architecture of St Mark's we notice the influence of the East. 4. We spent a couple of hours admiring the shops in the colonnade. 5. Venice grew rich carrying on a trade with the East. 6. We were looking at the pigeons when he arrived. 7. We are writing this postcard as the gondola glides through the water of the Grand Canal. 8. The gondolier is using only one oar. 9. She spends hours every day admiring the masterpieces of the famous Venetian painters. 10. The prisoners used to go from the Doge's palace to the gaol across the Bridge of Sighs.

Exercise 2

Translate into Italian: 1. Seeing the goldsmiths on the Rialto reminds me (of) the Ponte Vecchio in Florence. 2. We love crossing the canals in gondolas. 3. Some people prefer using bridges—there are hundreds of them in Venice. 4. Before going to Italy I learnt Italian for a year. 5. One can book rooms in a small boarding house instead of living in a large hotel. 6. Some people set out on holiday without booking any rooms. 7. After having visited Venice we understood why it is called the Queen of the Adriatic. 8. We spent our time between admiring churches and palaces and visiting museums and galleries. 9. We always love seeing beautiful things. 10. Visiting the cities and admiring the great masterpieces in their churches and galleries is the best way of studying art.

Exercise 3

Translate into Italian: 1. Having finished the fifth lesson the students passed to the following lesson. 2. Intelligent pupils are promoted without ever repeating a year. 3. If one studies one will learn. 4. Being able to speak many languages is very useful in travelling. 5. Did you know that Venice was founded by people fleeing from the mainland in front of the barbaric invasions? 6. Having finished our homework, we are going for a walk. 7. After leaving (finire) grammar schools, students usually attend a University. 8. Instead of being suspended from school as in Italy, our children, if they are undisciplined, receive corporal punishment. 9. Before commencing their studies at a secondary school pupils do an entrance exam. 10. At the end of every term pupils receive a report card containing their marks.

A. *Translate into English:* 1. Venezia, chiamata la Regina dell'Adriatico, fu per secoli una delle più famose repubbliche italiane. 2. Si racconta che essa fosse fondata sulle isolette della laguna veneta da gente, per lo più (mostly) pescatori, che fuggivano dinnanzi alle invasioni barbariche. 3. I periodi più importanti per l'architettura veneziana sono il '200, il '400 e il '500 e in questi periodi furono costruiti i palazzi più belli e le chiese più conosciute. 4. Chi ha visitato Venezia non può dimenticare Piazza

San Marco, con i suoi famosi colombi, la sua magnifica chiesa scintillante di mosaici, il campanile con il famoso orologio e i lunghi portici. 5. Le industrie principali di Venezia sono quella del vetro e quella dei merletti e passeggiando sotto i portici si vedono nei negozi, bicchieri, vasi, e bottiglie di vetro leggerissimo lavorati a Murano. 6. L'isola in cui si lavorano i merletti è Burano e le donne di Burano passano molte ore della loro giornata, dinnanzi alla loro casa, lavorando bellissimi merletti. 7. Col vetro si fanno anche collane e braccialetti che sono un altro degli oggetti preferiti dai forestieri. 8. Arrivando a Venezia in treno, si passa su un lunghissimo ponte che unisce la città alla terraferma. 9. L'acqua dei canali è verde scuro all'ombra, ma scintilla al sole come migliaia di pezzettini di vetro. 10. Le gondole scivolano sull'acqua; i gondolieri remano per la maggior parte in piedi, usando solamente un remo. 11. Dinnanzi ai meravigliosi palazzi del Canal Grande, che sembrano ornati di merletti di pietra, vi sono ancora molti pali a cui venivano legate le gondole dei visitatori. 12. I capi della città erano chiamati dogi e sotto di loro Venezia si arricchì esercitando il commercio con l'oriente. 13. Col commercio fiorirono le arti, specialmente la pittura e la scuola veneta può gloriarsi di famosi pittori come Tiziano Vecellio, Paolo Veronese, Tintoretto, Tiepolo e Canaletto. 14. Tiziano Vecellio è forse il più famoso tra i pittori veneti; si racconta che una volta essendogli caduto il pennello mentre stava dipingendo, Carlo V che gli era vicino, si chinasse a raccoglierlo. 15. I capelli delle donne nei quadri del Tiziano sono spesso di un biondo caldo e rossastro che è diventato famoso col nome di rosso tizianesco. 16. Il Tiepolo è specialmente conosciuto per gli affreschi con cui decorò i soffitti dei più celebri palazzi. 17. La Basilica di San Marco, scintillante di mosaici, fu costruita prima nell'829 e poi una seconda volta nel 1063 dal doge Contarini. 18. Tra i ponti più famosi di Venezia ci sono il Ponte di Rialto e quello dei Sospiri. 19. Questo ponte fu così chiamato perché attraverso di esso passavano i prigionieri che andavano dal palazzo dei Dogi alla prigione. 20. Veneto fu il Goldoni che nel '700 arricchì il teatro italiano di moltissime commedie, alcune delle quali si recitano ancora oggi.

B. *Translate into Italian:* 1. Up to the sixth century the little green islands of the lagoon(s) on which Venice is now built, were little known. 2. Some of the inhabitants were poor fishermen, others carried on a trade in salt. 3. Fleeing before the barbarians, the inhabitants of the mainland built their homes on these islands; this was the origin of Venice, now called the Queen of the Adriatic. 4. Being built on these small islands, the city has canals instead of streets, but there are numerous bridges by means of which people can cross the canals and go from one part of the city to another. 5. Two of the most famous bridges are the Rialto, at the centre, and the Bridge of Sighs, across which prisoners used to pass from the Doge's palace to the gaols. 6. Visiting one of the famous palaces along the Grand Canal, one leaves one's gondola tied to a pole, as one would leave a car in front of a house in our modern cities. 7. The architecture of these palaces and of the magnificent churches, especially that of St Mark with its five cupolas, has something (di) Eastern in its style. 8. This is natural since the Republic of Venice carried on a trade with the East for many centuries. 9. Venetian architecture and sculpture were possibly at their greatest (nel loro massimo splendore) in the 13th and 16th centuries when so many magnificent churches and palaces were built. 10. St Mark's Square is generally crowded with people admiring the huge basilica with its scintillating mosaics, the famous bell tower, the doge's palace and long colonnade. 11. These people love to watch the pigeons eating from their hands and washing themselves in the fountains. 12. There there are magnificent shops selling laces and objects in glass, the two most important industries of Venice. 13. Murano is the name of the island where glass is worked, and Murano vases and bottles, necklaces and bracelets are among the objects foreigners buy in Venice. 14. Among the islands around Venice Burano is famous for its laces; the women of Burano spend a large part of their day working these beautiful laces. 15. The heads of the Republic of Venice were called dogi and under them Venice became rich. 16. When Vasco da Gama opened a new route to (verso) the East, much of her trade passed from Venice to other cities leaving her much less rich than before. 17. But the flourishing of Venetian art continued till the 18th century when she could boast of the masterpieces of Tiepolo and Canaletto as in the 16th century those of Titian, Tintoretto and Veronese. 18. The reddish colour of women s hair in Titian paintings is still called Titian red and their magnificent clothes give us an idea of the rich silk and brocades of that period. 19. "The design of Michelangelo and the colour of Titian" was the motto that Tintoretto had on his studio wall. 20. Veronese's frescoes on the ceiling and walls of Venetian palaces are well known as are those of Tiepolo two centuries later.

C. Come si chiamano le varie parti del corpo umano?—What are the different parts of the human body called? Cominciamo dalla testa o capo.—Let us begin from the head. La parte superiore e posteriore della testa è costituita dal cranio che contiene il cervello e che è coperto esternamente dai capelli.—The upper and posterior part of the head comprises the skull which contains the brain and which is covered externally with hair. Di che colore sono i capelli?—What colour is hair? I capelli possono essere biondi, bruni, castani rossi, grigi, bianchi, brizzolati; possono anche essere lisci, ondulati, ricci o crespi, corti o lunghi.—Hair can be fair, dark, chestnut red, grey, white and greying; it can also be straight, wavy, curly, short or long. La parte anteriore della testa si chiama faccia o viso e se la pelle del viso è liscia e di un bel colore si dice che una persona ha una bella carnagione o un bel colorito.—The frontal part of the head is called face and if the skin is smooth and healthy looking we say that the person has a good complexion or a good colouring. Nella faccia ci sono gli occhi che possono essere neri, azzurri, verdi, grigi. In the face are the eyes which can be black, blue, green and grey. Quali sono le varie parti dell'occhio? Le pupille, le palpebre, le ciglia sono parti dell'occhio. Al di sopra degli occhi ci sono le sopracciglia.—What are the different parts of the eye? The pupils, the eye-lids, and the lashes are the different parts of the eye. Above the eyes are the eyebrows. Nella faccia ci sono anche il naso, le guancie, la bocca in cui ci sono la lingua, il palato e i denti, e il mento. Sul mento degli uomini cresce la barba.—The face is also made up of the nose, the cheeks, the mouth in which are the tongue, the palate and the teeth, and the chin. A beard grows on men's chins. Ai lati della testa ci sono gli orecchi.—The ears are on the side of the head. La testa è unita al tronco per mezzo del collo. The head is joined to the body by the neck. Quali sono le varie parti del tronco?—What are the various parts of the trunk? Nel tronco distinguiamo le spalle, il petto, lo stomaco e il ventre.—In the trunk we have the shoulders, the chest, the stomach and the abdomen. Come si chiamano le braccia e le gambe? Si chiamano gli arti e sono attaccate al tronco.—What are our arms and legs called? They are called our limbs and they are attached to the trunk. Le braccia si piegano formando i gomiti: le mani sono attaccate alle braccia per mezzo dei polsi.—The arms bend forming the elbows: the hands are joined to the arms by the wrists. Le gambe si piegano al ginocchio e ad esse per mezzo delle caviglie sono attaccati i piedi.—The legs bend at the knee and the feet are joined to the legs by the ankles. Quali sono le varie parti delle mani? Le mani hanno il dorso e la palma: esse hanno cinque dita: il pollice, l'indice, il medio, l'anulare e il mignolo.—What are the various parts of the hand? The hands have a back and a palm: they have five fingers: the thumb, the index finger, the middle finger, the fourth or ring finger and the little finger. Come si chiamano le varie parti del piede?—What are the different parts of the foot called? Nei piedi il dito più grosso si chiama alluce e la parte posteriore calcagno o tallone.—The biggest toe is called the big toe and the back part of the foot is called the heel. Il punto debole di un uomo si chiama 'tallone di Achille'.—A person's weak spot is called 'Achilles' heel'. Di una persona maldicente si dice che è una cattiva lingua o che ha la lingua lunga.—We say of a slanderous person that they have an evil tongue or a long tongue. Che cosa si dice di una persona che non sente bene? Si dice che ha l'orecchio duro.—What do we say of a person who does not hear well? We say that they have a hard ear. Di una persona che parla apertamente? Che non ha peli sulla lingua.—Of a person who speaks openly? that they have no hairs on their tongue. Chiamiamo testa balzana una persona un po' matta.—We call a crazy head someone who is a bit mad. Chi è curioso e indiscreto è spesso chiamato ficcanaso.—One who is curious and interfering is often called Nosey Parker. Che cosa si dice di una persona che ruba? Si dice che ha la mano lesta o le mani lunghe.—What does one say about a person who steals? that they have quick or long hands. Di una persona che spende troppo? Che ha le mani bucate.—Of a person who spends too much? that they have holes in their hands. Che vuole dire 'andare con i piedi di piombo'? Significa agire con prudenza.—What does 'to go with leaden feet' mean? It means to act with prudence. Entrare in punta di piedi significa to enter on tiptoes. Ventre a terra è una espressione equivalente a 'a grande velocità'.—With belly on the ground is an expression signifying 'at great speed'. A mano destra significa on the right. Mancino è chi usa la mano sinistra per scrivere, mangiare, tagliare, etc.—'Mancino'is one who writes, eats, cuts, etc., with the left hand. Un colpo mancino è un colpo inaspettato.—A left handed blow is an unexpected or unfair blow. Prendere per i capelli o per la gola significa forzare qualcuno o fargli pagare troppo.—To take someone by the hair or throat means to force, or to make someone pay too much. Che significa 'Tirare gli orecchi'? What does to pull the ears mean? to box one's ears or to scold one. Che significa 'portare in palma di mano'? Apprezzare o lodare qualcuno.—What does to 'carry in the palm of one's hand' mean? To appraise or praise someone. Essere o mettere all'indice significa essere proibito.—To be or to put on the index means to be forbidden. Segnare a dito significa to point. Fare l'occhio di triglia means to have a 'come hither' look. Fare l'occhio, l'occhiolino o strizzare l'occhio to make eyes or to 'squeeze' the eye means to wink. Aggrottare le ciglia—to knit the brows or to frown. Storcere la bocca, il naso—to turn up one's nose. Aguzzare gli occhi—to peer. 'Che barba' significa che noia! What a 'beard' means what a nuisance. Pregare a mani giunte—to pray insistently. Un uomo di polso—a man of strong will. Un colpo di testa is a harsh decision against someone's authority. Testa dura is a thick head. 'A braccetto' means arm in arm. 'Fare la pelle a qualcuno' means to kill somebody. Squadrare qualcuno dalla testa ai piedi is to look someone up and down. Che cosa si dice se uno non si sente bene? —What do people say if they do not feel well? Mi fa male la testa, la gola, lo stomaco.—I have a headache, a sore throat, stomach pains. Mi fanno male gli orecchi—I have earache. Ho un dolore alla spalla, al braccio, in questa gamba.—I have a pain in the shoulder, the arm, this leg.

D. *Accidɛnti*! etc.

Accidɛnti! L'ho dimenticato a casa—Damn! I've left it at home
Accidɛnti! Guarda quella bionda!—Whew! Look at that blonde!
Accidɛnti a lui!—Damn the man!
Cɔsta un accidɛnte—It costs a hell of a lot (also cɔsta un ɔcchio della tɛsta and cɔsta l'ɔsso del cɔllo).

LESSON XXX

Indefinite Pronouns and Adjectives

Indefinite pronouns, so called because they do not refer to particular persons or things, and adjectives of the same kind, can be grouped as follows:

1. Pronouns and adjectives used only in the singular.

Pronouns		Adjectives	
ognuno -a	everyone	ogni	every
qualcuno -a	somebody, anybody	qualche	some, any
qualcheduno -a		qualunque	whatever
chiunque	whoever, whomsoever	qualsiasi	of some sort, of any sort
ciascuno -a	each, everyone		

With the exception of *ognuno*, *qualcuno* and *ciascuno* that have a feminine form, all others are invariable.

Ciascheduno, *chicchessia*, *checché* (each, whoever, whatever) are forms of written Italian which are falling into disuse:

Ognuno l'ammirava.	Everyone admired him.
Qualcuno arrivò in ritardo.	Somebody arrived late.
Chiunque arrivi.	Whoever arrives.
Ciascuno ne comprò due.	Each one bought two.
Usciva ogni giorno.	He went out every day.
Compriamo qualche cartolina.	Let us buy some postcards.
Cerca una qualunque soluzione.	Find some sort of solution.
Qualsiasi ragione.	Whatever reason.

2. Pronouns and adjectives used both in the singular and the plural.

uno -a -i -e (pron.)	one, ones
altro -a -i -e (pron. & adj.)	other, others, else
altrui (inv. pron.)	of others, to others
certo -a -i -e (pron. & adj.)	certain
tale, tali (pron. & adj.)	such, somebody

Uno besides being an article and a numeral, when used in the sense of 'a certain', is an indefinite pronoun. In the plural it is always preceded by the definite article and is used in conjunction with *altri*:

Uno mi raccontò.
Someone told me.

Gli uni leggevano, gli altri scrivevano.
Some were reading, others writing.

Altro -a -i -e can be used both as a pronoun and an adjective:

Parliamo d'altro.	Let us talk of something else.
Un'altra vɔlta.	Another time.

L'un l'altro translates each other, reciprocally.

Si aiutarono l'un l'altro. They helped each other.

Altrui is invariable and used only of persons, signifying *di altri*, *ad altri*:

Rispɛtta la rɔba altrui. Respect other people's property.

Cɛrto -a -i -e in the singular, preceded by the indefinite article, is an adjective only. Used in the plural it can be both adjective and pronoun:

Un cɛrto giorno.	A certain day.
Cɛrti lo stimano molto.	Certain people esteem him highly.
Cercava cɛrte ɛrbe.	He was looking for certain herbs.

Tale -i can be used both as a pronoun and an adjective:

Incontrai un tale.	I met somebody, a person.
Quei tali libri	Those (particular) books.

3. Compound of *uno* used almost exclusively in the plural:

alcuno -a -i -e (pron. & adj.)	someone, some
taluno -a -i -e (pron. & adj.)	certain people, somebody, certain
certuno -a -i -e (pron. & adj.)	someone, somebody

Alcuno with few exceptions is used always in the plural in the spoken language:

	Alcuni dicono.	Some say.
but:	Non ho alcun dubbio.	I have no doubt.

Certuni and *taluni* are used mostly in writing:

Certuni pensano. Some people think.

Niɛnte and *nulla* are equivalent to *nessuna cɔsa* and are invariable pronouns.

Veruno (nobody) and *cadauno* (each) are literary and obsolete.

4. The following adjectives of quantity, when used as substantives are also considered to be indefinite pronouns:

pɔco -a pɔch -e	few, little
molto -a -i -e	much, many
parecchio -a -i -e	a good deal, some, several
trɔppo -a -i -e	too, too much, too many
tutto -a -i -e	all, whole
tanto -a -i -e	so much, so great, so many
alquanto -a -i -e	some, several

Fra pɔco giungerà.	He will arrive shortly.
Parecchi erano partiti.	Several had left.
Molti sono chiamati.	Many are called.

Absolute Construction

The absolute construction, derived from Latin, is so called because the phrase concerned, although equal to a dependent clause, is in Italian as in Latin, independent of the rest of the sentence.

It is a very common construction in Italian and consists in omitting the auxiliary verb (ɛssere or avere) and using the past participle alone in place of the perfect participle (gerundio composto).

Rule for the Agreement of the Participle

When the verb of the participial phrase is intransitive and applies to the subject of the main clause, the past participle agrees in gender and number with that subject:

Partita di buɔn mattino, essa camminò per tre ore.
Having left early in the morning she walked for three hours.

Arrivati in cima alla collina si riposarono.
Having arrived at the summit of the hill, they rested.

When the verb in the participial phrase is transitive, the past participle agrees in gender and number with the object it governs.

Salutata la commessa, uscirono dal negɔzio.
Having greeted the assistant, they left the shop.

Scritte le lɛttere andò ad imbucarle.
Having written the letters he went to post them.

Vocabulary XXX

glɔria glory; (adj. **glorioso**)
g*u*glia spire, pinnacle
tetto roof
turista (m. & f.) tourist
lato side
descrizione (f.) description
gioiɛllo jewel
gioielliɛre jeweller
mattone (m). brick
refettɔrio refectory
impressione (f.) impression
luɔgo di ritrɔvo meeting place
stɔria story, history
aeroplano aeroplane
regalo present, gift
ricchezza richness
lago lake
capitale (f.) capital
romanzo novel
poɛsia poems, poetry
aperitivo aperitif, drink
affare (m.) business, affair
gala gala
scopɛrta discovery
abbondanza abundance
fiume (m.) river
banc*a*rio (adj.) banking
econɔmico (adj.) economic
gɔtico (adj.) gothic
immɛnso (adj.) immense
maestoso (adj.) majestic
intatto (adj.) intact
architettɔnico (adj.) architectural
favorito (adj.) favourite

puro (adj.) pure
Lombardia Lombardy (adj. **lombardo**)
Ambrogio Ambrose
sfortunatamente (adv.) unfortunately

scoprire to discover, come upon
innalzarsi to rise
scomparire* to fade out
coltivare to grow
accorgersi to notice

Exercise 1

Translate into English: 1. Non parlarne a chicchessia. 2. Checché egli ne pensi. 3. In qualsiasi posto. 4. Danne due per ciascuno. 5. Ad alcune ragazze. 6. Senza alcun disegno. 7. Chiunque lo veda. 8. Se ognuno pensasse agli affari propri. 9. Lo comprava ogni giorno. 10. In qualunque negozio. 11. Qualsiasi regalo. 12. Qualcuno li aspetta. 13. Gli affari altrui. 14. Certuni arrivano in ritardo. 15. Telefona sempre ad una certa ora. 16. In qualche piazza. 17. Tali francobolli. 18. Alcuni arrivavano altri partivano. 19. Nessuno lo capiva. 20. Ognuno comprò il biglietto.

Exercise 2

Translate into Italian: 1. Having admired the picture they went into the other room. 2. Having arrived late she did not find a seat. 3. Having fled from the mainland, they built their homes on these islands. 4. Having failed his exam., he repeated the class. 5. Having finished his Moses, Michelangelo asked the statue why it did not speak. 6. Having recovered from her cold, the girl returned to school. 7. Having received his answer they left immediately. 8. Having arrived at the station too soon, they waited in the waiting room. 9. Having looked at the windows, they entered the shop. 10. Having paid the bill they left a tip on the table.

Exercise 3

Translate into Italian: 1. In whatever country of the world. 2. Whoever built it. 3. Without any reason. 4. Other people's lives. 5. Certain places of interest. 6. Such buildings. 7. Any steamer at all. 8. Everyone admired it. 9. He bought some books. 10. Somebody was writing to the papers. 11. Each one rose. 12. Every spire. 13. Was there not a distinction of some sort? 14. Some spoke English, others French. 15. They understood each other. 16. He was looking for a certain novel. 17. Those (particular) stamps. 18. A certain person. 19. I shall return shortly. 20. I have no idea. 21. Wherever you arrive. 22. Some people are always late. 23. Without any system. 24. Of any masterpiece. 25. Some other time.

A. *Translate into English:* 1. Milano, capitale della Lombardia, è uno dei centri commerciali e industriali più importanti di Italia. 2. Chiunque arrivi a Milano osserva subito il maggiore traffico, le strade più affollate, la fretta dei passanti che camminano velocemente, le vetrine dei negozi piene di tante belle cose. 3. La chiesa che è una delle glorie di Milano è il Duomo, di stile gotico, che s'innalza con le sue guglie e la sua maestosa facciata ornate di statue. 4. Milano è il centro di numerose industrie tra le quali quella della seta, della lana, delle automobili. 5. Uno dei luoghi di ritrovo più conosciuti è la Galleria, nella quale i Milanesi si incontrano o si danno appuntamento per prendere l'aperitivo o per parlare di affari. 6. Nella vicina piazza c'è la Scala, il teatro famoso in tutto il mondo per le opere che vi si danno. 7. Per quanto sia difficile avere i biglietti senza prenotarli molto tempo prima, ogni turista dovrebbe cercare di andare una volta alla Scala in una serata di gala; quante signore eleganti e quanti meravigliosi gioielli! 8. Lombardi furono alcuni tra i più grandi poeti e scrittori italiani. 9. Alessandro Manzoni è famoso per il suo romanzo 'I Promessi Sposi', una storia del tempo in cui Milano era sotto il governo degli Spagnuoli. 10. Alcuni pensano che 'I Promessi Sposi' sia un romanzo un po' pesante ma leggendo questo libro ci accorgiamo che il Manzoni usò in esso una lingua e uno stile purissimi. 11. Il capolavoro del Parini è 'Il Giorno' in cui il poeta mostra, criticandoli, i costumi del mondo elegante nel '700. 12. La sua opera fu molto importante perché egli nelle sue poesie mostrò anche le nuove scoperte della scienza. 13. Chi non ha sentito parlare dell'Ultima Cena di Leonardo da Vinci? 14. Sfortunatamente questo celebre dipinto di Leonardo da Vinci su una delle pareti del refettorio di Santa Maria delle Grazie è stato molto rovinato dal tempo. 15. Alcuni pensano che se Leonardo non avesse usato dei colori preparati da lui stesso, l'affresco si sarebbe conservato meglio. 16. In alcune parti della pianura lombarda, per l'abbondanza delle acque portate dai molti fiumi che scendono dalle Alpi, si può coltivare il riso. 17. Il risotto alla milanese è una delle specialità di Milano e chiunque lo assaggi sarà d'accordo nel trovarlo molto buono. 18. La campagna lombarda ha paesaggi meravigliosi e in questa parte d'Italia vi sono dei laghi bellissimi. 19. Il Manzoni comincia il suo celebre romanzo con una descrizione di uno di questi laghi: il lago di Como. 20. Como è anche famosa per essere il centro principale dell'industria della seta.

B. *Translate into Italian:* 1. Milan, although it is not the capital of Italy, has become the economic capital and the greatest industrial, commercial and banking centre of the country. 2. Its principal architectural glory is the magnificent cathedral, a wonderful example of Gothic architecture with its 135 little spires which rise towards the sky. 3. Everyone admires its facade of white marble and the thousands of statues with which its roofs and walls are adorned. 4. It was begun about 1386 and was finished at the beginning of the 20th century. Inside there is room for 40,000 people and, after St Peter's, it is the largest church in the world. 5. A very famous place in Milan is the Vittorio Emmanuele Gallery with its great glass roof and its cupola almost 50 metres high. 6. It is a favourite meeting place for the Milanese who meet there to have an aperitif or to talk business. 7. In the restaurants of this famous gallery one can sample some of the dishes for which Milan is noted; for example risotto alla Milanese and cotoletta alla Milanese. 8. This region of Italy gives us many fine cheeses: Mascarpone, Robiola, Bel Paese and Stracchino. 9. Through the Vittorio Emanuele Gallery we enter Piazza della Scala whose world famous theatre has given its name to the square. 10. Among the many other old churches, that founded by St Ambrose in the 4th century and rebuilt of (in) red brick in the 12th, is now a modern basilica in which is the tomb of the saint. 11. Thousands of visitors go to Milan every year to see Leonardo da Vinci's 'Last Supper' painted on the wall of the Refectory beside the church of Santa Maria della Grazia. 12. Unfortunately this painting, one of his greatest masterpieces, has been much destroyed by time and one day will certainly fade out completely. 13. Certain people consider that the best collection of paintings in Italy is in the Uffizi in Florence but the Brera palace in Milan can boast of a very fine collection also. 14. Some of the walls built by the Spaniards in the 16th century are still almost intact. 15. Milan is the centre of the silk trade and today as in the past its beautiful brocades, velvets and rich silks are appreciated all over the world. 16. Some of the other industries by which she has enriched herself are those of machinery, motor cars and aeroplanes. 17. The Naviglio, a large canal which once divided the city in two parts, is now no longer used. 18. From the Alps several rivers flow (scendere) through the Po valley (pianura padana) in which, because of the (its) natural richness and of the abundance of water, rice can be grown. 19. Lombardy can boast of some of the most celebrated writers and poets, such as Manzoni and Parini: the former is famous for his masterpiece 'I Promessi Sposi' the latter for 'Il Giorno'. 20. Parini, in his poem, criticized the customs and the life of society in the 18th century.

C. Da quanto tempo l'Italia è una nazione unita e c'è nessuna traccia delle antiche divisioni?—How long has Italy been a united nation and do no traces of the former divisions remain? L'Italia fu divisa per secoli e secoli in molti stati e benché dal 1870 essa sia ormai unita in una nazione sola, tracce delle antiche divisioni sono ancora visibili nelle differenze esistenti tra il Nord e il Sud.—Italy was divided for centuries into many states and although from 1870 onwards it has been united into one single nation, traces of the old divisions are still visible in the differences existing between the North and the South. Quale parte del paese ha il livello di vita più alto? Il livello di vita, d'istruzione e di igiene è certo più alto nell'Italia Settentrionale che nell'Italia Meridionale e tra i problemi più gravi del Mezzogiorno ci sono quelli dell'analfabetismo, della disoccupazione e della riforma agraria.—Which part of the country has the higher standard of living? The level of life, of education and of hygiene is certainly higher in the North than in the South of Italy, and among the gravest problems of the south are illiteracy, unemployment and agrarian reform. I Settentrionali sono differenti in aspetto dai Meridionali?—Do the people from the north look different from those of the south? Gli Italiani del Nord si chiamano Settentrionali, quelli del Sud, Meridionali e spesso essi sono molto differenti sia in apparenza che in cara[illegible].—The Italians of the north are called 'Settentrionali', those of the [illegible] are very different both in appear[illegible] vereste?—How would you descri[illegible] lmente più alti, biondi e con gli oc[illegible] runi e con occhi neri.—The northe[illegible] h blue eyes, the southerners are sh[illegible] E quali sono le differenze di caratt[illegible] character? I Settentrionali sono [illegible] fari; i Meridionali sognatori eloqu[illegible] erners are considered active, pract[illegible] ers are dreamy, eloquent and full [illegible] te il Mezzogiorno?—Where exact[illegible] dove esattamente cominci il Mez[illegible] n Italia si dice scherzando che i Mi[illegible] cominci da Milano in giù e i Rom[illegible] lem to state exactly where the south begins, because they say for a joke in Italy that the people of Milan claim that the south begins from Milan down, and the Romans from Rome down. Si può capire dal modo di parlare a che regione appartenga una persona?—Can you tell from his speech to which district an Italian belongs? I dialetti cambiano da regione a regione e a volte nella stessa regione ogni provincia ha dialetto e cadenza differenti tranne la Toscana in cui anche il popolo parla in italiano puro.—Dialects change from one region to another and at times from province to province, each having its own dialect and intonation except Tuscany where even the common people speak pure Italian. Siena è considerata la città in cui si parla meglio.—Siena is considered the city where the best Italian is spoken. Il clima contribuisce alla differenza di temperamento e carattere?—Does the climate contribute to the difference of temperament and character? Anche il clima varia molto divenendo più mite e moderato dal Nord al Sud e dall'interno alla costa.—The climate also varies a lot becoming milder from north to south and from the interior to the coast. I contadini della pianura pugliese sono tanto differenti dai montanari che abitano nelle Alpi quanto gli abitanti di paesi diversi.—The inhabitants of the plain of Apulia are as different from the mountain dwellers who live on the Alps as inhabitants of different countries. Che cosa hanno in comune tutti gli Italiani? In tutti gli Italiani è comune il grande amore per la loro patria. —What have all Italians got in common? Common to all Italians is a great love for their fatherland.

D. *Rɔba da matti*! *Cɔse da pazzi*! *Cɔse turche*!
Sai che l'ha pagato cεnto milioni? Rɔba da matti!
Do you know that he paid a hundred million lire for it? Incredible!

LESSON XXXI

General Observations on Irregular Verbs

Italian irregular verbs are to the foreign student the most difficult part of the language to master. Many of them, however, are hardly ever used, quite a number show—as we shall see later—distinct similarities which lend themselves to grouping, others are simply derived from an original irregular verb and, on the whole, follow its irregularities. The irregularities occur almost entirely in the stem and—with the exception of *ɛssere* and the four irregular verbs of the first conjugation: *dare*, *andare*, *fare* and *stare*—only in a few tenses.

The mood and tenses in which irregularities occur are:

Infinitive

The present infinitive being the tense from which all other tenses are usually formed can hardly be described as irregular; there are six verbs however and their derivatives, which are peculiar in having most of their tenses formed from the original Latin infinitive stem and some others (future and conditional) from the contracted Italian one. In such contracted infinitives a syllable is dropped and sometimes an additional *r* is inserted:

fa(ce)re	fare	to do	condu(ce)re	condurre	to lead
be(ve)re	bere	to drink	po(ne)re	porre	to put
di(ce)re	dire	to say	tra(he)re	trarre	to draw

Present Indicative

The 2nd person plural is always regular; in other persons the irregularity as shown in: *faccio* (fare), *vado* (andare), *pɔsso* (potere), *dɛbbo* (dovere), varies and does not lend itself to grouping, except in certain verbs as will be shown later.

Past Descriptive

Past descriptive is always regular; in contracted verbs keeps to the stem of the original infinitive and, in those which have changed conjugation, the original 2nd conjugation.

facevo (facere)   conducevo (conducere)

Past Absolute

Is the tense in which irregularity occurs most commonly but presents a certain uniformity which renders grouping easy. The key to the irregularity is the 1st person singular, from which the 3rd person singular and the 3rd person plural are derived. The other three persons are regular. The stem of the first person must always be supplied; the endings, invariable throughout the conjugations, are: *i*, *e*, *ero* respectively.

fec-i	*scriss-i*
fac-esti	scriv-esti
fec-e	*scriss-e*
fac-emmo	scriv-emmo
fac-este	scriv-este
fec-ero	*scriss-ero*

Future and Conditional

Apart from the six verbs with contracted infinitives, which show (with the exception of *bere*) the same irregularity in the future and in the conditional, other verbs whose infinitives are regular can have a similar contraction in these two tenses. This irregularity affects the stem only, never the endings,

fare	farò	farɛi
bere	berrò	berrɛi
andare	andrò	andrɛi
vedere	vedrò	vedrɛi

Present Subjunctive

The irregularity of the present subjunctive is, for the most part, strictly connected with that of the present indicative, being formed, with few exceptions, on the same stem. The endings *a*, *a*, *a*, *iamo*, *iate*, *iano*, common to regular and irregular verbs of the 2nd and 3rd conjugations, are used also in the four irregular verbs of the 1st conjugation:

fare	faccio	faccia
andare	vado	vada

Imperfect Subjunctive

The imperfect subjunctive, almost always regular, is formed on the same stem as the 2nd person singular of the past absolute and thus, with few exceptions (*stare*, *dare*) shows trace of the original Latin infinitive.

fare (facere)	facessi
bere (bevere)	bevessi

Past Participle

Past participle is irregular in a variety of ways, though sometimes it is formed on the irregular past absolute.

fare	feci	fatto
scrivere	scrissi	scritto
scendere	scesi	sceso

Irregular Verbs of the First Conjugation (*continued*)

The following list completes the irregular forms of the four irregular verbs of the 1st conjugation:

FUTURE

andare: andrò, andrai, andrà, andremo, andrete, andranno.
dare: darò, darai, darà, daremo, darete, daranno.
fare: farò, farai, farà, faremo, farete, faranno.
stare: starò, starai, starà, staremo, starete, staranno.

CONDITIONAL

andare: andrεi, andresti, andrεbbe, andremmo, andreste, andrεbbero.
dare: darεi, daresti, darεbbe, daremmo, dareste, darεbbero.
fare: farεi, faresti, farεbbe, faremmo, fareste, farεbbero.
stare: starεi, staresti, starεbbe, staremmo, stareste, starεbbero.

PRESENT SUBJUNCTIVE

andare: vada, vada, vada, andiamo, andiate, vadano.
dare: dia, dia, dia, diamo, diate, diano.
fare: faccia, faccia, faccia, facciamo, facciate, facciano.
stare: stia, stia, stia, stiamo, stiate, stiano.

IMPERFECT SUBJUNCTIVE

andare (regular)
dare: dessi, dessi, desse, dessimo, deste, dessero.
fare: facessi, facessi, facesse, facessimo, faceste, facessero.
stare: stessi, stessi, stesse, stessimo, steste, stessero.

IMPERATIVE

andare: va', vada, andiamo, andate, vadano.
dare: da', dia, diamo, date, diano.
fare: fa', faccia, facciamo, fate, facciano.
stare: sta', stia, stiamo, state, stiano.

PAST ABSOLUTE

andare (regular)
dare: diεdi or dεtti, desti, diεde or dεtte, demmo, deste, diεdero or dεttero.
fare: fεci, facesti, fεce, facemmo, faceste, fεcero
stare: stεtti, stesti, stεtte, stemmo, steste, stεttero

PAST PARTICIPLE
andare (regular)
dare: (regular)
fare: fatto
stare: (regular)

Fare

Fare followed by the infinitive is the construction used to render 'to have something done' or 'to make someone do something' or 'to get something done'. Noun objects follow the infinitive.

Feci spedire il mio bagaglio. I had my luggage forwarded.

When both verbs have an object, the object of *fare* becomes indirect.

Faccia scrivere agli alunni questa poesia.
Get the pupils to write this poem.

Contrary to the rule that conjunctive pronouns follow the infinitive form of the verb, in this construction they precede *fare*.

L'ho fatto mandare a casa.	I have had it sent home.
Gli feci studiare la lezione.	I made him study the lesson.
Gliela feci studiare.	I made him study it.

Stare

Stare—to be, to be on the point, to stay, to suit, replaces in many cases, as in the progressive form, the verb *to be* and, according to the noun or verb which follows it, takes different meanings.

Stare per partire	to be on the point of leaving.
stare in piɛdi, seduto, alla finɛstra	to stand, sit, be at the window.
stare a guardare, sentire	to look, to listen.
stare in campagna, di casa	to be, to live in the country, to live at.
stare bɛne	to be well, to suit, to serve right.

Andare

Similarly *andare* can alter its meaning according to the noun or phrases which follow it.

andare a piɛdi	to walk.
andare a cavallo	to ride.
andare in bicicletta	to ride a bicycle.
andare in trɛno, in automɔbile, etc.	to go by train, by car.
andare bɛne	to go well, to fit.

Exercise 1

Repeat orally: The imperfect tense of: *fare, andare, dare*; the future of: *andare, stare*; the present conditional of: *fare, andare*; the present subjunctive of: *fare, dare, stare, andare*; the imperfect subjunctive of *stare, fare, dare*; the imperative of: *andare, fare, dare, stare.*

Exercise 2

Translate into Italian: 1. Let us go. 2. Do not do it. 3. They have made it. 4. You would stand. 5. I shall go there. 6. Let them make it. 7. Although he gave it to her. 8. They will make them (f.) 9. So that he might stay. 10. We were giving them (f.) to him. 11. He will be better soon. 12. Go there at once. 13. Do it as well as possible. 14. You would make. 15. Let them stay. 16. They made a mistake. 17. He gave us everything. 18. Before he went. 19. Even if they stayed. 20. In order that you might go. 21. Give it to me at once. 22. He fears that she has gone. 23. It seems that he has given it to her. 24. Let us do it now. 25. Give it to him.

Exercise 3

Translate into Italian: 1. Get the pupil to read this novel. 2. We had the house built. 3. I shall make him write it (f.) at once. 4. Although he had it (m.) made, it does not suit him. 5. Where is your luggage? We had it forwarded. 6. I was on the point of phoning you when you rang the bell. 7. Gondoliers always row standing in their boats. 8. Do you know Florence well? We live near the Duomo. 9. He was writing when we arrived. 10. If that boy is suspended for a day or two it will serve him right. 11. When it is good weather, my friends cycle to school. 12. I always used to travel by train, now I prefer to fly. 13. One sees more by walking than when one goes by car. 14. It is better to learn to ride when one is very young. 15. How are things going? 16. Where is your cousin now? She is in the country with my aunt. 17. Is your dress a model? No but I had it copied from a model. 18. She was listening without understanding. 19. This dress does not fit you, it is too large. 20. She made them eat it.

A. *Translate into English:* Il mio cane non era riguardato come un cane normale, ma come un essere straordinario, diverso da tutti gli altri cani, e degno di essere particolarmente onorato. Anch'io, del resto, ho sempre pensato che in lui ci fosse un elemento infantilmente angelico o demoniaco, e che i contadini non avessero torto nel trovargli quella ambiguità che obbliga all'adorazione. Già, la sua origine era misteriosa. Questo cane era stato trovato in treno, sulla linea che da Napoli va a

Taranto, con un cartellino appeso al collare che diceva: "Il mio nome è Barone. Chi mi trova abbia cura di me." Non si seppe dunque mai di dove venisse; forse dalla grande città, poteva essere il figlio di un rè. Lo presero i ferrovieri, e lo tennero qualche tempo alla stazione di Tricarico; quelli di Tricarico lo regalarono ai ferrovieri della stazione di Grassano. Il podestà di Grassano lo vide, se lo fece dare dai ferrovieri, e lo tenne nella sua casa con i suoi bambini, ma poiché faceva troppo chiasso, ne fece dono a suo fratello, segretario del sindacato dei contadini di Grassano, che lo portava sempre con sé, nei suoi giri per la campagna. Tutti conoscevano Barone, e tutti, a Grassano, lo consideravano un essere straordinario.

In verità era forse un cane da pastore, ma di una razza o incrocio non comune: non ne ho mai incontrati altri identici. Era di media grandezza, tutto bianco, con una macchia nera sulla punta delle orecchie, che aveva lunghissime e pendenti ai lati del viso. Questo era molto bello, come quello di un drago cinese, spaventoso nei momenti di furore, o quando mostrava i denti, ma con due occhi rotondi e umani, color nocciola, coi quali mi seguiva senza voltare il capo, pieno volta a volta di dolcezza, di libertà e di una certa infantile misteriosa arguzia. Il pelo era lungo quasi fino a terra, ricciuto, morbido e lucente come la seta: la coda, che egli portava arcuata e svolazzante come un pennacchio di guerriero orientale, era grossa come quella di una volpe. Era un essere allegro, libero e selvaggio: si affezionava, ma senza servilità; ubbidiva, ma conservava la sua indipendenza; una specie di folletto o di spiritello familiare, bonario, ma, in fondo, irraggiungibile. Più che camminare, saltava, a grandi balzi, con un ondeggiare delle orecchie e del pelo; inseguiva le farfalle e gli uccelli, spaventava le capre, lottava con i cani e coi gatti, correva da solo pei campi guardando le nuvole, sempre pronto, scattante, in un continuo gioco aereo, come seguisse il filo ondulante di un innocente pensiero inumano, l'elastico incarnarsi di un bizzarro spirito dei boschi.

(Carlo Levi: from *Cristo si è fermato a Eboli.*)

B. *Translate into Italian:* As the Count was standing one day in the large and beautiful square of Forli, there came a certain peasant who presented him with a basket of fruit. And when the Count said, "Stay and sup with me," the peasant answered, "My lord, I wish to go home before it rains, for assuredly there will be much rain to-day." The Count then sent for[1] his friend, the learned Guido, and said to him, "Dost thou hear what this man says?" Guido answered, "He does not know what he is saying; but wait a little." He carefully[2] observed the appearance of the sky, and then said it was impossible that it should rain that day. The

[1] mandare a chiamare [2] attentamente

peasant, however, obstinately maintained what he had said and when Guido asked him, "How dost thou know?" he replied that his ass, on coming out of the stable that morning, had shaken his head; and that whenever he did this, it was a certain sign that the weather would soon change. Then he took leave[1] of the Count, and departed in haste, much fearing the rain, though the sun was shining and the sky without a cloud. And an hour afterwards it began to thunder, and the rain fell in torrents until long after the setting of the sun. But Guido was greatly angered that the donkey of an ignorant peasant should seem wiser than he.

D. *Meno male*

Meno male che l'avevi avvertito.

Just as well that you had warned him.

[1] accomiatarsi

LESSON XXXII

Irregular Verbs with Contracted Infinitives

Irregular verbs with contracted infinitives (*dire*, *condurre*, *bere*, *trarre*, *porre*) have the following similarities which permit their being grouped:

(1) The future and the conditional are formed on the contracted stem.

(2) All other tenses are formed, almost entirely, on the original Latin stem.

(3) In all, the past absolute has the usual irregularity; in two, *trarre* and *porre*, a double *g* or a single *g* appears in the 1st person singular and 3rd plural of the present indicative; 1st, 2nd, 3rd singular and 3rd plural of the present subjunctive and in the 3rd singular and 3rd plural of the imperative.

Dire[1] **(dicere)**—to say or tell

Tenses formed on contracted stem:
Future: dirò, dirai, dirà, diremo, direte, diranno.
Conditional: dirɛi, diresti, dirɛbbe, diremmo, direste, dirɛbbero.

Tenses formed on the stem of the original verb:
Present Indicative: dico, dici, dice, diciamo, dite[2], dicono.
Imperfect: dicevo, dicevi, diceva, dicevamo, dicevate, dicevano.
Past Absolute: dissi, dicesti, disse, dicemmo, diceste, dissero.
Present Subjunctive: dica, dica, dica, diciamo, diciate, dicano.
Imperfect Subjunctive: dicessi, dicessi, dicesse, dicessimo, diceste, dicessero.
Imperative: di', dica, diciamo, dite, dicano.
Present Participle: dicɛnte.
Gerund: dicɛndo.
Past Participle: detto.

Note idiomatic constructions of *dire:* Dire di sì, di no—to say yes, no. Dire bene, male di—To speak well, ill of. Cosa vuɔl dire?—What does it mean? Dirɛi di sì.—I should think so.

[1] The commonest compound verbs identically conjugated are: *adire, addirsi, benedire, contraddire, disdire, indire, maledire, ridire.*
[2] The forms not based on the original stem are underlined.

Condurre[1] **(conducere)—To conduct, to lead**

Tenses formed on the contracted stem:

Future: **condurrò, condurrai, condurrà, condurremo, condurrete, condurranno.**

Conditional: **condurrɛi, condurresti, condurrɛbbe, condurremmo, condurreste, condurrɛbbero.**

Tenses formed on the original stem:

Present Indicative: **conduco, conduci, conduce, conduciamo, conducete, conducono.**

Imperfect: conducevo, conducevi, conduceva, conducevamo, conducevate, conducevano.

Past Absolute: condussi, conducesti, condusse, conducemmo, conduceste, condussero.

Present Subjunctive: conduca, conduca, conduca, conduciamo, conduciate, conducano.

Imperfect Subjunctive: conducessi, conducessi, conducesse, conducessimo, conduceste, conducessero.

Imperative: conduci, conduca, conduciamo, conducete, conducano.

Present Participle: conducɛnte.

Gerund: conducɛndo.

Past Participle: condotto.

Bere (bibere-bevere)—to drink

Tenses formed on the contracted stem:

Future: berrò, berrai, berrà, berremo, berrete, berranno.

Conditional: berrɛi, berresti, berrɛbbe, berremmo, berreste, berrɛbbero

Tenses formed on the original stem:

Present Indicative: bevo, bevi, beve, beviamo, bevete, bevono.

Imperfect: bevevo, bevevi, beveva, bevevamo, bevevate, bevevano.

Past Absolute: bevvi, bevesti, bevve, bevemmo, beveste, bevvero.

Present Subjunctive: beva, beva, beva, beviamo, beviate, bevano.

Imperfect Subjunctive: bevessi, bevessi, bevesse, bevessimo, beveste, bevessero.

Imperative: bevi, beva, beviamo, bevete, bevano.

Present Participle: bevɛnte.

Gerund: bevɛndo.

Past Participle: bevuto.

Trarre[2] (trahere)—To draw, to pull

Tenses formed on the contracted stem:

Future: trarrò, trarrai, trarrà, trarremo, trarrete, trarranno.

[1] The following verbs are identically conjugated: *addurre, dedurre, indurre, produrre, ridurre, tradurre.*

[2] The commonest compound verbs identically conjugated are: *astrarre, attrarre, contrarre, distrarre, detrarre, estrarre, protrarre, ritrarre, sottrarre.*

Conditional: trarrεi, trarresti, trarrεbbe, trarremmo, trarreste. trarrεbbero.

Tenses formed on the original stem: (the *h*, no longer pronounced, has disappeared in some persons or has been substituted by a double *g*)

Present Indicative: traggo, trai, trae, traiamo, traete, traggono.

Imperfect: traevo, traevi, traeva, traevamo, traevate, traevano.

Past Absolute: trassi, traesti, trasse, traemmo, traeste, trassero.

Present Subjunctive: tragga, tragga, tragga, traiamo, traiate, traggano.

Imperfect Subjunctive: traessi, traessi, traesse, traessimo, traeste, traessero.

Imperative: trai, tragga, traiamo, traete, traggano.

Present Participle: traεnte.

Gerund: traεndo.

Past Participle: tratto.

Porre[1] (ponere)—To put

Tenses formed on the contracted stem:

Future: porrò, porrai, porrà, porremo, porrete, porranno.

Conditional: porrεi, porresti, porrεbbe, porremmo, porreste, porrεbbero.

Tenses formed on the original stem: (with the insertion of a *g* in certain persons)

Present Indicative: pongo, poni, pone, poniamo, ponete, pongono.

Imperfect: ponevo, ponevi, poneva, ponevamo, ponevate, ponevano.

Past Absolute: posi, ponesti, pose, ponemmo, poneste, posero.

Present Subjunctive: ponga, ponga, ponga, poniamo, poniate, pongano.

Imperfect Subjunctive: ponessi, ponessi, ponesse, ponessimo, poneste ponessero.

Imperative: poni, ponga, poniamo, ponete, pongano.

Present Participle: ponεnte.

Gerund: ponεndo.

Past Participle: posto.

Prepositions

The prepositions studied in Lesson V (di, a, da, in, con, su, per, fra, tra) are regarded in Italian as prepositions proper, that is to say they are always used with nouns and pronouns and denote the relationship between them. As such they are distinguished from other prepositions like: *vicino*—near; *avanti*—before, in front; *lungo*—along, etc., which have an

[1] The commonest compound verbs identically conjugated are: *apporre, comporre, deporre, disporre, esporre, frapporre, interporre, predisporre, preporre, proporre, scomporre, sottoporre, supporre.*

adverbial function also. As their meanings overlap, the subtle variety of functions allotted to each must be learned to ensure their being used idiomatically correctly.

Da—from, by, at, etc. It is used in Italian to express

(1) (a) Motion from a place: Partì da Roma. He set out from Rome.

Motion to a person: Verrò da te. I shall come to you.

(b) or rest in a place: Sto da mia zia. I am staying with my aunt. (only in idiomatic phrases where *da* is followed by a noun or a pronoun referring to a person).

(2) The doer of an action: È amato da tutti. He is loved by all.

(3) The cause:

Trɛma dal freddo.	He is trembling with cold.
Muɔre dalla paura.	He is scared to death.
Cade dal sonno.	He is dropping with sleep.
Crɛpa dalla rabbia.	He is bursting with anger.
Muɔre dalla vɔglia di . . .	He is dying to . . .

(4) The origin:

Leonardo da Vinci.
Iacopo da Lentini.
Antonello da Messina.

(5) Extent of time:

da qualche giorno	for some days
da tre mesi	since three months (ago)
da un po' di tɛmpo	for a short while

(6) Purpose:

carta da macero	waste paper
biglietto da visita	a visiting card
casa da affittare	house to rent
sala da ballo	ball room
legna da ardere	firewood
uva da tavola	table grapes
servizio da caffè	coffee set

(7) Quality:

un tɛmpo da cani	very bad weather
cɔse da pazzi	mad, incredible things
un vestito da pierrot	a pierrot costume

(8) A physical quality or detail of clothing:

l'uɔmo dal naso aquilino	the man with the aquiline nose

la fanciulla dai capelli biondi	the girl with fair hair
il cavaliɛre dall'elmo piumato	the knight with the plumed helmet

(9) In phrases like:

fare da guida	to act as a guide
agire da gentiluɔmo	to behave like a gentleman
da questa parte	on this side, this way

Exercise 1

(a) *Repeat orally the following tenses:*

dire: present indicative, past absolute, imperative.
condurre: conditional, present subjunctive, imperfect subjunctive.
bere: future, imperfect indicative, past absolute.
trarre: present indicative, present subjunctive, past absolute.
porre: present indicative, present subjunctive, past absolute.

(b) *Give:* the present participle, gerund and past participle of above five verbs.

Exercise 2

Translate into Italian: 1. You tell. 2. They will conduct. 3. He was drinking. 4. We shall pull. 5. Let them place. 6. Tell us. 7. He led. 8. I shall drink. 9. You were pulling. 10. Although they might place. 11. They said. 12. Let us conduct. 13. He drank. 14. They are pulling. 15. We have placed. 16. He will tell us. 17. They conducted him there. 18. They dragged the boat ashore. 19. Let us drink another glass. 20. Let them not place it there. 21. I should drink a sweet wine. 22. Mary, tell me (it) at once. 23. We shall conduct them there. 24. Even if it was placed there. 25. We shall put it out. 26. (No sooner) said (than) done. 27. I could not drink alone. 28. We were placed last on the list. 29. Boys, pull it ashore. 30. They always place it here.

Exercise 3

Translate into Italian: 1. We departed from Rome. 2. We are staying with my cousin. 3. He is feared by all. 4. They were trembling with cold. 5. He has been (say: is) in this town for three weeks. 6. A house for sale; a bathroom; a wine glass; a night-dress. 7. It is a mad thing: I cannot believe it. 8. The young lady with the white hat. 9. She acts as a guide. 10. He spoke like a gentleman. 11. They get off the bus at the next stop. 12. He was admired by all. 13. Have you stayed here long? For three years. 14. The little girl with the fair hair. 15. A shop for sale; a flat to let; a dance hall.

A. *Translate into English:* Incamminatosi per una ripida mulattiera che saliva alla montagna, si guardava attorno a osservare il paesaggio. Ma, nonostante il sole, provava un senso di delusione. Aveva sperato che il posto fosse in una romantica valle con boschi di pini e di larici, recinta da grandi pareti. Era invece una valle di prealpi, chiusa da cime tozze, a panettone, che parevano desolate e torve. Un posto da cacciatori, pensò il Gaspari, rimpiangendo di non esser mai potuto vivere, neppure per pochi giorni, in una di quelle valli, immagini di felicità umana, sovrastate da fantastiche rupi, dove candidi alberghi a forma di castello stanno alla soglia di foreste antiche, cariche di leggende. E con amarezza considerava come tutta la sua vita fosse stata così: niente in fondo gli era mancato ma ogni cosa sempre inferiore al desiderio, una via di mezzo che spegneva il bisogno, mai gli aveva dato piena gioia.

Intanto era salito un buon tratto e, voltatosi indietro, stupì di vedere il paese, l'albergo, il campo da tennis, già così piccoli e lontani. Stava per riprendere il cammino quando, di là di un basso costone, udì alcune voci.

Per curiosità lasciò allora la mulattiera e, facendosi strada tra i cespugli, raggiunse la schiena della ripa. Là dietro, sottratto agli sguardi di chi seguiva la via normale, si apriva un selvatico valloncello, dai fianchi di terra rossa, ripidi e crollanti. Qua e là un macigno che affiorava, un cespuglietto, i resti secchi di un albero. Una cinquantina di metri più in alto il canalone piegava a sinistra, addentrandosi nel fianco della montagna. Un posto da vipere, rovente di sole, stranamente misterioso.

A quella vista egli ebbe una gioia; e non sapeva neanche lui il perché. Il valloncello non presentava speciale bellezza. Tuttavia gli aveva ridestato una quantità di sentimenti fortissimi, quali da molti anni non provava; come se quelle ripe crollanti, quella abbandonata fossa che si perdeva chissà verso quali segreti, le piccole frane bisbiglianti giù dalle arse prode, egli le riconoscesse. Tanti anni fa le aveva intraviste, e quante volte, e che ore stupende erano state; propriamente così erano le magiche terre dei sogni e delle avventure, vagheggiate nel tempo in cui tutto si poteva sperare. (Dino Buzzati: from *Paura alla Scala: Il borghese stregato.*)

B. *Translate into Italian:* During the wars in Italy, a gentleman who was returning home was robbed of his cloak by some soldiers. He complained to the chief of the brigands, telling him that some of his men had taken his cloak, and that he hoped the general would not let them go unpunished. The chief, looking at the gentleman, asked him how he was dressed when he had been robbed of his cloak. "Just as I am at present," replied he. "Then," said the chief, "you have not been robbed by my men, for I am sure that there is not one among them who would have left you so good a coat upon your back[1] as that you wear now."

This speech so incensed Harry, that he raised his hand in a violent fury, and gave the old judge a box on the ear.[2] Thereupon the judge ordered him to be taken to prison for having struck one of the officers[3] of the law.

When the old man informed the King how he had acted, the King praised him, and made[4] the Prince ask for pardon. Harry, who saw how much he was to blame, willingly confessed his fault, and humbly begged the judge to forgive him.

This noble action so delighted the King that he said—"I am a happy King to have so honest a judge, who was not afraid to send my son to jail; but I am a happier father to have so good a son, who is not ashamed to acknowledge his fault, and submit himself to the laws."

D. *Già, Eh già*

Vuole fare sempre il comodo suo. Eh, già!

He always wants to have his own way. Just so!

[1] addosso [2] schiaffo [3] rappresentante
[4] costringere .. a

LESSON XXXIII

Irregular Verbs (*Continued*)

The following 5 verbs: ***tenere, rimanere, valere, venire, dolersi,*** follow the same rules as the contracted verb ***porre*** in the future and conditional and in the tenses where the ***g*** appears: two, ***tenere*** and ***venire*** in the 2nd and 3rd person singular of the present indicative and 2nd singular of the imperative insert an ***i*** in the stem. ***Dolersi*** inserts a ***u*** in the same persons and same tenses.

Tenere[1]—to keep

Future: **terrò, terrai, terrà, terremo, terrete, terranno.**

Conditional: **terrɛi, terresti, terrɛbbe, terremmo, terreste, terrɛbbero.**

Pres. Indicative: **tɛngo, tiɛni, tiɛne, teniamo, tenete, tɛngono.**

Past Absolute: **tenni, tenesti, tenne, tenemmo, teneste, tennero.**

Pres. Subjunctive: **tɛnga, tɛnga, tɛnga, teniamo, teniate, tɛngano.**

Imperative: **tiɛni, tɛnga, teniamo, tenete, tɛngano.**

Note the idiomatic use of *tenere*: tenere in mano—to hold in one's hand; tenere qualcɔsa nascosto—to keep something hidden; tenere la prɔpria mano—to keep to one's own side (of the road); tenerci a—to have at heart; tenere in ordine—to keep tidy; tenersi al sicuro—to keep safe.

Rimanere[2]—to remain

Future: **rimarrò, rimarrai, rimarrà, rimarremo, rimarrete, rimarranno.**

Conditional: **rimarrɛi, rimarresti, rimarrɛbbe, rimarremmo, rimarreste, rimarrɛbbero.**

Pres. Indicative: **rimango, rimani, rimane, rimaniamo, rimanete, rimangono.**

Past Absolute: **rimasi, rimanesti, rimase, rimanemmo, rimaneste, rimasero.**

Pres. Subjunctive: **rimanga, rimanga, rimanga, rimaniamo, rimaniate, rimangano.**

Imperative: **rimani, rimanga, rimaniamo, rimanete, rimangano.**

Past Participle: **rimasto.**

Note the idiomatic use of *rimanere*: rimanere di sasso, di stucco—to be dumbfounded; rimanere sorpreso—to be surprised; rimanere a colazione —to stay for lunch; che mi rimane?—what is there left for me?

Verbs identically conjugated: [1] ***appartenere, astenersi, contenere, detenere, mantenere, ottenere, ritenere, trattenere***; [2] ***permanere.***

Valere[1]—to be worth

Future: varrò, varrai, varrà, varremo, varrete, varranno.
Conditional: varrɛi, varresti, varrɛbbe, varremmo, varreste, varrɛbbero
Pres. Indicative: valgo, vali, vale, valiamo, valete, valgono.
Past Absolute: valsi, valesti, valse, valemmo, valeste, valsero.
Pres. Subjunctive: valga, valga, valga, valiamo, valiate, valgano.
Imperative: vali, valga, valiamo, valete, valgano.
Past Participle: valso.

Venire[2]—to come

Future: verrò, verrai, verrà, verremo, verrete, verranno.
Conditional: verrɛi, verresti, verrɛbbe, verremmo, verreste, verrɛbbero.
Pres. Indicative: vɛngo, viɛni, viɛne, veniamo, venite, vɛngono.
Past Absolute: venni, venisti, venne, venimmo, veniste, vennero.
Pres. Subjunctive: vɛnga, vɛnga, vɛnga, veniamo, veniate, vɛngano.
Imperative: viɛni, vɛnga, veniamo, venite, vɛngano.

Dolersi—to mourn, complain.

Future: mi dorrò, ti dorrai, si dorrà, ci dorremo, vi dorrete, si dorranno.
Conditional: mi dorrɛi, ti dorresti, si dorrɛbbe, ci dorremmo, vi dorreste, si dorrɛbbero.
Pres. Indicative: mi dɔlgo, ti duɔli, si duɔle, ci dogliamo, vi dolete, si dɔlgono.
Past Absolute: mi dɔlsi, ti dolesti, si dɔlse, ci dolemmo, vi doleste, si dɔlsero.
Pres. Subjunctive: mi, ti, si dɔlga, ci dogliamo, vi dogliate, si dɔlgano.
Imperative: duoliti, si dɔlga, dogliamoci, doletevi, si dɔlgano.
Past Participle: dolutosi.
Gerundio: dolɛndosi.

Prepositions

A—to, at, etc. is used in Italian to express:

(1) Indirect object:

Scrivevo a Maria. I was writing to Maria.

(2) Motion towards a place:

Vado a Roma. I am going to Rome.

(3) State in which:

Resterò a casa. I shall stay at home.

(4) The means:

scrivere a matita to write in pencil

Verbs identically conjugated: [1] *prevalere.* [2] *avvenire, convenire, divenire, prevenire, provenire, sovvenire, svenire.*

camminare a piɛdi	to go on foot
andare a cavallo	to go on horseback

(5) The manner:

andarsene all'inglese	to depart without a farewell
chiuso a chiave	locked
maccheroni al burro	macaroni with butter
camminare a passi lɛnti	to walk slowly
imparare a pɔco a pɔco	to learn gradually
a quadri, a pallini, a righe, a fiori	checked, spotted, striped, flowered
a pɔco a pɔco	little by little, gradually
a centinaia, a migliaia	in hundreds, in thousands
andavano a due a due	they went in twos

(6) The cause:

Al tremɛndo rumore mi svegliai	At the terrific noise I woke up.

(7) The time:

ad un tratto	suddenly
a vent'anni	at twenty, when one is twenty
alle tre	at three o'clock.

(8) The penalty:

condannato a mɔrte	condemned to death
a diɛci anni di prigione	to ten years' imprisonment

Exercise 1

Repeat orally the following tenses:

tenere: conditional, present indicative, present subjunctive, imperative, past absolute.

rimanere: future, present subjunctive, past absolute, present indicative.

valere: conditional, present indicative, imperative, past participle, past absolute.

venire: future, present subjunctive, past absolute, imperative.

dolersi: present indicative, conditional, past absolute, imperative.

Exercise 2

Translate into Italian: (a) 1. You would remain. 2. They will keep. 3. He complained. 4. We shall come. 5. Let them remain. 6. Keep it. 7. He remained. 8. I shall complain. 9. You were coming. 10. Although they are worth. 11. They kept. 12. Let us not complain. 13. She came. 14. They are coming. 15. We have remained.

(b) 1. He will complain to him. 2. They are not worth so much. 3. Let us not remain too long. 4. How much would it be worth? 5. How long will you remain there? 6. Tell him to come. 7. I don't know if it is worth less. 8. Ask them if they would keep it. 9. We hoped you would come. 10. He told me he would complain to them. 11. I believe they have remained at home. 12. Do you know where he keeps his car? 13. We hope that she might come to-day. 14. He ordered them to remain where they were. 15. Do you think they would come? 16. He is keeping it hidden. 17. She was very surprised. 18. Keep to the left. 19. Stay for dinner. 20. There is nothing left but to leave. 21. I think he has it at heart. 22. She kept it in her pocket.

Exercise 3

Translate into Italian: 1. They departed without a farewell. 2. It was locked. 3. He ordered a Milanese cutlet. 4. They walked slowly. 5. Write it in ink (in pen). 6. A checked shirt. 7. She is cleaning the house gradually. 8. We go to Naples next month. 9. Have you sent the parcel to Julia? 10. A striped suit. 11. When can I find them at home? 12. They ride every day. 13. A flowered scarf. 14. What time did she come? 15. They were condemned to 7 years' imprisonment. 16. At those words he got up and left the room. 17. A spotted tie. 18. I have an appointment at five o'clock. 19. I shall take them with butter. 20. We shall go there on foot.

A. *Translate into English:* Le persone non sono ridicole se non quando vogliono parere o essere ciò che non sono. Il povero, l'ignorante, il malato, il vecchio, non sono mai ridicoli finché si contentano di parer tali, e non tentano di oltrepassare i limiti di questi loro difetti, ma lo sono quando il vecchio vuol parer giovane, il malato sano, il povero ricco, l'ignorante vuol far l'istruito. Gli stessi difetti corporali, per gravi che siano, non destano che un riso passeggero se uno non si sforza di nasconderli, cioè non vuole nasconderli e sembrare diverso da quel ch'egli è. E generalmente il voler essere ciò che non siamo, guasta ogni cosa al mondo: e non per altra ragione riesce insopportabile una quantità di persone, che sarebbero amabilissime se si contentassero di essere ciò che sono. Questo non avviene solamente per gli individui ma anche per intere popolazioni: io conosco città di provincia colte e floride, che sarebbero assai piacevoli per chi vi abita, se non cercassero di imitare ciò che si fa nelle metropoli. (Giacomo Leopardi.)

B. *Translate into Italian:* Tom had not heard[1] anything from home for some weeks—a fact which did not distress him, for his father and mother

[1] non avere alcuna notizia.

were not apt[1] to manifest their affection in unnecessary letters—when, to his great surprise, on the morning of a dark[2] cold day near[3] the end of November, he was told, soon after entering the study at nine o'clock, that his sister was in the drawing-room. It was Mrs Stelling who had come into the study to tell him, and she left him to enter the drawing-room alone. Maggie . . . was tall now, almost as tall as Tom, though she was only thirteen; and she really looked older than he did at the moment. She had thrown off her bonnet, her heavy braids were pushed back from her forehead, as if it would not bear that extra[4] load, and her young face had a strangely worn look[5] as her eyes turned anxiously towards the door. When Tom entered she did not speak, but only went up[6] to him, put her arms round his neck and kissed him . . . "Why, how is it you're not at school? The holidays have not begun yet?"—"Father wanted me at home," said Maggie, with a slight trembling[7] of the lip. "I came home three or four days ago." (George Eliot: *The Mill on the Floss.*)

D. *Per forza*

Hai dovuto pagare per tutti? Per forza!

Did you have to pay for all of them? I had to!

[1] incline. [2] grigio. [3] verso.
[4] altro. [5] aspetto. [6] andare vicino.
[7] tremore.

LESSON XXXIV

Irregular Verbs (*Continued*)

Six verbs—*vedere*, *sapere*, *vivere*, *cadere*, *potere* and *dovere* lose their *e* in the future and the conditional. The first four have an irregular past absolute; *potere*, *dovere* and *sapere* reflect in the present subjunctive and the imperative the irregularity already displayed in the present indicative.

Vedere[1]—to see

Future: vedrò, vedrai, vedrà, vedremo, vedrete, vedranno.
Conditional: vedrɛi, vedresti, vedrɛbbe, vedremmo, vedreste, vedrɛbbero.
Past Absolute: vidi, vedesti, vide, vedemmo, vedeste, videro.

Sapere—to know, know how

Future: saprò, saprai, saprà, sapremo, saprete, sapranno.
Conditional: saprɛi, sapresti, saprɛbbe, sapremmo, sapreste, saprɛbbero.
Past Absolute: sɛppi, sapesti, sɛppe, sapemmo, sapeste, sɛppero.
Pres. Subjunctive: sappia, sappia, sappia, sappiamo, sappiate, sappiano.
Imperative: sappi, sappia, sappiamo, sappiate, sappiano.

Vivere[2]—to live

Future: vivrò, vivrai, vivrà, vivremo, vivrete, vivranno.
Conditional: vivrɛi, vivresti, vivrɛbbe, vivremmo, vivreste, vivrɛbbero.
Past Absolute: vissi, vivesti, visse, vivemmo, viveste, vissero.
Past Participle: vissuto.

Cadere[3]—to fall, sink

Future: cadrò, cadrai, cadrà, cadremo, cadrete, cadranno.
Conditional: cadrɛi, cadresti, cadrɛbbe, cadremmo, cadreste, cadrɛbbero.
Past Absolute: caddi, cadesti, cademmo, cadeste, caddero.

Potere—to be able

Future: potrò, potrai, potrà, potremo, potrete, potranno.
Conditional: potrɛi, potresti, potrɛbbe, potremmo, potreste, potrɛbbero.

Verbs identically conjugated: [1] *avvedersi, prevedere, provvedere, ravvedersi, rivedere, travedere*; [2] *convivere, rivivere;* [3] *accadere, decadere.*

Pres. Subjunctive: pɔssa, pɔssa, pɔssa, possiamo, possiate, pɔssano.

Imperative: pɔssa, possiamo, possiate, pɔssano.

Note the idiomatic uses of *Potere*: Si può?—May I come in?; Non pɔsso farne a meno—I cannot do without; Cɔsa pɔsso farci?—What can I do?; Non ne pɔsso più—I have had enough, I cannot bear any more; Può darsi, può ɛssere—it may very well be.

Dovere—to be obliged, must, have to

Future: dovrò, dovrai, dovrà, dovremo, dovrete, dovranno.

Conditional: dovrɛi, dovresti, dovrɛbbe, dovremmo, dovreste, dovrɛbbero.

Pres. Subjunctive: dɛva (or dɛbba), dɛva, dɛva, dobbiamo, dobbiate, dɛvano.

Imperative: dɛva, dobbiamo, dobbiate, dɛvano.

Note the idiomatic uses of *Dovere*: Che ora è? Dɛvono ɛssere quasi le tre.—What time is it? It must be nearly 3 o'clock. Gli dɛvo la mia fortuna—I owe him my fortune. Dɛve ɛssere pazzo—He must be crazy.

Prepositions

Di of, from, for, with, at, etc., is used in Italian to express:

(1) Possession:

il libro di Giovanni — John's book

(2) Cause:

morì di crepacuɔre — He died of a broken heart

(3) Means:

coprirsi di ridicolo — to make oneself a laughing stock

(4) Matter:

argomento d'attualità — current topic

(5) Material:

un piatto d'argɛnto	a silver plate
di seta	of silk
di cotone	of cotton
di lana	of wool

(6) Motion from a place:

uscire di casa	to go out
ɛssere fuɔri di sé	to be beside oneself

(7) Manner:

arrivare di corsa — to arrive running

(8) Time:

di mattina	in the morning
di sera	in the evening

di pomeriggio	in the afternoon
di nɔtte	at night
d'estate	in summer

(9) To render the second term of a comparison:

È più gentile di te. He is kinder than you.

(10) As a link between certain verbs and their dependent infinitives:

Vi prɛgo di non parlare. I beg you not to speak.

Note idiomatic:

Dire di sì, di no	to say yes, no
spero di no	I hope not
dare del tu, del voi, del lɛi	to address by tu, voi, lei.

Exercise 1

Repeat orally the following tenses:

vedere, sapere, vivere, cadere: future, conditional and past absolute.
potere, dovere: future, conditional, present indicative, present subjunctive and imperative.

Exercise 2

Translate into Italian: (a) 1. You would see (2nd s.). 2. They will live. 3. She fell. 4. We shall be able. 5. That they may be obliged. 6. He lived. 7. You must know (imperative 2nd s.). 8. I shall know. 9. They lived. 10. They knew. 11. You (3rd s.) will have to. 12. I saw. 13. He could. 14. Would they live? 15. They were obliged to.

(b) 1. Although she knows. 2. Long may he live. 3. I do not know if they must pay at once. 4. I hoped he would live longer. 5. I believe they know everything. 6. Whoever must do it. 7. He fell from this window. 8. Do you know if he can come? 9. Can you (2nd s.) tell me? 10. I do not know if they would live in the country. 11. Ask him if he knows it. 12. Do you (3rd s.) know if they are remaining at home this morning or if they are coming here? 13. If they could they would come. 14. Could you (3rd s.) tell me where they live? 15. Although he knows it he cannot tell me. 16. I don't owe him anything. 17. May I come in? 18. What time is it? It must be about eight. 19. It might very well be. 20. I cannot bear it any more.

Exercise 3

Translate into Italian: 1. A silk dress. 2. He went out in great haste. 3. In winter days are shorter. 4. Is he coming? I hope he is. 5. Do not say no, please. 6. Let us address each other with tu. 7. It is a very topical matter. 8. She arrived running. 9. He has made a fool of himself. 10. He asked her not to go out.

A. *Translate into English:* Il cielo prometteva una bella giornata: la luna, in un canto, pallida e senza raggio, pure spiccava nel campo immenso d'un bigio ceruleo, che, giù giù verso l'oriente, s'andava sfumando leggermente in un giallo roseo. Più giù, all'orizzonte, si stendevano, a lunghe falde ineguali, poche nuvole, tra l'azzurro e il bruno, le più basse orlate al di sotto d'una striscia quasi di fuoco, che di mano in mano si faceva più viva e tagliente: da mezzogiorno, altre nuvole ravvolte insieme, leggiere e soffici, per dir così s'andavan lumeggiando di mille colori senza nome: quel cielo di Lombardia, così bello quand'è bello, così splendido, così in pace. (Alessandro Manzoni.)

Il contadino che non sa scrivere, e che avrebbe bisogno di scrivere, si rivolge a uno che conosca quell'arte, scegliendolo, per quanto può, tra quelli della sua condizione, perché degli altri si perita o si fida poco; l'informa, con più o meno ordine e chiarezza, degli antecedenti: e gli espone, nella stessa maniera, la cosa da mettere in carta. Il letterato, parte intende, parte fraintende, dà qualche consiglio, propone qualche cambiamento, dice: lasciate fare a me ....: perché, non c'è rimedio,[1] chi ne sa più degli altri non vuol essere strumento materiale nelle loro mani; e quando entra negli affari altrui, vuole anche fargli andare un po' a modo suo. (Alessandro Manzoni.)

B. *Translate into Italian:* At the entrance to the little court he hesitated. Dusk was coming rapidly now, and he could see only dimly[2] the stone wall, and beyond it the huddled[3] dark mass of the house, its line ragged against the sky. A little wind had come[4] with the evening, and was whistling and whining over the ground, a tune[5] so familiar to him in its thin desolation, mingled as it was with the rhythm of running[6] water and the chill of oncoming night, that it was like the hand-grip of a friend. But it was not the wind to which he was now listening. How often during these last years, he had waited thus on his return!

Sometimes he had been absent only a week, sometimes months, and once, directly[7] after her flight, nearly a year had passed. Always the same. Listening, his hand on the gate that was swinging now on its hinges, because he must postpone a little longer the moment when he would put it to test[8] whether she were waiting for him or no. One day it would be

[1] it cannot be helped. [2] vagamente. [3] confuso.
[4] levarsi. [5] suono. [6] scorrente.
[7] subito. [8] sapere.

—of that he had no doubt—but how soon? How soon? Could he endure this time the blow of the disappointment? He set back his shoulders,[1] looked up to the last yellow strands that struck like whips across the darkening sky, then went forward[2] with a firm tread. The door was open. He could see the familiar things, the old armour, the yellow-faced[3] clock like a moon against the shadow, and he could hear the sounds, the clock's voice, a banging door monotonously complaining, and the stir that there was always about the old house, rats in the wainscot, maybe, and the dust of the years sifting[4] from ceiling to floor. (Hugh Walpole: *Rogue Herries*.)

D. *Tutti quanti*

Andiamoci, tutti quanti! Let's go, all of us!

[1] raddrizzarsi. [2] avanzarsi.
[3] dal quadrante giallo. [4] cadere.

LESSON XXXV

Irregular Verbs (*Continued*)

Four verbs—*giacere, piacere, tacere* and *nuɔcere*, double the *c* of the stem in the 1st person singular (1st pers. plural optional) and the 3rd person plural of the present indicative: in the 1st, 2nd and 3rd person singular and 3rd person plural of the present subjunctive and in the 3rd person singular and plural of the imperative. They all present the usual irregularity in the past absolute. *Nuɔcere* (from Latin nocere) changes the original *o* into a diphthong whenever the stress, originally falling on the ending of the infinitive, moves to another syllable or vowel. (See lesson XXXVII.)

Giacere[1] to lie

Pres. Indicative: giaccio, giaci, giace, giaciamo or giacciamo, giacete, giacciono.
Pres. Subjunctive: giaccia, giaccia, giaccia, giaciamo, giaciate, giacciano.
Imperative: giaci, giaccia, giaciamo (giacciamo), giacete, giacciano.
Past Absolute: giacqui, giacesti, giacque, giacemmo, giaceste, giacquero.
Past Participle: giaciuto.

Piacere[2] —to please

Pres. Indicative: piaccio, piaci, piace, piaciamo or piacciamo, piacete, piacciono.
Pres. Subjunctive: piaccia, piaccia, piaccia, piaciamo, piaciate, piacciano.
Imperative: piaci, piaccia, piaciamo, piacete, piacciano.
Past Absolute: piacqui, piacesti, piacque, piacemmo, piaceste, piacquero.
Past Participle: piaciuto.

Tacere—to keep silent

Pres. Indicative: taccio, taci, tace, taciamo, tacete, tacciono.
Pres. Subjunctive: taccia, taccia, taccia, taciamo, taciate, tacciano.
Imperative: taci, taccia, taciamo, tacete, tacciano.
Past Absolute: tacqui, tacesti, tacque, tacemmo, taceste, tacquero.
Past Participle: taciuto.

Nuɔcere—to hurt, injure (Lat. Nocere)

Pres. Indicative: nuɔccio, nuɔci, nuɔce, nociamo, nocete, nuɔcciono.
Pres. Subjunctive: nuɔccia, nuɔccia, nuɔccia, nociamo, nociate, nuɔcciano.

Verbs identically conjugated: [1] ***soggiacere.*** [2] ***compiacere, dispiacere.***

Imperative: nuɔci, (noccia or) nuɔccia, nociamo, nocete, nuɔcciano.
Past Absolute: nɔcqui, nocesti, nɔcque, nocemmo, noceste, nɔcquero.
Past Participle: nociuto.

Prepositions

In in, into, etc., is used in Italian to express:

(1) Place / State } in or at which:

Sono in casa	I am at home
Vive in città	He lives in the city
Abito in campagna	I live in the country
Rεsta in Italia	He stays in Italy
Sorprεndere in fallo	To catch out
Cɔgliere in flagrante	To catch red handed

(2) Place to which:

Vado in città	I am going to town
Vanno in montagna	They go into the hills
Vai in vacanza?	Do you go on holiday?
Vado in Francia	I am going to France

With the names of towns, however, motion towards is expressed by *a*:

Andare a Roma   To go to Rome

(3) Manner:

Mangiare in fretta	To eat in a hurry
Aspettare in piεdi	To stand waiting
Mettere in luce	To stress, to emphasize
Arrivare in ritardo, in orario	To arrive late, on time
Viaggiare in trεno	To travel by train
Stare in ansia	To be anxious
Ɛssere in cɔllera	To be in a rage
Ci andarono in tre	Three of them went

(4) Time:

In autunno	In autumn
In primavεra	In spring
In pɔchi minuti	In a few minutes
In maggio	In May
Nell'anno 1955	In 1955

Exercise 1

Repeat orally the following tenses:
giacere, piacere, tacere, nuocere: present indicative, present subjunctive, imperative, past absolute, past participle.

Exercise 2

Translate into Italian: (a) 1. I lie. 2. Let us keep silent. 3. He pleased. 4. They hurt (P. Abs.). 5. We have kept silent. 6. Lie down. 7. I am keeping silent. 8. He did not lie down. 9. Has he liked it? 10. Keep silent.

(b) 1. She thinks he likes it. 2. I hope it does not hurt him. 3. I do not know if they have kept silent. 4. If he had liked it he would have remained there longer. 5. He complained that she had kept silent with him. 6. Ask her if she likes my paintings. 7. Will he come tomorrow if he likes the programme? 8. He ordered them to keep silent. 9. It is better if he keeps silent. 10. I think that it has not hurt them.

Exercise 3

Translate into Italian: 1. We are at home on Mondays. 2. Did you catch him out? 3. Do you live in town or in the country? 4. We live in town but we always go to the country on holiday. 5. If she pulls his leg he gets into a rage. 6. Where did they go last year? They went to Italy but could not go to Rome. 7. Do not wait standing. 8. Let us eat quickly; I want to arrive there in time. 9. Do not be so anxious; I am sure they are all right. 10. In 1956 we moved into the new house. 11. The four will go there. 12. They always travel by train.

A. *Translate into English:* Sul lettino bianco, rigidamente stirato, il cadavere della madre, con un'enorme cuffia in capo dalle tese inamidate.

Non vide altro, in prima, il professor Gori, entrando. In preda a quell'irritazione crescente, di cui, nello stordimento e nell'impaccio, non riusciva a rendersi esatto conto, con la testa che già gli fumava, anziché commuoversene, se ne sentì irritare, come per una cosa veramente assurda: stupida e crudele soperchieria della sorte, che, no, perdio, non si doveva a nessun costo lasciar passare!

Tutta quella rigidità della morta gli parve di parata, come se quella povera vecchia si fosse distesa da sé, là, su quel letto, con quella enorme cuffia inamidata, per prendersi lei, a tradimento, la festa preparata per la figliuola, e quasi quasi al professor Gori venne la tentazione di gridarle:

—Su via, si alzi, mia cara vecchia signora! Non è il momento di fare scherzi di codesto genere!—

Cesara Reis stava per terra, caduta sui ginocchi; è tutta aggruppata, ora, presso il lettino su cui giaceva il cadavere della madre, non piangeva più, come sospesa in uno sbalordimento grave e vano. Tra i capelli neri, scarmigliati, aveva alcune ciocche ancora attorte dalla sera avanti in pezzetti di carta, per farsi i ricci.

Ebbene, anziché pietà, provò anche per lei quasi dispetto il professor Gori. Gli sorse prepotente il bisogno di tirarla su da terra, di scuoterla da quello sbalordimento. Non si doveva darla vinta al destino, che favoriva così iniquamente l'ipocrisia di tutti quei signori radunati nell'altra stanza! No, no: era tutto preparato, tutto pronto; quei signori là erano venuti in marsina come lui per le nozze: ebbene, bastava un atto di volontà in qualcuno; costringere quella povera fanciulla, caduta lì per terra, ad alzarsi; condurla, trascinarla, anche così mezzo sbalordita, a concludere quelle nozze per salvarla dalla rovina. (Luigi Pirandello. Novelle: *Marsina stretta*: Soc. Editrice Mondadori—Milano.)

B. *Translate into Italian:* Had Elizabeth's opinions been all drawn[1] from her own family, she could not have formed a very pleasing picture of conjugal felicity or domestic comfort. Her father, captivated by youth and beauty, and that appearance of good humour which youth and beauty generally give, had married a woman whose weak understanding[2] and illiberal mind[3] had very early in their marriage put an end to all real affection for her. Respect, esteem, and confidence had vanished for ever; and all his views[4] of domestic happiness were overthrown.[5] But Mr Bennet was not of a disposition to seek comfort for the disappointment which his own imprudence had brought on[6] in any of those pleasures which too often console the unfortunate for their folly or their vice. He was fond[7] of the country and of books; and from these tastes had arisen[8] his principal enjoyments. To his wife he was very little otherwise indebted[9] than as her ignorance and folly had contributed to his amusement. This is not the sort of happiness which a man would in general wish to owe to his wife; but, where other powers of entertainment are wanting,[10] the true philosopher will derive benefit from such as are given.[11] (Jane Austin: *Pride and Prejudice*.)

D. *Mi raccomando*

Venite presto, mi raccomando. Be sure to come in good time.

[1] derivare. [2] scarsa intelligenza. [3] mentalità ristretta.
[4] idea. [5] distrutte. [6] causare.
[7] amare. [8] derivare. [9] dovere.
[10] mancare. [11] concedere.

LESSON XXXVI

Irregular Verbs (*Continued*)

The irregularity of the following group of verbs consists in certain similar changes of consonants:

gl becomes *lg* in *scegliere*, *sciɔgliere*, *tɔgliere*, *cɔgliere* and their compounds.
gn becomes *ng* in *spɛgnere.*
l becomes *gl* in *volere*, *solere.*
l becomes *lg* in *salire.*
ll becomes *lg* in *svɛllere.*

Such changes take place in the 1st person singular and 3rd person plural of the present indicative (1st person singular, 1st and 3rd person plural for *volere* and *solere*); in the 1st, 2nd and 3rd person singular and 3rd person plural of the present subjunctive (all persons for *volere* and *solere*), and the 3rd person singular and plural of the imperative (all persons for *volere* and *solere*)

With the exception of *salire* (regular) and *solere* (defective), all of them have an irregular past absolute: *scelsi, sciɔlsi, tɔlsi, cɔlsi, spensi vɔlli, svelsi.*

Volere has the future and the conditional like contracted verbs, viz.: *vorrò* and *vorrɛi* and all, except *volere* and *salire* have an irregular past participle: *scelto, sciɔlto, tolto, cɔlto, spento, solito, svɛlto.*

Scegliere[1]—to select, choose (gl, lg)

Pres. Indicative: scelgo, scegli, sceglie, scegliamo, scegliete, scelgono.
Pres. Subjunctive: scelga, scelga, scelga, scegliamo, scegliate, scelgano.
Imperative: scegli, scelga, scegliamo, scegliete, scelgano.
Past Absolute: scelsi, scegliesti, scelse, scegliemmo, sceglieste, scelsero.
Past Participle: scelto.

Sciɔgliere[2]—to untie, melt, dissolve (gl, lg)

Pres. Indicative: sciɔlgo, sciɔgli, sciɔglie, sciogliamo, sciogliete, sciɔlgono.
Pres. Subjunctive: sciɔlga, sciɔlga, sciɔlga, sciogliamo, iscogliate, sciɔlgano.
Imperative: sciɔgli, sciɔlga, sciogliamo, sciogliete, sciɔlgano.

Compound verbs identically conjugated: [1] *prescegliere.* [2] *disciɔgliere.*

Past Absolute: sciɔlsi, sciogliesti, sciɔlse, sciogliemmo, scioglieste, sciɔlsero.

Past Participle: sciɔlto.

Tɔgliere[1]—to take from (gl, lg)

Pres. Indicative: tɔlgo, tɔgli, tɔglie, togliamo, togliete, tɔlgono.

Pres. Subjunctive: tɔlga, tɔlga, tɔlga, togliamo, togliate, tɔlgano.

Imperative: tɔgli, tɔlga, togliamo, togliete, tɔlgano.

Past Absolute: tɔlsi, togliesti, tɔlse, togliemmo, toglieste, tɔlsero.

Past Participle: tɔlto.

Cɔgliere[2]—to gather, pick up (gl, lg)

Pres. Indicative: cɔlgo, cɔgli, cɔglie, cogliamo, cogliete, cɔlgono.

Pres. Subjunctive: cɔlga, cɔlga, cɔlga, cogliamo, cogliate, cɔlgano.

Imperative: cɔgli, cɔlga, cogliamo, cogliete, cɔlgano.

Past Absolute: cɔlsi, cogliesti, cɔlse, cogliemmo, coglieste, cɔlsero.

Past Participle: cɔlto.

Spegnere—to extinguish, put off, put out (gn, ng)

Pres. Indicative: spɛngo, spɛgni, spɛgne, spegniamo, spegnete, spɛngono.

Pres. Subjunctive: spɛnga, spɛnga, spɛnga, spegniamo, spegniate, spɛngano.

Imperative: spegni, spenga, spegniamo, spegnete, spengano.

Past Absolute: spɛnsi, spegnesti, spɛnse, spegnemmo, spegneste, spɛnsero.

Past Participle: spɛnto.

Volere—to will, wish, want (l, lg)

Pres. Indicative: Vɔglio, vuɔi, vuɔle, vogliamo, volete, vɔgliono.

Pres. Subjunctive: vɔglia, vɔglia, vɔglia, vogliamo, vogliate, vɔgliano.

Past Absolute: vɔlli, volesti, vɔlle, volemmo, voleste, vɔllero.

Past Participle: voluto.

Future: vorrò, vorrai, vorrà, vorremo, vorrete, vorranno.

Conditional: vorrɛi, vorresti, vorrɛbbe, vorremmo, vorreste, vorrɛbbero.

Note idiomatic uses of *volere*: Voler bɛne (a)—to love, to be fond of. Ci vuɔle paziɛnza—One must be patient. Voler male—to wish ill. Quanto ci vuɔle per arrivare?—How long to arrive? Ci vɔgliono tre quarti d'ora—three quarters of an hour. Che ci vuɔle! non ci vuɔl molto—Come on, it is not difficult.

Solere—to be accustomed (l, gl)[3]

Pres. Indicative: sɔglio, suɔli, suɔle, sogliamo, solete, sɔgliono.

Verbs identically conjugated: [1] *distɔgliere, ritɔgliere.* [2] *accɔgliere, incɔgliere, raccɔgliere.*

[3] For appearance of *u* in certain forms compare *Dolersi*—lesson XXXIII.

Pres. Subjunctive: **sɔglia, sɔglia, sɔglia, sogliamo, sogliate, sɔgliano.**
Past Participle: **solito.**

Salire[1]**—to climb, go up, ascend (l, lg).**

Pres. Indicative: **salgo, sali, sale, saliamo, salite, salgono.**
Pres. Subjunctive: **salga, salga, salga, saliamo, saliate, salgano.**
Imperative: **sali, salga, saliamo, salite, salgano.**

Svellere—to root out (ll, lg)

Pres. Indicative: **svɛllo or svɛlgo, svɛlli, svɛlle, svelliamo, svellete, svɛllono or svɛlgono.**
Pres. Subjunctive: **svɛlga, svɛlga, svɛlga, svelliamo, svelliate, svɛlgano.**
Imperative: **svɛlli, svɛlga, svelliamo, svellete, svɛlgano.**
Past Absolute: **svɛlsi, svellesti, svɛlse, svellemmo, svelleste, svɛlsero.**
Past Participle: **svɛlto.**

Prepositions

Per through, for, by, on account, etc., is used to express:

(1) Motion through a place:

S'avviò per una stradina	He made his way through a narrow street
Vagava per i campi	She wandered through the fields

(2) Motion to a place after the verb *partire*:

Partire per la guɛrra	To go off to the war
Partire per la spiaggia	To set out for the beach

(3) Duration:

Parlò per due ore	He spoke for two hours

(4) Cause:

Peccò per trɔppa bontà	He sinned by over kindness
Lo faccia per piacere	Do it as a favour

(5) Means:

Lo tirò per i capelli	He pulled him by the hair
La prɛnde per mano	He takes her by the hand

(6) Manner:

Lo incontrai per caso	I met him by chance
Per fortuna la vidi	Luckily I saw her

(7) Price:

Le compriamo per pɔchi sɔldi	We buy them for a few coppers

(8) End:

Trappola per i tɔpi	A mousetrap

[1] Verbs identically conjugated: *assalire, risalire, trasalire.*

Note the idiomatic:

Per me è uno sbaglio	In my judgement it is a mistake;
and: Per lεi è una questione finita	As far as she is concerned the matter is ended.

Exercise 1

Repeat orally the following tenses:

scegliere: pres. indicative, past participle, imperative, past absolute, and pres. subjunctive.

sciogliere: present subjunctive, imperative, past absolute, pres. indicative and past participle.

togliere: past participle, past absolute, pres. indicative, imperative, and pres. subjunctive.

cogliere: pres. subjunctive, imperative, past absolute, past participle and pres. indicative.

spegnere: past absolute, past participle, present subjunctive, imperative and pres. indicative.

volere: pres. indicative, pres. subjunctive, imperative, past absolute, past participle, conditional and future.

solere: pres. indicative, pres. subjunctive, past participle.

salire: pres. indicative, pres. subjunctive and imperative.

svellere: present indicative, pres. subjunctive, imperative, past absolute and past participle.

Exercise 2

Translate into Italian: 1. You would not want it (2nd pers. sing.). 2. They choose them. 3. He picked it up. 4. Let them come up. 5. Did you (2nd pers. plu.) root it out? 6. Take it away from her (2nd pers. sing.). 7. He is accustomed to getting up late. 8. Put it off immediately (3rd pers. sing.). 9. They climb up the stairs slowly. 10. Did they pick it up this morning? 11. You (2nd pers. sing.) must dissolve it in water. 12. Put off the light (2nd pers. sing.) 13. Have you (2nd pers. sing.) chosen it now? 14. He has just put it off. 15. Unless he wants it. 16. Tell her to take it away from here. 17. Please choose (3rd pers. sing.) what you want. 18. I do not know what he wants. 19. Did you (2nd pers. sing) put it off? 20. He has just taken it from there. 21. They wish us ill. 22. She is very fond of him. 23. One must be patient. 24. How long to the station? 25. Only five minutes.

Exercise 3

Translate into Italian: 1. They left for the seaside. 2. He was walking through the main street. 4. She held him by the hand. 4. Luckily we understand it. 5. In my judgement it is too late. 6. She was pulling him by his jacket. 7. They have done it out of kindness. 8. I shall go (passare) through Rome on the 5th April. 9. Please, shut the door. 10. He was waiting at the stop for 20 minutes.

A. *Translate into English:* A mezzogiorno camminavo sulle colline libere, e tedeschi e repubblichini li avevo lasciati chissà dove nella valle. Avevo perduto la strada maestra: gridai a certe donne che voltavano il fieno in un prato, per dove si andasse nel paese vicino al mio. Mi fecero segno di tornare alla valle. Gridai di no, che la mia strada era attraverso le colline. Coi forconi mi dissero di proseguire.

Non si vedevano paesi, solamente cascine sui versanti selvosi e calcinati. Per raggiungerne qualcuna avrei dovuto dilungarmi sui sentieri ripidi, nell'afa delle nuvole basse. Scrutavo attento i lineamenti delle creste, gli anfratti, le piante, le distese scoperte. I colori, le forme, il sentore stesso dell'afa, mi erano noti e familiari: in quei luoghi non ero mai stato, eppure camminavo in una nube di ricordi. Certe piante di fico contorte, modeste, mi sembravano quelle di casa, del cancello dietro il pozzo. Prima di notte, mi dicevo, sono al Belbo.

Una casetta sulla strada, annerita, sfondata, mi fermò e fece battere il cuore. Pareva un muro sinistrato di città. Non vidi anima viva. Ma la rovina non era recente; sulla parete, dove prima era una vite, spiccava appena la macchia azzurra del verderame. Pensai all'eco dei clamori, al sangue sparso, agli spari. Quanto sangue, mi chiesi, ha già bagnato queste terre, queste vigne. Pensai che era sangue come il mio, ch'erano uomini e ragazzi cresciuti a quell'aria, a quel sole, dal dialetto e dagli occhi caparbi come i miei. Era incredibile che gente come quella, che mi vivevano nel sangue e nel chiuso ricordo, avessero anche loro subito la guerra, la ventata, il terrore del mondo. Per me era strano, inaccettabile, che il fuoco, la politica, la morte sconvolgessero quel mio passato. Avrei voluto trovar tutto come prima, come una stanza chiusa. Era per questo, non soltanto per vana prudenza, che da due giorni non osavo nominare il mio paese: tremavo che qualcuno dicesse: "È bruciato. C'è passata la guerra." (Cesare Pavese: from *Prima che il gallo canti.*)

B. *Translate into Italian:* One afternoon (I had been three weeks at Lowood), as I was sitting with a slate in my hand, puzzling[1] over a sum in long division, my eyes, raised in abstraction[2] to the window, caught sight[3] of a figure just passing; I recognized almost instinctively that gaunt outline; and when, two minutes after, all the school, teachers included, rose en masse, it was not necessary for me to look up in order to ascertain whose entrance they thus greeted. A long stride measured the school-

[1] stillarsi il cervello. [2] distrattamente. [3] scorgere.

room, and presently beside Miss Temple, who herself had risen, stood the same black column which had frowned[1] on me so ominously from the hearth-rug[2] of Gateshead. I now glanced sideways at this piece of architecture. Yes, I was right; it was Mr Brocklehurst, buttoned up[3] in a surtout,[4] and looking[5] longer, narrower, and more rigid than ever. He stood at Miss Temple's side; he was speaking low[6] in her ear: I did not doubt he was making disclosures of my villainy; and I watched her eye with painful anxiety, expecting every moment[7] to see its dark orb[8] turn on me a glance of repugnance and contempt. (Charlotte Brontë: *Jane Eyre*.)

D. *Tanto per cambiare*
Tanto per cambiare, piove. It's raining, just for a change (ironical).
Tanto
È inutile darle dei consigli, tanto non li ascolta.
It's useless to advise her, she never pays any attention.

[1] squadrare. [2] presso il caminetto. [3] sino al mento.
[4] spolverino. [5] con un aspetto. [6] a bassa voce.
[7] da un momento all'altro. [8] pupilla.

LESSON XXXVII

Irregular Verbs (*Continued*)

The following six verbs, *morire*, *udire*, *uscire*, *cuɔcere*, *apparire*, and *parere*, differing from one another in some of their irregularities, are grouped because of the changes that take place in the vowels of their stem. Such changes happen when the stress shifts from the vowel on which it fell in the infinitive to another vowel, producing either a diphthong or a change of vowel. e.g.

morire becomes muɔio, muɔri, muɔre
but moriamo, morite and again muɔiono
uscire becomes ɛsco, ɛsci, ɛsce
but usciamo, uscite and again ɛscono
udire becomes ɔdo, ɔdi, ɔde
but udiamo, udite and again ɔdono

In *cuɔcere* the change though apparently the reverse (from a diphthong to a simple vowel) is in reality the same, when we consider the original Latin infinitive *coquere*. Coquere has come into Italian as *cuɔcere*, i.e. a single vowel has become a diphthong. The real difference is that the change takes place in this verb *not* when the stress moves from the original syllable to another, but when it remains on the original syllable.

Morire—to die

Pres. Indicative: muɔio, muɔri, muɔre, moriamo, morite, muɔiono.
Pres. Subjunctive: muɔia, muɔia, muɔia, moriamo, moriate, muɔiano.
Imperative: muɔri, muɔia, moriamo, morite, muɔiano.
Past Participle: mɔrto.

Udire—to hear, listen

Pres. Indicative: ɔdo, ɔdi, ɔde, udiamo, udite, ɔdono.
Pres. Subjunctive: ɔda, ɔda, ɔda, udiamo, udiate, ɔdano.
Imperative: ɔdi, ɔda, udiamo, udite, ɔdano.

Uscire[1]—to go out

Pres. Indicative: ɛsco, ɛsci, ɛsce, usciamo, uscite, ɛscono.
Pres. Subjunctive: ɛsca, ɛsca, ɛsca, usciamo, usciate, ɛscano.
Imperative: ɛsci, ɛsca, usciamo, uscite, ɛscano.

[1] Verbs identically conjugated: *riuscire*.

Cuɔcere—to cook

Pres. Indicative: cuɔcio, cuɔci, cuɔce, cociamo cocete, cuɔciono.

Pres. Subjunctive: cuɔcia, cuɔcia, cuɔcia, cociamo, cociate, cuɔciano.

Imperative: cuɔci, cuɔcia, cociamo, cocete, cuɔciano.

Imperfect Indicative: cocevo, cocevi, coceva, cocevamo, cocevate, cocevano.

Future: cocerò, cocerai, cocerà, coceremo, cocerete, coceranno.

Conditional: cocerɛi, coceresti, cocerɛbbe, coceremmo, cocereste, cocerɛbbero.

Pres. Participle: cocɛnte.

Gerund: cocɛndo.

Past Absolute: cɔssi,[1] cocesti, cɔsse,[1] cocemmo, coceste, cɔssero.[1]

Past Participle: cɔtto.[1]

Apparire[2]—to appear

Pres. Indicative: appaio (apparisco), appari, appare, appariamo, apparite, appaiono.

Pres. Subjunctive: appaia (apparisca), appaia, appaia, appariamo, appariate, appaiano.

Imperative: appari (apparisci), appaia, appariamo, apparite, appaiano.

Past Absolute: apparsi or apparvi or apparii, apparisti, apparse, etc.

Pres. Participle: apparɛnte (apparent) or appariscɛnte (showy).

Past Participle: apparso.

Parere—to seem, appear

Pres. Indicative: paio, pari, pare, paiamo, parete, paiono.

Pres. Subjunctive: paia, paia, paia, paiamo, pariate, paiano.

Future: parrò, parrai, parrà, parremo, parrete, parranno.

Conditional: parrɛi, parresti, parrɛbbe, parremmo, parreste, parrɛbbero.

Past Absolute: parvi, paresti, parve, paremmo, pareste, parvero.

Past Participle: parso.

Prepositions

Con with is used in Italian to express:

(1) Means:

Lo vidi con i miɛi ɔcchi.	I saw it with my own eyes.
Mi salutò a lungo con la mano.	He waved to me for a long time.

(2) Company:

Partirà con me. He will leave with me.

1 Exceptions to the given rule.
2 Verb identically conjugated: *scomparire*.

(3) Manner:

Mi salutò con molta cordialità.	He greeted me warmly.
Lo disse con aria contenta.	He said it with a pleased air.

Fra, tra—among, between, in, within, to, amid

Both above prepositions are used to express:

(1) Time:

Fra poco	in a short while, soon
Tra l'alba e il tramonto	between dawn and sunset

(2) Relationship:

Fra me e te	between you and me, us
Tra di loro	between them

(3) Manner:

Tra l'allegro e il triste a mixture of gay and sad

(4) Place:

Fra due montagne between two mountains

Su—on, upon, over, above

The preposition *su* is used to express:

(1) Place:

Sulla montagna	on the mountain
Sul giornale	in the newspaper

(2) Topics:

Parlò su Michelangelo.	He spoke on Michelangelo.
Fece una conferenza sull'Alfieri.	He gave a lecture on Alfieri.

Exercise 1

Repeat orally the following tenses:

morire: pres. indicative, imperative, past absolute, pres. subjunctive, pres. participle and past participle.

udire: imperative, pres. subjunctive, pres. indicative.

uscire: pres. subjunctive, pres. indicative, imperative.

cuocere: pres. subjunctive, past absolute, future, imperative, conditional, pres. participle, gerund, past participle.

apparire: pres. indicative, imperative, pres. subjunctive, past absolute, past participle, pres. participle.

parere: past absolute, pres. indicative, future, past participle, conditional, pres. subjunctive.

Exercise 2

Translate into Italian: 1. It would appear. 2. They die in hundreds. 3. Listen! 4. Come out with me. 5. Cook (2nd pers. sing.) it slowly. 6. It will appear strange. 7. He appeared and then disappeared after five minutes. 8. Have you cooked it enough? 9. I want him to go out with you. 10. He died this morning. 11. I hear somebody coming up the stairs. 12. They appeared to me (to be) very kind. 13. It seems (use parere) to me that they stay (rimanere) too long. 14. Do you hear anything? 15. Everybody seems to become silent when I appear. 16. How long did you cook it? 17. I hope that they go out together. 18. He seemed (past absolute) tired to me. 19. Let us hope that they have not died in vain. 20. I am going out shortly.

Exercise 3

Translate into Italian: 1. In a few minutes. 2. On the other hand. 3. Over the mantelpiece. 4. Between you and me. 5. A book on Machiavelli. 6. He walked with a stick. 7. Cut it with a knife. 8. She eats it with the spoon. 9. Shortly. 10. On the balcony.

A. *Translate into English:* Finito il pranzo, sorbito il caffè, egli si ritira di nuovo nello studio. Qui si assopisce ritto nella poltrona, la testa un po' reclinata verso la spalla, la bocca semiaperta sotto il naso paonazzo. Non dorme proprio, è una specie di ronzante torpore, ogni tanto la mano gli va nel cassetto a prendere un biscotto che non finisce di masticare e di inghiottire: di modo che le briciole gli cascano dalle labbra sulla cravatta. Ma poi ad un tratto si sveglia di soprassalto, subito, come ispirato, si leva con decisione ed esce dallo studio. Furtivo, proiettando un'ombra grottesca sopra le buie mura dei corridoi domestici, striscia sino alla dispensa, un camerotto senza finestre, quadrato, con tante mensole intorno le pareti, accende una gialla lampada e s'avventa sui piatti. È appena un'ora che si è levato da tavola, ma che importa? tutto è buono per lui e a tutte l'ore: una crosta inseccolita di formaggio, quattro fagiuoli freddi cagliati nel sugo coagulato, un rimasuglio di insalata russa impastricciata di maionese, l'avanzo unto e gelato di un pasticcio di maccheroni. In piedi nel camerotto ermetico, in quell'agro odore di muffa e di bisunto il notaio spizzica, rosicchia, assaggia, mastica, ingolla, con strani gesti frenetici, strani schiocchi di lingua e scricchiolii di mascelle, ancor più strani roteamenti di pupille. Perché come tutti i viziosi il notaio è un solitario, ama il sotterfugio e il batticuore; e però trova più gusto a ingozzarsi di nascosto in quel ripostiglio che a mangiare a tavola alle ore debite, tra la sua gente. (Alberto Moravia: *I sogni del Pigro.*)

B. *Translate into Italian:* As he was turning the handle of the door, his eye fell upon the portrait Basil Hallward had painted of him. He started back[1] as if in surprise. Then he went on into his own room, looking somewhat puzzled.[2] After he had taken[3] the buttonhole out of his coat, he seemed to hesitate. Finally he came back,[4] went over[5] to the picture, and examined it. In the dim light that struggled[6] through the cream-coloured silk blinds, the face appeared to him to be a little changed. The expression looked different. One would have said that there was a touch of cruelty in the mouth. He turned round, and, walking to the window, drew up the blind. The bright dawn[7] flooded the room . . . but the strange expression that he had noticed in the face of the portrait seemed to linger there, to be more intensified even. He rubbed his eyes, and came[5] close to the picture, and examined it again. There were no signs of any change when he looked into the actual painting, and yet there was no doubt, that the whole expression had altered.

He threw himself into a chair, and began to think. Suddenly there flashed across his mind what he had said in Basil Hallward's studio the day the picture had been finished. Yes, he remembered it perfectly. He had uttered a mad wish that he himself might remain young, and the portrait grow old;[8] that his own beauty might be untarnished, and the face on the canvas bear the burden of his passions and his sins; that the painted image might be seared with the lines of suffering and thought, and that he might keep all the loveliness of his boyhood. Surely his wish had not been fulfilled? (Oscar Wilde: *The Picture of Dorian Gray.*)

D. *Che bellezza*

Che bellezza! Domani è vacanza!
It's wonderful! Tomorrow is a holiday!

[1] indietreggiare. [2] con un'aria alquanto perplessa.
[3] togliersi il fiore dall'occhiello. [4] ritornare indietro. [5] avvicinarsi.
[6] filtrare. [7] luce dell'alba. [8] invecchiare.

LESSON XXXVIII

Irregular Verbs (*Continued*)

Apart from the verbs already studied and some defective verbs, the majority of irregular verbs are irregular in the past absolute and in the past participle. At times the irregularity of the past absolute is repeated in the past participle:

accɛndere to kindle accesi acceso

at other times the irregularity varies:

assumere to assume assunsi assunto

and therefore while we print here a list of irregular verbs for consultation, we have used italics to denote the commonest ones which should be learned by heart:

1. accadere to happen (impersonal); *see* cadere
2. accɛdere to accede; *see* concɛdere
3. *accɛndere* to light; p. abs. accesi, accendesti, etc.; p. part. acceso
4. *accludere* to enclose; *see* alludere
5. accɔgliere to receive; *see* cɔgliere
6. *accɔrgersi* to perceive; *see* scɔrgere
7. accorrere to run up; *see* correre
8. accrescere to increase; *see* crescere
9. addirsi (=addicersi) to suit; *see* dire
10. addurre (=adducere) to convey; pres. ind. adduco, etc; p. abs. addussi, adducesti, etc.; p. part. addotto; fut. addurrò; pres. subj. adduca, adduciamo, adduciate, adducano; impve. adduci, adduca, adduciamo, adducete, adducano.
11. affiggere to stick, fasten; p. abs. affissi, affiggesti, etc.; p. part. affisso.
12. affliggere to afflict; p. abs. afflissi, affliggesti, etc.; p. part. afflitto
13. aggiungere to add; *see* giungere
14. alludere to allude; p. abs. allusi, alludesti, etc.; p. part. alluso
15. ammettere to admit; *see* mettere
16. andare to go; pres. ind. vado *or* vɔ, vai, va, andiamo, andate, vanno; fut. andrò; pres. subj. vada, andiamo, andiate, vadano; impve. va', vada, andiamo, andate, vadano.
17. annɛttere to annex; p. abs. annɛssi *or* annettei, annettesti, etc.; p. part. annɛsso

18. *apparire* to appear; pres. ind. appaio *or* apparisco, appari *or* apparisci, appare *or* apparisce, appariamo, apparite, appaiono *or* appariscono; p. abs. apparsi *or* apparvi *or* apparii, apparisti, etc.; p. part. apparso *or* apparito; pres. subj. appaia *or* apparisca, appariamo, appariate, appaiano *or* appariscano; impve. appari *or* apparisci, appaia *or* apparisca, appariamo, apparite, appaiano *or* appariscano
19. appartenere to belong; *see* tenere
20. *appɛndere* to hang; appesi, appendesti, etc.; p. part. appeso
21. apporre (=apponere) to affix; *see* porre
22. apprɛndere to learn; *see* prɛndere
23. *aprire* to open; p. abs. apɛrsi *or* aprii, apristi, etc.; p. part. apɛrto
24. ardere to burn; p. abs. arsi, ardesti, etc.; p. part. arso
25. ascendere to ascend; *see* scendere
26. aspɛrgere to sprinkle p. abs. aspɛrsi, aspergesti, etc.; p. part. aspɛrso
27. assalire to assail, assault; *see* salire
28. assidersi to sit; p. abs. mi assisi, ti assidesti, etc.; p. part. assiso
29. assistere to be present at; p. abs. assistetti; p. part. assistito
30. assɔlvere to absolve; p. abs. assɔlsi or assolvei *or* assolvɛtti, assolvesti, etc.; p. part. assoluto *or* assɔlto
31. *assumere* to assume; p. abs. assunsi assumesti, etc.; p. part. assunto
32. astenersi to abstain; *see* tenere
33. astrarre (=astraere) to abstract; *see* trarre
34. attɛndere to attend, wait; see tɛndere
35. attingere to draw up; *see* tingere
36. avvedersi to perceive; *see* vedere
37. avvenire to happen (impersonal); *see* venire
38. avvincere to bind; *see* vincere
39. avvɔlgere to fold, to wind; *see* vɔlgere
40. benedire to bless; *see* dire
41. *bere* (=bevere) to drink; pres. ind. bevo; p. abs. bevvi *or* bevei *or* bevɛtti, bevesti, etc.; p. part. bevuto; fut. berrò pres. subj. beva; impve. bevi, beva, beviamo, bevete, bevano.
42. *cadere* to fall; p. abs. caddi, cadesti, etc.; fut. cadrò
43. *chiɛdere* to ask; pres. ind. chiɛdo *or* chiɛggo, chiɛdi, chiɛde, chiediamo, chiedete, chiɛdono *or* chiɛggono; p. abs. chiɛsi, chiedesti, etc.; p. part. chiɛsto; pres. subj. chiɛda *or* chiɛgga; impve. chiɛdi, chiɛda, chiediamo, chiedete, chiɛdano.
44. *chiudere* to close; p. abs. chiusi, chiudesti, etc.; p. part. chiuso
45. cingere to gird, embrace; p. abs. cinsi, cingesti, etc.; p. part. cinto
46. cɔgliere *or* cɔrre to gather; pres. ind. cɔlgo, cɔgli, cɔglie, cogliamo, cogliete, cɔlgono; p. abs. cɔlsi, cogliesti, etc.; p. part. cɔlto; pres. subj. cɔlga; impve. cɔgli, cɔlga, cogliamo, cogliete, cɔlgano.

47. coincidere to coincide; p. abs. coincisi, coincidesti, etc.; p. part. coinciso
48. commettere to commit; *see* mettere
49. commuɔvere to move, affect; *see* muɔvere
50. comparire to appear; *see* apparire
51. compiacere to please; *see* piacere
52. compiangere to pity; *see* piangere
53. comporre (=componere) to compose; *see* porre
54. comprɛndere to comprehend, understand; *see* prɛndere
55. comprimere to compress; p. abs. comprɛssi, comprimesti, etc.; p. part. comprɛsso
56. *concɛdere* to concede, grant; p. abs. concɛssi *or* concedei *or* concedɛtti, concedesti, etc.; p. part. concɛsso *or* conceduto
57. *concludere or* conchiudere to conclude; *see* alludere
58. concorrere to concur; *see* correre
59. condolersi to complain, condole with; *see* dolere
60. condurre (=conducere) to conduct; *see* addurre
61. configgere to drive in; *see* figgere
62. confondere to confound; *see* fondere
63. congiungere to join, match; *see* giungere
64. connɛttere to connect; *see* annɛttere
65. conoscere to know; p. abs. conobbi, conoscesti, etc.
66. consistere to consist; *see* assistere
67. contɛndere to contend; *see* tɛndere
68. contenere to contain; *see* tenere
69. contɔrcere to twist; *see* tɔrcere
70. contradire to contradict; *see* dire
71. contraffare (=contraffacere) to counterfeit; *see* fare
72. contrarre (=contraere) to contract; *see* trarre
73. convenire to agree; *see* venire
74. convincere to convince; *see* vincere
75. *coprire* to cover; *see* aprire
76. corrɛggere to correct; *see* rɛggere
77. correre to run; p. abs. corsi, corresti, etc.; p. part. corso
78. corrispondere to correspond; *see* rispondere
79. corrompere to corrupt; *see* rompere
80. costringere to force; *see* stringere
81. costruire to construct, build; p. abs. costrussi, costruisti, etc.; p. part. costrutto *or* costruito
82. *crescere* to grow, raise; p. abs. crebbi, crescesti, etc.
83. *cuɔcere* to cook; pres. ind. cuɔcio, cuɔci, cuɔce, cociamo, cocete, cuɔciono; p. abs. cɔssi, cocesti, etc.; p. part. cɔtto; pres. subj. cuɔcia, cociamo, cociate, cuɔciano; impve. cuɔci, cuɔcia, cociamo cocete, cuɔciano

84. *dare* to give; pres. ind. dɔ, dai da, diamo, date, danno; p. abs. diεdi *or* dεtti, desti, etc.; p. part. dato; fut. darò; pres. subj. dia, diamo, diate, diano *or* dieno; impve. da', dia, diamo, date, diano
85. *decidere* to decide; p. abs. decisi, decidesti, etc.; p. part. deciso
86. decrescere to decrease; *see* crescere
87. dedurre (=deducere) to deduce, deduct; *see* addurre
88. deludere to delude, beguile; *see* alludere
89. deporre (=deponere) to depose, bear witness; *see* porre
90. deprimere to depress; *see* comprimere
91. deridere to deride; *see* ridere
92. desumere to infer; *see* assumere
93. descrivere to describe; *see* scrivere
94. detεrgere to clean; *see* tεrgere
95. *difεndere* to defend; p. abs. difesi, difendesti, etc.; p. part. difeso
96. diffondere to diffuse; *see* fondere
97. dipεndere to depend; *see* appεndere
98. dipingere to paint; *see* pingere
99. *dire* (=dicere) to say, tell; pres. ind. dico, dici, dice, diciamo, dite, dicono; p. abs. dissi, dicesti, etc.; p. part. detto; fut. dirò; pres. subj. dica, diciamo, diciate, dicano; impve. di', dica, diciamo, dite, dicano
100. *dirigere* to direct; p. abs. dirεssi, dirigesti, etc.; p. part. dirεtto
101. discendere to descend; *see* scendere
102. dischiudere to disclose, open; *see* chiudere
103. disciɔgliere to untie; *see* sciɔgliere
104. discorrere to talk; *see* correre
105. *discutere* to discuss; p. abs. discussi, discutesti, etc.; p. part. discusso
106. disfare (=disfacere) to undo; *see* fare
107. disgiungere to disjoint, separate; *see* giungere
108. disilludere to disappoint; *see* illudere
109. dispεrdere to disperse; *see* pεrdere
110. dispiacere to displease; *see* piacere
111. disporre (=disponere) to dispose; *see* porre
112. dissuadere to dissuade; *see* persuadere
113. distεndere to stretch; *see* tεndere
114. *distinguere* to distinguish; p. abs. distinsi, distinguesti, etc.; p. part. distinto
115. distɔgliere *or* distɔrre to dissuade, divert from; *see* tɔgliere
116. distrarre (=distraere) to distract, divert; *see* trarre
117. distruggere to destroy; *see* struggere
118. divellere to uproot; p. abs. divεlsi, divellesti; p. part. divεlto
119. divenire to become; *see* venire
120. *dividere* to divide; p. abs. divisi, dividesti, etc.; p. part. diviso

121. dolere to ache, pain; pres. ind. dɔlgo, duɔli, duɔle, doliamo, dolete, dɔlgono; p. abs. dolsi, dolesti, etc.; fut. dorrò; pres. subj. dɔlga, doliamo, doliate, dɔlgano
122. dovere to have to, be obliged, must; pres. ind. dɛvo *or* dɛbbo, dɛvi, dɛve, dobbiamo, dovete, dɛvono *or* dɛbbono; fut. dovrò; pres. subj. dɛva *or* dɛbba, dobbiamo, dobbiate, dɛvano *or* dɛbbano
123. effondere to pour out; *see* fondere
124. elɛggere to elect; *see* lɛggere
125. elidere to elide; p. abs. elisi, elidesti, etc.; p. part. eliso
126. eludere to elude; *see* alludere
127. emɛrgere to emerge; p. abs. emɛrsi, emergesti, etc.; p. part. emɛrso
128. emettere to emit; *see* mettere
129. ɛrgere to erect, raise; p. abs. ɛrsi, ergesti, etc.; p. part. ɛrto
130. erigere to erect, raise; *see* dirigere
131. *escludere* to exclude; *see* alludere
132. esigere to exact, cash; p. part. esatto
133. espellere to expel; p. abs. espulsi, espellesti, etc.; p. part. espulso
134. esplɔdere to explode; p. abs. esplɔsi, esplodesti, etc.; p. part. esplɔso
135. esporre (=esponere) to expose; *see* porre
136. esprimere to express; *see* comprimere
137. estɛndere to extend; *see* tɛndere
138. estinguere to extinguish; *see* distinguere
139. estrarre (=estraere) to extract; *see* trarre
140. evadere to evade; p. abs. evasi, evadesti, etc.; p. part. evaso
141. *fare* (=facere) to do, make; pres. ind. faccio *or* fɔ, fai, fa, facciamo, fate, fanno; p. abs. feci, facesti, etc.; p. part. fatto; fut. farò; pres. subj. faccia, facciamo, facciate, facciano; impve. fa', faccia, facciamo, fate, facciano
142. figgere to fix; p. abs. fissi, figgesti, etc.; p. part. fitto
143. *fingere* to feign, pretend; *see* cingere
144. fondere to melt; p. abs. fusi, fondesti, etc.; p. part. fuso
145. frammettere to interpose, insert; *see* mettere
146. frangere to break; p. abs. fransi, frangesti, etc.; p. part. franto
147. frapporre (=frapponere) to interpose, insert, *see* porre
148. friggere to fry; p. abs. frissi, friggesti, etc.; p. part. fritto
149. fungere to act as; p. abs. funsi, fungesti, etc.
150. *giacere* to lie; pres. ind. giaccio, giaci, giace, giaciamo *or* giacciamo, giacete, giacciono; p. abs. giacqui, giacesti, etc.; pres. subj. giaccia; impve. giaci, giaccia, giaciamo *or* giacciamo, giacete, giacciano
151. *giungere* to arrive, join (the hands) (giungere in the sense of—to arrive, takes the auxiliary essere) p. abs. giunsi, giungesti, etc.; p. part. giunto

152. godere to enjoy; fut. godrò; condit. godrɛi
153. illudere to delude, beguile; *see* alludere
154. immɛrgere to immerse, plunge; *see* emɛrgere
155. imporre (= imponere) to impose; *see* porre
156. imprimere to imprint, impress; *see* comprimere
157. incidere to cut; *see* decidere
158. includere to include; *see* alludere
159. incorrere to incur; *see* correre
160. increscere to cause sorrow; *see* crescere
161. incutere to strike; *see* discutere
162. indulgere to indulge; p. abs. indulsi, indulgesti, etc.
163. indurre (= inducere) to induce; *see* addurre
164. inferire to infer; p. abs. infersi *or* inferii, inferisti, etc.; p. part. inferto *or* inferito
165. infliggere to inflict; *see* affliggere
166. infrangere to break; *see* frangere
167. infondere to infuse; *see* fondere
168. insistere to insist; *see* assistere
169. intɛndere to intend, understand; *see* tɛndere
170. intercɛdere to intercede; *see* cɛdere
171. interdire (= interdicere) to interdict, prohibit; *see* dire
172. interporre (= interponere) to interpose; *see* porre
173. interrompere to interrupt; *see* rompere
174. intervenire to intervene; *see* venire
175. intraprɛndere to undertake; *see* prɛndere
176. intridere to temper; p. abs. intrisi, intridesti, etc.; p. part. intriso
177. introdurre (= introducere) to introduce; *see* addurre
178. intrudere to intrude; p. abs. intrusi, intrudesti, etc.; p. part. intruso
179. invadere to invade; *see* evadere
180. invɔlgere to wrap; *see* vɔlgere
181. irrompere to rush in upon; *see* rompere
182. iscrivere to inscribe; *see* scrivere
183. istruire to instruct; *see* costruire
184. lɛdere to hurt, offend; p. abs. lɛsi, ledesti, etc.; p. part. lɛso
185. *lɛggere* to read; p. abs. lɛssi, leggesti, etc.; p. part. lɛtto
186. maledire to curse; *see* dire
187. mantenere to maintain; *see* tenere
188. *mettere* to put; p. abs. misi *or* messi, mettesti, etc.; p. part. messo
189. mɔrdere to bite; p. abs. mɔrsi, mordesti, etc.; p. part. mɔrso
190. morire to die; pres. ind. muɔio, muɔri, muɔre, moriamo, morite, muɔiono; p. part. mɔrto; fut. morirò *or* morrò; pres. subj. muɔia, moriamo, moriate, muɔiano; impve. muɔri, moriamo, morite, muɔiano

191. *muɔvere or* mɔvere to move; pres. ind. muɔvo *or* mɔvo, muɔvi *or* mɔvi, muɔve *or* mɔve, moviamo, movete, muɔvono *or* mɔvono; p. abs. mɔssi, movesti, etc.; p. part. mɔsso; pres. subj. muɔva *or* mɔva, moviamo, moviate, muɔvano *or* mɔvano; impve. muɔvi *or* mɔvi, muɔva, moviamo, movete, muɔvano
192. mungere to milk; p. abs. munsi, mungesti, etc.; p. part. munto
193. *nascere* to be born; p. abs. nacqui, nascesti, etc.; p. part. nato
194. *nascondere* to hide, conceal; p. abs. nascosi, nascondesti, etc.; p. part nascosto
195. nuɔcere *or* nɔcere to hurt, prejudice; pres. ind. nuɔccio *or* nɔccio, nuɔci, nuɔce, nociamo, nocete, nuɔcciono *or* nɔcciono; p. abs. nɔcqui, nocesti, etc.; pres. subj. nuɔccia *or* nɔccia, nociamo, nociate, nuɔcciano *or* nɔcciano; impve. nuɔci, nuɔccia *or* nɔccia, nociamo, nocete, nuɔcciano *or* nɔcciano
196. occorrere to be necessary; (impersonal); *see* correre
197. offɛndere to offend; *see* difɛndere
198. *offrire* to offer; p. abs. offɛrsi *or* offrii, offristi, etc.; p. part. offɛrto
199. omettere to omit; *see* mettere
200. opporre (= opponere) to oppose; *see* porre
201. opprimere to oppress; *see* comprimere
202. ottenere to obtain; *see* tenere
203. *parere* to seem, appear; pres. ind. paio, pari, pare, paiamo, parete, paiono; p. abs. parvi *or* parsi, paresti, etc.; p. part. parso; fut. parrò; pres. subj. paia, paiamo, pariate, paiano
204. percorrere to run over; *see* correre
205. percuɔtere to strike; p. abs. percossi, percotesti, etc.; p. part. percosso
206. *pɛrdere* to lose; p. abs. pɛrsi *or* perdei *or* perdɛtti, perdesti, etc.; p. part. pɛrso *or* perduto
207. permettere to permit; *see* mettere
208. persuadere to persuade; p. abs. persuasi, persuadesti, etc.; p. part. persuaso
209. pervenire to arrive at; *see* venire
210. *piacere* to please; pres. ind. piaccio, piaci, piace, piacciamo, piacete, piacciono; p. abs. piacqui, piacesti, etc.; pres. subj. piaccia, piacciamo, piacciate, piacciano; impve. piaci, piaccia, piaciamo, piacete, piacciano
211. piangere to cry, weep; p. abs. piansi, piangesti, etc.; p. part. pianto
212. pingere to paint; p. abs. pinsi, pingesti, etc.; p. part. pinto
213. piɔvere to rain (impersonal); p. abs. piɔvve
214. pɔrgere to present, offer; p. abs. pɔrsi, porgesti, etc.; p. part. pɔrto

215. *porre* (=ponere) to put; pres. ind. pongo, poni, pone, poniamo, ponete, pongono; p. abs. posi, ponesti, etc.; p. part. posto; fut. porrò; pres. subj. ponga, poniamo, poniate, pongano; impve. poni, ponga, poniamo, ponete, pongano
216. posporre (=posponere) to postpone; *see* porre
217. possedere to own, possess; *see* sedere
218. potere to be able, may, can; pres. ind. pɔsso, puɔi, può, possiamo, potete, pɔssono; fut. potrò, pres. subj. pɔssa, possiamo, possiate, pɔssano
219. prediligere to prefer; p. abs. predilɛssi, prediligesti, etc.; p. part. predilɛtto
220. predire (=predicere) to predict; *see* dire
221. prefiggersi to take into one's head; *see* affiggere
222. preludere to forecast; *see* alludere
223. *prɛndere* to take; p. abs. presi, prendesti, etc.; p. part. preso
224. preporre (=preponere) to prefer; *see* porre
225. prescegliere to choose from among; *see* scegliere
226. prescrivere to prescribe; *see* scrivere
227. presiedere to preside; *see* sedere
228. presumere to presume; *see* assumere
229. pretɛndere to pretend; *see* tɛndere
230. prevalere to prevail; *see* valere
231. prevedere to foresee; *see* vedere
232. prevenire to anticipate; *see* venire
233. produrre (=producere) to produce; *see* addurre
234. profferire to utter; *see* inferire
235. profondere to pour out; *see* fondere
236. promettere to promise; *see* mettere
237. promuɔvere *or* promɔvere to promote; *see* muɔvere
238. proporre (=proponere) to propose; *see* porre
239. prorompere to burst out; *see* rompere
240. proscrivere to proscribe; *see* scrivere
241. *protɛggere* to protect; p. abs. protɛssi, proteggesti, etc.; p. part. protɛtto
242. provenire to proceed from; *see* venire
243. provvedere to provide; *see* vedere
244. pungere to sting; p. abs. punsi, pungesti, etc.; p. part. punto
245. racchiudere to include; *see* chiudere
246. raccɔgliere to gather; *see* cɔgliere
247. radere to shave; p. abs. rasi, radesti, etc.; p. part. raso
248. raggiungere to overtake; *see* giungere
249. rapprɛndere to congeal; *see* prɛndere
250. rattenere to restrain; *see* tenere

251. rattɔrcere to wring; *see* tɔrcere
252. rattrarsi (=rattraersi) to shrink; *see* trarre
253. ravvedersi to repent; *see* vedere
254. ravvɔlgere to wrap up; *see* vɔlgere
255. recidere to cut off; *see* decidere
256. redigere to write; p. part. redatto
257. redimere to redeem; p. abs. redɛnsi, redimesti, etc.; p. part. redɛnto
258. reggere to support; p. abs. rɛssi, reggesti, etc.; p. part rɛtto
259. *rɛndere* to render; p. abs. resi, rendesti, etc.; p. part. reso
260. reprimere to repress; *see* comprimere
261. rescindere to rescind; *see* scindere
262. respingere to push back; *see* spingere
263. restringere *or* ristringere to restrain; *see* stringere
264. retrocɛdere to retrocede; *see* cɛdere
265. ricadere to fall again; *see* cadere
266. richiɛdere to request; *see* chiɛdere
267. riconoscere to recognize; *see* conoscere
268. ricoprire to cover again; *see* coprire
269. ricorrere to run again, have recourse; *see* correre
270. ridere to laugh; p. abs. risi, ridesti, etc.; p. part. riso
271. ridire (=ridicere) to say again; *see* dire
272. ridurre (=riducere) to reduce; *see* addurre
273. rifare (=rifacere) to do again, make again; *see* fare
274. riflɛttere to reflect; p. part. riflettuto *or* riflɛsso
275. rifrangere to refract; *see* frangere
276. rifulgere to shine; p. abs. rifulsi, rifulgesti; p. part. rifulso
277. *rimanere* to remain; pres. ind. rimango, rimani, rimane, rimaniamo, rimanete, rimangono; p. abs. rimasi, rimanesti, etc.; p. part. rimasto; fut. rimarrò, pres. subj. rimanga, rimaniamo, rimaniate, rimangano; impve. rimani, rimanga, rimaniamo, rimanete, rimangano
278. rimettere to replace, set again; *see* mettere
279. rimɔrdere to bite again, feel remorse; *see* mɔrdere
280. rimpiangere to regret; *see* piangere
281. rinascere to be born again; *see* nascere
282. rinchiudere to shut in, enclose; *see* chiudere
283. rincrescere to regret (impersonal); *see* crescere
284. rinvenire to find again; *see* venire
285. ripercuɔtere to repercuss, strike back; *see* percuɔtere
286. riporre (=riponere) to put again; *see* porre
287. riprɛndere to retake, recover; *see* prɛndere
288. riprodurre (=riproducere) to reproduce; *see* addurre
289. riscuɔtere to collect; *see* scuɔtere
290. risɔlvere to resolve; *see* assɔlvere

291. risorgere to rise up again; *see* sorgere
292. *rispondere* to answer, reply; p. abs. risposi, rispondesti, etc.; p. part. risposto
293. ristare to cease; *see* stare
294. ristringere to restrain; *see* stringere
295. ritenere to retain; *see* tenere
296. ritrarre (=ritraere) to draw; *see* trarre
297. riuscire to succeed; *see* uscire
298. rivedere to see again; *see* vedere
299. rivivere to live again; *see* vivere
300. rivɔlgere to turn; *see* vɔlgere
301. rodere to gnaw; p. abs. rosi, rodesti, etc.; p. part. roso
302. rompere to break; p. abs. ruppi, rompesti, etc.; p. part. rotto
303. salire to ascend, climb; pres. ind. salgo, sali, sale, saliamo, salite, salgono; pres. subj. salga, saliamo, saliate, salgano; impve. sali, salga, saliamo, salite, salgano
304. *sapere* to know, know how; pres. ind. sɔ, sai, sa, sappiamo, sapete, sanno; p. abs. sɛppi, sapesti, etc.; fut. saprò; pres. subj. sappia, sappiamo, sappiate, sappiano; impve. sappi, sappia, sappiamo, sappiate, sappiano
305. scadere to fall due; *see* cadere
306. *scegliere* to select; pres. ind. scelgo, scegli, sceglie, scegliamo, scegliete, scelgono; p. abs. scelsi, scegliesti, etc.; p. part. scelto; pres. subj. scelga, scegliamo, scegliate, scelgano; impve. scegli, scelga, scegliamo, scegliete, scelgano
307. *scendere* to descend; p. abs. scesi, scendesti, etc.; p. part. sceso
308. schiudere to disclose; *see* chiudere
309. scindere to separate; p. abs. scissi, scindesti, etc.; p. part, scisso
310. *sciɔgliere* to untie, melt; pres. ind. sciɔlgo, sciɔgli, sciɔglie, sciogliamo, sciogliete, sciɔlgono; p. abs. sciɔlsi, sciogliesti, etc.; p. part. sciɔlto; pres. subj. sciɔlga, sciogliamo, sciogliate, sciɔlgano; impve. sciɔgli, sciɔlga, sciogliamo, sciogliete, sciɔlgano
311. scommettere to bet; *see* mettere
312. scomparire to disappear; *see* apparire
313. scomporre (=scomponere) to undo; *see* porre
314. sconfiggere to defeat; *see* figgere
315. sconnɛttere to disconnect; *see* annɛttere
316. sconoscere to pay with ingratitude; *see* conoscere
317. scontɔrcere to contort, twist; *see* tɔrcere
318. sconvɔlgere to overturn; *see* vɔlgere
319. *scoprire* to discover; *see* aprire
320. scɔrgere to perceive; p. abs. scɔrsi, scorgesti, etc.; p. part. scɔrto
321. scorrere to flow; *see* correre

322. *scrivere* to write; p. abs. scrissi, scrivesti, etc.; p. part. scritto
323. scuɔtere to shake; pres. ind. scuɔto, scuɔti, scuɔte, scotiamo, scotete, scuɔtono; p. abs. scɔssi, scotesti, etc.; p. part. scɔsso; fut. scoterò; pres. subj. scuɔta, scotiamo, scotiate, scuɔtano; impve. scuɔti, scuɔta, scotiamo, scotete, scuɔtano
324. sedere to sit; pres. ind. siɛdo *or* seggo, siɛdi, siɛde, sediamo, sedete, siɛdono *or* sɛggono; pres. subj. siɛda *or* sɛgga, sediamo, sediate, siɛdano *or* sɛggano; impve. siɛdi, sɛgga, sediamo, sedete, sɛggano.
325. seppellire to bury; p. part. seppellito *or* sepolto
326. smettere to cease; *see* mettere
327. smuɔvere to move; *see* muɔvere
328. socchiudere to half shut; *see* chiudere
329. soccorrere to assist; *see* correre
330. soddisfare (=soddisfacere) to satisfy; *see* fare
331. soffrire to suffer; p. abs. soffɛrsi *or* soffrii, etc.; p. part. soffɛrto
332. soggiungere to add; *see* giungere
333. solere to be accustomed; pres. ind. sɔglio, suɔli, suɔle, sogliamo, solete, sɔgliono; pres. subj. sɔglia, sogliamo, sogliate, sɔgliano; p. part. sɔlito
334. sɔlvere to untie; *see* assɔlvere
335. sommɛrgere to submerge; *see* emɛrgere
336. sopprimere to suppress; *see* comprimere
337. sorgere to arise; p. abs. sorsi, sorgesti, etc.; p. part. sorto
338. sorprɛndere to surprise; *see* prɛndere
339. sorrɛggere to support; *see* rɛggere
340. sorridere to smile; *see* ridere
341. sospɛndere to suspend; *see* appɛndere
342. sospingere to push; *see* spingere
343. sostenere to support; *see* tenere
344. sottintɛndere to imply; *see* tɛndere
345. sovvenire to aid; *see* venire
346. spandere to shed; p. part. spanto
347. spargere to shed, scatter; p. abs. sparsi, spargesti, etc.; p. part. sparso
348. sparire to disappear; p. abs. sparii *or* sparvi, sparisti, etc.
349. *spɛgnere or* spɛngere to extinguish, put off; pres. ind. spɛngo, spɛgni *or* spɛngi, spɛgne *or* spɛnge, spegniamo *or* spengiamo, spegnete *or* spengete, spɛngono; p. abs. spɛnsi, spɛgnesti *or* spɛngesti; pres. subj. spɛnga, spegniamo, spegniate, spɛngano; p. part. spɛnto
350. *spɛndere* to spend; p. abs. spesi, spendesti, etc.; p. part. speso
351. spɛrdersi to disappear; *see* pɛrdere
352. spiacere to displease; *see* piacere
353. *spingere* to push; p. abs. spinsi, spingesti, etc.; p. part. spinto

354. spɔrgere to hold out; *see* pɔrgere
355. *stare* to stay, stand, be; pres. ind. sto, stai, sta, stiamo, state, stanno; p. abs. stɛtti, stɛsti, etc.; pres. subj. stia, stiamo, stiate, stiano; fut. starò; impve. sta', stia, stiamo, state, stiano
356. stɛndere to stretch out; *see* tɛndere
357. stɔrcere to wrest, twist; *see* tɔrcere
358. stringere to bind fast; p. abs. strinsi, stringesti, etc.; p. part. stretto
359. struggere to melt, pine away; p. abs. strussi, struggesti, etc.; p. part. strutto
360. succɛdere to succeed, happen; *see* concɛdere
361. supporre (=supponere) to suppose; *see* porre
362. svɛllere to root out; pres. ind. svɛllo (svɛlgo), svɛlli (svɛlgi), svɛlle, svelliamo, svellete, svɛllono, (svɛlgono); p. abs. svɛlsi, svellesti, etc.; p. subj. svɛlga, svelliamo, svelliate, svɛlgano; impve. svɛlli, svɛlga, svelliamo, svellete, svɛlgano
363. svenire to faint away; *see* venire
364. svɔlgere to unfold; *see* vɔlgere
365. *tacere* to pass over in silence, not to say; pres. ind. taccio, taci, tace, taciamo, tacete, tacciono; p. abs. tacqui, tacesti, etc.; pres. subj. taccia, taciamo, taciate, tacciano; impve. taci, taccia, taciamo, tacete, tacciano
366. tɛndere to tend; p. abs. tesi, tendesti, etc.; p. part. teso
367. *tenere* to hold, have; pres. ind. tɛngo, tiɛni, tiɛne, teniamo, tenete, tɛngono; p. abs. tenni, tenesti, etc.; fut. terrò; pres. subj. tɛnga, teniamo, teniate, tɛngano; impve. tiɛni, tɛnga, teniamo, tenete, tɛngano
368. tɛrgere to dry; p. abs. tɛrsi, tergesti, etc.; p. part. tɛrso
369. tingere to dye; p. abs. tinsi, tingesti, etc.; p. part. tinto
370. *tɔgliere or* tɔrre to take from; pres. ind. tɔlgo, tɔgli, tɔglie, togliamo, togliete, tɔlgono; p. abs. tɔlsi, togliesti, etc.; p. part. tɔlto; pres. subj. tɔlga, togliamo, togliate, tɔlgano; impve. tɔgli, tɔlga, togliamo, togliete, tɔlgano
371. tɔrcere to twist, writhe; p. abs. tɔrsi, torcesti, etc.; p. part. tɔrto.
372. tradurre (=traducere) to translate; *see* addurre
373. trafiggere to run through; *see* figgere
374. transigere to come to terms; *see* esigere
375. *trarre* (=traere) to draw, pull; pres. ind. traggo, trai, trae, traiamo, traete, traggono; p. abs. trassi, traesti, etc.; p. part. tratto; fut. trarrò; pres. subj. tragga, traiamo, traiate, traggano; impve. trai, tragga, traiamo, traete, traggano
376. trascorrere to pass over; *see* correre
377. trascrivere to transcribe; *see* scrivere

378. trasmettere to transmit, send; *see* mettere
379. trasparire to shine forth; *see* apparire
380. trattenere to entertain; *see* tenere
381. travedere to see dimly; *see* vedere
382. *uccidere* to kill; p. abs. uccisi, uccidesti, etc.; p. part. ucciso
383. udire to hear; pres. ind. ɔdo, ɔdi, ɔde, udiamo, udite, ɔdono; pres. subj. ɔda, udiamo, udiate, ɔdano; impve. ɔdi, ɔda, udiamo, udite, ɔdano
384. ungere to grease; p. abs. unsi, ungesti, etc.; p. part. unto
385. uscire to go out; pres. ind. ɛsco, ɛsci, ɛsce, usciamo, uscite, ɛscono; pres. subj. ɛsca, usciamo, usciate, ɛscano; impve. ɛsci, ɛsca, usciamo, uscite, ɛscano
386. *valere* to be worth; pres. ind. valgo, vali, vale, valiamo, valete, valgono, p. abs. valsi, valesti, etc.; p. part. valso; fut. varrò; pres. subj. valga, valiamo, valiate, valgano
387. *vedere* to see; p. abs. vidi, vedesti, etc.; p. part. visto *or* veduto; fut. vedrò
388. *venire* to come; pres. ind. vɛngo, viɛni, viɛne, veniamo, venite, vɛngono; p. abs. venni, venisti, etc.; p. part. venuto; fut. verrò; pres. subj. vɛnga, veniamo, veniate, vɛngano; impve. viɛni, vɛnga, veniamo, venite, vɛngano
389. vincere to win; p. abs. vinsi, vincesti, etc.; p. part. vinto
390. *vivere* to live; p. abs. vissi, vivesti, etc.; p. part. vissuto
391. *volere* to will, wish, want; pres. ind. vɔglio, vuɔi, vuɔle; vogliamo, volete, vɔgliono; p. abs. vɔlli, volesti, etc.; fut. vorrò; pres. subj. vɔglia, vogliamo, vogliate, vɔgliano; impve. vɔgli, vɔglia, vogliamo, vogliate, vɔgliano
392. vɔlgere to turn, revolve; p. abs. vɔlsi, volgesti, etc.; p. part. vɔlto

Exercise 1

Give the past absolute and past participle of the following verbs: uccidere, vincere, venire, tingere, vivere, togliere, spegnere, scrivere, stare, stringere, tacere, spingere, reggere, rimanere, sapere, porre, prendere, scegliere, rompere, ridere, mettere, parere, nascere, permettere, giungere, leggere, affiggere, espellere, diffondere, difendere, discutere, dolersi, maledire, immergere, accorrere, coincidere, opprimere, riconoscere, appendere, nascondere, ridurre.

Exercise 2

Translate into Italian: 1. He killed. 2. Having won. 3. Did he come? 4. I came, I saw, I conquered. 5. Did you take it? (togliere). 6. After having pushed it. 7. I did not take it. 8. Where did he put them? 9. They kept silent. 10. We have discussed enough. 11. They complained to (con) me. 12. How long did she stay (rimanere) there? 13. As soon as he recognised her he went up to her (andare incontro). 14. Who divulged the news? 15. He wrote the letter, reread it and put it on the table. 16. Did she take her coat when she went out? 17. They arrived (giungere) late. 18. Have you hidden my hat? No, I hung it in the hall. 19. When he was expelled he did not defend himself, he did not discuss it, he was not sorry, he went on living as he had lived till then. 20. Did she ever laugh? 21. He was born in 1925. 22. What did she do when she knew? She laughed. 23. Nobody defended them. 24. We have been oppressed all our life. 25. It had been dyed green. 26. They put it off. 27. Where did you take them? 28. How did he conclude his speech? 29. She did not put on the light. 30. Enclosed, you will find her photograph.

Exercise 3

Translate into Italian: 1. Although he does not go out often . . . 2. Did she look happy to you? 3. Let us hope that he does not die. 4. It will seem (parere) strange. 5. I hope it will not be overcooked. 6. I did not like it at all. 7. Unless it displeases you. 8. I would not know. 9. When did he live? 10. I hope he knows it. 11. I do not think it has been born yet. 12. You will tell me if it has been translated well. 13. Do you know if he was acquitted? 14. I believe that they kept them hidden throughout the war. 15. She does not believe he drank it alone. 16. I hope he shut the door properly (say well). 17. Do you want me to tell her? 18. He does not think they discussed it. 19. I believe he pretended to be interested in it. 20. They fear she has not put it in a safe place.

A. *Translate into English:* Voi che siete nati nelle piccole e nelle grandi città, voi non sapete la dolcezza, l'orgoglio, la necessità, il privilegio d'essere 'paesani'. Voi non sapete come sia fatto l'amore per il paese dove si è nati e cresciuti, perché la città natia, anche piccola, è sempre troppo grande, e il paese, il borgo, il villaggio, il 'paesello' delle canzonette e della retorica umile s'ama casa per casa, gronda per gronda, sasso per sasso, direi anche viso per viso. Voi non sapete che cosa sia possedere il proprio luogo d'origine, perché le vostre strade, le vostre piazze, i vostri crocicchi, son sempre di tutti, anche di chi arriva dalla stazione in questo momento, mentre il paese è proprio nostro, di noi che ci viviamo, di noi che ce ne siamo impossessati per diritto di nascita, e il forestiere che ciondola per la contrada con la valigetta in mano è nostro ospite e non ci fa nessuna invidia, povero pellegrino, ma forse una grande pietà. Voi non sapete che cosa sia nel borgo selvaggio il mutarsi del cielo, l'avvicendarsi delle stagioni, l'arrivo e la partenza delle rondini, il passaggio del postino amico di tutti, la distribuzione del giornale, un temporale, un corteo, un organetto, una carrozza, una nuvola; tutte cose bellissime che ci fanno ancora impressione, che hanno ancora un significato, poiché in ciascuno di noi ci sarà sempre tanta rusticità da goderne. Chi di voi sa d'aver sotto la sua gronda a livello della sua finestra, da tempo immemorabile, dacché fu ridipinta la casa, un nido di rondini? E che cos'è un nido di rondini in città se non una bozza sudicia che, a vederla di giù, deturpa un bel cornicione? Ma gli è che voi avete i bei cornicioni! (Marino Moretti: *Il paese natale*: from *Il tempo felice*: Treves, Milano.)

B. *Translate into Italian:* The fact of the matter[1] is that Beethoven's deafness and its influence on his art, have always been greatly exaggerated by sentimental biographers understanding nothing of a great composer's method of work. It is absurd to suppose that such a consummately gifted composer as Beethoven was in the degree dependent on external aids to composition, or that he was unable to reproduce in his mind's ear the exact equivalent of the notes which he wrote down. Practically none of the touching complaints that he makes about his affliction[2] in correspondence and conversation has any reference to his art; they are almost entirely concerned with the disabilities that it involved on the human and social side of his existence. No doubt he would have liked to hear music occasionally, but inability[3] to do so is not necessarily a great deprivation; many composers in full possession of their faculties never enter a concert-hall from one year's end to the other.[4] (Cecil Gray: *A History of Music.*)

In a society which is as indifferent to works of art as our modern industrialism it seems paradoxical[5] that artists of all kinds should loom so large[6] in the general consciousness of mankind; that they should be remembered with reverence and boasted[7] of as national assets when statesmen, lawyers and soldiers are forgotten. The great mass of modern men could rub along[8] happily enough without works of art or at least without new ones, but society would be sensibly more bored[9] if the artist died out[10] altogether. The fact is that every honest bourgeois, however sedate and correct his life, keeps a hidden and scarce-admitted[11] yearning for that other life of complete individualism which hard necessity or the desire for success has denied him. In contemplating the artist he tastes vicariously these forbidden joys. He regards the artist as a strange species,[12] half idiot, half divine, but above all irredeemably himself. He

1 la verità dei fatti
2 infermità
3 impossibilità
4 da un capo all'altro dell'anno
5 paradosso
6 avere un posto così predominante
7 vantare
8 continuare a vivere
9 annoiarsi
10 sparire
11 inconfessato
12 essere

seems equally strange in his outrageous egoism and his superb devotion to an idea. (Roger Fry: *Vision and Design.*)

D. *Va a finire che . . .*
Va a finire che dovrò pagare io.
In the end I'll be left to pay.

LESSON XXXIX

Prepositions

Prepositions which join an infinitive to the noun, adjective or verb on which the infinitive depends, vary considerably and consequently do not lend themselves to definite groupings. The following observations are therefore intended as helps to students and are not to be regarded as rules.

Prepositions Used when an Infinitive depends on a Noun

If the purpose or object of the noun is indicated, the dependent infinitive is commonly governed by *da*: if a precise specification is indicated, the infinitive is generally governed by *di*. *Per* and *a* are very occasionally found.

appartamento *da* vendere	flat for sale.
macchina *da* cucire	sewing machine.
acqua *da* bere	drinking water.
una ragazza *da* maritare	an eligible girl.
desidɛrio *di* riuscire	wish to succeed.
orrore *di* peccare	horror of sinning.
brama *di* arricchire	longing to enrich.
il mɔdo *di* conquistarlo	the way to win it.
l'aspirazione *a* vincere	the yearning to conquer.
la strada *per* arrivare alla cima	the way to the summit.

Prepositions Used when an Infinitive depends on an Adjective

At times no preposition is required with certain adjectives like: *giusto ingiusto*, *facile*, *difficile*, *importante*, *utile*, *inutile*, *necessario*.

Sarebbe giusto avvertirlo.	It would be fair to warn him.
È supɛrfluo raccomandarglielo.	It is pointless to recommend it to him.

The commonest preposition is *di* which again here indicates some specification. A few adjectives, for the most part past participles, take *a*: *avvezzo*—accustomed, *abituato*—used to, *assuefatto*—accustomed, *autorizzato*—authorised.

Sono liɛto *di* conoscerla	Glad to meet you.
abituato *ad* alzarsi prɛsto	used to getting up early.
avvezzo a lavorare	accustomed to work.

Prepositions Used when an Infinitive depends on a Verb

As was the case with adjectives, some verbs do not require prepositions. The most common of these are: *dovere*, *potere*, *volere*, *solere*, *bisognare*, *sembrare*, *parere*, *bastare*, *sentire*, *udire*, *vedere*, *osare*, *sapere*, *lasciare*, *preferire*, etc.

Ɔsa sfidarmi	He dares to defy me.
Preferisco tacere	I prefer to keep silent.

The preposition *a* is generally used with verbs which signify movement, help, beginning or continuation of an action, invitation, encouragement, instruction.

Impara *a* lεggere	He is learning to read.
Gli insegnò *a* scrivere	He taught him to write.

di,[1] also very common, is used with a variety of verbs.

Ti consiglio *di* partire	I advise you to leave.
Gli promise *di* aspettarlo	He promised to wait for him.
Speri *di* vederlo?	Do you hope to see him?

The following list of the constructions of the commonest verbs will be most useful for study and reference.

abbassarsi a to lower oneself to, to condescend to
abbandonarsi a to give way to, to surrender to
abbonarsi a to subscribe
abituare (si) a to accustom (oneself) to
accanirsi a to go on trying desperately
accettare di to agree to, undertake to
accingersi a to get ready, set about
acconsentire a to consent, accede
accordare di to grant
accostumarsi a to accustom oneself to
addestrarsi a to train oneself to
affaticarsi a to strive, tire oneself out to
affrettarsi a to hasten to, hurry
agognare di to covet, strive for
aiutare a to assist, help
amare to love
ammonire di non to warn, admonish
andare a to go and . . .
apparecchiarsi a to prepare
applicarsi a to apply oneself to
apprεndere a to learn
apprestarsi a to get ready to
***ardire di** to dare
arrabbattarsi a to bestir oneself, endeavour
arrischiarsi a to venture, dare
arrivare a to succeed in
aspettare di to wait
assuefare (si) a to accustom (oneself) to
attεndersi di to expect
autorizzare a to authorise

[1] di is always used in dependent clauses when the subject is the same as that of the main clause (see Lesson XXIII).

aver cura **di** to take care to . . .
avere da to have to
aver bisogno **di** to need to . . .
aver agio **di** to have the opportunity to, to be able
aver paura **di** to be afraid to . . .
avvezzare (si) **a** to accustom (oneself) to
azzardarsi **a** to venture
badare **a** to take care to (negative —di non)
bastare **di** to suffice
bisognare to be obliged to, it is necessary
bramare **di** to long for
cercare **di** to try, strive to
cessare **di** to cease, leave off
chiedere **di** to beg
comandare **di** to order
cominiciare **a** to begin to
compiacersi **di** or **nel** to be pleased to, to take pleasure in
concedere **di** to concede, admit
condannare **a** to condemn
condurre **a** to drive, induce
confortare **a** to encourage
consentire **a** or **di** to consent, agree
consigliare **di** to advise
continuare **a** to continue, resume
*contribuire **a** to contribute, to have part in
convenire **di** to agree
convenire **a** to suit
correre **a** to hasten
cospirare **a** to conspire, plot
costringere **a** to force, compel
credere **di** to believe, consider
curarsi **di** to pay heed to, take care of
decidere **di** to decide
degnarsi **di** to deign, condescend
deliberare **di** to resolve to
desiderare (**di**) to desire, to wish
destinare **a** to mean to, to allocate
determinare **di** to determine, resolve (when conjugated with essere takes ***a***)
dilettarsi **a**, **di** to delight to or in
dimenticare **di** to forget to
dire **di** to tell, bid
disegnare **di** to plan, resolve
disporre **di** to arrange to
disporsi **a** to prepare oneself to
divisare **di** to plan
domandare **di** to ask, demand
dovere to owe, have to
dubitare **di** to hesitate
eccitare **a** to incite, provoke, rouse
essere contento, lieto **di** to be glad to
esitare **a** to hesitate, waver
esortare **a** to exhort, urge
far conto **di** to imagine, suppose, rely
far meglio **a** to be better to
far piacere **di** to like to
far a meno **di** to refrain from, to do without
fermarsi **a** to stop
figurarsi **di** to imagine, fancy, suppose
fingere **di** to pretend, feign
*finire **di** to finish, leave off, cease
forzare **a** to force, compel
giovare **di** to help
giovarsi to avail oneself of
giustificarsi **di** to justify oneself
godere **di** to rejoice, enjoy
guardare **di** to take care
guardarsi **da** to forbear, beware
immaginare **di** to imagine
imparare **a** to learn
*impedire **di** to prevent, hinder
impegnarsi **di**, **a** to undertake
impiegare **a** to employ, spend
imporre **di** to enjoin, command

imprendere **a** to undertake, begin
incitare **a** to incite, instigate
inclinare **a** to incline, bend
incoraggiare **a** to encourage
indugiare **a** to delay
indurre **a** to lead, induce
insegnare **a** to teach, show
intendere **di** to intend, mean, require
intendersela **con** to come to terms with
invitare **a** to invite, request
invogliare **a** to induce, lead, tempt
lasciare **(a)** to let, allow, permit
mancare **di** to be lacking, wanting
mandare **a** to send for
meditare **di** to plan, design
meravigliarsi **di** to wonder, be surprised, be astonished
meritare **di** to deserve, require, want
mettersi **a** to begin, start, set in, set out
muovere **a** to move, stir
obbligare **a, di** to oblige, compel, bind
occorrere **di** to be necessary, required, to happen
occuparsi **di** to busy oneself with, occupy oneself with
offrire **di** to offer, afford, bid
ordinare **di** to order, arrange, ordain
osare **di** to dare, venture
ostinarsi, **a** to persist, insist
parere **di** to appear, seem
passare **a** to go on to
penare **a** to find it difficult, suffer
pensare **a** to think
pensare **di** to resolve, mean
pentirsi **di** to repent, regret
permettere **di** to allow, permit
persistere **a, nel** to persist
persuadere **a, di** to persuade, convince
pervenire **a** to arrive, reach, attain
piacere **di** to like
potere to be able
*preferire **di** to prefer
pregare **di** to request, beg, invite
prendere **a** to start, begin, to get into the habit
prepararsi **a** to prepare, get ready
resumere **di** to presume, conjecture, rely on
pretendere **di** to profess, pretend, claim
principiare **a** to commence, begin, start
procurare **di** to try
*proibire **di** to forbid, prohibit
promettere **di** to promise
proporre **di** to propose, propound
provarsi **a** to try
rallegrarsi **di** to rejoice, be glad
rassegnarsi **a** to resign oneself to, submit
ricordarsi **di** to remember, recollect
ricusare **di** to refuse, deny
rifiutare **di** to refuse, decline
rimanere **a** to remain, stay, stop
rincrescersi **di** to cause regret, displease
rinunziare to renounce, give up
ripugnare **di** to disgust, to be repugnant
risolvere **di** to resolve, solve, settle
risolversi **a** to decide
rispondere **di** to reply, agree to take responsibility for
ritornare **a** to return, go back, recur
riuscire **a, di** to succeed
sapere **di** to know, to be aware of

scongiurare **di** to implore
scrivere **di** to write
sdegnare **di** to disdain, scorn, refuse, to be scornful of
seguitare **a** to keep on, continue
sembrare **di** to seem, appear
sentire to feel, hear, learn
servire **a** to serve, contribute, be of use to
servirsi **di** to make use of, to use
sfidare **a** to defy, challenge, dare
sforzarsi **a, di** to exert oneself, strive
smaniare **di** to rave, to be crazy for
smettere **di** to stop, cease, give up
solere **(di)** to be accustomed to
sollecitare **a** to hasten, urge, entreat
sognare **di** to dream of, imagine
sperare **di** to hope for, expect, rely on
spiacersi **di** to displease, to be sorry
spingere **a** to push, shove, thrust
spronare **a** to spur, goad
stare **a** to stand, stay
stimolare **a** to stimulate, urge, encourage
*suggerire **di** to suggest, prompt
supplicare **a, di** to beg, implore, entreat
tardare **a** to delay, retard, linger, loiter
temere **di** to dread, shrink from
tentare **di** to attempt, try
toccare **a . . . di** to fall to one's lot
tornare **a** to return to it
udire to hear
usare to use to, have the habit
valere to be worth
vedere to see
venire **a** to come
vergognarsi **di** to be ashamed
vietare **di** to forbid, prohibit

Exercise 1

Translate into Italian: 1. House to sell. 2. Have you anything to say? 3. Her wish to forget. 4. It is not fair to remind him. 5. Firewood. 6. Sewing machine. 7. Is it necessary to tell him? 8. He is used to going dancing every night. 9. I am surprised to find you here. 10. It would be useful to know it. 11. Bathroom. 12. It is easy to learn it by heart. 13. Teacups. 14. He is authorised to sell. 15. It is her intention to leave.

Exercise 2

Translate into Italian: 1. Can you come? 2. I must leave. 3. She did not hear him coming. 4. Will he dare to follow her? 5. They prefer to stay at home. 6. Do you want to learn Italian? 7. I have seen him arrive. 8. We must (bisognare) go. 9. She saw them climbing up the stairs. 10. He used to go out every day.

Exercise 3

Translate into Italian: 1. She agreed (accettare) to carry on the job. 2. They hastened to refuse. 3. Help them to open the parcel. 4. Try to find him. 5. Did he order them to wait for him? 6. They will start building it. 7. When will she stop talking? 8. You are forcing him to stop working. 9. Will you go on writing? 10. We have decided to buy it. 11. I wish to sell them. 12. They have forgotten to telephone her. 13. Did *she* tell you to post it? 14. She will ask him to do it. 15. Do not pretend to ignore it. 16. You are preventing her from working. 17. They were teaching him to swim. 18. We invited them to come with us. 19. Will you allow them to go out? 20. Although he promised to come back. 21. He succeeded in finding the place. 22. Can he write? 23. She is afraid of not arriving in time. 24. Try to tell him. 25. Do not forbid them to see the show.

A. *Translate into English:* S'andava[1] fuori d'ogni stagione, ma quando riaccendo i ricordi non vedo che inverno e autunno o primavera piovosa: cieli coperti, uniti, grigi, chiusi; vento mordente o la quiete fredda e imbronciata della terra che pena e lavora nel profondo. Non vedo mai sole; non sento mai caldo; o vedo un solicello annacquato che viene a occhiate di tra le nubi in viaggio e fa sembrar più nera la terra ogni volta che risparisce. Vedo la campagna come sotto un cielo di nord, con tutto il raccoglimento e il deserto dell'anno che finisce, dopo che l'ultimo ramicello dimenticato è raggrinzito sui tralci secchi della vite. E mi ricordo bene di certe corte e ventose giornate di gennaio e di febbraio, quando si camminava[2] via lesti per le strade dure, ghiacciate, che risonavano sotto passi, fra muri asciutti che rimandavan gli echi, sotto le sfilaccicature[3] bianche delle nuvole alte. A forza di camminare tornavo a casa coi piedi brucianti e il viso acceso, tutto vibrante e vigoroso come se tornassi da una vittoria. E la casa povera e buia, e la mia cameruccia fredda e arruffata, con una lucernina a olio, d'ottone, che dava poco lume e un non so che di mortorio, mi pareva il ritorno alla mediocrità, alla schiavitù—alla morte. Allora prendevo un libro e leggevo alla fiochissima luce di quella funebre lucerna e a poco a poco tutto il mio corpo si raffreddava, i piedi tornavan gelati, la tristezza raddoppiava ed io mi buttavo sul letto a seppellir nel sonno i desideri inespressi e i sogni indeterminabili di una vita troppo diversa da questa—e da ogni vita. (Giovanni Papini: from *Un uomo finito*, Firenze, Vallecchi, 1922.)

B. *Translate into Italian:* We have mentioned Borgia. It is impossible not to pause for a moment on the name of a man in whom the political morality of Italy was so strongly personified, partially blended with the sterner lineaments of the Spanish character. On two important occasions Machiavelli was admitted to his society[4]; once, at the moment when his splendid villany achieved its most signal triumph, when he caught in one

[1] we went [2] we walked [3] fringe [4] presenza

snare and crushed at one blow all his most formidable rivals; and again when, exhausted by disease and overwhelmed by misfortunes, which no human prudence could have averted, he was the prisoner of the deadliest enemy of his house.

From some passages in The Prince, and perhaps also from some indistinct traditions, several writers have supposed a connection between those remarkable men much closer than ever existed. The Envoy has even been accused of prompting the crimes of the artful and merciless tyrant. But from the official documents it is clear that their intercourse, though ostensibly amicable, was in reality hostile. It cannot be doubted, however, that the imagination of Machiavelli was strongly impressed, and his speculations on government coloured[1] by the observations which he made on the singular character and equally singular fortunes of a man who under such disadvantages[2] had achieved such exploits.[3]

Some of those crimes of Borgia which to us appear the most odious would not have struck an Italian of the fifteenth century with equal horror. Patriotic feeling also might induce Machiavelli to look with some indulgence and regret on the memory of the only leader who could have defended the independence of Italy against the confederate spoilers of Cambray. (Macaulay: *Essays Historical and Literary*.)

D. *Per di più*

E per di più, mi aveva perduto il passaporto.

And on top of everything, he had lost my passport.

Per lo più

Per lo più resto a casa. I usually stay at home.

Tanto più che

Tanto più che glielo avevo detto.

Especially as I had told him.

[1] influenzate [2] condizioni contrarie [3] risultati

LESSON XL

Letter Writing

In Italian, more than in other languages, the written language differs from the spoken language, in a greater formality of style. Such formality is accentuated in letter writing, particularly in the fixed formulae used in official letters. The beginning and end of a letter, together with the pronoun used throughout, vary according to the type of letter and to the relationship between the writer and the recipient. We shall distinguish between (1) a letter to a relative or intimate friend or to an acquaintance; (2) a letter to a person of importance, and (3) a letter to a business firm, a Corporation, the management of a hotel or a Ministry.

Type (1), if the recipient is a relative or a close friend, begins 'Caro Roberto' or 'Cara Maria': the second person singular is used throughout and the letter ends with 'Un affettuoso abbraccio' (an affectionate embrace) or 'Ti abbraccio affettuosamente', followed by the Christian name. If the recipient is a less close friend or an acquaintance, the letter begins 'Gentile amico (amica)', 'Gentile Signora', 'Gentile Avvocato', 'Gentile Professore', etc.; the 3rd person sing. is used (lɛi,[1] suo, suɔi, etc.) and it ends with 'Cordiali saluti' (cordial greetings), 'Salutandola cordialmente', 'Pregandola di porgere i miɛi cordiali saluti a suo marito' (please give my kindest regards to your husband) 'mi creda suo devotissimo' (yours very sincerely) with the Christian name and initial letter of the surname, according to the degree of friendship.

Type (2), to a person of standing, begins 'Egrɛgio Avvocato', 'Stimatissimo collɛga', 'Chiarissimo Professore', 'Signor Senatore', ('Signor Ministro', 'Signor Presidente', etc.). The courtesy form (Lɛi, suo, suɔi) is used, with 'Ella' frequently replacing 'Lɛi' when addressed directly to the recipient, and the letter ends 'Con devɔti ossɛqui' (sincerely and respectfully), 'Con deferɛnti ossɛqui', 'Mi creda con i migliori saluti suo devotissimo' and the writer ends by signing his full name.

Type (3)—business letter—has the recipient's designation written near the top of the page to the left, preceded by 'Spettabile'

e.g. Spettabile Direzione della FIAT S.p.A.
Spettabile Direzione dell'Albergo Croce di Malta.
Spettabile Officina Salimbeni—Ufficio Vendite.

[1] Sometimes, as a token of respect, these personal pronouns, possessive pronouns and possessive adjectives are spelt with initial capital letters; this applies also to the suffix form, e.g. SalutandoLa cordialmente.

The customary salutation is omitted: the 2nd person plur. is used (Voi, vostre, etc.) and a common opening formulae are:

'In riscontro (acknowledgement) alla Vostra del 15 ultimo scorso', 'Con riferimento alla Vostra del 4 corrente', 'Facendo seguito alla nostra (following ours), etc.', and the letter ends 'In attesa di pronto (or sollecito) (speedy) riscontro, Vi salutiamo distintamente', or 'Distinti saluti' followed by the name of the firm or person who signs for it. If the letter concerns a request to a Minister or a Government Office, it is headed 'Onorevole Ministero del Commercio Estero' and it begins 'Il sottoscritto fa istanza (application) a che gli venga concessa . . .', it ends 'Con osservanza (respect)', 'Con ossequio'.

All letters are dated in the top right corner thus:

2 gennaio 1953
11 marzo 1955
1º (primo) settembre 1957

Envelopes are addressed according to the profession, importance, etc. of the recipient. 'Presso' stands for c/o.

e.g. Gentile Signora X Y (to a lady)
Piazza Esquilino, 28
Roma

Egregio Avvocato Francesco Capaldi (to a man of standing)
Via Ostiense 53
Roma

Dott. Mario Ansaldi (Avv. Mario Ansaldi, Ing. Mario Ansaldi)
Viale Aventino 12
Roma

Business letters are addressed in the same way as the heading inside the letter, viz. 'Spettabile Direzione, etc.'

The Italian method of beginning, ending and addressing letters strikes foreigners accustomed to simpler formulae as a little pompous, but it is current usage in Italy and reflects the good manners associated with an educated person.

(1) Le Scalette—Fiesole
18 settembre 1957

Cara Tina,

avevamo sperato di averti qui con noi per qualche giorno durante il mese di agosto, ma poiché non sei riuscita a risolvere il problema di essere contemporaneamente a Sanremo con Gianni, qui con noi e a Roma, speriamo almeno che, finiti gli esami, tu venga a fare compagnia per qualche giorno a papà e a me. Delia e i bambini partono venerdì e noi ci sentiremo molto soli senza di loro. Ti telefoneremo domani sera a casa per sentire se puoi venire subito. Naturalmente se Elena non è ancora partita per Londra ci farà molto piacere avere anche lei qui.

Un caro abbraccio.

Nadia.

(2)

Gentile Professore,

La ringrazio infinitamente per la cortesia e la premura con cui ha risposto alla mia lettera. Le informazioni che Ella mi dà sono del più grande interesse e mi saranno di prezioso aiuto nel mio lavoro.

Pregandola di accettare l'espressione della mia devozione, mi creda.

Sua, X.Y.

(3) Spettabile Direzione
dell'Albergo Riviera,
Riccione.

Vi saremmo grati se poteste riservarci una camera matrimoniale ed una singola, entrambe con acqua corrente, dal 16 al 30 stetembre. Desidereremmo conoscere il prezzo della pensione completa e della mezza pensione, compreso il servizio e la tassa di soggiorno, ed anche quanto costerebbe avere un bagno privato.

In attesa di un Vostro sollecito riscontro, con distinti saluti.

Dott. Francesco Betti.

Commonest Idioms

The following verbs, *fare*, *stare*, *andare*, *dare*, *restare*, *avere*, together with an adjective, an adverb or a noun, form some of the more frequently used idioms; some of the commonest are grouped in this lesson.

Fare

far conto   to reckon, to assume
far a meno   to go without
fare attenzione   to pay attention
fare bancarotta   to become insolvent
fare l'avvocato, il dottore   to be a lawyer, a doctor
far piacere (refl.)   to be pleased
fare la spola   to go to and fro
fare disonore   to disgrace
fare del bene   to help
fare una cura   to have treatment
fare bel tempo   to be good weather
fare esercizio   to practise
fare fronte   to cope, face up to
fare furore   to be all the rage
fare invidia   to be envied
fare a metà   to share, go half
fare naufragio   to be shipwrecked
fare il biglietto   to buy a ticket
fare presto   to be quick
fare tardi   to be late
fare senza   to do without
fare il sordo   to turn a deaf ear to
fare la corte   to court
fare poco caso   to make light of
far freddo, caldo   to be cold, hot
far fuoco   to fire
fare un giro   to go around

fare la barba to shave
fare a mɔdo prɔprio to have one's way
fare una passeggiata to go for a walk
fare a pɛzzi to tear to pieces
fare a pugni to box
fare silɛnzio to keep silent
fare tɔrto to wrong
fare onore to be a credit

Farsi

farsi fɔrza to pull oneself together
farsi coraggio to give oneself courage
farsi compagnia to keep company
farsi avanti to step forward
farsi strada to get along; to make a success of one's career
farsi sera, scuro to become dark
farsi vivo to turn up
farsi tardi to get late
farsi giɔco, beffe to mock
farsi male to hurt oneself
farsi vɛcchio to get old
farsi un dovere di to take it upon oneself

Stare

stare attɛnto to take care, pay attention
stare a disagio to be ill at ease
star fresco to be in a pretty plight
stare in ginɔcchio, in piɛdi, seduto to kneel, stand, sit
stare di casa to live, to dwell
stare lì lì (per) to be on the point of
stare sulle spine to be on tenterhooks
star mɛglio, pɛggio to be better, worse
stare buɔno to be good
stare muto to keep silent
stare zitto to be silent
stare bɛne to be well
stare in ɔzio to be idle
stare in pena to be anxious
stare comodo to be comfortable

Andare

andare a gɛnio to be liked by, to take to
andare a piɛdi, a cavallo, in macchina to walk, ride, drive
andare a rɔtoli, in malora to go from bad to worse, to go to ruin
andare a tentoni to feel one's way, to proceed with caution
andare all'altro mondo to die
andar a monte to come to nothing
andare a gonfie vele to go very well
andare a zonzo, in giro to wander
andare al passo, al trɔtto, al galɔppo to walk, trot, gallop
andare avanti e indiɛtro to go to and fro
andare con i piɛdi di piombo to be very cautious
andare d'accɔrdo to get on well
andare per i fatti prɔpri to go about one's own business
andare a fondo to get to the root of the matter
andare a picco to sink
andare a rɛmi, a vela, a vapore to row, sail, steam
andare in bestia to get very cross
andare a spasso to go for a walk
andare via (refl.) to leave
andare alla deriva to drift
andare (montare) su tutte le furie to get very cross

Restare (rimanere)

restare male to take it badly
restare di stucco, di sasso to be taken aback

restare stupito, sorpreso to be taken aback

restare al verde to be hard up

Avere

avere sete to be thirsty

avere tɔrto to be wrong

avere fretta to be in a hurry

avercela con qualcuno to be angry with somebody

aver a cuɔre to take to heart

aver agio to have the opportunity

aver a che dire to quarrel

avere vergogna to be ashamed

aver paura to be afraid

aver ragione to be right

averne abbastanza to be fed up

aver caro to hold dear

avere in prɛgio to hold in esteem

aver vent'anni to be twenty

Dare

dare rɛtta to listen to

dar la baia to mock

dare il buongiorno to wish good day

dare nell'ɔcchio to attract attention

dare uno schiaffo to slap somebody's face

dare del ladro, del bugiardo, etc. to call somebody a thief, a liar

dare un calcio, un pugno to kick, punch

dare fastidio to annoy, bother

dare la caccia to hunt, chase

dare motivo to give cause

dare la mano to shake hands

dare di piglio to get hold

dare un esame to sit an exam

Darsi

darsi da fare to busy oneself with

darsi delle arie to give oneself airs

darsela a gambe to run away

darsi la mano to shake, hold hands

darsi d'attorno to busy oneself with

darsi alla macchia to hide

darsi bɛl tɛmpo to have a good time

può darsi it might well be

Exercise 1

Translate into English: 1. Fa' del bene e poi dimenticalo. 2. Che cosa fa suo padre? Fa l'avvocato. 3. Fa sempre a modo suo. 4. Quando andrete a fare il biglietto? 5. Non fare il sordo. 6. Si fece gioco di lui. 7. Ti sei fatto male? 8. Pazienza! Fanne senza. 9. Faceva una passeggiata ogni mattina. 10. Dove vai? Vado a fare un giretto. 11. Quando fu a tre passi di distanza, fece fuoco. 12. Quella ragazza fa furore. 13. Fecero naufragio quando erano quasi in porto. 14. Facciamo a metà. 15. Domani farà bel tempo. 16. Sta' attento! 17. Stavi in pena? 18. Stava lì lì per rispondere. 19. Non sta comodo? 20. Se aspetti che ti aiuti, stai fresco. 21. Dove sta di casa? 22. Sta' buono. 23. Non mi va a genio. 24. Va a zonzo tutto il giorno. 25. Quando si sposano? Purtroppo il matrimonio è andato a monte. 26. Meglio così, non andavano affatto d'accordo; lui andava su tutte le furie per niente. 27. Ce l'hai con me? Hai torto. Io ho a cuore la tua salute. 28. Ne ho abbastanza, me ne vado. 29. Non ti dare delle arie, non vedi che ti danno la baia? 20. Cerca di non dare troppo nell'occhio. 31. Se la dette a gambe. 32. Dagli la mano. 33. Prima gli dette uno schiaffo, poi dette di piglio a un bastone e gli dette la caccia. 34. Facesti male a dargli del ladro. 35. Può darsi, ma lui me ne aveva dato motivo. 36. Dammi retta, non dargli fastidio. 37. Quando la vide, restò di stucco. 38. Se ti dai bel tempo e spendi tanto, resterai al verde. 39. Sarebbe meglio andare a fondo in questa questione. 40. Perché? Hanno avuto a che dire?

Exercise 2

Write a letter to an hotel booking rooms and asking prices.

Exercise 3

Write a composition using as many idioms as you can.

A. *Translate into English:* Ogni paese ha il suo vento, ogni terra si riconosce al modo come respira; è il fiato che schiarisce le foglie degli olivi, gonfia le chiome dei pini, liscia le pietre dei muri e l'intonaco delle case, arruffa i capelli sulla fronte delle ragazze, e pulisce il cielo nei torbidi giorni di Marzo, è l'alito stesso di quella terra, il suo profondo respiro.

Anche la Toscana ha il suo modo di respirare, assai diverso da quello della Liguria, dell'Emilia, della Romagna, dell'Umbria, del Lazio, che le fanno siepe intorno. Ma dire diverso è poco; si dovrebbe dire contrario. Ed è lo stesso modo col quale respirano i suoi abitanti, le sue pietre, le sue piante, i suoi fiumi, il suo mare. Quattro sono, anche in Toscana, i venti cardinali, e sono il grecale, il libeccio, lo scirocco, e il tramontano. Ma non son questi i venti che fanno il carattere della Toscana, che le danno quel colore, quel respiro, quel tono della pelle e della terra, degli occhi e delle foglie. . . .

Poi c'è un venticello minore, che non si sa che sia, non si sa che nome dargli, e alcuni lo chiamano il briachino[1], altri il pazzerello, ma i più lo chiamano il passerotto: e saltella davvero come un passerotto, via per i campi e le siepi, ad accarezzare il viso alle massaie, a lustrare il pelo dei buoi e dei cavalli, a ripulire i vetri delle finestre, le mezzine di rame sul muricciolo del pozzo, e fa dei chicchi[2] d'uva tanti occhietti lustri e vispi che ti sbirciano tra i pampani. Il venticello che fa bene agli ulivi, e non sai di dove venga. C'è chi dice che viene dall'Umbria, chi di più lontano, dalle Marche o giù di lì. Ma io direi che viene dalle parti di Perugia, perché è pulito, chiaro e civile, un vento che fa dimagrire, e ti rende semplice e ordinato: e solo quando fa il pazzerello mi par che venga da

[1] tipsy [2] each grape

quelle parti dell'Umbria dove stanno di casa i matti di Gubbio. È il vento che piace ai senesi, e lo vedi dipinto nelle tele di quei pittori, lo senti soffiare nella parlata di San Bernardino, l'odi scorrere come un'acqua viva lungo le facciate di marmo delle chiese e i muri del conventi. Piace ai senesi, come agli aretini e ai viareggini il libeccio, ai maremmani il grecale. E come lo scirocco piace ai ladri, agli spergiuri, ai marinai briachi, e ai toscani barlacci.[1] (Curzio Malaparte: from *Maledetti Toscani.*)

B. *Translate into Italian:* Ferocity and insolence were not among the vices of national character. To the discriminating cruelties of politicians, committed for great ends on select victims, the moral code of the Italians was too indulgent. But though they might have recourse[2] to barbarity as an expedient, they did not require it as a stimulant. They turned[3] with loathing from the atrocity of the strangers who seemed to love blood for its own sake,[4] who not content with subjugating, were impatient to destroy, who found a fiendish pleasure in razing magnificent cities, cutting the throats of enemies who cried for quarter,[5] or suffocating[6] an unarmed population by thousands in the caverns to which it had fled for safety.[7] Such were the scenes which daily excited the terror and disgust of a people among whom, till lately, the worst that a soldier had to fear in a pitched battle was the loss of his horse and the expense of his ransom. The wealth which had been accumulated during centuries of prosperity and repose was rapidly melting away. The intellectual superiority of the oppressed people only rendered them more keenly sensible[8] of their political degradation. . . . Yet a discerning eye might even then have seen that genius and learning would not long survive the state of things from which they had sprung[9], that the great men whose talents gave lustre to that melancholy[10] period had been formed under the influence of happier days and would leave no successors behind them. (Macaulay, *Essays Historical and Literary.*)

D. *Te lo dico io*

Quello è in malafede, te lo dico io.

I can assure you that that man is acting in bad faith.

[1] bad
[2] ricorrere
[3] rifuggire
[4] per se stesso
[5] implorare mercè
[6] sterminare
[7] rifugiarsi per cercare scampo
[8] consapevole
[9] derivare
[10] triste

ESSERE—TO BE / AVERE—TO HAVE

INDICATIVE MOOD

Present	Present Perfect		Present	Present Perfect	
I am	*I have been*		*I have*	*I have had*	
sono	sono		ho	ho	
sɛi	sɛi	stato (a)	hai	hai	
è	è		ha	ha	avuto
siamo	siamo		abbiamo	abbiamo	
siɛte	siɛte	stati (e)	avete	avete	
sono	sono		hanno	hanno	

Past Descriptive	Past Perfect		Past Descriptive	Past Perfect	
I was being, used to be	*I had been*		*I was having, used to have*	*I had had*	
ɛro	ɛro		avevo	avevo	
ɛri	ɛri	stato (a)	avevi	avevi	
ɛra	ɛra		aveva	aveva	avuto
eravamo	eravamo		avevamo	avevamo	
eravate	eravate	stati (e)	avevate	avevate	
ɛrano	ɛrano		avevano	avevano	

Past Absolute	2nd Past Perfect		Past Absolute	2nd Past Perfect	
I was	*I had been*		*I had*	*I had had*	
fui	fui		ɛbbi	ɛbbi	
fosti	fosti	stato (a)	avesti	avesti	
fu	fu		ɛbbe	ɛbbe	avuto
fummo	fummo		avemmo	avemmo	
foste	foste	stati (e)	aveste	aveste	
furono	furono		ɛbbero	ɛbbero	

Future	Future Perfect		Future	Future Perfect	
I shall be	*I shall have been*		*I shall have*	*I shall have had*	
sarò	sarò		avrò	avrò	
sarai	sarai	stato (a)	avrai	avrai	
sarà	sarà		avrà	avrà	avuto
saremo	saremo		avremo	avremo	
sarete	sarete	stati (e)	avrete	avrete	
saranno	saranno		avranno	avranno	

SUBJUNCTIVE MOOD

Present	Present Perfect		Present	Present Perfect	
(that) I may be	*I may have been*		*(that) I may have*	*I may have had*	
sia	sia		abbia	abbia	
sia	sia	stato (a)	abbia	abbia	
sia	sia		abbia	abbia	avuto
siamo	siamo		abbiamo	abbiamo	
siate	siate	stati (e)	abbiate	abbiate	
siano	siano		abbiano	abbiano	

Past	Past Perfect		Past	Past Perfect	
(*that*) *I might be*	*I might have been*		(*that*) *I might have*	*I might have had*	
fossi	fossi	stato (a)	avessi	avessi	avuto
fossi	fossi		avessi	avessi	
fosse	fosse		avesse	avesse	
fossimo	fossimo	stati (e)	avessimo	avessimo	
foste	foste		aveste	aveste	
fossero	fossero		avessero	avessero	

CONDITIONAL MOOD

Present	Perfect		Present	Perfect	
I should be	*I should have been*		*I should have*	*I should have had*	
sarεi	sarεi	stato (a)	avrεi	avrεi	avuto
saresti	saresti		avresti	avresti	
sarεbbe	sarεbbe		avrεbbe	avrεbbe	
saremmo	saremmo	stati (e)	avremmo	avremmo	
sareste	sareste		avreste	avreste	
sarεbbero	sarεbbero		avrεbbero	avrεbbero	

IMPERATIVE (Present)

Be

—
sii
sia
siamo
siate
siano

IMPERATIVE (Present)

Have

—
abbi
abbia
abbiamo
abbiate
abbiano

INFINITIVE

Pres: εssere—*to be*
Perf: εssere stato—*to have been*

INFINITIVE

Pres: avere—*to have*
Perf: avere avuto—*to have had*

"PARTICIPIO"

Pres: ——
Past: stato—*been*

"PARTICIPIO"

Pres: avεnte—*having*
Past: avuto—*had*

"GERUNDIO"

Pres: εssendo—*being*
Past: εssendo stato—*having been*

"GERUNDIO"

Pres: avεndo—*having*
Past: avεndo avuto—*having had*

FIRST CONJUGATION

AMARE—TO LOVE

INDICATIVE MOOD

Present	**Present Perfect**	
I love	*I have loved*	
am o	ho	amato
am i	hai	amato
am a	ha	amato
am iamo	abbiamo	amato
am ate	avete	amato
am ano	hanno	amato

Past Descriptive	**Past Perfect**	
I was loving, used to love	*I had loved*	
am avo	avevo	amato
am avi	avevi	amato
am ava	aveva	amato
am avamo	avevamo	amato
am avate	avevate	amato
am avano	avevano	amato

Past Absolute	**2nd Past Perfect**	
I loved	*I had loved*	
am ai	ɛbbi	amato
am asti	avesti	amato
am ò	ɛbbe	amato
am ammo	avemmo	amato
am aste	aveste	amato
am arono	ɛbbero	amato

Future	**Future Perfect**	
I shall love	*I shall have loved*	
am erò	avrò	amato
am erai	avrai	amato
am erà	avrà	amato
am eremo	avremo	amato
am erete	avrete	amato
am eranno	avranno	amato

SUBJUNCTIVE MOOD

Present	**Present Perfect**	
(that) I may love	*I may have loved*	
am i	abbia	amato
am i	abbia	amato
am i	abbia	amato
am iamo	abbiamo	amato
am iate	abbiate	amato
am ino	abbiano	amato

Past	**Past Perfect**	
(that) I might love	*I might have loved*	
am assi	avessi	amato
am assi	avessi	amato
am asse	avesse	amato
am assimo	avessimo	amato
am aste	aveste	amato
am assero	avessero	amato

CONDITIONAL MOOD

Present	**Perfect**	
I should love	*I should have loved*	
am erɛi	avrɛi	amato
am eresti	avresti	amato
am erɛbbe	avrɛbbe	amato
am eremmo	avremmo	amato
am ereste	avreste	amato
am erɛbbero	avrɛbbero	amato

IMPERATIVE (Present)

Love

am a
am i

am iamo
am ate
am ino

INFINITIVE

Pres: am are—*to love* **Perf:** avere amato—*to have loved*

"PARTICIPIO"

Pres: am ante—*loving* **Past:** am ato—*loved*

"GERUNDIO"

Pres: am ando—*loving* **Past:** avɛndo amato—*having loved*

SECOND CONJUGATION

TEMERE—TO FEAR

INDICATIVE MOOD

Present	**Present Perfect**	
I fear	*I have feared*	
tɛm o	ho	temuto
tɛm i	hai	
tɛm e	ha	
tem iamo	abbiamo	
tem ete	avete	
tɛm ono	hanno	

Past Descriptive	**Past Perfect**	
I was fearing, used to fear	*I had feared*	
tem evo	avevo	temuto
tem evi	avevi	
tem eva	aveva	
tem evamo	avevamo	
tem evate	avevate	
tem evano	avevano	

Past Absolute	**2nd Past Perfect**	
I feared	*I had feared*	
tem ei (ɛtti)	ɛbbi	temuto
tem esti	avesti	
tem é (ɛtte)	ɛbbe	
tem emmo	avemmo	
tem este	aveste	
tem erono (ɛttero)	ɛbbero	

Future	**Future Perfect**	
I shall fear	*I shall have feared*	
tem erò	avrò	temuto
tem erai	avrai	
tem erà	avrà	
tem eremo	avremo	
tem erete	avrete	
tem eranno	avranno	

SUBJUNCTIVE MOOD

Present	**Present Perfect**	
(that) I may fear	*I may have feared*	
tɛm a	abbia	temuto
tɛm a	abbia	
tɛm a	abbia	
tem iamo	abbiamo	
tem iate	abbiate	
tɛm ano	abbiano	

Past	**Past Perfect**	
(that) I might fear	*I might have feared*	
tem essi	avessi	temuto
tem essi	avessi	
tem esse	avesse	
em essimo	avessimo	
tem este	aveste	
tem essero	avessero	

CONDITIONAL MOOD

Present	**Perfect**	
I should fear	*I should have feared*	
tem erɛi	avrɛi	temuto
tem eresti	avresti	
tem erɛbbe	avrɛbbe	
tem eremmo	avremmo	
tem ereste	avreste	
tem erɛbbero	avrɛbbero	

(IMPERATIVE) **Present**

Fear

tɛm i
tɛm a
tem iamo
tem ete
tɛm ano

INFINITIVE

Pres: tem ere—*to fear* **Perf:** avere temuto—*to have feared*

"PARTICIPIO"
Pres: tem ɛnte—*fearing* **Past:** tem uto—*feared*

"GERUNDIO"
Pres: tem ɛndo—*fearing* **Past:** avɛndo temuto—*having feared*

THIRD CONJUGATION

DORMIRE—TO SLEEP

INDICATIVE MOOD

Present	**Present Perfect**	
I sleep	*I have slept*	
dɔrm o	ho	
dɔrm i	hai	
dɔrm e	ha	dormito
dorm iamo	abbiamo	
dorm ite	avete	
dorm ono	hanno	

Past Descriptive	**Past Perfect**	
I was sleeping, used to sleep	*I had slept*	
dorm ivo	avevo	
dorm ivi	avevi	
dorm iva	aveva	dormito
dorm ivamo	avevamo	
dorm ivate	avevate	
dorm ivano	avevano	

Past Absolute	**2nd Past Perfect**	
I slept	*I had slept*	
dorm ii	ɛbbi	
dorm isti	avesti	
dorm ì	ɛbbe	dormito
dorm immo	avemmo	
dorm iste	aveste	
dorm irono	ɛbbero	

Future	**Future Perfect**	
I shall sleep	*I shall have slept*	
dorm irò	avrò	
dorm irai	avra i	
dorm i rà	avrà	dormito
dorm iremo	avremo	
dorm irete	avrete	
dorm iranno	avranno	

SUBJUNCTIVE MOOD

Present	**Present Perfect**	
(that) I may sleep	*I may have slept*	
dɔrm a	abbia	
dɔrm a	abbia	
dɔrm a	abbia	dormito
dorm iamo	abbiamo	
dorm iate	abbiate	
dɔrm ano	abbiano	

Past	**Past Perfect**	
(that) I might sleep	*I might have slept*	
dorm issi	avessi	
dorm issi	avessi	
dorm isse	avesse	dormito
dorm issimo	avessimo	
dorm iste	aveste	
dorm issero	avessero	

CONDITIONAL MOOD

Present	**Perfect**	
I should sleep	*I should have slept*	
dorm irɛi	avrɛi	
dorm iresti	avresti	
dorm irɛbbe	avrɛbbe	dormito
dorm iremmo	avremmo	
dorm ireste	avreste	
dormi rɛbbero	avrɛbbero	

IMPERATIVE **(Present)**

Sleep
—
dɔrm i
dɔrm a
dorm iamo
dorm i te
dɔrm ano

INFINITIVE

Pres: dorm ire—*to sleep* **Perf:** avere dormito—*to have slept*

"PARTICIPIO"

Pres: dorm ɛnte—*sleeping* **Past:** dorm ito—*slept*

"GERUNDIO"

Pres: dorm ɛndo—*sleeping* **Past:** avɛndo dormito—*having slept*

THIRD CONJUGATION (II)

CAPIRE—TO UNDERSTAND

INDICATIVE MOOD

Present	Present Perfect	
I understand	*I have understood*	
cap isc o	ho	capito
cap isc i	hai	
cap isc e	ha	
cap iamo	abbiamo	
cap ite	avete	
cap isc ono	hanno	

Past Descriptive	Past Perfect	
I was understanding, used to understand	*I had understood*	
cap ivo	avevo	capito
cap ivi	avevi	
cap iva	aveva	
cap ivamo	avevamo	
cap ivate	avevate	
cap ivano	avevano	

Past Absolute	2nd Past Perfect	
I understood	*I had understood*	
cap ii	ɛbbi	capito
cap isti	avest i	
cap ì	ɛbbe	
cap immo	avemmo	
cap iste	aveste	
cap irono	ɛbbero	

SUBJUNCTIVE MOOD

Present	Present Perfect	
(that) I may understand	*I may have understood*	
cap isc a	abbia	capito
cap isc a	abbia	
cap isc a	abbia	
cap iamo	abbiamo	
cap iate	abiate	
cap isc ano	abbiano	

Past	Past Perfect	
(that) I might understand	*I might have understood*	
cap issi	avessi	capito
cap issi	avessi	
cap isse	avesse	
cap issimo	avessimo	
cap iste	aveste	
cap issero	avessero	

CONDITIONAL MOOD

Present	Perfect	
I should understand	*I should have understood*	
cap irɛi	avrɛi	capito
cap iresti	avresti	
cap irɛbbe	avrɛbbe	
cap iremmo	avremmo	
cap ireste	avreste	
cap irɛbbero	avrɛbbero	

Future	**Future Perfect**		IMPERATIVE **(Present)**
I shall understand	*I shall have understood*		*Understand*
cap irò	avro	capito	
cap irai	avrai	capito	cap isc i
cap irà	avrà	capito	cap isc a
cap iremo	avremo	capito	cap iamo
cap irete	avrete	capito	cap ite
cap iranno	avranno	capito	cap isc ano

INFINITIVE
Pres: capire—*to understand* **Perf:** avere capito—*to have understood*

"PARTICIPIO"
Pres:—— **Past:** cap ito—*understood*

"GERUNDIO"
Pres: cap ɛndo—*understanding* **Past:** avɛndo capito—*having understood*

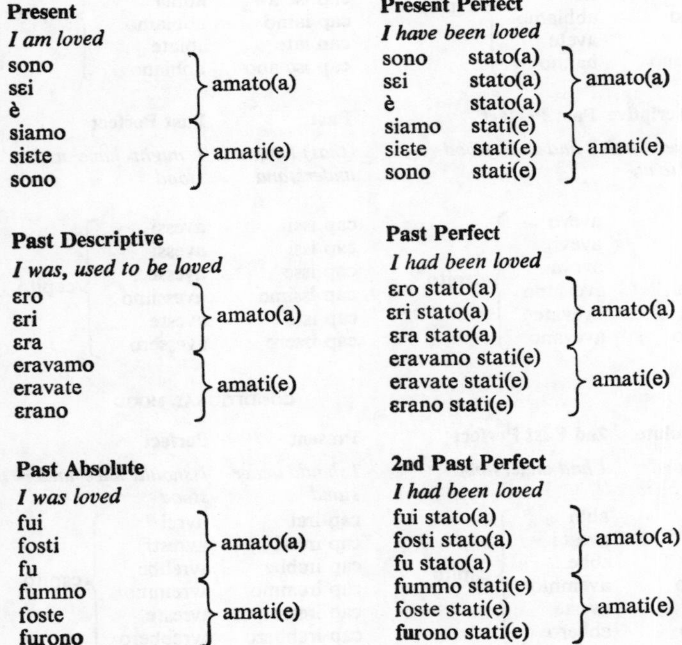

PASSIVE VOICE

INDICATIVE MOOD

Present		**Present Perfect**	
I am loved		*I have been loved*	
sono	amato(a)	sono stato(a)	amato(a)
sɛi	amato(a)	sɛi stato(a)	amato(a)
è	amato(a)	è stato(a)	amato(a)
siamo	amati(e)	siamo stati(e)	amati(e)
siɛte	amati(e)	siɛte stati(e)	amati(e)
sono	amati(e)	sono stati(e)	amati(e)

Past Descriptive		**Past Perfect**	
I was, used to be loved		*I had been loved*	
ɛro	amato(a)	ɛro stato(a)	amato(a)
ɛri	amato(a)	ɛri stato(a)	amato(a)
ɛra	amato(a)	ɛra stato(a)	amato(a)
eravamo	amati(e)	eravamo stati(e)	amati(e)
eravate	amati(e)	eravate stati(e)	amati(e)
ɛrano	amati(e)	ɛrano stati(e)	amati(e)

Past Absolute		**2nd Past Perfect**	
I was loved		*I had been loved*	
fui	amato(a)	fui stato(a)	amato(a)
fosti	amato(a)	fosti stato(a)	amato(a)
fu	amato(a)	fu stato(a)	amato(a)
fummo	amati(e)	fummo stati(e)	amati(e)
foste	amati(e)	foste stati(e)	amati(e)
furono	amati(e)	furono stati(e)	amati(e)

Future		**Future Perfect**	
I shall be loved		*I shall have been loved*	
sarò	amato(a)	sarò stato(a)	amato(a)
sarai		sarai stato(a)	
sarà		sarà stato(a)	
saremo	amati(e)	saremo stati(e)	amati(e)
sarete		sarete stati(e)	
saranno		saranno stati(e)	

SUBJUNCTIVE MOOD

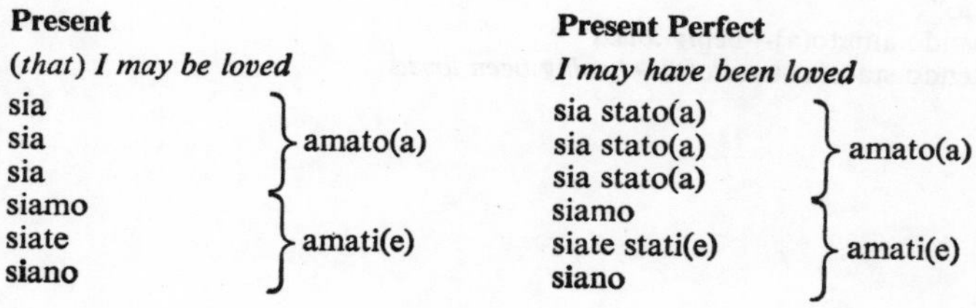

Present		**Present Perfect**	
(that) I may be loved		*I may have been loved*	
sia	amato(a)	sia stato(a)	amato(a)
sia		sia stato(a)	
sia		sia stato(a)	
siamo	amati(e)	siamo	amati(e)
siate		siate stati(e)	
siano		siano	

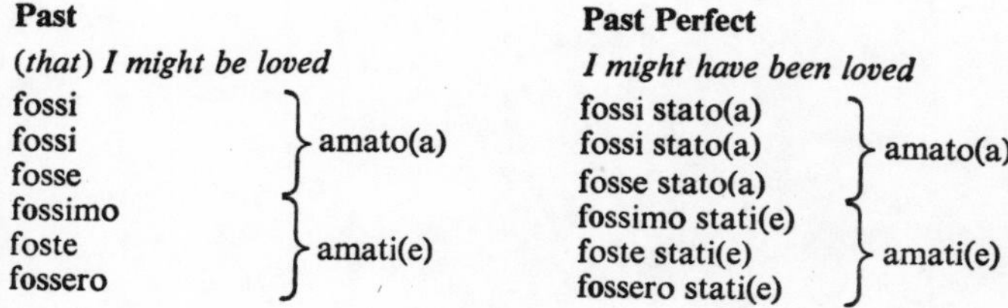

Past		**Past Perfect**	
(that) I might be loved		*I might have been loved*	
fossi	amato(a)	fossi stato(a)	amato(a)
fossi		fossi stato(a)	
fosse		fosse stato(a)	
fossimo	amati(e)	fossimo stati(e)	amati(e)
foste		foste stati(e)	
fossero		fossero stati(e)	

CONDITIONAL MOOD

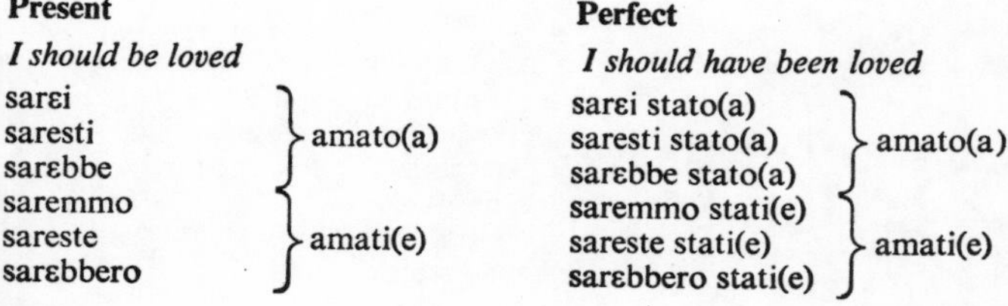

Present		**Perfect**	
I should be loved		*I should have been loved*	
sarεi	amato(a)	sarεi stato(a)	amato(a)
saresti		saresti stato(a)	
sarεbbe		sarεbbe stato(a)	
saremmo	amati(e)	saremmo stati(e)	amati(e)
sareste		sareste stati(e)	
sarεbbero		sarεbbero stati(e)	

IMPERATIVE

Present

be loved

sii	**amato(a)**
sia	
siamo	**amati(e)**
siate	
siano	

INFINITIVE

Pres: essere amato—*to be loved* **Perf: essere stato amato—*to have been loved***

"PARTICIPIO"

Pres: —— **Past: stato(a) amato(a)**

"GERUNDIO"

Pres: essendo amato(a)—*being loved*

Past: essendo stato(a) amato(a)—*having been loved*

GENERAL VOCABULARY

Italian – English

A

a (prep.) to, at, in
abbaco ready reckoner
abbandonare to abandon, leave
abbastanza (adv.) enough, fairly, somewhat
abbondanza abundance
abitante (m. & f.) inhabitant, resident
abitare to live in
abituare to accustom
acacia acacia
accademia academy
accadere to happen, occur
accarezzare to caress, fondle
accendere to light
accento accent
accettare to accept, agree to, approve
acciocché (conj.) in order that
accompagnare to accompany, escort
accorgersi to notice
acqua water
acre (adj.) acrid
adatto (adj.) suitable
adorazione (f.) worship
addentrarsi to penetrate
Adriatico Adriatic
ad un tratto suddenly
aereo (adj.) airy
aeroplano aeroplane
afa sultriness, closeness
affare (m.) business, affair
affatto (adv.) entirely, at all
affezionarsi to become fond of
affinché (conj.) in order that
affiorare to come to the surface
affittare to rent
affliggere to afflict, distress
affollato (adj.) crowded
affrancatura postage
affresco fresco (painting)
affrettarsi to make haste, hurry
aggruppato (adj.) bunched up
agitato (adj.) rough (sea) worried (man)
aglio garlic
agnello lamb
agosto August
agro (adj.) sour
aiutare to help
aiuto help
alba dawn
albergo hotel
albero tree
albicocca apricot
alcuno (adj.) some, any
alito gentle breeze
allegro (adj.) gay
Alpi (f. pl.) the Alps (adj. **alpino**)
alpinismo mountaineering
alquanto (adj. & pron.) some, several
alto (adj.) high, tall
altro (adj.) other; (pron.) something else
altrui (pron. inv.) of others, to others
alunno pupil
alzarsi to get up, rise
amaca hammock
amabile (adj.) amiable
amare to love; **amanti**, lovers
amarezza bitterness
ambedue (pron.& adj. inv.) both
ambiguita ambiguity
Ambrogio Ambrose
amico, a friend
ammirare to admire
ammissione (f.) admission, entrance
ammonire to admonish
ampio (adj.) wide, spacious
amore (m.) love
analisi (f.) analysis
anatra duck
anche (adv.) also, too
ancora (adv.) still, yet, again
andare to go (*see* pp. 198, 259)
andarsene to depart
anfratto ravine

angelico (adj.) angelic
angolo corner
anima soul
Anna Anne
annacquato (adj.) watery, pale
annerito (adj.) blackened
anno year (adj. **annuale**)
annoiarsi to be bored
antecedente precedent
antico (adj.) old, ancient
Antonio Antony
anziché (conj.) rather than
aperitivo drink, aperitif
aperto (adj.) open, opened; **all'a,** in the open air
apparecchiare to set the table
apparire to appear
appartamento flat, apartment
appena (adv.) hardly, scarcely
appena che (conj.) as soon as
appendere to hang
applaudire* to applaud, cheer
apprezzare to appreciate
appuntamento appointment, date
aprico (adj.) sunny
aprile (m.) April
aprire to open
aragosta lobster
aranceto orange-grove
aranciata orangeade
arancia orange
arbitro referee, umpire
archeologo archaeologist
architetto architect
architettura architecture (adj. **architettonico**)
arcicontento (adj.) very happy
arcuato (adj.) arched, curled up
ardere to burn
Aretini people of Arezzo
argomento subject, theme, topic
arguzia wit
aria air
armadio wardrobe, cupboard
aromatico (adj.) sweet, aromatic
arredamento furnishing
arricchirsi to become rich
arrivare . . . a to arrive
arrivo arrival
arrosto (n. & adj.) roast, roasted
arruffare to ruffle
arso (adj.) burnt
arte (f.) art, skill
artista (m. & f.) artist
ascensore (m.) lift
asciugare to dry (adj. **asciutto**)
ascoltare to listen to (n. **ascoltatore**)
asino-ello ass, donkey
aspettare to wait, wait for
aspirazione (f.) yearning
assaggiare to sample, taste
assai (adv.) very, quite
assiduamente (adv.) assiduously
assieme (adv.) together
assopirsi to doze, fall asleep
assortimento selection, assortment
assuefatto (adj.) accustomed
assurdo (adj.) absurd
a tradimento treacherously
attento (adj.) attentive
attorcere to curl
attore, attrice actor, actress
attraversare to cross
attraverso (prep.) across
audacia audacity; (pl.) daring deeds
audace (adj.) bold, valiant
autobus (m. inv.) bus
automobile (f.) car
autorimessa garage
autorizzato (adj.) authorized
autunno autumn
avanti (adv. & prep.) before
avanzo left overs, remains
avere to have (*see* p. 261)
— appetito to have an appetite
— bisogno di to need
— fame to be hungry
avvenire to happen, occur
avventarsi to rush
avventura adventure
avvertire to warn
avvezzo (adj.) accustomed
avviarsi to make one's way
avvicendarsi (n.) succession
avvocato lawyer
azzurro (adj.) blue

B

babbo daddy
bagaglio luggage
bagnare soak
balcone (m.) balcony
ballare to dance
ballo ball, dance, dancing

balzo leap, jump
bambino, -i little child, children
banca, bancario bank, banking
bar (m. inv.) bar
barbabietola (m.) beetroot
barbaro barbarian (adj. **barbarico**)
barca boat
barocco (adj.) baroque (style)
basilica basilica
basso (adj.) low
bastare to be enough
battere to beat
batticuore (m.) palpitation
Battistero Baptistery
baule (m.) trunk
belga, belgi (m.) Belgian
bello (adj.) beautiful (n. **bellezza**)
benché (conj.) although
bene (adv.) well; **ben presto**, pretty soon
bere to drink
biancheria underwear, linen
bianco (adj.) white, sullen
bicchiere (m.) glass
bigio (adj.) grey
biglietto ticket, card
binario rails, platform
biondo (adj.) fair, blond
biro (f.) biro
bisbigliare to whisper
biscotto biscuit
bisognare to be necessary
bisogno need; **avere —**, to need
bisunto grease
bizzarro (adj.) bizarre
bocca mouth
bocciato failed, rejected (v. **bocciare**)
boia (m.) executioner
bonario (adj.) good natured, amiable
borgo village
borsetta handbag
bosco wood
bottega little shop
bottiglia bottle
bozza lump
braccialetto bracelet
braccio arm
brama longing, desire
breve (adj.) short; **tra —, in —**, shortly
briachino, briaco tipsy
briciola crumb
broccato brocade
brodo broth, clear soup
bronchite (f.) bronchitis
bruciare burn
bruno (adj.) dark
brutto (adj.) ugly
buca delle lettere letter-box
bue (m.) ox (pl. **buoi**)
bugia lie
buio (adj.) dark
buono (adj.) good
burro butter
bussare to knock
busta envelope
buttarsi to throw oneself

C

cabina telefonica telephone box
cacciagione (f.) game
cacciatore (m.) hunter
cadavere (m.) corpse
cadere to fall, drop
caduco (adj.) transient
caffè (m.) coffee, café
— e latte white coffee
caffettiera coffee-pot
cagliare to clot, curdle
calcinato chalky
calcio football
caldo (adj.) hot, warm
calmo (adj.) calm
calza, calzino stocking, sock
calzoleria shoeshop, bootmaker's
cambiamento change (v. **cambiare**)
camera da letto bedroom
cameriere (m.) waiter
camice (m.) surplice
camicetta blouse
camicia shirt
— da notte night-dress
caminetto fireplace, mantelpiece
camminare to walk
cammino way, road, journey
campagna country
campana bell
campanello bell
Campania Campania
campanile (m.) belfry, bell-tower
campo field, course
canale (m.) canal, channel
canalone (m.) rift
cancello gate

cane (m.) dog
candelabro chandelier
candido (adj.) white
canottaggio rowing
cantare to sing
canto canto, chant, corner, side
canzone (f.) song
caparbio (adj.) self-willed, obstinate
capello hair
capire* to understand
capitale (f.) capital
capitolo chapter
capo head, chief; **Capo d'anno,** New Year's Day
capolavoro masterpiece
Cappella Sistina Sistine Chapel
cappello hat; **cappellino,** smart little hat
cappotto coat, topcoat
capro, a goat
carattere (m.) character
caratteristico (adj.) characteristic
carciofo artichoke
cardinale (adj.) chief, principal
carico (adj.) laden
Carlo Charles
carne (f.) meat
caro (adj.) dear; **carino,** pretty
carota carrot
carretto trolley
carrozza cab, carriage
carrozza ristorante dining-car
carta paper; **— da lettere,** notepaper
cartellino label, ticket
cartolaio stationer
cartoleria stationery
cartolina postcard
casa house
casalingo (adj.) home-made, homely
cascare to fall, drop
cascina dairy-farm
cassetto drawer
cassettone (m.) chest of drawers
castello castle, palace
catalogo catalogue
cattivo (adj.) bad; **cattivello,** naughty
cavaliere (m.) knight, horseman, rider
cavallo horse; **cavalletto,** easel
cavolfiore (m.) cauliflower
cavolo cabbage
ce (pron. & adv.) us, to us, there
celebre (adj.) famous
celeste (adj.) pale blue
cenare to dine
cenere (f.) ashes, cinders
centimetro centimetre, tape-measure
centinaio about a hundred
centro centre; **in centro,** in town
cercare to look for; **cercare di,** to try
certo (pron. & adj.) certain, reliable
certuno (pron.) someone
ceruleo (adj.) sky blue
cespuglio bush, thicket
cestino da viaggio packed lunch
cetriolo cucumber
che (adj., inter. pron., conj.) what? that
checché (pron.) whatever
chi (inter. pron.) who, whom (he who)
chiamare to call
chiamarsi to be called
chiarezza clarity, clearness
chiaro (adj.) clear, pale
chiasso din, uproar
chiave (f.) key
chicchessia (pron.) anyone
chiedere . . . a to ask
chiesa church
chilo kilo (2·25 lbs.)
chilometro kilometre
chimico (n. & adj.) chemist, chemical
chinarsi to bend, stoop
chioma hair
chirurgo surgeon
chissà who knows
chiunque (pron.) whoever
chiuso (adj.) closed
ci (pron. & adv.) us, to us, there
ciascheduno, ciascuno (pron.) each one
ciclista (m. & f.) cyclist
cicoria chicory, endive
cielo sky
ciliegia cherry
cima top, summit
cinema (m.) cinema
cinese (adj.) Chinese
ciò (pron.) that (referring to a statement)
ciò che that which, what
ciocca lock of hair
ciondolare to dawdle, stroll
cipolla onion
circa (adv. & prep.) about

circostante (adj.) surrounding
città city, town
civile (adj.) civil
clamore (m.) noise
classe (f.) class, rank
classico (adj.) classic, classical
clima (m.) climate
coagulato coagulated
coda tail
codesto (adj.) that, those
cogliere to catch, gather, pick up
cognato, a brother-, sister-in-law
colà (adv.) there
colazione (f.) lunch, breakfast
colei che she who
collana necklace
collare (m.) collar
collega (m. & f.) colleague
collera rage
colletto collar
collina hill, height
colombo pigeon
colonna column, pillar
colonnato colonnade
colorato (adj.) coloured
colore (m.) colour
coloro che those who
coltello knife
coltivare to cultivate
colto (adj.) cultivated, educated
colui che he who
comandare to order
come (adv.) how, as
cominciare . . . a to begin
commedia comedy, play
commemorare to commemorate
commercio trade, commerce (adj. **commerciale**)
commesso, a shop assistant
commissione (f.) errand, commission (v. **commissionare**)
commuovere to move, touch
comodino bedside-table
comodo (adj.) comfortable
compire to complete, fulfil
compito task, homework
compleanno birthday
completamente (adv.) completely
composto composed
comprare to buy
comprendere to understand, consist of
comune (adj.) common
comunque (adv.) however
con (prep.) with
concludere to effect, conclude
condannare to condemn
condizione (f.) condition
conducente (m.) driver
condurre to lead, conduct
confettura jam
confrontare to compare
conoscente acquaintance
conoscere to know, be acquainted with
conquistare to win
consegnare to hand in, give, deliver
conservare to keep, put away
considerare to consider
consigliare a . . . di to advise
consiglio advice
consistere to consist of
contadino peasant
contadinotto sturdy little peasant
contagioso (adj.) infectious
contare to reckon, count; **— su,** to rely on
conte (m.) count
contenere to contain, hold
contentarsi to be content
contento . . . di (adj.) glad
continuare to continue (adj. **continuo**)
conto bill; **rendersi** to realize
contorno side-dish
contorto twisted
contrada quarter of a town
contrario (adj.) contrary, harmful
contro (prep.) against
convenire to be fitting
convento convent, monastery
conversazione (f.) conversation, talk
coperta blanket, rug, counterpane
coperto (adj.) covered; (n.) place at table, cover
coppia couple
coprire to cover
corallo coral
cornicione (m.) rone, gutter
corpo body; (adj.) **corporale**
correre to run
corridoio corridor
corsa race
corteo procession

cortese (adj.) kind
corto (adj.) short
cosa thing
così (adv.) so, as, therefore
costà (adv.) there
costa coast, shore, rib
costare to cost (n. **costo**)
costei (f.) this woman
costì (adv.) there
costone (m.) prominence
costoro (m. & f. pl.) these men, women
costringere to force, compel
costruire* to build, erect
costruzioni navali (f. pl.) shipbuilding
costui (m.) this man
costume (m.) costume, custom
cotoletta alla milanese milanese cutlet . . .
cotone (m.) cotton
cozze mussels
cravatta tie
credenza sideboard
credere to believe, think
crepacuore (m.) broken heart
crepare to split, burst
crescere to grow
cresta crest, ridge
cristallo crystal
Cristo Christ
criticare to criticize
crocicchio cross-roads, crossings
crollare to fall down, crumble
crosta crust
crudeltà cruelty (adj. **crudele**)
cucchiaino da tè, da caffè tea-, coffee-spoon
cucchiaio spoon
cucina kitchen, cuisine, cooking
cucinare to cook
cucire to sew
cuffia cap, bonnet
cugino, a cousin
cui (rel. pron.) whom, which
cuocere to cook
cuore (m.) heart
cupola dome, cupola
cura care
curare to treat, cure
curiosità curiosity
cuscino pillow, cushion

D

da (prep.) by, from
dacché (conj.) since
dare to give (*see* p. 261)
data date
dato che (conj.) supposing that, given
davanti (prep.) in front of
davvero (adv.) really
debito (adj.) due
debole (adj.) weak
decina about ten
decisione (f.) decision
decorare to decorate
degno (adj.) worthy
delusione (f.) delusion, deception
demolire* to demolish
demoniaco (adj.) demoniac(al)
denaro money
dente (m.) tooth
dentro (adv.) inside, within
derivare to spring, originate
descrivere to describe (n. **descrizione** (f.))
deserto wilderness
desiderare to desire, wish, want
desiderio desire
desolato (adj.) desolate, forlorn
destare to wake, rouse
destino destiny, fate
detto saying; (adj.) called
deturpare to disfigure, spoil
di (prep.) of
dialetto dialect
dialogo dialogue
dicembre (m.) December
dietro (prep. & adv.) behind, back
difetto defect
differente (adj.) different
difficile (adj.) difficult
diligente (adj.) diligent
dilungarsi to digress, move away
diluviare to pour with rain
dimagrire to make, become lean
dimenticare to forget
di modo che so that
dinamo (f.) dynamo
di nuovo again
dinnanzi (adv.) in front, before
Dio God
dipingere to paint
dire to say, tell
dirigere to direct, manage, conduct

diritto (adj.) straight
disastro disaster
disciplina discipline
disciplinare to discipline (adj. **disciplinato**)
discreto (adj.) discreet
disegno design, pattern
dispensa pantry, distribution
dispetto annoyance, spite
dispiacere to displease
distanza distance, range
distendere stretch out
distesa expanse, range
distinzione (f.) distinction
distribuire* to distribute, give, issue
distribuzione (f.) distribution, delivery (postal)
distruzione (f.) destruction
dito finger
diurno by day
divano divan
diventare to become
diverso (adj.) different, severa
divertente (adj.) amusing
divertirsi to enjoy oneself
dividere to divide
documentario documentary
doge (m.) doge
dolce (m.) sweet, cake; **dolcezza,** sweetness
dolersi to mourn, complain
domandare . . . a to ask
domani (adv.) tomorrow
domenica Sunday
domestico (adj.) domestic, tame
dominare to dominate
donna woman
dono gift
dopo (prep. & adv.) after
doppio double
dormire to sleep
dottore (m.) doctor
dove (adv.) where
dovere to be obliged, must, have to
dovunque (conj.) wherever
dozzina dozen, about twelve
drago dragon
drogheria, droghiere (m.) grocer's shop, grocer
dubbio doubt
duca (m.) duke
dunque (adv.) therefore
duomo cathedral
durante (prep.) during
durare to last
duro (adj.) hard, stiff, harsh

E

e, ed (conj.) and
ebbene (conj.) well, well then
eccetto (adv.) except
ecco (adv.) here is, here are
eco echo
economico (adj.) economic
edicola paper-stall
edificio building
egli (pron.) he
egregio (adj.) distinguished
elastico (n. & adj.) elastic
elegante (adj.) elegant, smart
elementare (adj.) elementary
elmo helmet
Emanuele (m.) Emmanuel
elemento element, unit
Elena Helen
ella (pron.) she
Enea (m.), **Eneide** (f.) Aeneas, the Aeneid
enorme (adj.) huge, enormous
entrambi (pron.) both
entrare . . . in to enter, go into
epilogo epilogue
epoca epoch, period, age
eppure (conj.) and yet
erba grass
Ercolano Herculaneum
ermetico (adj.) air-tight, close
eruzione (f.) eruption
esame (m.) examination
esatto (adj.) exact, precise
esempio example
esercitare to practise
esporre to expose, display
esposizione (f.) exhibition
espresso express letter
essa, e (pron.) she, it, they
essere to be; **— in ritardo,** to be late (n.) being
esso, i (pron.) he, it, they
estate (f.) summer

F

fa (adv.) ago
facchino porter
facciata front, façade

facile (adj.) easy
facoltà faculty, power
fagiano pheasant
fagiolino French bean; **fagiolo,** bean
falda flake, layer
falò bonfire
fallo fault, error, slip
famiglia family
familiare (adj.) familiar, intimate
famoso (adj.) famous
fanciullo child
fantastico (adj.) fantastic, fanciful
fare to make, do (*see* pp. 259–60)
farfalla butterfly
farina flour
farmácia chemist's shop
farmacista (m.) chemist
fase (f.) stage
fattorino conductor
favore favour; **per —, please**
favorire to favour, encourage
favorito (adj.) favourite
fazzoletto handkerchief, scarf, head-square
febbraio February
febbre (f.) fever
fedele (adj.) faithful
federa pillowslip
felice (adj.) happy
felicità (f.) happiness
fermata stop, stopping-place
fermare to stop
ferroviere (m.) railwayman
fertile (adj.) fertile (n. **fertilità**)
festa festival, celebration, party
fianco flank, side
fiato breath
fico fig
fidarsi to rely on
fieno hay
figlio, a son, daughter
Filippo Philip
film (m.) film
filo thread
filovia cable railway
finché (conj.) until
finestra window; **finestrino,** of a train
finire* to finish, end
fino . . . a until, as far as
finocchio fennel
fioco (adj.) hoarse, weak, feeble
fiore (m.) flower; **a fiori,** flowered
fiorentino (adj.) Florentine
fioritura blossoming (v. **fiorire**)
Firenze (f.) Florence
firma signature; **firmare,** to sign
fischiare to hiss
fitto (adj.) thick, dense
fiume (m.) river
flanella flannel
flessibile (adj.) flexible, pliable
florido (adj.) flourishing
focaccia yeast savoury cake
foglia leaf
foglietto sheet of note paper
folletto sprite, elf
fondare to build
fondo (n. & adj.) bottom, deep
fontana fountain
forchetta fork
forcone (m.) pitchfork
foresta forest
forestiere (m.) visitor, stranger, guest
forma shape, form
formaggio cheese
fornitore (m.) tradesman
forse (adv.) perhaps
forte (adj.) strong
forza strength; **a — di,** by dint of
fossa ditch
fotografia photograph
fra (prep.) in, within, between, among
fragola strawberry
fraintendere to misunderstand
frana landslide
Francesco Francis
francese (adj.) French; **Francia,** France
francobollo stamp
fratello brother
freddo (adj.) cold
frenetico (adj.) frantic, frenzied
frequente (adj.) frequent; **di —,** frequently
fresco (adj.) cool, fresh
fretta haste, hurry
frigorifero refrigerator
fritto (n. & adj.) fried
fronte (f.) forehead
fruttivendolo fruiterer
frutto fruit (pl. **frutta, frutti**)
fuggiasco fugitive, runaway
fuggire to flee, run away
fumare to smoke, fume

funebre (adj.) funereal
fuoco fire
fuori . . . di (prep. & adv.) outside
furore (m.) fury, rage
furtivo (adj.) furtive, stealthy

G

gala gala
galleria gallery, arcade
garofano carnation
gatto cat
gelare to freeze
generalmente (adv.) generally
genere (m.) kind, sort
genero son-in-law
genitore (m.) parent
gennaio January
gente (f.) people
gentile (adj.) kind, courteous
gentiluomo gentleman
gesto gesture, sign
ghiacciare to freeze
già (adv.) already, once
giacere to lie
giallo (adj.) yellow
giardino garden
ginocchio knee
giocare to play
gioia joy
gioielliere, gioiello jeweller, jewel
gioco game, play, sport; **— di società,** parlour-game
Giorgio George
giornale (m.) newspaper
giorno day; **giornata**, duration
giovane (adj.) young
Giovanni John
giovedì Thursday
giro tour, drive, run
giù (adv.) down
giugno June
Giulia Julia
Giulio Julius
giungere to arrive, join
gli (pron.) to him, it; (def. art.) the
gloria glory (adj. **glorioso**)
gloriarsi to boast
gnomo gnome
godersi to enjoy
golfo bay, gulf
gondola; gondoliere (m.) gondola; gondolier
gonfiare to swell, inflate
gonna skirt
gotico (adj.) gothic
governo government
grado degree
Gran Bretagna Great Britain
grande (adj.) big, great (n. **grandezza**)
grandinare to hail
grandine (f.) hail
grasso (adj.) fat, plump
grave (adj.) serious, grave, heavy
grazie (f. pl.) thanks, thank you
grecale (m.) north-east wind
Grecia Greece (adj. **greco**)
gridare to cry out, scold
grigio (adj.) grey
gronda gutter, rone
grosso (adj.) big, thick, coarse
grottesco (adj.) grotesque
gruppo group
guanto glove
guardare to look, look at
guarire* to cure, recover
guastare to spoil, mar
guerra; guerriero war; warrior
guglia spire, pinnacle
guida guide, guide-book
guidare to drive, guide
gusto taste; **trovare** to like

I

I (def. art.) the (pl.)
idea idea
identico (adj.) identical
ieri (adv.) yesterday
ignorante (adj.) ignorant
il (def. art.) the
imballaggio packing
imbronciato (adj.) sullen, surly
imbucare to post
imitare to imitate
immaginare to imagine
immagine (f.) image
immemorabile (adj.) immemorial
immenso (adj.) immense
impaccio hindrance, encumbrance embarrassment
imparare to learn
impastricciato mixed up
impegno engagement
impermeabile (m.) raincoat
impiegato clerk

impiego employment, job
importanza importance
importare to matter
impossessarsi to take possession
impossibile (adj.) impossible
impressione (f.) impression
improvviso (adj.) sudden, unexpected; **all'improvviso,** suddenly
in (prep.) in, into, on, at; **in piedi** standing
inaccettabile (adj.) unacceptable
inamidare to starch
inaspettatamente (adv.) unexpectedly
incamminarsi to set out
incarnare to incarnate, embody
incontrare to meet
incredibile (adj.) unbelievable
incrocio crossing
indeterminabile (adj.) indefinable
indifferente (adj.) indifferent
indipendenza independence
indirizzo address
indisciplinato (adj.) unruly
individuo individual, fellow
industria industry (adj. **industriale)**
ineguale (adj.) unequal
inespresso (adj.) unexpressed
infantile (adj.) childish
inferiore (adj.) lower
inferno hell, inferno
infimo (adj.) lowest
influenza influence, influenza
informazione (f.) information (v. **informare)**
ingegneria engineering
Inghilterra England (adj. **inglese)**
inghiottire to swallow
ingiusto (adj.) unjust
ingollare to gulp, gobble
ingozzare to cram, devour
ingresso hall, admission, entrance
iniquamente (adv.) wrongly, wickedly
in iscatola tinned
inizio beginning
innalzarsi to rise
innocente (adj.) innocent
inoltre (adv.) besides
insalata salad; **i. russa** Russian salad
inseccolito dried up
insegnante (m. & f.) teacher (v. **insegnare . . . a)**
inseguire to pursue, follow
insieme (adv.) together
insopportabile (adj.) unbearable
intatto (adj.) intact
intelligente (adj.) intelligent
intendere to understand
interessante (adj.) interesting
interno interior; (adj.) inner, inland; **all'interno,** inside
intero (adj.) entire, whole
interrogare to question
intervallo interval
intonaco plaster
intorno (adv.) around; **— . . . a** (prep.). around
intravisto (adj.) glimpsed
intreccio plot
inumano (adj.) inhuman
inutile (adj.) useless
invasione (f.) invasion
invece di instead of
inverno winter
invidia envy
invitare to invite, request
invitato guest
invito invitation
io (pron.) I
Ionio Ionian Sea
irragiungibile (adj.) unattainable
irritare to irritate
irritazione (f.) irritation
ipocrisia hypocrisy
isola island
Ispirato inspired
istituto tecnico technical college
istruito educated, learned
istruzione (f.) instruction, education
Italia Italy
italiano (adj.) Italian
iugoslavo Yugoslav

L

la (pron.) her, it, you; (def. art.) the
labbro lip
ladro thief
lago lake
lagnarsi to complain
laguna lagoon
lampada lamp
lampeggia there is lightning (v. **lampeggiare)**
lampone (m.) raspberry
lana wool

largo (adj.) wide, broad
larice (m.) larch
lasciare to leave, let
latino Latin
lato side
lattaio, latteria milkman, dairy
latte (m.) milk
lattiera milk-jug
lattuga lettuce
lava lava
lavarsi to wash oneself
lavorare to work; **lavoro,** toil, work, task
le (pron.) them, you; to her, to it, to you; (def. art.) the
legare to bind, tie
legge (f.) law
leggenda legend
leggere to read
leggero (adj.) light, slight, frivolous
legume (m.) vegetable (pulse)
lei (pron.) her, you
lentamente (adv.) slowly (adj. **lento**)
lenzuolo sheet
lesto (adj.) quick, brisk
lettera letter
letterario (adj.) literary
letterato (adj.) cultured; (n.) a literary person
letteratura literature
letto bed
levarsi to rise, get up
lezione (f.) lesson
li (pron.) them; **lì** (adv.), there, here
libeccio south-west wind
libero (adj.) free; **libertà,** freedom
libreria book-case, book-shop
libro book
licenza leave, permission
liceo grammar-school
limitato limited
limite (m.) limit, extent
limonata lemonade
linea line; **lineamento,** feature
lingua language, tongue
lira lira (Italian money); lyre
lisciare to smooth
liscio (adj.) smooth, glossy
lista menu
livello level
lo (pron.) him, it
loggia loggia
logico (adj.) logical
Londra London
lontano (adj.) distant, remote
loro (pron.) they, them, to them, you, to you
— (poss. adj. & pron.) their, theirs
lotta struggle (v. **lottare**)
luce (f.) light
lucente (adj.) shining, bright
lucerna lamp
luglio July
lui (pron.) he, him
Luigi Louis
Luisa Louise
lume (m.) light, lamp
lumeggiare to illuminate
luna moon
lunedì (m.) Monday
lungo (prep.) along; (adj.) long
luogo place; — **di nascita,** birthplace
lustrare to clean, polish
lustro (adj.) shiny, glittering

M

ma (conj.) but
macchia spot, stain, blot
maccheroni macaroni
macedonia di frutta fruit salad
macellaio, macelleria butcher, butcher's shop
macigno block of stone
madre (f.) mother
maestoso (adj.) majestic
maestro (n. & adj.) master, teacher, principal
maggio May
maggiore (adj.) bigger
magico (adj.) magic, magical
magnifico (adj.) magnificent
mai (adv.) ever, (negatively) never
maiale pork
maionese mayonnaise
malato (n. & adj.) ill, sick
malattia illness, sickness, disease
male (adv.) badly
malora ruin, peridition
mamma mummy
mancare to lack, miss, be in want of
mancia tip
mandare to send

mandarino mandarin
mangiare to eat
maniera manner
mano (f.) hand
manoscritto manuscript
manto mantle, cloak
manzo beef
marciapiede (m.) pavement
mare (m.) sea
maremmano of the Maremma
Maria Mary
marinaio sailor, seaman
marito husband
marmellata marmalade, jam
marmo marble
marrone (adj.) brown
marsina evening-dress, dress-coat (men's)
martedì (m.) Tuesday
marzo March
mascella jaw
massaia housewife
massimo (adj.) very big, **maximum** most
masticare to chew
matematica mathematics
materasso mattress
materia subject, matter, substance
materiale (adj.) material, physical
matita pencil
mattina morning
matto fool, madman
mattone (m.) brick
me (pron.) me
medicina medicine
medico doctor
medio (adj.) secondary, middle, average
mediocrità mediocrity
medioevale (adj.) mediaeval
meglio (adv.) better
mela apple; **melone** (m.), melon
membro member
memoria memory
meno (adj., adv.) less, minus
a meno che non unless
mensola bracket, corbel
mentre (conj.) while, as, whereas
meraviglioso (adj.) marvellous, wonderful
mercoledì (m.) Wednesday
meridionale (adj.) south, southern
merito merit
merletto lace
merluzzo cod
mescolanza blend, mixture
mese (m.) month (adj. **mensile**)
metà half
metro metre, tape-measure
metropoli (f. inv.) metropolis
metropolitano policeman
mettere to put
mezzina jug, pitcher
mezzo (adj.) half; (n.) middle, means
mezzogiorno midday
mi (pron.) me, to me, myself
migliaio about a thousand
miglio mile
migliore (adj.) better
milione (m.) million
minestra soup
minimo (adj.) very small, minimum, least
minore (adj.) smaller
minuto minute
mio, a, ei, e (adj.) my, mine
misura measurement
misterioso (adj.) mysterious
mite (adj.) mild, gentle, moderate
mittente (m. & f.) sender
mobile (m.) piece of furniture
mobilia furniture
moda fashion; **di —**, fashionable
modello model, model clothes
moderato (adj.) moderate
moderno (adj.) modern
modesto (adj.) plain, simple, quiet
modo way, manner, means, **di modo che** so that
moglie (f.) wife (pl. **mogli**)
molle (adj.) soft
molto (adj.) much, many; (adv.) very
momento moment
mondo world (adj. **mondiale**)
monologo monologue
montagna mountain
monte (m.) mountain, bulk
montone (m.) mutton
monumento monument
morbido (adj.) soft, weak, morbid
mordente biting
morire to die
morte (f.) death

mortorio funeral (procession)
mosaico mosaic
mostrare . . . a to show
motto motto
movimento movement
mucchio heap, stack, pile
muffa mould, must
mulattiera mule-track
muro wall; **muricciolo,** low wall
museo museum
mutarsi to change

N

Napoli (f.) Naples (adj. **napoletano**)
nascere to be born
nascita birth
nascondere to hind, conceal; **di nascosto,** secretly, by stealth
naso nose
natio (adj.) native
nato born
natura nature (adj. **naturale**), (adv. **naturalmente**)
nazionale (adj.) national
ne (pron.) of him, her, it, them; (adv.) from there
né . . . né (conj.) neither . . . nor
neanche (conj.) not even
nebbia fog, haze, mist
necessario (adj.) necessary
necessità necessity, need
negozio shop
nemmeno (conj.) not even
neppure (conj.) not even
nero (adj.) black
nessuno (pron.) nobody; (adj.) no
nevicare to snow (n. **neve** (f.))
nido nest
niente (pron.) nothing
nipote (m. & f.) nephew, niece; grandchild
no (adv.) no
nocciola nut, hazelnut
noioso (adj.) annoying, boring
nome (m.) name
nominare to name, nominate
non (adv.) not
nonno, a, i grandfather, -mother, -parents
nonostante (prep. & adv.) notwithstanding, nevertheless; **— che** (conj.), although
normale (adj.) normal
nord (m.) north
nostro, i, a, e (adj. & pron.) our, ours
notaio notary
notte (f.) night; **notturno** (adj.), nightly
noto (adj.) known
novembre (m.) November
nozze (f. pl.) wedding, marriage
nube (f.) cloud
nulla (pron.) nothing
numero number
numeroso (adj.) numerous
nuocere to hurt, injure
nuora daughter-in-law
nuotare to swim
nuovo (adj.) new, **di —** again
nuvola cloud

O

o (conj.) or; **o . . . o,** either . . . or
obbligare to oblige
obbligatorio (adj.) obligatory, compulsory
obbligo duty, obligation
obelisco obelisk
occhiata glance, quick look
occhio eye
occorrere to be necessary
ode (f.) ode
odiare to hate
odio hatred
odore (m.) smell, odour, scent
offrire to offer
oggetto object, article
oggi (adv.) today
ogni (adj. inv.) every, each
ognuno (pron.) everyone
olio oil
olivo olive tree
oltrepassare to surpass, go beyond
ombra shade, shadow
ombrellone (m.) parasol, large umbrella
omicida (m. & f.) murderer
onda wave
ondeggiare to wave, flap
ondulante (adj.) undulating
onesto (adj.) honest
onorare (v.) to honour
onore (m.) honour
opaco (adj.) opaque
opera work, composition

ora (adv.) now; (n.) time, hour, o'clock
orale (adj.) oral
orario periods, hours of lessons, timetable
ordinare to order, tidy up
ordinato (adj.) tidy
ordine (m.) order, rank
orecchio ear
orefice (m.) goldsmith, jeweller
organetto barrel-organ
orgoglio pride
Oriente (m.) East (adj. **orientale**)
origine (f.) origin, cause
orizzonte (m.) horizon
orlare to border
ornare to adorn, ornament
orologio watch
orrore (m.) horror
osare to dare
oscuro (adj.) dark
ospite (m. & f.) guest, host, hostess
osservare to observe, remark
osteria inn, pub
ostrica oyster
ottimamente (adv.) very well
ottimo (adj.) very good
ottobre (m.) October
ottone (m.) brass
ovale (adj.) oval

P

pacco parcel
pace (f.) peace
Padova Padua
padre (m.) father
paesaggio landscape, scenery
paesano countryman
paese (m.) country; **paesello**, village
pagare to pay
pagella report, certificate
paio pair
palazzo palace
pallido (adj.) pale
pallino little ball
palo pole, stake, post
pampano vine leaf
pane (m.) bread
panetteria baker's shop
panettone (m.) large (Milanese) cake
paniere (m.) basket
panini imbottiti sandwiches
pantaloni (m.) trousers
Paolo Paul
paonazzo (adj.) violet, peacock-blue
paragrafo paragraph
parata display
parco park, grounds
parecchio (adv. & adj.) much; several, considerable
parente (m. & f.) relative
parere to seem, appear
parete (f.) wall (of a room)
Parigi (f.) Paris
parlare . . . con to speak, talk to
parlata conversation, dialect, lingua
parola word
parte (f.) part, side; **in —** (adv.) partly
partecipare to take part in
partenza departure
particolare (adj.) particular, peculiar
partire to leave, set out
partita match
Pasqua Easter
passaggio passage
passare to spend, pass by
passato past
passeggero (n. & adj.) passenger, brief
passeggiare to go for a walk
passeggiata walk (**fare una —**)
passerotto young sparrow
passo step, stride, pace
pasta asciutta macaroni
pasticceria, pasticciere (m.) cakeshop, pastrycook
pasticcio pie
pastore (m.) shepherd
patata potato
patria fatherland
paura fear
pavimento floor
pazzerello (n. & adj.) fool, mad, silly
peccare to sin
pedagogo tutor, pedagogue
pedone (m.) pedestrian
peggio (adv.) worse
peggiore (adj.) worse
pelle (f.) skin
pellegrino pilgrim, traveller
pelo hair, fur, coat
penare labour
pendente (adj.) hanging
penna stilografica fountain pen

pennacchio plume
pennello brush
pensare to think, consider, believe
pensiero thought
pensione (f.) boarding-house, pension
pentirsi to repent
pepe (m.) pepper
peperone (m.) capsicum
per (prep.) for; **— quanto** (conj.), although
pera pear
perché (conj. & adv.) because, in order that, why
perdere to lose, miss, waste
perdio by Jove
perdonare to forgive, excuse
pericolo danger
periodo period, time
peritarsi to be shy
permettere to allow
però (adv.) however, but, yet
persona person; (pl.) people
pesante (adj.) heavy
pesca peach
pescare to fish
pescatore fisherman
pesce (m.) fish
pescivendolo fishmonger
pessimo (adj.) very bad
Pesto Paestum
pettinarsi to comb one's hair
pezzo piece
piacere to please
piacevole (adj.) pleasant, agreeable
piangere to weep, cry
piano (adj.) level; (n.) storey, floor
pianta plant, plan, map
pianura plain
piattino saucer
piatto plate, dish, course
piazza square, market place
piccolo (adj.) small, little
piede (m.) foot; **a —**, on foot, **in —** standing
piegare to fold, bend, turn
pieno (adj.) full
pierrot pierrot
pietà pity, mercy, piety
pietra stone
Pietro Peter
pigiama (m.) pyjamas (pair of)
pino pine tree
Pio Pius
pioggia rain (adj. **piovoso**, v. **piovere**)
pisello pea
pista ski track, trail
pittore (m.) painter
pittura painting, picture
più (adv.) more; (adj. inv.) several; **i —**, most people
piumato plumed
piumino quilt, eiderdown
po', poco (pron., adj. & adv.) little, few
podestà administrative head of a commune
poesia poems, poetry
poeta (m.) poet; **poetastro**, worthless poet
poi (adv.) then, after; **poiché** (conj.), since
politica politics, policy
pollame (m.) poultry; **pollo**, chicken
poltrona armchair, seat
pomeriggio afternoon
pomodoro tomato
Pompei Pompeii
ponte (m.) bridge
popolare (adj.) popular
popolazione (f.) population
porcellana porcelain, china
porco pig
porre to put
porta door
portare to carry, take, wear
portico porch; (pl.) colonnade
porto port, harbour
porzione (f.) helping, portion
posata cutlery
possedere to possess
possibile (adj.) possible
posta mail, post office
posteggio parking place
postino postman
posto place, spot, site
potere to be able, can
povero (adj.) poor, unfortunate
pozzo well
pranzo dinner, lunch
pratico (adj.) practical
prato meadow, lawn
prealpi (f.) foothills of Alps
preda booty, prey
preferire* to prefer

pregare to pray, beg; **Prego!**, don't mention it!
premiare to award a prize
premura haste
prendere to catch, take
— l'impegno to undertake
prenotare to book, reserve
preparare to prepare
prepotente (adj.) arrogant, overbearing
presentare to present, offer
presso (prep.) near, beside; c/o (letters)
presto (adv.) early
prezzemolo parsley
prezzo price
prigione (f.) prison, gaol
prigioniero prisoner
prima (adv.) first of all, before
p. di (prep.), **p. che** (conj.) before
primavera spring
primo (adj.) first
principale (adj.) principal, chief
privato (adj.) private
privilegio privilege
probabile (adj.) likely
problema (m.) problem
procaccia (m.) rural postman
proda edge, border, bank
professione (f.) profession
professore (m.) professor
profondo (adj.) deep, profound, (n.) depth
proiettare to cast, throw
prologo prologue
promettere to promise
promosso promoted (n **promozione** (f.))
prontezza quickness, readiness
pronto (adj.) ready (telephone: Hello!)
proporre to propose
propriamente (adj.) just
proprio (adj.) one's own, (adv.) just
proseguire to continue, go on
prossimo (adj.) next, nearest
protetto protected
provare to try, try on, feel
provincia province
provviste (f. pl.) provisions
prudente (adj.) careful, prudent
prudenza prudence
psichiatra (m.) psychiatrist
psicologo psychologist
pubblico (adj.) public
pudico (adj.) modest
pulire* to clean
punta point, tip, end
puntuale (adj.) punctual
punizione (f.) punishment
pupilla pupil (eye)
purché (conj.) provided that
pure (adv. & conj.) also, even
puro (adj.) pure
purtroppo (adv.) unfortunately

Q

qua (adv.) here
quadrato (adj.) square
quadro painting, square; **a —**, checked
qualche (adj.) some, any; **— volta**, sometimes
qualcuno (pron.) someone, anybody
quale (adj.) which, which?
qualsiasi (adj.) of some sort, of any sort whichever
qualunque (adj.) whichever
quando (adv.) when?
quantità quantity, amount
quanto (adj.) how much, how many, as
quantunque (conj.) although
quasi (adv.) almost, nearly, as if
quegli (pron.) that man
quello (pron. & adj.) that
quercia oak
questione (f.) question, matter
questo (adj.) this
qui (adv.) here
quiete (f.) quiet, calm
quindicina about fifteen

R

rabbia rage, anger
raccoglimento concentration
raccogliere to pick up
raccolto crop, harvest
raccomandare to recommend
raccomandata registered letter
raccontare to tell, relate
raddoppiare to redouble
radicale (adj.) radical
radio (f.) radio
radunare to assemble, collect
raffreddare to get cold

raffreddore (m.) cold, chill (adj. **raffreddato**)
ragazzo, a boy, girl
raggio ray
raggiungere to rejoin, reach
raggrinzire to shrivel up
ragione (f.) reason
rallegrarsi to rejoice
rame copper
ramicello small branch, twig
ramo branch, bough
rapa turnip
ravanello radish
ravvolgere to wrap up, envelop
razza race, breed
rè (inv.) king
recente (adj.) recent
recentemente (adv.) recently
recinto enclosed
recitare to perform, play, act
reclinare to recline, rest
refettorio refectory
regalare to give (n. **regalo**)
regina queen
regione (f.) region
registro register, book
remare to row; **remo,** oar
rendere to make; **restituire**
rendersi conto to realize
repubblica republic
repubblichini people who had joined the fascist republic
respirare to breathe (n. **respiro**)
restare to stay
resto (**del resto**) rest, remainder, change (however)
retorica rhetoric
riaccendere to rekindle
ricchezza richness
riccio curl (adj. **ricciuto**)
ricco (adj.) rich
ricerca research, investigation
ricevere to receive
ricevimento reception, party
ricevuta receipt
richiedere to require, request
ricompensare to reward
riconoscente (adj.) grateful
riconoscere to recognize
ricordare to remember, remind
ricordo memory, recollection, record
ricostruire* to reconstruct
ridestare to re-awaken, arouse
ridicolo (adj.) ridiculous
ridipinto repainted
rifugio mountain inn
riforma reform
rigidità rigidity, stiffness, rigour
rigido (adj.) severe, stiff
riguardare to consider, regard
rimandare to send back, postpone
rimanere to remain
rimasuglio remnant, left over
rimpiangere to lament over, regret
Rinascimento Renaissance
rincrescere to regret
ripa ridge
ripetere to repeat
ripido (adj.) steep
riposare to rest
ripostiglio lumber-room, recess
riprendere to resume, take up again
ripulire to clean
riscuotere to cash
riso rice, laughter
risonare to resound
risparire to disappear again
rispettare to respect
rispondere . . . a to answer
risposta answer
ristorante (m.) restaurant
ritardo; essere in ritardo delay; to be late
ritirare to withdraw
ritto (adj.) upright, erect
ritornare to come back (n. **ritorno**)
riuscire to succeed, result, turn out
rivista magazine, review
rivolgersi to apply to, turn to
roba property, goods, stuff
Roberto Robert
roccia rock (adj. **roccioso**)
romani the Romans
romantico (adj.) romantic
romanzo novel
rondine (f.) swallow
ronzare to buzz, hum
rosa rose; (adj. inv.) pink
rosato (adj.) pinkish
roseo (adj.) rosy, rose-coloured
rosicchiare to nibble
rosso (adj.) red
roteamento rolling
rotondo (adj.) round

rovente (adj.) red-hot, scorching
rovina ruin (v. **rovinare**)
rumoroso (adj.) noisy
rupe (f.) rock, cliff
russo Russian
rusticità rusticity

S

sabato Saturday
sabbia sand
sala d'aspetto, — da pranzo waiting-, dining-room
salame (m.) salami
salato (adj.) savoury
sale (m.) salt
salire to rise, go up
salotto drawing-room
saltare to skip, hop
saltellare to hop
salubre (adj.) healthy
salumeria, salumaio Italian warehouse, man
salutare to greet, say good-bye
salvare to save
sangue (m.) blood
sano (adj.) healthy
santo (n. & adj.) saint, holy
sapere to know how, be aware of, to know
sapere di to taste of
sapore (m.) flavour, taste
Sardegna Sardinia
sarto tailor, dressmaker
sasso stone, rock
sbaglio mistake
sbalordimento amazement
sbalordito (adj.) stunned, amazed
sbirciare to cast sidelong glances
scaffale (m.) bookcase (open)
scala staircase, steps (pair of)
scalata a climb (v. **scalare**)
scalatore (m.) climber
scampi crayfish
scarmigliare to ruffle
scarpa shoe
scattare to spring up
scegliere to choose, select
scellino shilling
scendere . . . da to descend, come down, get off
scherzo joke, trick
schiarire to clear
schiavitù (f.) slavery
schiena back, back-bone
schiocco smack, crack, snap
sci (m. inv.) ski (v. **sciare**)
sciarada charade
scienza science (adj. **scientifico**)
scintillare to sparkle
sciogliere to untie, melt, dissolve
scirocco south-east wind of Mediterranean
scivolare to slip, slide, glide
scolaro pupil
scomparire* to fade out
scompartimento compartment
sconto discount
sconvolgere to upset, turn upside down
scopare to sweep
scoperta discovery
scoperto discovered, open
scoprire to discover, come upon
scoraggiare to discourage, daunt
scorrere to flow, run, scour
scorso (adj.) last
scricchiolio creaking
scritto written
scrittore (m.) writer
scrivania writing-desk
scrivere to write
scrutare to scrutinize, investigate
scultore (m.) sculptor
scultura sculpture
scuola school (**— magistrale,** for training elementary school teachers)
scuotere to shake, rouse
scuro (adj.) dark, deep
scusarsi to apologize
sé (pron.) oneself, himself, herself, itself, themselves
se (conj.) if, whether; **— pure** (conj.), even if
sebbene (conj.) although
secco (adj.) dry, withered
secolo century
secondo (prep.) according to
sedano celery
sedia chair; **— a sdraio,** deck chair
sega saw
segno sign, motion, signal
segretario secretary
segreto secret
seguente (adj.) following (v. **seguire**)
selvaggio (adj.) wild, savage

selvatico (adj.) wild, uncultivated
selvoso (adj.) wooded
semaforo traffic lights
sembrare to seem, appear
semiaperto half open
semplice (adj.) simple
sempre (adv.) always
senese (m. & f.) Sienese
sentiero footpath, track
sentimento feeling, sentiment
sentire to feel, hear
senso sense, feeling
sentore (m.) smell, scent, feeling
senza (prep.) without
seppellire to bury
sera evening, night
serata evening; — party; — performance
sereno (adj.) clear, cloudless
serie (f.) series
servilità servility
servire to serve, be of use, attend to
seta silk
settembre (m.) September
settimana week
sfondato (adj.) bottomless, roofless
sfortunatamente (adv.) unfortunately
sforzarsi to try
sfumare to vanish, evaporate
sguardo look, glance
sì (adv.) yes
si (pron.) oneself, himself, herself, itself, themselves; one, people, they; each other
sibilla sibyl
siepe (f.) hedge, wall, barrier
significato meaning, sense
signora lady, Mrs
signorina young lady, Miss
signore (m.) gentleman, Mr., sir
sindacato trade union, syndicate
sinistra left hand, left
sinistrare to damage
sino . . . a (conj.) until
sistema (m.) system
società society, community, partnership
soffiare to blow, blow out
soffice (adj.) soft
soffitto ceiling
soffocante (adj.) stifling, oppressive
soglia threshold
sogliola sole
sogno dream
solamente (adv.) only
sole (m.) sun
solere to be accustomed
solicello faint, wintry sun
solingo lonely
solitario lonely person; (adj.) lonely
solo (adj.) only
soltanto (adv.) only
sonno sleep
soperchieria insolence, outrage
sopportare to bear, endure
sopra (prep.) on, upon, over, beyond
sopraffino first quality
soprassalto start, sudden movement
sorbire to sip, swallow
sorella sister
sorgere to rise, stand
sorta kind, sort
sorte (f.) fate
sosia (m. & f.) double
sospeso suspended
sospiro sigh
sotterfugio subterfuge
sotto (prep.) under
sottrarre . . . a to conceal from
sovrastare to overhang
spagnuolo (adj. & n.) Spanish, Spaniard
spalla shoulder
sparecchiare to clear the table
spargere to spread
sparo shot
spaventare to terrify, scare
spaventoso (adj.) fearful, dreadful
spazio space
specchiarsi to look at oneself, be reflected
specchio mirror
speciale (adj.) special, particular
specialità speciality
specialmente (adv.) especially
specie (f. inv.) kind, sort
spedire* to forward, send, dispatch
spegnere to put out, extinguish
sperare to hope
spergiuro (adj. & n.) perjured, perjurer, perjury
spesso (adv.) often
spettacolo show, play
spettatore (m.) spectator
spiaggia beach, sea-side

spiccare to be conspicuous, stand out
spiegare to explain, unfold, display, spread out
spinace spinach
spiritello sprite
spirito spirit
spizzicare to pinch, nibble
splendido (adj.) magnificent, gorgeous
splendore (m.) splendour, magnificence
spolverare to dust
sport (m.) sport
sportello carriage door; office window
sportivo (adj. & n.) sporting, sports
squadra team
stadio playing ground
stagione (f.) season
stanco (adj.) tired
stanza room (in general) — **da bagno**, bathroom
stare to stay, be (*see* pp. 198 and 259)
starna partridge
starnutare to sneeze
statua statue
stazione (f.) station
stendere to spread, stretch out, extend
stesso (adj.) same
stile (m.) style
stimare to esteem
stirare to iron
stirato (adj.) stiff, ironed
stoffa material, fabric
stordimento dizziness, dullness, stupefaction
storia story, history
strada street, roadway
straniero (adj. & n.) foreign, foreigner
strano (adj.) strange, odd
straordinario (adj.) extraordinary
straricco very rich
strascico trail
strato layer
stravecchio very old
stretto (adj.) narrow, tight
striscia streak, stripe
strisciare crawl, shuffle
strumento tool, implement
studiare to study
studio study (adj. **studioso**)
stupendo (adj.) wonderful, marvellous
stupido (adj.) idiotic, foolish
stupire to be astonished
su (prep.) on; **su via** come on
subire to bear, undergo
subito (adj. & adv.) sudden; soon, at once
succedere to happen, occur
sudicio (adj.) dirty, foul, filthy
sufficiente (adj.) sufficient
sugo (tomato) sauce, juice
suo (adj.) her, her, its, your
suocero, a father-, mother-in-law
suonare to ring, play
superficie (f.) surface
superiore (adj.) higher
supremo (adj.) very high
susina plum
svellere to root out
svegliare to wake, waken
sviluppo development, expansion
svolazzare to flutter, hover

T

tabaccaio tobacconist
tabaccheria tobacconist shop
tacchino turkey
tacere to keep silent
tagliatelle (f. pl.) home-made macaroni
tagliente (adj.) cutting, sharp
tale (adj. & pron.) such, like, as, so somebody
taluno (pron. & adj.) certain people
tanto (adv. & adj.) so much, so many as much
tappeto carpet, rug, mat
tardi (adv.) late
tartaruga tortoiseshell
tavola table
tavolino small table
taxi (m. inv.) taxi
tazza cup
te (pron.) you
tè (m.) tea
teatro theatre
tedesco (adj.) German
teiera tea-pot
tela canvas
telefono telephone; — **pubblico**, public telephone

telefonare to telephone
telegramma (m.) telegram
temere to fear
temperatura temperature
tempio temple
tempo time, weather
temporale (m.) storm; (adj.) secular
tenda curtain
tendina screen
tenere to hold
tentare to try, test
tentazione (f.) temptation
terra earth, ground
terrazza terrace
terrore (m.) dread, terror
tesa border
tesi (f. inv.) thesis
testa head
tetto roof
ti (pron.) you, to you
tipo type
tirare to draw, pull, drag
tirare vento to be windy
tizianesco (adj.) as depicted by Titian
togliere to take from
toletta dressing-table
tomba tomb, grave
tono tone
topo mouse
torbido (adj.) muddy, troubled
tornare to return, go back
torpore (m.) lethargy
torto wrong; **avere —**, to be wrong
torvo (adj.) grim, surly
Toscana Tuscany
tosse (f.) cough (v. **tossire**)
tovaglia tablecloth
tovagliolo napkin
tozzo (adj.) squat, thick-set
tra (prep.) between, among
tradimento treason, betrayal, **a —** treacherously
traffico traffic
tralcio branch
tram (m. inv.) tramcar
tramontana north wind
tramonto sunset
tranne che (conj.) except
trappola pitfall, trap
trarre to draw, pull
trascinare to drag
tratto distance; **ad un —** suddenly
trattoria restaurant (modest)
tremare to tremble
treno train
— diretto, espresso express train
triglia red mullet
trimestre (m.) term
triste (adj.) sad; **tristezza,** sadness
troppo (adv. & adj.) too much, too many
trovare to find
truppe (f.) troops, forces
tu (pron.) you
tuo, a, oi, e (adj.) your
tuonare to thunder (weather)
turista (m. & f.) tourist
tuttavia (adv.) however
tutto (adj.) all; **— il,** the whole

U

ubbidire* to obey
ubbriaco (adj.) drunk
uccello bird
udire to hear
ufficio postale post office
ulivo olive tree
ultimo (adj.) last, latest, top
umanità humanity, mankind
umano (adj.) human
Umberto Hubert
umido (adj.) damp, wet
umile (adj.) simple, lowly
un, una, o (indef. art.) a, an
unico (adj.) only, sole
unire* to unite, join
unito united
università university
unto (adj.) greasy, dirty
uomo man (pl. **uomini**)
uovo egg
usare to use
uscire to go out
utensile (m.) tool
utile (adj.) useful
uva (f.) grape, grapes

V

vacanza holiday
vagare to wander
vagheggiare to gaze fondly at, wish for, dream of
vaglia (m.); **— postale** money order; postal order; **— telegrafico,** by wire

vagone (m.), **letto** sleeping car, sleeper
valere to be worth
valigetta small suit-case
valigia suit-case
valle (f.) valley
valloncello glen
vano (adj.) empty, useless
vantarsi to boast
vaporetto steamer
vario (adj.) different, several
vaso vase
vassoio tray
Vaticano Vatican
ve (pron.) you, to you; (adv.) there
vecchio (adj.) old
vedere to see
velluto velvet
velocemente (adv.) quickly
vendere to sell
Veneto (n. & adj.) Venice (region)
Venezia Venice (adj. **veneziano**)
venire to come
ventata gust
venticello breeze, light wind
vento wind (adj. **ventoso**)
Vera Vera
verbo verb
verde (adj.) green
verderame (m.) verdigris
verdura vegetables (greens)
vergognarsi to be ashamed
verità truth (adj. **vero**)
versante (m.) slope, side
verso (prep.) towards, against
vestirsi to dress oneself
vestito dress; (pl.) clothes
— a giacca suit
Vesuvio Vesuvius
vetrina shop window, glass show-case
vetro glass
vettura coach
vi (pron.) you, to you; (adv.) here, there
via (n. & adv.) road; away
viaggiare to travel
viaggio journey, travel
viale (m.) avenue
vibrante quivering
vicino (adj. & adv.) near, nearby
vicino . . . a (prep.) near
vigliacco coward
vigna vineyard
vigneto vineyard
vigoroso (adj.) strong, vigorous
villa villa
villaggio hamlet
vincere to conquer, defeat
vino wine
vinta (darla —) give in
violento (adj.) violent
violinista (m. & f.) violinist
vipera viper, adder
Virgilio Virgil
virtù (f. inv.) virtue
visitare to visit
visitatore (m.) visitor
viso face
vispo (adj.) lively, brisk
vista view, sight
vita; vitalità life; vitality
vite (f.) vine
vitello veal, calf
vittoria victory
vivace (adj.) gay, lively
vivere to live
vivo (adj.) living, alive
vizioso (adj.) vicious
voce (f.) voice
voglia wish, desire
voi (pron.) you
volere to want, wish, be willing
volontà (inv.) will
volpe (f.) fox
volta time, turn
voltare to turn
volume (m.) volume
vongola cockle
vostro, a, i, e (adj.) your, yours
voto mark
vulcano volcano

Z

zeppo (adj.) crammed, full
zero nought, zero
zio, a uncle, aunt
zuccheriera sugar-basin
zucchero sugar
zuppa soup
zuppa inglese trifle

English – Italian

A

a, an (indef. art.) un, uno, una, un'
able (adj.) abile; **to be —**, potere
about (adv. & prep.) circa; **to be —** esserci
above (prep.) sopra
abroad all'estero
abruptly (adv.) a picco
absent (adj.) assente
absurd (adj.) assurdo
abundance abbondanza
acacia acacia
academy accademia
accent accento
accept (v.) accettare
accompany (v.) accompagnare
according (prep.) secondo
accumulate (v.) accumularsi
accuse (v.) accusare, incolpare
accustom (v.) abituare
achieve (v.) raggiungere, realizzare
acknowledge (v.) riconoscere
acquaintance conoscente (m. & f.)
acrid (adj.) acre
across (prep.) attraverso
act (v.) recitare, agire; (n.) atto
action azione (f.)
actor attore (m.)
actress attrice (f.)
actual (adj.) proprio
address indirizzo
admire (v.) ammirare
admission ingresso
admit (v.) ammettere
admonished ammonito
adorn (v.) adornare, ornare
Adriatic Adriatico
advice consiglio
advise (v.) consigliare
aeroplane aeroplano
affair affare (m.)
affection affezione (f.)
afflict (v.) affliggere
afraid (to be) aver paura, timore
after (prep. & adv.) poi, dopo
afternoon pomeriggio
afterwards (adv.) dopo
again (adv.) ancora, di nuovo
against (prep.) contro
age età, periodo, epoca
ago (adv.) fa
agreeable (adj.) piacevole
agree (v.) essere d'accordo, approvare
aid aiuto
acknowledge (v.) riconoscere
all (adj.) tutto
allow (v.) permettere
almost (adv.) quasi
alone (adj. & adv.) solo
along (prep.) lungo
Alps Alpi
already (adv.) già
also (adv. & conj.) anche
alter (v.) cambiare, alterarsi
although (conj.) sebbene, quantunque
altogether (adv.) completamente
always (adv.) sempre
Ambrose Ambrogio
amicable (adj.) amichevole
among (prep.) fra, tra
amusement divertimento
amusing (adj.) divertente
analysis analisi (f.)
and (conj.) e, ed
Ann Anna
anger (v.) irritare, infuriare; (n.) rabbia
annoying (adj.) noioso
Antony Antonio
answer (v.) rispondere; (n.) risposta
anxiously (adv.) ansiosamente
anxiety ansietà
any (adj.) qualche, ogni
anybody (pron.) nessuno, alcuno, qualcuno
anything (pron.) nulla
aperitif aperitivo
apologize (v.) scusarsi
appear (v.) apparire, sembrare
appearance aspetto, apparenza
appetite appetito
applaud (v.) applaudire

apple mela
appointment appuntamento, nomina
appreciate (v.) apprezzare
approve (v.) approvare
apricot albicocca
April aprile
arcade galleria
archaeologist archeologo
architect architetto
architecture architettura
architectural (adj.) architettonico
arm braccio
armchair poltrona
armour armatura
around (adv. & prep.) attorno, intorno
arrive (v.) arrivare
art arte (f.)
artful (adj.) astuto
artichoke carciofo
article articolo, oggetto
artist artista
as (conj.) mentre
ascertain (v.) assicurarsi
ashamed (to be) vergognarsi
ashes cenere (f.)
ask (v.) domandare, chiedere
ass asino
asset gloria, vantaggio
assiduously (adv.) assiduamente
assistant commesso
assortment assortimento
assuredly (adv.) certamente
at (prep.) a, in
at least (adv.) almeno
atrocity atrocità
attend (v.) frequentare
August agosto
aunt zia
Autumn autunno
avenue viale (m.)
avert (v.) allontanare, evitare

B

back (adv.) indietro, dietro
bad (adj.) cattivo
baker fornaio
baker shop panetteria
balcony balcone (m.)
ball ballo, palla
bang (v.) sbattere; (n.) scoppio, rumore
bank banca
banking (adj.) bancario
Baptistery Battistero
bar bar (m. inv.)
barbarian barbaro
barbaric (adj.) barbaro
barbarity barbarie (f.)
barbarous (adj.) barbaro
baroque (adj.) barocco
basilica basilica
basket paniere (m.)
bathroom stanza da bagno
battle battaglia
bay baia
be (v.) essere, stare
beach spiaggia
bean fagiolo
bear (v.) sopportare
beauty bellezza
beautiful (adj.) bello
because (conj.) perché
become (v.) diventare
bed letto
bedroom camera da letto
bedside table comodino
beef manzo
beetroot barbabietola
before (prep.) prima
beg (v.) pregare
begin (v.) cominciare
beginning principio, inizio
behind (prep.) dietro
believe (v.) credere, pensare
belfry campanile (m.)
Belgian (adj.) belga (inv.)
bell campanello, campana
bell tower campanile (m.)
bend (v.) curvarsi; (n.) curva
benefit beneficio
beside (prep.) accanto . . . a
besides (adv.) inoltre
best (adj.) il migliore
between (prep.) fra, tra
better (adj.) migliore
beyond (prep.) oltre, dietro
big (adj.) grosso, grande
bigger (adj.) maggiore
biggest (adj.) il maggiore
bill conto
bind (v.) legare
biographer biografo
biro biro (f.)

birthday compleanno
birth place luogo di nascita
black (adj.) nero
blame (v.) biasimare; (n.) biasimo; **am I to blame?** è colpa mia?
blanket coperta
blend (v.) mescolare; (n.) mescolanza, mistura
blind (n.) tendina, persiana; (adj.) cieco
blood sangue (m.)
blouse camicetta
blue (adj.) azzurro; **pale —,** celeste;
blond (adj.) biondo
blow (v.) soffiare; (n.) colpo
boarding house pensione (f.)
boat barca, battello
boast (v.) vantarsi, gloriarsi
book (v.) prenotare; (n.) libro
book-case libreria; **open —,** scaffale (m.)
bookshop libreria
bonfire falò (m. inv.)
bonnet cappello
bored (to be) annoiarsi; (adj.) annoiato
boring (adj.) noioso
bottle bottiglia
bourgeois (adj.) borghese
box scatola
boy ragazzo
boyhood fanciullezza, giovinezza
bracelet braccialetto
braid treccia
branch ramo, succursale (f.)
bread pane (m.)
break intervallo; (v.) rompere
breakfast colazione (f.)
brick mattone (m.)
bridge ponte (m.)
brief (adj.) breve
brigand brigante (m.)
bright (adj.) brillante
broad (adj.) largo
brocade broccato
bronchitis bronchite (f.)
broth brodo
brother fratello
brother-in-law cognato
brown (adj.) marrone
brush (v.) spazzolare; (n.) pennello, spazzola
build (v.) costruire*
building costruzione (f.), casa
burden peso
bus autobus (m. inv.)
business affare (m.)
but (adv.) ma, però
butcher macellaio
butcher shop macelleria
butter burro
button (v.) abbottonare; **buttonhole** (m.) occhiello
buy (v.) comprare
by (prep.) da; (adv.) vicino

C

cabbage cavolo
cable railway filovia
Caesar Cesare
café caffè (m. inv.)
cake dolce, torta
cake-shop pasticceria
call (v.) chiamare; (n.) chiamata
called detto
calm (adj.) calmo
can (v.) potere, sapere
canal canale (m.)
canvas tela
capital capitale (f. & m.)
capsicum peperone (m.)
captivate (v.) attrarre
car automobile (f.)
card biglietto
careful (adj.) prudente
carnation garofano
carpet tappeto
carriage carrozza
carriage-door sportello
carrot carota
carry (v.) portare
cash (v.) incassare, riscuotere; (n.) cassa
catalogue catalogo
catch (v.) prendere, catturare
cauliflower cavolfiore (m.)
cause causa
cavern caverna
ceiling soffitto
celery sedano
centimetre centimetro
centre centro
century secolo

certain (adj.) certo
certainly (adv.) certamente
chair sedia
chandelier candelabro
change (v.) cambiare; (n.) cambiamento alterazione (f.) (n.) resto, spiccioli
channel canale (m.)
chapter capitolo
character carattere (m.)
characteristic caratteristico
charade sciarada
cheese formaggio
cheer (v.) applaudire; (n.) applauso
chemical (adj.) chimico
chemist farmacista
chemist shop farmacia
cherry ciliegia
chest-of-drawers cassettone (m.)
chicory cicoria
chicken pollo
chief (n.) capo; (adj.) principale
child bambino, a
chill raffreddore, fresco
chilled (adj.) raffreddato
china porcellana
Chinese (adj.) cinese
church chiesa
Christmas Natale
cathedral cattedrale (f.)
cinder cenere (f.)
cinema cinema (m. inv.)
city città
class classe (f.)
classic (adj.) classico
clean (adj.) pulito; (v.) pulire*
clear (adj.) chiaro, sereno
clear soup brodo
clear (the table) sparecchiare
clerk impiegato, commesso
climate clima (m.)
climb (v.) scalare; (n.) scalata
climber scalatore (m.)
cloak mantello
clock orologio
close (v.) chiudere; (adv. & adj.) vicino
closed chiuso
clothes vestiti
cloud nuvola
cloudless (adj.) sereno
cloudy (adj.) nuvoloso
coach vettura
coal carbone (m.)
coast costa, riva
coat cappotto
cockle vongola
cod merluzzo
code codice (m.)
coffee caffè (m.)
coffee-pot caffettiera
cold (adj.) freddo; (n.) raffreddore (m.)
collar colletto
colleague collega (m. & f.)
colonnade colonnato, portico
colour colore (m.)
coloured (adj.) colorato
column colonna
comb (v.) pettinare; (n.) pettine (m.)
come (v.) venire
come back ritornare
comedy commedia
comfort comodità, conforto
comfortable (adj.) comodo
commemorate (v.) commemorare
commerce commercio
commission (v.) commissionare
commit (v.) commettere
common (adj.) comune
compare (v.) confrontare
compartment scompartimento
complain (v.) lamentarsi, lagnarsi
complaint lamentela, lagnanza
complete (adj.) completo
completely (adv.) completamente
composer compositore (m.)
composition composizione (f.)
compulsory (adj.) obbligatorio
comprehend (v.) comprendere
concern (v.) concernere
concert hall sala da concerto
conductor fattorino
confederate (adj.) alleato
confess (v.) confessare
confidence confidenza
confront (v.) confrontare
conjugal (adj.) coniugale
connection legame (m.), vincolo
consciousness coscienza
consist (v.) consistere
console (v.) consolare
consummately (adv.) completamente
contagious (adj.) contagioso
contain (v.) contenere

contemplate (v.) contemplare
contempt disprezzo
content contenuto
continue (v.) continuare
contribute (v.) contribuire*
convenient (adj.) comodo
conversation conversazione (f.)
cook (v.) cucinare; (n.) cuoco . . . a
cooking cucina
cool (adj.) fresco
coral corallo
corner angolo
corporal (adj.) corporale
correct (v.) correggere; (adj.) corretto
correspondence corrispondenza
courteous (adj.) cortese
cost (v.) costare; (n.) costo
cotton cotone (m.)
cough (v.) tossire;* (n.) tosse (f.)
count (v.) contare; (n.) conte (m.)
counterpane coperta
country paese (m.), campagna
couple coppia
courage coraggio, audacia
course piatto, portata, campo
court cortile (m.)
cousin cugino . . . a
cover (v.) coprire
covered (adj.) coperto
coward (adj.) vigliacco
crayfish scampi (m. pl.)
cream (adj.) crema
crime crimine (m.)
criticize (v.) criticare
crop raccolto
cross (v.) attraversare; (n.) croce (f.)
crossing traversata, incrocio
crowd folla
crowded (adj.) affollato
cruelty crudeltà
crush (v.) schiacciare
crystal cristallo
cucumber cetriolo
cuisine cucina
cup tazza
cupboard armadio
cupola cupola
cure (v.) guarire; (n.) cura
curtain tenda
cushion cuscino
custom costume (m.)
cut (v.) tagliare
cutlery posate (f. pl.)
cutlet cotoletta
cyclist ciclista (m. & f.)

D

daddy papà (m.), babbo
daily (adv.) giornalmente; (adj.) giornaliero, quotidiano
dairy latteria
damp (adj.) umido
dance (v.) ballare; (n.) ballo
dancing (n.) ballo
danger pericolo
daring (adj.) coraggioso, audace
dark (adj.) scuro
darkening (adj.) che diventa scuro
date data
daughter figlia
daughter-in-law nuora
daunt (v.) scoraggiare
dawn alba
day giorno, giornata
deadly (adj.) mortale
deafness sordità
dear (adj.) caro
December dicembre
deck-chair sedia a sdraio
decorate (v.) decorare
defend (v.) difendere
degradation degradazione (f.)
degree grado, laurea
delight (v.) deliziare, piacere; (n.) delizia
deliver (v.) consegnare
dense (adj.) denso
demolish (v.) demolire*
deny (v.) negare
depart (v.) partire
dependent (adj.) dipendente
deprivation privazione (f.)
derive (v.) derivare, ricavare
descend (v.) scendere
describe (v.) descrivere
description descrizione (f.)
design (v.) disegnare; (n.) disegno
desire desiderio
desolation desolazione (f.)
destroy (v.) distruggere
destruction distruzione (f.)
development sviluppo
devotion devozione (f.)
dialogue dialogo

die (v.) morire
different (adj.) differente
difficult (adj.) difficile
diligent (adj.) diligente
dim (adj.) fioco
dine (v.) pranzare
dining-car vettura ristorante
dining-room sala da pranzo
dinner pranzo, cena
direct (v.) dirigere, guidare; (adj.) diretto
disability incapacità
disappointment delusione (f.)
discerning (adj.) acuto
discipline disciplina
disclosure rivelazione (f.)
discount sconto
discover (v.) scoprire
discovery scoperta
discreet (adj.) discreto
discriminating (adj.) calcolato
disease malattia
disgust disgusto
dish piatto
dispatch (v.) spedire; (n.) dispaccio
displease (v.) dispiacere
disposition disposizione (f.), carattere (m.)
distance distanza
distinguished distinto (adj.)
distress (v.) affliggere, preoccupare; (n.) infelicità
distribute (v.) distribuire
district quartiere (m.), distretto
divan divano
divide (v.) dividere
divine (adj.) divino
division divisione (f.)
do (v.) fare
doctor dottore (m.), dottoressa (f.), medico
document documento
documentary documentario
Doge doge (m.)
dome cupola
domestic (adj.) domestico
dominate (v.) dominare
donkey asino, asinello
door porta
double doppio, sosia (m. & f. inv.)
doubt (v.) dubitare; (n.) dubbio
down (adv.) giù
dozen dozzina
draft (v.) stendere
drafting stesura, bozza
draw (v.) tirare
drawer cassetto
drawing-room salotto
dress (v.) vestirsi; (n.) vestito
dressing-table toletta
dressmaker sarta
drink (v.) bere; (n.) bevanda, aperitivo
drive (v.) guidare
driver conducente (m.)
drop (v.) cadere; (n.) goccia
drunk (adj.) ubbriaco
dry (v.) asciugare; (adj.) asciutto
Duke duca (m.)
during (prep.) durante
dusk tramonto, oscurità
dust (v.) spolverare; (n.) polvere (f.)
duty dovere (m.)
dynamo dinamo (f. inv.)

E

each (adj.) ogni (inv.)
each one (pron.) ognuno
ear orecchio
early (adv.) presto
easel cavalletto
east oriente
Easter Pasqua
eastern (adj.) orientale
easy (adj.) facile
eat (v.) mangiare
economic (adj.) economico
education istruzione (f.)
egg uovo
egoism egoismo
elegant (adj.) elegante
elementary (adj.) elementare
eiderdown piumino
either . . . or o . . . o
employment impiego
end (v.) finire*; (n.) fine (f.)
endure (v.) sopportare
enemy nemico
engagement impegno, fidanzamento
engineer ingegnere (m.)
engineering ingegneria
England Inghilterra
enjoy (v.) divertirsi
enjoyment godimento
enormous (adj.) enorme

enough (adv.) abbastanza
enter (v.) entrare
entertainment divertimento
entirely (adv.) interamente
entrance ingresso, ammissione (f.)
envelope busta
envoy ambasciatore (m.)
epilogue epilogo
epoch epoca
equal (adj.) eguale
equally (adv.) egualmente
equivalent (adj. & m.) equivalente
erect (v.) erigere, costruire
eruption eruzione (f.)
escort (v.) accompagnare
especially (adv.) specialmente
esteem stima
even (adv.) perfino
evening sera, serata
evening party serata
ever (adv.) sempre, mai
every (adj.) ogni (inv.)
everyone (pron.) ognuno
exact (adj.) esatto, preciso
exaggerate (v.) esagerare
examination esame (m.)
examine (v.) esaminare
example esempio
except (prep. & conj.) tranne, eccetto
excite (v.) eccitare
executioner boia (m.)
exist (v.) esistere
existence esistenza
exhausted (adj.) esaurito, esausto
exhibition esposizione (f.)
expansion espansione (f.)
expect (v.) aspettare
expedient espediente (m.)
expense spesa
expensive (adj.) caro
explain (v.) spiegare
express (n. & adj.) espresso
express letter espresso
express train treno diretto, espresso
expression espressione (f.)
external (adj.) esterno
eye occhio

F

fabric stoffa
facade facciata
face faccia, viso

fact fatto
faculty facoltà
fade out (v.) svanire, scomparire
failed (adj.) bocciato
fair (adj.) giusto, biondo
fairly (adv.) abbastanza
fall (v.) cadere; (n.) caduta
familiar (adj.) familiare
family famiglia
famous (adj.) famoso, celebre
fashion moda
fashionable (adj.) di moda, alla moda
father padre (m.)
father-in-law suocero
fatherland patria
fault sbaglio, colpa
favour favore (m.)
favourite (adj.) favorito
fear (v.) temere; (n.) paura, timore (m.)
February febbraio
feel (v.) sentire
feel better stare meglio
feeling sentimento
felicity felicità
fennel finocchio
ferocity ferocia
festival festival (m.)
fever febbre (f.)
few (adj.) pochi
field campo
fiendish (adj.) diabolico
fig fico
figure figura, cifra
film film (m. inv.)
finally (adv.) finalmente
find (v.) trovare
finger dito
finish (v.) finire*
fire (v.) sparare; (n.) fuoco
fireplace caminetto
firm (n.) ditta, società; (adj.) solido
first (adj.) primo
fish (v.) pescare; (n.) pesce (m.)
fisherman pescatore (m.)
fishmonger pescivendolo
fitting (to be) convenire
flannel flanella
flash (v.) balenare
flat (n.) appartamento; (adj.) piatto
flavour sapore (m.)
flee (v.) fuggire

flexible (adj.) flessibile
flight fuga, volo
flood (v.) inondare; (n.) inondazione (f.)
floor pavimento
Florence Firenze
Florentine fiorentino
flour farina
flower fiore (m.)
fog nebbia
follow (v.) seguire
following (adj.) seguente
folly follia
fond (to be) amare
foot piede (m.)
football calcio
for (prep.) per; (conj.) perché
forbid (v.) proibire, vietare
forehead fronte (f.)
foreign (adj.) forestiero, straniero
foreigner straniero
forget (v.) dimenticare
forgive (v.) perdonare
fork forchetta
form (v.) formare
formidable (adj.) formidabile
fortune fortuna
forward (v.) inoltrare, spedire
fountain fontana
fountain-pen penna stilografica
France Francia
Francis Francesco
free (adj.) libero
freeze (v.) gelare
French (adj.) francese
frequent (v.) frequentare; (adj.) frequente
frequently (adv.) spesso, di frequente
fresco affresco
fresh (adj.) fresco
Friday venerdì
fried (adj.) fritto
friend amico, a
frivolous (adj.) frivolo, leggero
from (prep.) da, dopo, di
front davanti, facciata, fronte (m.)
fruit frutto
fruiterer fruttivendolo
fruit salad macedonia di frutta
fugitive (adj.) fuggiasco
fulfil (v.) compiere, esaudire
full (adj.) pieno
furnishing arredamento
furniture mobilia
furniture (piece of) mobile (m.)
fury furia

G

gala serata di gala
gallery galleria
game gioco, partita, cacciagione
gaol carcere (m.), prigione (f.)
garage autorimessa, garage (m.)
garden giardino
garlic aglio
gate cancello
gaunt (adj.) scarno, secco
gay (adj.) gaio, allegro
general (adj. & n.) generale
generally (adv.) generalmente, di solito
genius genio
gentle (adj.) mite, gentile
gentleman gentiluomo, signore (m
George Giorgio
German tedesco
get off scendere
gift regalo, dono
gifted (adj.) dotato
girl ragazza
give (v.) dare, consegnare
glad (adj.) contento, lieto
glance (v.) dare un occhiata; (n.) occhiata
glass bicchiere, vetro
glass window vetrina
glide (v.) scivolare
glorious (adj.) glorioso
glory gloria
glove guanto
glue colla
go (v.) andare; **go on** andare avanti, procedere, continuare
God Dio
goldsmith orefice (m.)
gondola gondola
gondolier gondoliere (m.)
good (adj.) buono, bravo
Gothic (adj.) gotico
government governo
grammar grammatica
grammar school liceo
grandchild nipote (m. & f.)
grandfather nonno

grandmother nonna
grapes uva
grass erba
grateful grato, riconoscente
grave tomba
great (adj.) grande
greatly (adv.) grandemente
Great Britain Gran Bretagna
Greece Grecia
Greek (adj.) greco
green (adj.) verde
greens verdura
greet (v.) salutare
grey (adj.) grigio
grieve (v.) dispiacere
grocer droghiere (m.)
grocer's shop drogheria
ground terreno, parco
ground floor pianterreno
group gruppo
grow (v.) crescere, coltivare
guest ospite (m. & f.), invitato, visitatore (m.)
guide (v.) guidare; (n.) guida
gulf golfo

H

hail (v.) grandinare; (n.) grandine (f.)
hair capello
half metà, mezzo
hall ingresso
hammock amaca
hand mano (f.)
hand-bag borsetta, borsa
hand in (v.) consegnare
handgrip stretta di mano
handkerchief fazzoletto
handle maniglia, manico
hang (v.) appendere
happen (v.) accadere, avvenire, succedere
happily (adv.) felicemente
happiness felicità
happy (adj.) felice
hard (adj.) duro
Harry (Henry) Enrico
harvest raccolto
haste fretta
hat cappello
hate (v.) odiare
hatred odio
have (v.) avere
have, to (v.) druere
haze nebbia, foschia
he (pron.) egli, lui
head testa, capo
headsquare fazzoletto
healthy (adj.) salubre, sano
heap mucchio
hear (v.) sentire, udire
heart cuore (m.)
heavy (adj.) pesante
height altura, altezza
Helen Elena
hell inferno
help (v.) aiutare; (n.) aiuto
helping porzione (f.)
her (pron.) essa, lei, la; **herself** lei stessa
her (adj.) suo, -ua, -uoi, -ue
hesitate (v.) esitare
hide (v.) nascondere; **hidden** nascosto
high (adj.) alto
higher (adj.) più alto, superiore
highest (adj.) il più alto, supremo
hill colle (m.), collina
him (pron.) lo lui
himself (pron.) lui stesso, si
hinge cardine (m.)
his (adj. & pron.) suo, -ua, -uoi, -ue
hiss (v.) fischiare
history storia
holiday vacanza
holy (adj.) santo, sacro
home casa
home-made fatto in casa, casalingo
home-work compito
honest (adj.) onesto, integro
hope (v.) sperare; (n.) speranza
horror orrore (m.)
horse cavallo
hospital ospedale (m.)
host ospite (m.)
hostess ospite (f.)
hostile (adj.) ostile
hotel albergo
hour ora
house casa
how (adv.) come
how much (adv. & adj.) quanto
how often quante volte ?
how soon (adv.) tra quanto
however (adv.) però, tuttavia per quanto

Hubert Umberto, Uberto
huge (adj.) enorme
human (adj.) umano
humanity umanità
humbly (adv.) umilmente
humour spirito, umore (m.)
hundred cento, centinaio
hunger fame (f.)
hungry (adj.) affamato
hungry (to be) aver fame
hurry (v.) affrettarsi; (n.) fretta
hurry (to be in a) aver fretta
husband marito

I

I (pron.) io; mi, me
idea idea
idiot idiota (m. & f.)
if (conj.) se
ignorance ignoranza
ignorant (adj.) ignorante
ill (adj.) malato
illness malattia
image immagine (f.)
imagination immaginazione (f.)
imagine (v.) immaginare
immediately (adv.) immediatamente
immense (adj.) immenso
impatient (adj.) impaziente
importance importanza
important (adj.) importante
impossible (adj.) impossibile
impudence impudenza
impress (v.) impressionare
impression impressione (f.)
imprudence imprudenza
in (prep.) in
incense (v.) infuriare
include (v.) includere
indifferent (adj.) indifferente
independence indipendenza
indistinct (adj.) confuso
individualism individualismo
induce (v.) indurre
indulgence indulgenza
indulgent (adj.) indulgente
industrial (adj.) industriale
industrialism industrialismo
industry industria
infectious (adj.) infettivo
inferno inferno
influence influenza
influenza influenza
inform (v.) informare
information informazione (f.)
inhabitant abitante (m. & f.)
inn osteria, locanda
inside (adv. & prep.) dentro
insolence insolenza
instruction istruzione (f.)
instinctively (adv.) istintivamente
intact (adj.) intatto
intellectual (adj.) intellettuale
intelligent (adj.) intelligente
intensified (adj.) intensificato
intercourse relazione (f.)
interest interesse (m.)
interesting (adj.) interessante
interior (n. & adj.) interno
interval intervallo
into (prep.) in, dentro
invasion invasione (f.)
investigation investigazione (f.), ricerca
invitation invito
invite (v.) invitare
involve (v.) comportare
Ionian Sea Ionio
iron ferro
irredeemably (adv.) inevitabilmente
island isola
issue (v.) distribuire
Italian (adj.) italiano
Italian warehouse salumeria
Italian warehouseman salumaio, salumiere
Italy Italia
it (pron.) esso, a; egli, lo, la
its (adj. & pron.) suo, -ua, -uoi, -ue

J

jail prigione (f.), carcere (m.)
jam confettura, marmellata
January gennaio
jewel gioiello
jeweller gioielliere (m.), orefice (m.)
job impiego, lavoro
John Giovanni
join (v.) unire
journey viaggio
joy gioia
judge giudice (m.)
Julia Giulia
July luglio

June giugno
just (adv.) proprio

K

keen (adj.) acuto, vivo; **keenly** (adv.) acutamente
keep conservare
kilogramme chilo
kilometre chilometro
kind (adj.) gentile; (n.) tipo, specie (f.)
kindly (adv.) gentilmente
king re (m. inv.)
kiss (v.) baciare; (n.) bacio
kitchen cucina
knee ginocchio
knife coltello
knock (v.) bussare; (n.) colpo
know conoscere, sapere

L

lace merletto
laden (adj.) carico
lady signora
lagoon laguna
lake lago
lamb agnello
lamp lampada, lume (m.)
landscape paesaggio
language linguaggio, lingua
large (adj.) grande, largo
last (v.) durare; (adj.) ultimo, scorso
late (adv.) tardi
late (to be) essere in ritardo
lately (adv.) ultimamente, recentemente
Latin (adj.) latino
laugh (v.) ridere; (n.) riso
lava lava
law legge (f.)
lawyer avvocato
layer strato
leader capo, condottiero
learn (v.) imparare
learned dotto
learning sapere (m.)
least (adj. & adv.) meno; **at least** almeno
leave (v.) partire, lasciare; (n.) licenza
leaving certificate licenza
left (adj.) sinistro
lemonade limonata
less (adv.) meno

11*

lesson lezione (f.)
let (v.) permettere, lasciare
letter lettera
letter-box buca delle lettere
lettuce lattuga
level livello
library biblioteca
lie (v.) giacere, sdraiarsi; (n.) bugia
life vita
lift (v.) alzare; (n.) ascensore, passaggio
light (n.) luce (f.); (adj.) leggero
lightning lampo
like (v.) piacere; (prep.) come
likely (adv.) probabile
limited (adj.) limitato
line linea, ruga
lineament lineamento
linen biancheria
linger (v.) indugiare
lip labbro
lira lira
listen (v.) ascoltare
literary (adj.) letterario
literature letteratura
little (adj.) piccolo; (adv.) poco
live (v.) abitare, vivere
lively (adj.) vivace
load peso, carico
loathing odio
lobster aragosta
loggia loggia
logical (adj.) logico
Lombardy Lombardia
London Londra
lonely (adj.) solitario, solo
long (adj.) lungo
look (v.) guardare, sembrare; (n.) aspetto
look for (v.) cercare
lord signore (m.)
loss perdita
Louise Luisa
love (v.) amare; (n.) amore
loveliness incanto, bellezza
lovely (adj.) bello, incantevole
lover amante (m. & f.)
low (adj.) basso
lower (adj.) inferiore
lowest (adj.) infimo
luck fortuna
luggage bagaglio

lunch colazione (f.)
lustre lustro

M

macaroni maccheroni, pasta asciutta
mad (adj.) pazzo
magazine rivista
magnificent (adj.) magnifico
magnificently (adv.) magnificamente
maid cameriera
mail posta
mainland terraferma
maintain (v.) mantenere, sostenere
majestic (adj.) maestoso
make (v.) fare, rendere
man uomo
mankind umanità
manifest (v.) manifestare; (adj.) manifesto
manner maniera, modo
mantelpiece caminetto
manuscript manoscritto
many (adj.) molti
marble marmo
March marzo
mark voto
market-place mercato, piazza
marmelade marmellata
marriage matrimonio
marry (v.) sposare
marvellous (adj.) meraviglioso
Mary Maria
mass massa, messa
masterpiece capolavoro
mat tappetino
match partita, incontro
material stoffa
mathematics matematica
matter (v.) importare; (n.) affare (m.)
mattress materasso
May maggio
maybe (adv.) forse
me (pron.) mi
mean (v.) significare
means mezzo
meat carne (f.)
measure (v.) misurare
measurement misura
mediaeval (adj.) medioevale
medicine medicina
meet (v.) incontrare, conoscere
melon melone (m.)
melt (v.) sciogliere, sciogliersi, svanire
member membro
memory memoria
mention (v.) menzionare, citare
menu lista
merciless (adj.) spietato
merit merito
method metodo
metre metro
mild (adj.) mite
mile miglio
milk latte (m.)
milk-jug lattiera
milkman lattaio
mind mente (f.)
mine (pron.) mio, a, ei, ie
mingle (v.) mescolare
minute minuto, bozza
mirror specchio
misfortune sfortuna
miss signorina
mist nebbia
mistake sbaglio
mister signore (m.)
mistress signora
mixture mescolanza
model modello
moderate (adj.) moderato, mite
modern (adj.) moderno
modest (adj.) modesto, pudico
moment momento
Monday lunedì
money denaro
money order vaglia (m. inv.)
monologue monologo
monotonously (adv.) monotonamente
month mese (m.)
monthly (adv.) mensile
monument monumento
moon luna
moral (adj.) morale
morality moralità
more (adv.) piú
morning mattina
mother madre (f.)
mother-in-law suocera
motto motto
mount monte (m.)
mountain montagna
mountain-inn rifugio
mountaineering alpinismo
mouth bocca

mosaic mosaico
movement movimento
Mr, Mrs Signor(e), Signora
much (adj. & adv.) molto
murderer assassino
museum museo
music musica
mussel cozza
must (v.) dovere
mutton montone (m.)
my (adj.) mio, a, ei, e

N

name nome (m.)
napkin tovagliuolo
Naples Napoli
narrow (adj.) stretto
national (adj.) nazionale
native (adj.) nativo, natio
natural (adj.) naturale
naturally (adv.) naturalmente
nature natura
Neapolitan (adj.) napoletano
near (adv. & prep.) vicino
nearly (adv.) quasi
necessary (adj.) necessario
necessarily (adv.) necessariamente
necessity necessità
neck collo
necklace collana
need (v.) aver bisogno; (n.) bisogno
neither . . . nor né . . . né
nephew nipote (m. & f.)
never (adv.) mai
new (adj.) nuovo
news notizia, informazione (f.)
newspaper giornale (m.)
newsvendor giornalaio
next (adj.) prossimo
night notte (f.), sera
night-dress camicia da notte
no (adv.) no; (adj.) nessuno
noble (adj.) nobile
nobody (pron.) nessuno
none (pron.) nessuno
note (v.) notare; (n.) nota
not even (adv.) neanche
note-paper carta da lettere
nothing niente
notice (v.) notare; (n.) avviso
nought zero
novel romanzo
November novembre
now (adv.) ora
number numero
numerous (adj.) numeroso

O

oak quercia
oar remo
obelisk obelisco
object oggetto
obligatory (adj.) obbligatorio
obliged obbligato
obscure (adj.) oscuro
observation osservazione (f.)
observe (v.) osservare
obstinately (adv.) ostinatamente
occasion occasione (f.)
occasionally (adv.) ogni tanto
occur (v.) accadere, succedere, avvenire
o'clock ora, ore
October ottobre
odious (adj.) odioso
of (prep.) di
offend (v.) offendere
offer (v.) offrire; (n.) offerta
office ufficio
office door sportello
officer ufficiale
official (adj.) ufficiale
often (adv.) spesso
old (adj.) vecchio, antico
ominously (adv.) minacciosamente
on (prep.) su
once (adv.) una volta
one (people) si
oncoming (adj.) che sopraggiunge
onion cipolla
only (adv.) solamente, soltanto
open (v.) aprire; (adj.) aperto
opinion opinione (f.)
oppressed oppresso
or (conj.) o
oral (adj.) orale
orange arancio
orangeade aranciata
orange grove aranceto
order (v.) ordinare; (n.) ordine (m.); **in —** per
origin origine (f.)
ostensibly (adv.) ostentatamente
other (adj.) altro

otherwise (adv.) altrimenti
our (adj.) nostro
ours (pron.) nostro
outcast paria (m. inv.)
outline figura
outrageous (adj.) offensivo, oltraggioso
outside (prep. & adv.) fuori
oval (adj.) ovale
over (prep.) sopra
overwhelmed sopraffatto
owe (v.) dovere
own (adj.) proprio
ox bue (pl. buoi)
oyster ostrica

P

Padua Padova
packing imballaggio
painful (adj.) penoso
paint (v.) dipingere; (n.) pittura, tinta
painter pittore (m.)
painting pittura
pair paio
palace palazzo
pale (adj.) pallido
paper carta
paper-stall edicola
paragraph paragrafo
parasol ombrellone (m.)
parcel pacco
pardon perdono
parent genitore (m.)
Paris Parigi
park parco
parking place posteggio
parlour game gioco di società
parsley prezzemolo
part parte (f.)
partially (adv.) parzialmente
partnership società
partridge starna
party ricevimento, partito
pass (v.) passare
passage passaggio
passenger passeggero
passion passione (f.)
pastry cook pasticciere (m.)
patient (n. & adj.) paziente (m. & f.)
patriotic (adj.) patriottico
pattern disegno
Paul Paolo
pause (v.) soffermarsi; (n.) pausa
pavement marciapiede (m.)
pay (v.) pagare
pea pisello
peach pesca
pear pera
peasant contadino
pedagogue pedagogo
pedestrian pedone (m.)
pen penna
pencil matita
pension pensione (f.)
people gente (f.), popolo
pepper pepe (m.)
perfectly (adv.) perfettamente
perform (v.) recitare
perhaps (adv.) forse
period periodo, epoca, ora di lezione
permission permesso
person persona
personified personificato
pheasant fagiano
Philip Filippo
philosopher filosofo
photograph fotografia
pick up (v.) raccogliere
picture quadro, pittura
piece pezzo
pig porco, maiale (m.)
pigeon piccione (m.), colombo
pile mucchio
pillar colonna
pillow cuscino, guanciale (m.)
pillow slip federa
pink (adj.)· rosa (inv.)
pinkish (adj.) rosato
pinnacle guglia
pitched (adj.) campale
place posto, luogo
plain pianura
plate piatto
platform binario, marciapiede (m.)
play (v.) giocare, suonare, recitare; (n.) commedia
playing ground stadio
pleasant (adj.) piacevole
please per piacere, per favore
pleasing (adj.) piacevole
pleasure piacere (m.)
plot intreccio
plum susina, prugna
plump (adj.) grasso, grassoccio

poem poesia, poema
poet poeta (m.)
poetry poesia
pole palo, polo
policeman metropolitano, guardia
political (adj.) politico
politician uomo politico
poor (adj.) povero
popular (adj.) popolare
population popolazione (f.)
porcelain porcellana
porch portico
pork maiale (m.)
port porto
porter facchino
portion porzione (f.)
portrait ritratto
possession possesso
post (v.) imbucare, impostare; (n.) posta
postage affrancatura
postal order vaglia postale
postcard cartolina
postman postino
post office ufficio postale, posta
postpone (v.) posporre, rimandare
potato patata
pour (v.) diluviare, versare
power potere (m.), facoltà
practical (adj.) pratico
practically (adv.) praticamente
practise (v.) esercitare
praise (v.) lodare; (n.) lode (f.)
precise (adj.) preciso, esatto
prefer (v.) preferire*
prepare (v.) preparare
present (v.) regalare; (n.) regalo; at — ora
presently (adv.) tra poco, poco dopo
prince principe (m.)
principal (adj.) principale
prison prigione (f.), carcere (m.)
prisoner prigioniero
private (adj.) privato
prize premio
problem problema (m.)
procession processione (f.), corteo
profession professione (f.)
professor professore (m.)
programme programma (m.)
progress (in) in via di attuazione
prologue prologo
promoted (adj.) promosso
promotion promozione (f.)
prompt (v.) suggerire*
prosperity prosperità
protect (v.) proteggere
province provincia
provision provviste (f. pl.)
prudence prudenza
prudent (adj.) prudente
psychiatrist psichiatra (m.)
psychologist psicologo
public (adj.) pubblico
public house osteria
punctual (adj.) puntuale
punishment punizione (f.)
pupil scolaro, alunno
pure (adj.) puro
push (v.) spingere; **push back** respingere
put (v.) mettere
pyjamas pigiama (m.)

Q

quarter quarto, quartiere (m.)
queen regina
question (v.) interrogare; (n.) domanda
quickly (adv.) presto, velocemente
quilt piumino
quite recently (adv.) poco tempo fa

R

race corsa
radical (adj.) radicale
radio radio (f.)
radish ravanello
ragged (adj.) tagliato, frastagliato
rails binario, rotaie
rain (v.) piovere; (n.) pioggia
raincoat impermeabile (m.)
rainy (adj.) piovoso
raise (v.) alzare, sollevare, aumentare
range distanza
rank rango, classe (f.)
ransom riscatto
rapidly (adv.) rapidamente
raspberry lampone (m.)
rat ratto, topo
raze (v.) radere al suolo
read (v.) leggere
ready (adj.) pronto
ready reckoner abbaco

real (adj.) reale, vero
reality realtà
receipt ricevuta
receive (v.) ricevere
recently (adv.) recentemente
reception ricevimento
recognize (v.) riconoscere
recommend (v.) raccomandare
reconstruct (v.) ricostruire*
recover (v.) guarire*
red (adj.) rosso
red mullet triglia
refectory refettorio
referee arbitro
reference riferimento
reform riforma
refrigerator frigorifero
regard (v.) considerare
region regione (f.)
register registro
registered letter raccomandata
regret (v.) rincrescere, rimpiangere; (n.) rimpianto
rejoice (v.) rallegrarsi
relative parente (m. & f.)
reliable (adj.) attendibile, certo
rely (v.) contare . . . su
remain (v.) rimanere
remainder resto
remark (v.) osservare; (n.) osservazione (f.)
remarkable (adj.) notevole
remember (v.) ricordare
remind (v.) ricordare
Renaissance Rinascimento
render (v.) rendere
repeat (v.) ripetere
repent (v.) pentirsi
reply (v.) rispondere; (n.) risposta
report pagella
repose pace (f.), quiete (f.)
reproduce (v.) riprodurre
republic repubblica
repugnance ripugnanza
require (v.) aver bisogno
research ricerca
reserve (v.) prenotare, riservare
respect rispetto
rest (v.) riposare; (n.) riposo
restaurant ristorante (m.)
return (v.) ritornare; (n.) ritorno
reverence riverenza
review rivista
rhythm ritmo
rib costa, costola
rice riso
rich (adj.) ricco
richness ricchezza
right (adj.) destro, giusto; **to be —** avere ragione
rigid (adj.) rigido
ring (v.) suonare; (n.) anello
rise (v.) sorgere, alzarsi, salire
rival (adj.) rivale
river fiume (m.)
road strada, via
roast (n. & adj.) arrosto
rob (v.) derubare, rubare
Robert Roberto
rock roccia
rocky (adj.) roccioso
Rome Roma
Roman (adj.) romano
roof tetto
room stanza, posto
rose rosa
round (adj.) rotondo; (prep.) attorno
. . . a (adv.) intorno
rough (adj.) rozzo; **(of the sea)** agitato
row (v.) remare; (n.) fila, lite (f.)
rowing canottaggio
rub (v.) strofinare, stropicciare
rug tappeto
ruin (v.) rovinare; (n.) rovina

S

saint (adj.) santo
salad insalata
salami salame (m.)
salt sale (m.)
same (adj.) stesso
sample (v.) assaggiare; (n.) campione (m.)
sand sabbia
sandwich panino imbottito
Sardinia Sardegna
Saturday sabato
saucer piattino
savoury (adj.) salato
saw sega
say (v.) dire, raccontare
saying detto
scarf fazzoletto, sciarpa
scene scena

scenery scenario, paesaggio
school scuola
schoolroom aula
science scienza
scientific (adj.) scientifico
screen paravento, tendina
sculptor scultore (m.)
sculpture scultura
sea mare (m.)
sear (v.) devastare, solcare
sea-side al mare
seat (n.) sedile (m.)
second (adj.) secondo
secondary (adj.) secondario
section sezione (f.)
sedate (adj.) calmo
see (v.) vedere
seek (v.) ricercare
seem (v.) sembrare, parere
select (v.) scegliere; (adj.) scelto
selection assortimento
sell (v.) vendere
send (v.) mandare
sender mittente (m. & f.)
sensibly (adv.) sensatamente, sensibilmente
sentimental (adj.) sentimentale
September settembre
series serie (f. inv.)
serve (v.) servire
set the table apparecchiare
setting tramonto
set out (v.) partire
several (adj.) molti, parecchi, diversi
severe (adj.) severo, rigido
shade ombra
shadow ombra
shake (v.) scuotere
she (pron.) essa, ella, lei
sheet lenzuolo
sheet of paper foglio di carta
shine (v.) splendere
ship building costruzioni navali
shirt camicia
shoe scarpa
shoe shop calzoleria
shop negozio, magazzino
shop assistant commesso
shop window vetrina
shore costa, riva
short (adj.) corto, breve
shortly (adv.) in breve
show (v.) mostrare; (n.) mostra, spettacolo
show-case vetrina
shrine tempio
shut (v.) chiudere; (past. p.) chiuso
sick (adj.) malato
sickness malattia
side parte (f.), lato
sideboard credenza
side-dish contorno
sideways (adv.) di traverso, di sbieco
sigh (v.) sospirare; (n.) sospiro
sign (v.) firmare; (n.) segno, indizio
signal (v.) segnalare; (n.) segnale (m.)
signature firma
silk seta
simple (adj.) semplice
sin peccato
sing (v.) cantare
singular (adj.) singolare
sister sorella
sister-in-law cognata
Sistine Chapel Cappella Sistina
sit (v.) sedere
sitting-room salotto
ski (v.) sciare; (n.) sci
skill arte (f.), abilità
skin pelle (f.)
ski-track pista
skirt sottana, gonna
sky cielo
slate lavagna
sleep (v.) dormire; (n.) sonno
sleeping car vagone letto
slide (v.) scivolare
slight (adj.) leggero
slip (v.) scivolare
slowly (adv.) lentamente
small (adj.) piccolo
smart (adj.) elegante
smooth (adj.) liscio
snare trappola
sneeze (v.) starnutare, (n.) starnuto
snow (v.) nevicare; (n.) neve (f.)
snowy (adj.) nevoso
so (adv.) cosi; (conj.) perciò, dunque
social (adj.) sociale
society società
sock calzino
soft (adj.) morbido
softly (adv.) mollemente, dolcemente

soldier soldato
sole sogliola
some (adj.) qualche, alcuno
somebody (pron.) qualcuno
something (pron.) qualcosa
sometimes (adv.) a volte
somewhat (adv.) alquanto, abbastanza
son figlio
song canto, canzone (f.)
son-in-law genero
soon (adv.) presto
sort genere (m.), sorte (f.), sorta
sound (v.) suonare; (n.) suono
soup minestra, zuppa
southern (adj.) meridionale
spacious (adj.) spazioso
Spaniard Spagnuolo
Spanish (adj.) spagnuolo
sparkle (v.) scintillare; (n.) scintilla
speak (v.) parlare
speciality specialità
specially (adv.) specialmente
spectator spettatore (m.)
speculation speculazione (f.)
speech discorso
spend (v.) spendere
spinach spinaci
spire guglia
splendid (adj.) splendido
splendour splendore (m.)
spoiler saccheggiatore (m.)
spoon cucchiaio
sport sport (m. inv.)
sporting (adj.) sportivo
Spring primavera
square (adj.) quadrato; (n.) piazza
stable stalla
stack mucchio
stadium stadio
stage palcoscenico
staircase scala
stale (adj.) passato, vecchio, stantio
stamp francobollo
stand (v.) stare in piedi, ergersi, sorgere
state stato
statesman uomo di stato
station stazione (f.)
stationer cartolaio
stationery cartoleria
statue statua
stay (v.) stare, restare
steamer vaporetto
step scalino
steps (pair of) scala a piuoli
stern (adj.) duro
stiff (adj.) rigido
still (adv.) ancora
stimulant (adj. & n.) stimolante
stir (v.) girare, mescolare; (n.) movimento
stocking calza
stone pietra
stop (v.) fermare; (n.) fermata
storm temporale (m.)
story storia, racconto
straight (adj.) dritto
strand striscia
strange (adj.) strano
strangely (adv.) stranamente
stranger straniero, visitatore (m.)
strawberry fragola
street strada, via
stride passo
strike (v.) colpire, impressionare, (n.) sciopero
strong (adj.) forte
strongly (adv.) fortemente
struggle lotta
student studente (m.)
studio studio
studious (adj.) studioso
study (v.) studiare; (n.) studio
style stile (m.)
subject soggetto, materia
subjugate (v.) soggiogare, sottomettere
submit (v.) sottomettere
success successo
successor successore (m.)
such (adj.) tale
sudden (adj.) improvviso
suddenly (adv.) improvvisamente
suffering sofferenza
sufficient (adj.) sufficiente
suffocating (adj.) soffocante
sugar zucchero
sugar basin zuccheriera
suit vestito, vestito a giacca
suitable (adj.) adatto
suitcase valigia
sum somma, calcolo
Summer estate
summit sommità, cima

sun sole (m.)
sunny (adj.) soleggiato
sup (v.) cenare
superb (adj.) superbo
superiority superiorità
suppose (v.) supporre
sure (adj.) certo, sicuro
surely (adv.) certo, certamente
surgeon chirurgo
surplice camice (m.)
surprise sorpresa
surprised sorpreso
surrounding (adj.) circostante
survive (v.) sopravvivere
suspended sospeso
sweep (v.) scopare
sweet (adj.) dolce
sweet herb erba aromatica
swim (v.) nuotare
swimming nuoto
swing (v.) sbattere, oscillare
sybil sibilla
system sistema (m.)

T

table tavola
tablecloth tovaglia
table d'hote dinner pranzo a prezzo fisso
tailor sarto
take (v.) prendere, portare
take part (v.) partecipare
talent talento
talk (v.) parlare; (n.) conversazione (f.)
tall (adj.) alto
tangerine mandarino
tape measure metro
task lavoro, compito
taste (v.) gustare, assaggiare; (n.) sapore (m.), gusto
taxi taxi (m. inv.)
tea te (n. inv.)
teach (v.) insegnare
teacher maestro . . . a, professore (m.)
team squadra
tea pot teiera
technical college istituto tecnico
telegram telegramma (m.)
telephone (v.) telefonare; (n.) telefono
telephone box cabina telefonica
tell (v.) raccontare, dire
temperature temperatura
term trimestre (m.)
terrace terrazza
terror terrore (m.)
than (conj. and prep.) che, di
thanks grazie (f. inv.)
that (conj.) che; (adj.) quello
the (def. art.) il, lo, l', la, i, gli, le
theatre teatro
their (adj.), **theirs** (pron.) loro
them (pron.) li, le; **to them,** loro
theme tema (m.), soggetto, motivo
then (adv.) allora, poi
there (adv.) lì, là, vi, ci
thereupon (adv.) al che
thesis tesi (f. inv.)
thick (adj.) denso
thin (adj.) magro, sottile
thing cosa
think (v.) pensare, credere
thirst sete (f.)
thirsty (adj.) assetato
this (adj.) questo
though (adv.) sebbene, benché
thought pensiero
throat gola
through (prep.) attraverso
throw (v.) gettare, scagliare
throw off (remove) togliere
thunder (v.) tuonare; (n.) tuono
Thursday giovedì
thus (adv.) così
ticket biglietto
tie (v.) legare; (n.) cravatta
tight (adj.) stretto
till (prep.) fino a, finché
time tempo stagione, (f.) volta
time-table orario
tinned (adj.) in iscatola
tip (v.) dare la mancia; (n.) mancia
tired (adj.) stanco
to (prep.) a, in, verso
tobacconist tabaccaio, tabaccheria
to-day (adv.) oggi
together (adv.) assieme
toil lavoro
tomato pomodoro
tomato sauce salsa, sugo di pomodoro
tomb tomba
tomorrow (adv.) domani
tongue lingua
too (adv.) anche, troppo

tool utensile (m.)
too much (adv.) troppo
top cima
top coat cappotto
topic argomento, soggetto
torrent torrente (m.)
tortoiseshell tartaruga
touch (v.) toccare; (n.) tocco
touching (adj.) commovente
tourist turista (m. & f.)
towards (prep.) verso
town città
trace traccia
trade commercio
tradesman fornitore (m.)
tradition tradizione (f.)
traffic traffico
traffic lights semaforo
trail pista
train treno, strascico
tramcar tram (m. inv.)
transient (adj.) caduco
travel (v.) viaggiare; (n.) viaggio
tray vassoio
tread passo, filo
treat (v.) curare
tree albero
trembling tremore (m.)
trifle zuppa inglese
triumph trionfo
trolley carrello, carretto
troop truppa
trousers calzoni, pantaloni
true (adj.) vero
trunk baule (m.)
try (v.) tentare, cercare . . . di
Tuesday martedì
turkey tacchino
turn (v.) voltare; (n.) voltata
turnip rapa
Tuscany Toscana
tutor tutore (m.), istitutore (m.)
type tipo
tyrant tiranno

U

ugly (adj.) brutto
umbrella ombrello
umpire arbitro
unable (adj.) incapace, impossibilitato
unarmed (adj.) inerme
uncle zio
under (prep.) sotto
understand (v.) capire*
undertake (v.) intraprendere, prendere l'impegno
underwear biancheria
undisciplined (adj.) indisciplinato
unexpectedly (adv.) inaspettatamente
unfold (v.) spiegare
unfortunate (adj.) sfortunato
unfortunately (adv.) sfortunatamente, purtroppo
unite (v.) unire
United States Stati Uniti
university università
unjust (adj.) ingiusto
unless (adv.) a meno che
unnecessary (adj.) inutile
unpunished (adj.) impunito
untarnished (adj) intatto
until (conj.) finché, fino a che, sino a
upon (prep.) su
us (pron.) ci, noi
usually (adv.) di solito
use (v.) usare; (n.) uso
useful (adj.) utile
useless (adj.) inutile
utter (v.) esprimere

V

valiant (adj.) audace
valley valle (f.)
vanish (v.) sparire,* svanire*
vase vaso
Vatican Vaticano
veal vitello
vegetable (pulse) legume (m.)
vegetables verdura
velvet velluto
Venetian (adj.) veneziano
Venice Venezia
Vera Vera
verb verbo
Vergil Virgilio
very (adv.) molto
vicariously (adj.) per procura
vice vizio
victim vittima
victory vittoria
villa villa
village villaggio
villany cattiveria, perfidia
vineyard vigneto

violent (adj.) violento
violinist violinista (m. & f.)
virtue virtù (f.)
visit (v.) visitare; (n.) visita
visitor visitatore (m.), forestiere (m.)
vitality vitalità
voice voce (f.)
volcano vulcano
volume volume (m.)

W

wainscot pannello di legno
wait (v.) aspettare
waiter cameriere (m.)
waiting room sala d'aspetto
walk (v.) camminare, passeggiare; (n.) passeggiata
wall muro, parete (f.)
want (v.) desiderare; (n.) bisogno
war guerra
wardrobe armadio
wash (v.) lavare; (n.) bucato
watch (v.) osservare, sorvegliare; (n.) orologio
water acqua
wave (v.) sventolare; (n.) onda
way modo, maniera
weak (adj.) debole
wealth prosperità, ricchezza
wear (v.) portare
weather tempo
Wednesday mercoledì
week settimana
weekly (adv.) settimanale
well (adv.) bene
wet (adj.) umido, bagnato
what (adj.) che; (pron.) che cosa
when (adv.) quando
whenever (adv.) ogni volta che
where (adv.) dove
whereas (conj.) mentre
wherever (conj.) dovunque
whether (conj.) se
which (adj.) quale; (pron.) che
whichever (adj.) qualunque
while (conj.) mentre
whine (v.) lamentarsi
whip (v.) frustare; (n.) frusta
whistle (v.) fischiare
white (adj.) bianco
who (pron.) il quale, etc.; (inter.) chi?
whoever (pron.) chiunque
whole (adj.) intero, tutto il, etc.
whom (pron.) che, chi
whose (pron.) di chi? di quale? del quale?
why (adv.) perché
wide (adj.) largo, ampio
wife moglie
wind vento
window finestra
willingly (adv.) volentieri
wine vino
Winter inverno
wise (adj.) saggio
wish (v.) desiderare; (n.) desiderio
wit spirito
with (prep.) con, da, presso
within (prep.) fra, entro, dentro
without (prep.) fuori, senza
woman donna
wonderful (adj.) meraviglioso
wood legno
woodcock beccaccia
wool lana
work (v.) lavorare; (n.) lavoro
world mondo
worn (adj.) consumato
worried (adj.) preoccupato
worse (adj.) peggiore
worst (adj.) il peggiore, pessimo
write (v.) scrivere
writer scrittore (m.)
writing desk scrivania
written scritto

Y

year anno
yearly (adj.) annuale
yearning anelito
yeast bun focaccia
yellow (adj.) giallo
yes (adv.) sì
yesterday (adv.) ieri
yet (adv.) ancora, tuttavia
you (pron.) tu, lei, voi; ti, la, vi, li, le
young (adj.) giovane
your (adj.) tuo, a, etc.; suo, a, etc., vostro, etc.
youth giovinezza
Yugoslav iugoslavo

Z

zero zero

INDEX

The numbers refer to pages